An Exceptional Law
Section 98 and the Emergency State, 1919–1936

During periods of intense conflict, either at home or abroad, governments enact emergency powers in order to exercise greater control over the society that they govern. The expectation though is that once the conflict is over, these emergency powers will be lifted.

An Exceptional Law showcases how the emergency law used to repress labour activism during the First World War became normalized with the creation of Section 98 of the Criminal Code, following the Winnipeg General Strike. Dennis G. Molinaro argues that the institutionalization of emergency law became intricately tied to constructing a national identity. Following a mass deportation campaign in the 1930s, Section 98 was repealed in 1936 and contributed to the formation of Canada's first civil rights movement. Portions of it were used during the October Crisis and recently in the Anti-Terrorism Act of 2015. Building on the theoretical framework of Agamben, Molinaro advances our understanding of security as ideology and reveals the intricate and codependent relationship between state formation, the construction of liberal society, and exclusionary practices.

(The Canadian Social History Series)

DENNIS G. MOLINARO is a lecturer at Trent University.

PATRONS OF THE SOCIETY

Blake, Cassels & Graydon LLP
Chernos, Flaherty, Svonkin LLP
The Law Foundation of Ontario
McCarthy Tétrault LLP
Osler, Hoskin & Harcourt LLP
Paliare Roland Rosenberg Rothstein LLP
Torys LLP
WeirFoulds LLP

The Osgoode Society is supported by a grant from
The Law Foundation of Ontario.

The Law Foundation of Ontario
Building a better foundation for justice in Ontario

The Society also thanks The Law Society of Upper Canada
for its continuing support.

An Exceptional Law

Section 98 and the Emergency State, 1919–1936

Dennis G. Molinaro

Published for The Osgoode Society for Canadian Legal History by
UNIVERSITY OF TORONTO PRESS
Toronto Buffalo London

© University of Toronto Press 2017
Toronto Buffalo London
www.utppublishing.com
www.osgoodesociety.ca
Printed in Canada

ISBN 978-1-4426-2957-8 (cloth)
ISBN 978-1-4426-2958-5 (paper)

Library and Archives Canada Cataloguing in Publication

Molinaro, Dennis G., 1974–, author
An exceptional law : Section 98 and the emergency state,
1919–1936 / Dennis G. Molinaro.

(Canadian social history series)
(Osgoode Society for Canadian Legal History)
Includes bibliographical references and index.
ISBN 978-1-4426-2957-8 (cloth). – ISBN 978-1-4426-2958-5 (paper)

1. Canada. Criminal Code.   2. War and emergency legislation – Canada –
History – 20th century.   3. War and emergency powers – Canada – History –
20th century.   I. Title.   II. Series: Canadian social history series   III. Series:
Osgoode Society for Canadian Legal History (Series)

KE4713.M65 2017   342'.71062   C2016-908084-6

This book has been published with the help of a grant from the Federation
for the Humanities and Social Sciences, through the Awards to Scholarly
Publications Program, using funds provided by the Social Sciences and
Humanities Research Council of Canada.

University of Toronto Press acknowledges the financial assistance to its
publishing program of the Canada Council for the Arts and the Ontario Arts
Council, an agency of the Government of Ontario.

Canada Council   Conseil des Arts
for the Arts   du Canada

ONTARIO ARTS COUNCIL
CONSEIL DES ARTS DE L'ONTARIO
an Ontario government agency
un organisme du gouvernement de l'Ontario

Funded by the   Financé par le
Government   gouvernement
of Canada   du Canada

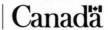

Forgetting, I would even say historical error, is an essential factor in the creation of a nation and it is for this reason that the progress of historical studies often poses a threat to nationality. Historical inquiry, in effect, throws light on the violent acts that have taken place at the origin of every political formation, even those that have been the most benevolent in their consequences. Unity is always brutally established.

Ernest Renan, "What Is a Nation?"

The exception is more interesting than the rule. The rule proves nothing; the exception proves everything.

Carl Schmitt, Political Theology, Four Chapters on
the Concept of Sovereignty

The tradition of the oppressed teaches us that the "state of emergency" in which we live is not the exception but the rule. We must attain to a conception of history that is in keeping with this insight. Then we shall clearly realize that it is our task to bring about a real state of emergency, and this will improve our position in the struggle against Fascism.

Walter Benjamin, "Theses on the Philosophy of History"

Contents

Foreword / ix

Acknowledgments / xi

Introduction: The Exception / 3

1 For the Protection of People and the State / 19

2 Defining Suspects / 57

3 The Trial / 86

4 Citizens of the World / 120

5 Outlaws / 146

6 Judgment / 185

Conclusion: Towards a Real State of Exception / 222

Appendix 1: Excerpt from the 1910 Immigration Act / 235

Appendix 2: Section 98 of the Criminal Code of Canada, Revised Statutes of Canada, 1927, ch. 36 / 239

Appendix 3: Excerpt from Memorandum for the Prime Minister Re: Bill 73: An Act to Amend Section 98 of the Criminal Code, 12 June 1936 / 243

Notes / 247

Bibliography / 299

Index / 321

Foreword

Section 98 of the Criminal Code of Canada was passed in 1919 following the Winnipeg General Strike. It was a law aimed at "unlawful associations." Section 98 was identical to a wartime order-in-council, and its inclusion in the Criminal Code, and thus its applicability in peacetime until it was repealed in 1936, makes it a most unusual measure and one deserving of deeper study. Its very broad definition of unlawful association meant that it could be used against a wide variety of opponents of the status quo, including left-leaning organizations of various kinds and labour leaders. Although it was justified as part of the state's "emergency powers," its applicability in non-emergency years requires us, Molinaro argues, to consider how it "normalized" the use of the criminal law for political activity and became part of the ordinary fabric of society's approach to dissent. Like other recent Osgoode Society publications, especially *Canadian State Trials, Volume IV: Security, Dissent, and the Limits of Toleration in War and Peace, 1914–1939, An Exceptional Law* provides a deeply researched historical account of a much-debated contemporary question – where is the line between freedom and security to be drawn in a liberal democracy?

The purpose of the Osgoode Society for Canadian Legal History is to encourage research and writing in the history of Canadian law. The Society, which was incorporated in 1979 and is registered as a charity, was founded at the initiative of the Honourable R. Roy McMurtry and officials of the Law Society of Upper Canada. The Society seeks to stimulate the study of legal history in Canada by supporting researchers, collecting oral histories, and publishing volumes that contribute to legal-historical scholarship in Canada. This year's books bring the total published to 105 since 1981, in all fields of legal history – the courts, the judiciary, and the legal profession, as well as on the history of crime and punishment, women and law, law and economy, the legal treatment of ethnic minorities, and famous cases and significant trials in all areas of the law.

Current directors of the Osgoode Society for Canadian Legal History are Susan Binnie, David Chernos, J. Douglas Ewart, Michael Fenrick, Timothy Hill, Ian Hull, Mahmud Jamal, William Kaplan, C. Ian Kyer, Virginia MacLean, The Hon. Roy McMurtry, Yasir Naqvi, Dana Peebles, The Hon. Paul Perell, The Hon. Paul Reinhardt, William Ross, Paul Schabas, The Hon. Robert Sharpe, Jon Silver, Alexander Smith, Lorne Sossin, Mary Stokes, and The Hon. Michael Tulloch.

The annual report and information about membership may be obtained by writing to the Osgoode Society for Canadian Legal History, Osgoode Hall, 130 Queen Street West, Toronto, Ontario, M5H 2N6. Telephone: 416-947-3321. E-mail: Osgoodesociety@lsuc.on.ca. Website: www.osgoodesociety.ca.

Robert J. Sharpe
President

Jim Phillips
Editor-in-Chief

Acknowledgments

This book originally began as a PhD dissertation, but in many ways it represents the culmination of my academic career to date. As a result, there are many people who deserve acknowledgments. I am thankful for the support of all of the individuals involved with this project, specifically Ian Radforth, Franca Iacovetta, Jim Phillips, Sean Mills, Gregory Kealey, and Steve Penfold for their comments and their critiques. My thanks to Michael Marrus and Wesley Wark for giving me a different perspective on intelligence and political trials and to Robert Wright, Ian McKay, and Kevin Sienna for their support. My thanks to Craig Heron, John McQuarrie, Mathieu Brûlé, Jennifer Stephen, Ester Reiter, and everyone in our labour studies group, the Osgoode Society for Canadian Legal History, and Rachel Horner and Marty Clark. The comments on previous drafts and chapters helped immensely. Thank you to Barry Wright, Susan Binnie, and Eric Tucker, whose comments on a different project indirectly helped me on this one. Thank you to Jason Radman, Ana Radman, Alex Zlatanovic and All Languages, Ben Bryce, Samira Samirano, and Eugienio, Rudolpho, and Sophie Badurina for their aid in translations.

This project benefitted from the funding provided by the Social Sciences and Humanities Research Council, the Federation for the Humanities and Social Sciences, the Ontario government, and the Department of History at the University of Toronto. Thank you to all of them for their generous support. My thanks to the archival staff at the Alberta, Saskatchewan, Ontario, and British Columbia archives and Library and Archives Canada, as well as the University of Toronto Press and staff, especially Len Husband, my editor, and Rebecca Russell, who did copy editing for the Press.

Many thanks to all my family and friends for believing in what I was doing, especially Scott Downie, Marino Osso, Tony Ricciardi, Marco Nave, Andrea Guglielmo, Kevin Hester, Michele, Lisa, Julian, Anthony, and Sebastian Molinaro, Phil and Theresa Downer, Travis Downer, Paige and Payson Marrett, and Miranda, Adam, and Ella Preston-Lord. Thank you to Leonardo and Andre for giving me inspiration to keep going and to Hailey for patiently listening to all my ideas. I owe much more than thanks to my partner in life, Nichole Molinaro. She has been unwavering in her love, support, patience, and dedication. None of what I have done would have been possible without her believing in me and supporting my efforts to continue doing it. I will always be forever grateful. My thanks to both of my parents, Krystyna and Gino Molinaro. As immigrants in a new land, they struggled and fought tenaciously in spite of the adversity they faced. Whether they know it or not, they imparted that spirit to me. This work is for them.

An Exceptional Law
Section 98 and the Emergency State, 1919–1936

Introduction:
The Exception

On 22 October 2014, Michael Zehaf-Bibeau drove his vehicle to the steps of Canada's National War Memorial in Ottawa and opened fire with a long-range rifle, killing Corporal Nathan Cirillo. He then drove to the front steps of Parliament, and after running inside, continued shooting until he was shot dead by Sergeant-at-Arms Kevin Vickers. The attack followed another incident that occurred two days earlier in Saint-Jean-sur-Richelieu, Quebec, when two Canadian Armed Forces personnel were attacked by Martin Couture-Rouleau when he attempted to run them over with his vehicle. After the officers had been struck, a police chase ensued. Couture-Rouleau lost control of his car, and after rolling his vehicle, he was shot dead by police but not before dashing out of the vehicle and making a last-ditch effort to attack a police officer with a knife. Warrant Officer Patrice Vincent, who was struck by Couture-Rouleau in his initial vehicle attack, died the following day in hospital.

Following the tragic loss of the soldiers, the government considered the events terrorist attacks because of the self-proclaimed ties the attackers claimed they had to Islamic extremism. The government stated that it would reinvestigate the issue of preventative arrest to decide whether existing Criminal Code powers to make such an arrest should be expanded. Forms of preventative arrest had been part of Canada's Criminal Code since the introduction of the Official Secrets Act of 1939, but the measure gained more attention when it was introduced into Canada's Criminal Code following the September 11th terrorist attacks in 2001. It enabled authorities to arrest anyone they believed was about to commit a crime, specifically a terrorist act. After an arrest the individual is brought before a judge who can impose conditions on their freedom. If the person refuses to comply, they could face one year in prison. The powers were originally tied to a sunset clause that expired in 2007, but in 2012 the powers were revived by the government following the breakup of a plot to attack a passenger train. On the basis of Section 83.28 of the Criminal Code, Canadian authorities presently have the power to arrest someone before they commit a crime. Christian Leuprecht of Queen's University and the Royal Military College stated that preventative arrest acts as a deterrent against terrorist behaviour and that the courts take the issue of preventative arrest seriously. Paradoxically, he surmised that the position of the courts was as follows: "if you're asking me to convict someone before they actually do something, you better have some pretty good evidence."[1] In the end, the government took things further with Bill C-51, or the Anti-Terrorism Act, 2015, which was a contentious piece of legislation that lowered the threshold for preventative arrest and further empowered Canada's intelligence agency to "disrupt" threats from anyone seeking to "undermine the security of Canada," with the definitions for disrupting and undermining security broadly defined.

How did we get here? How, in a liberal-democratic society, do the police have the power to arrest a person before they commit a crime? What type of legal framework is needed to process an accused for an offence that has not yet occurred? The more pressing point is, how is this legal?

Defenders of these laws often claim that the law has been rarely used and it is therefore not a problem. Such arguments were often made in Canada's past when politicians sought to defend extraordinary legal measures to curb sedition. The more important point is not the frequency of use, but rather how such a law can be created in a society that believes that a person has committed no crime until they actually do commit one, and that the state should have to prove that an offence has been committed, beyond a reasonable doubt, before an individual can be convicted. To dismiss such a law or the actions of state authorities in creating it as just "what states do" to combat challenges, perceived or otherwise, is to leave such actions unexamined and hence unchallenged if they are unwarranted.

To determine how Canada arrived at such a juncture, where extraordinary powers of the state normally reserved for times of emergency have achieved a level of normalcy (because they can be used even if no state of emergency is declared), we need historical analysis. We need to historicize the use of these powers to understand how they fit in relation to the law, the state, our democracy, our politics, and even our nationalism. At the same time we need theory to connect historical narrative to broader patterns and to help us make sense of these issues. A historical examination of repressive laws and responses, coupled with a new theoretical approach, can help us make sense of how the boundaries between the emergency and the normal have eroded over time and provide some insight into what to do about it now. History can be a project of reconnaissance where studying the past can not only better inform our present but can also help us find possible solutions to present-day problems.[2] Political violence and state repression have a long history in Canada.

From the rebellions of the 1830s to the Riel resistance movements and the Winnipeg General Strike, Canada's violent history of suppressing revolt and political activism runs deep. The interwar period was one of Canada's most turbulent times; the nation's temporary reprieve from international wars was plagued by another war, domestic in its locale and focused on internal enemies. The violence and militancy of the labour revolt (1917–1925) culminated in the Winnipeg strike of 1919. While the 1920s were relatively calm, there were still strikes and heated conflicts, notably in mining and steel-making communities in Nova Scotia. In Toronto, during the late 1920s, Communists and their supporters fought for free speech, while police attempted to quell the unrest.

The arrival of the Great Depression, which ushered in a new wave of unrest and violence, came upon Canadians quickly and ferociously. Within two years of the stock market crash of 1929, unemployment in Canada had surged to nearly 30 per cent. As the relief lines continued into the mid-1930s, labour militancy increased, and so did the state's attempts to crush it. The Canadian state outlawed the Communist Party of Canada (CPC), deported immigrants in unprecedented numbers, and made mass arrests of workers engaged in protests and strikes throughout the country. Police violence was at its height – most famously in places such as Estevan and Noranda. Royal Canadian Mounted Police (RCMP) detachments were being called in by civil authorities to quell violent marches of thousands of unemployed workers. Then there was the On-to-Ottawa Trek, where thousands of young, unemployed men marched towards the capital before they were met with police violence and gunfire, resulting in the Regina Riot. Canada's Conservative prime minister, Richard Bedford Bennett, ordered armoured cars and armed RCMP detachments to patrol Parliament. A present-day observer would scarcely recognize the Canada of the 1930s. Senator Gideon Robertson summed up the reasons for labour militancy when he told Bennett that workers "can hardly be expected to starve quietly."[3]

Within the many pages that historians have written about these events, there has always been mention of the "infamous" "legal sledgehammer" that was Section 98 of the Criminal Code of Canada. Labelled as Canada's "most repressive law," it is significantly understudied and misunderstood, as authors have referred to it as being "invoked" or "revived" to outlaw the CPC in 1931.[4] Historians have regarded it as an emergency power resurrected for repressive purposes, but it was only a section in Canada's Criminal Code and not part of Canada's emergency legislation at the time, the War Measures Act (WMA). A revised look at Section 98 that explains how and why it was created, how it operated, its effects on identity and society, and how it was challenged can shed insight into how emergency measures became regular features of Canada's Criminal Code in peacetime and the broader implications of this. It can also reveal broader patterns in the state's ability to create and use such powers and provide some understanding of how to resist them.

Section 98 was, in essence, a copy of Canadian wartime legislation that suppressed left-wing activism, namely Privy Council (PC) 2384, created in September 1918. It shared many similarities with Section 41 of the Immigration Act of 1910, which was based on US immigration law.[5] What makes Section 98 profoundly fascinating and significant is that it enabled the authorities to regulate Canadians politics during peacetime. I argue that the creation of Section 98 marked a watershed in Canadian history wherein the government began the process, and broader pattern, of normalizing emergency measures, which enabled it to legally engage in nation-building through repression. The state could regulate the political ideology of citizens and immigrants by way of the Criminal Code and exclude the undesirable. Communism was the authorities' principal target with Section 98, which gave them the power to target individuals or groups that expressed support for or advocated communism and to even control a person's entry to citizenship. The normalization of emergency law was the only way the state could legally sanction its ability to judge politics and use repression as a means of nation-building. It could use exceptional powers to legally and indefinitely control not only ideology, but political actions, such as strikes, it deemed illegitimate.[6]

What do I mean by the process of normalization? By this I mean the processes by which what were once regarded as emergency laws, laws that were designed to deal with a security threat, as defined by the state, in a specific time and place, lose any temporal grounding and become amorphous, existing everywhere and indefinitely. Before Section 98, exceptional legal measures were used to combat a *temporary* security threat.[7] The threat was specific, both in terms of time and place, and so was the state's response. Examples of exceptional legal measures being used in Canada's past are numerous, and one might even say Canada has, as Douglas Hay states, a "tradition" of using emergency measures. In 1794, the legislature of Lower Canada defined sedition as anything that disrupted the happiness of the Crown's subjects. In 1797, *habeas corpus* was suspended for cases of treasonable actions. The Better Preservation Act enabled the government to detain members of the House of Assembly without the House's approval. From 1818 to 1820, during Robert Gourlay's fight for political reform, an Upper Canadian statute treated all public political meetings as seditious ones. Lower Canada's court martial ordinance of 8 November 1833 provided for the death penalty and completely denied right to defence counsel.[8]

With the creation of Section 98, the government went beyond crafting a repressive law; it destroyed the linkages between time and crisis, altering the ways law was used to counter security threats. The crisis, as well as radical ideologies and their followers, now existed potentially everywhere in society and indefinitely. Through the classification of communism as a foreign invading ideology, the use of emergency measures normally reserved for war was justifiable to many, but now everyone was a potential Communist, everyone a potential enemy of the state – everyone a potential terrorist. Section 98 was a response to how security threats were defined. Law had to take the same shape and form as the threat to restore authorities' sense of security. Section 98 enabled the government to indefinitely and legally judge the lives of Canadians by way of their ideologies and thoughts because that was where the threat existed.

Canadian authorities' use of repression as a means of nation-building was not a straightforward process, because what the Canadian nation was in interwar Canada was a subject of much debate. Certainly, many lawmakers and members of government viewed the nation as an essentially white, patriarchal, liberal, and British one, complete with support for the monarchy, private property, and capitalism. In Quebec, the nation of Canada was British but also French. National identity was supposed to consist of a British and French partnership, that is, a partnership between English Canada and a largely French and Catholic Quebecois culture. But in both English Canada and in Quebec, government officials repressed communism with the intent of stamping it out and doing their part in preserving the nation as they saw it, which in both cases had no place for communists. To complicate matters further, Communists also had their own vision of Canadian nationhood. For them, Canada was to be a worker-led socialist republic, a multicultural nation united under socialism with equal status for men and women, opposed to imperialism around the world and allied with the Soviet Union. At the root of the repression of the interwar period was an attempt by Canadian authorities to preserve what they thought Canada was and expel that which it was not.

Understanding Section 98's origins and role in suppressing Canadians' civil rights is important given the heightened security climate of the present and governments' continued use of emergency measures to deal with security threats – real or exaggerated. By re-examining Section 98 as an emergency power turned normal feature of Canada's Criminal Code, we can better understand how current-day emergency powers, like preventative arrest and even widespread surveillance of civilian populations, have become normal and why we may see an individual law as unusual or exceptional but perceive the power to create it as acceptable and normal. I should add that I am not claiming that past governments or authorities had some grand plan to normalize emergency measures, nor am I seeking to judge past historical actors, agencies, or governments as misguided or foolishly overreacting to threats; my concerns are how a threat that was considered an emergency and worthy of being quelled by exceptional means continued to exist long past the end of the emergency, how the powers used to quell it were legally invoked, maintained, and accepted, and the effects of such actions on people and society. [9]

The security threat was also not geographically specific. It was everywhere. Governments, including those of Canada, the United States, and Britain, sought to harmonize their responses to communist activists. Those most vulnerable to state measures were internationalists; as transnational–immigrant activists they identified with no single homeland but with a broader communist movement.

These powers enabled authorities to legally reduce people to the status of what philosopher Giorgio Agamben has termed *homo sacer*, an individual subject to law but denied the protection of it.[10] Communists, and immigrant Communists especially (because they did not acquire citizenship and were not protected against measures like deportation), became security threats indefinitely. Through this identification of them and their ideology as a threat to security, immigrants and citizens knew which politics were acceptable, legal, and "Canadian" by virtue of what the government classified as illegal and "foreign." This type of nation-building was possible because law, in the service of sovereign power, enabled the state to reduce someone to the status of *homo sacer* because of their political ideology, thereby justifying the use of emergency measures against them.[11]

Previous works have briefly discussed Section 98 when relevant to a particular issue, such as labour unrest during the interwar period. In this context, some have argued that Section 98 was created to repress labour militancy but that its significance ended with its repeal. While its connections to PC 2384 have been documented, it has never been understood as anything other than a short-lived Criminal Code section. Viewing Section 98 as a reactionary law, drafted by the government to contend with a temporary emergency, is inadequate; such an interpretation downplays the significance of Section 98 as a bridge between the emergency and nonemergency state, as well as underestimating its long-lasting effects and role in nation-building.[12] Section 98's role in suppressing communism was more profound than the government's desire to contain it and more lasting than a reactionary law. As Carolyn Strange and Tina Loo argue, the effort to halt communism in this period "was an integral part of nation-building"; desired political values were encouraged by outlawing undesirable ones like communism. A politics that "was capitalist and not socialist," "Anglo-Saxon and not ethnic" was the ultimate goal. This book seeks to understand that process.[13]

Where does a study of Section 98 fit into the broader literature of state repression in Canada? By tracing the creation, use, and repeal of Section 98, this study makes a number of important contributions to legal, labour, immigration, intelligence, and human rights history, as well as contributing to a broader literature on state repression in Canada. The historical literature on this topic has undergone many changes over the years and has expanded in a multitude of directions.

Studies have often dealt with state repression as it pertained to a particular issue, such as Japanese Canadians' forced relocation during the Second World War. Although social historians have traditionally tended to focus on history "from below," much of the literature on state repression in Canada has centred on state policies and the reasons for their creation. For instance, early studies of Japanese forced relocation revealed how racism was endemic in the Canadian government and was the main motivating factor for the repressive policies that the Japanese faced.[14]

Other works have examined different groups, such as immigrant workers, which Avery argues were often viewed as "dangerous foreigners" because of their resistance to deplorable working conditions.[15] Class and gender were principal concerns of the state.

Working-class activism and demands for better conditions led to explosive confrontations with the government. During both world wars, the government interned a number of different groups as preventative security measures. Women faced repression in direct and subtle ways. Like their male counterparts, they could face repressive state measures if they expressed support for radical leftist politics and were subjected to moral regulation if their activities were perceived as attempts to challenge gender norms.[16]

Historians have studied the many ways the state engaged in repressive policies. Immigration laws reveal not only the racial biases of the state but its ideological biases.[17] Studies of repression in the Cold War demonstrate how the loyalty of citizens was important to security. The RCMP's dedication to stamping out communism was extended to surveillance of university campuses, the women's movement, and the civil rights movement – even the sexuality of citizens was under scrutiny.[18] The relentless fear of communism has led some scholars to conclude that the Canadian state was an "insecurity state."[19]

Cultural studies scholars have explored how culture was an integral part of repressive state actions, from regulating gender and sexuality, to policing leftist politics, to government censors hiding certain information from the public.[20] The influence of cultural studies has enabled scholars to examine how repression can be subtle rather than overt, as seen in the state's Canadianizing policies that were directed at post-war immigrants and how these immigrants resisted the aims of Canada's "gatekeepers."[21]

Studies on the history of human rights and civil liberties have detailed how individuals countered the state's encroachment on people's rights. Civil liberties groups organized opposition to laws or events such as the Padlock Law, the WMA during the Second World War, the Gastown Riot, and the October Crisis.[22]

More recently, Reg Whitaker, Gregory Kealey, and Andrew Parnaby have produced a new work on the history of "political policing" in Canada that argues that Canada has continually sought to police the politics of Canadians through the work of its security services, such as the RCMP and later the Canadian Security Intelligence Service (CSIS). Much of the focus of these agencies has been on curbing and halting the spread of communism, which became the RCMP's nemesis for much of the twentieth century. The authors explain the significance of the security services' relentless penetration into society by using Michel Foucault's work on modern society's push to create a panoptical society, with the security services being the all-seeing eye of the government.[23]

The historical literature has adequately documented and dealt with state repression as it pertained to individual groups or events of interest to scholars. We have a rich collection describing the various repressive actions undertaken by the Canadian state and a growing body of work detailing resistance to those activities. Yet we still know very little and do not have an adequate understanding of *how* repression was actually possible, how it worked, and how it connected more broadly to sovereignty and nationalism.

This work on Section 98 could be understood and situated as part of a broader process of state formation and the creation of a liberal order in Canada. Section 98 was a means of building the state as well as the nation and contributed to the construction of the security apparatus to deal with challenges to state power. It was a forceful means of protecting and preserving a liberal order as authorities saw it at the time, one where the values and culture of white, propertied, Christian men loyal to king and country were reflective of what the nation should be. When this was met with sustained opposition from people in the margins, such as immigrants, the working class, ethnic minorities, and women, the state undertook a process of passive resistance by folding Section 98 into other sections of Canada's Criminal Code. But if the application of Section 98 can be interpreted as part of state formation and the creation of a liberal order in Canada, this leads to larger questions, mainly, what kind of liberal order if repression was tied to its formation?

Repressive events remain opaque when we really try to understand them in relation to our conception of liberalism as being supportive and protective of Locke's inalienable rights, which include the right to freedom. We lack a means of connecting isolated repressive events and explaining the state's extraordinary power to crush dissent, often by powers reserved for wartime emergency, as anything other than a paradox in a liberal society and a product of overreacting to invisible threats or biases. Indeed, the ability of a liberal democracy to invoke a state of emergency and legally violate accepted legal norms is frequently condemned but remains unexamined in the historical literature.

By examining some of Canada's most repressive moments and by understanding that this ability to repress is integral to states and that the ability of states to exist and survive challenges is dependent on the right to control freedom, to restrict or even deny it, we can change our understandings of what a liberal state or liberal order is. A liberal state that can stamp out liberalism demands exploration that goes further than regarding it as a paradox. It compels us to reformulate how we define a liberal democratic state or even a liberal order where exclusion is fundamentally tied to inclusion. What Section 98's creation and use reveals is that liberalism relies and depends upon exclusion. There is no paradox.

The work of philosopher Giorgio Agamben has opened up new theoretical frameworks to address these issues. His theories make use of both Walter Benjamin and Benjamin's theoretical opponent of sorts, Carl Schmitt. Schmitt was a German theorist who argued that only the sovereign had the right to declare the state of exception and that it was the rule (which the Nazi regime used as justification for its state of exception and brutality). The leftist philosopher Benjamin countered Schmitt by arguing that the state of emergency should not be considered the rule. Agamben's theories are based on the work of both theorists, though his work is more aligned with Benjamin and Michel Foucault. He views himself as completing Foucault's work on biopolitics. Agamben argues that the intimate connection between life and politics mirrors the sovereign's relationship to law, which is one of inclusion and exclusion. For Agamben, these powers and the concept of biopolitics, or the idea that politics rules over life, predates the modern era and extends back to the very origins of liberal democratic theory. The sovereign (or the highest power in any nation, be it a president, parliament, or monarch) possesses the unique ability to withdraw itself from normal legal conventions and to exclude itself from judgment by creating a "state of exception" or state of emergency. These powers are ingrained in the very fabric of sovereignty and sovereign power, and they can always be invoked; thus the boundary that separates the emergency and the norm has always been artificial. In such a state, life gradually becomes law; all aspects of life become subject to law, a place of "nightmarish control." Sacrality is central in such a state, as the sovereign regards some things as sacred and in need of protection, while others are impure and need to be outlawed.[24] What is the effect of these powers on people? They enable the sovereign to create subjects that can be governed by law, but the sovereign also retains the power to exclude individuals from law. Agamben terms these nonbeings *homo sacer*, individuals who can be excluded from the protection of law but find themselves at the mercy of it. These beings can be killed without the sovereign being guilty of a homicide. For Agamben, the logic of sovereignty, and indeed sovereignty itself, is located in "the ban," or in the ability to create the exclusion.

The ability to kill without consequence is a power Agamben argues that only the sovereign possesses. For him, the real nature of law is not located in rule but in judgment. He contends that the sovereign's ability to declare and institute a "state of exception" has increasingly become, for Western liberal democracies, a "paradigm of governance."[25] He argues that the First World War marked a stark acceleration in the blurring of the exception and the norm after governments gave themselves extraordinary wartime powers. When applied to Canada's history of repression, this new theoretical approach provides us with a way of linking seemingly isolated repressive events by understanding them as an escalation in the merging of the emergency and the norm.

The most important contribution of this theoretical framework to a historical study of Section 98 is that it enables us to see that these exceptional legal measures form an important basis for how Canadian identity and sovereignty are practised and maintained. Creating exceptional legal measures is itself an act of sovereignty, as is the creation of *homo sacer*. Canadian political identity is then founded upon that which it excludes, what the sovereign considers *homo sacer*, and this process is deeply ingrained in law and the structure of our political system. If, as Agamben states, the logic of sovereignty is found in "the ban," in the place that is "a threshold in which life is both inside and outside the juridical order," then those that are placed within the sovereign ban (*homo sacer*) are also not totally excluded from the sovereign. The act of exclusion "preserves the memory of the originary exclusion through which the political dimension was first constituted."[26] Put more simply, by excluding communists from Canada's political identity, the state was defining it, and as a result, Canadian sovereignty became bound up with the exclusion, that is, with communism. Canadian identity could never truly separate itself from communism since the "memory" of the exclusion was preserved in the sovereign's understanding of itself. The exception (communists) proves the rule (Canadian sovereignty).[27] This framework allows us to completely reconceptualize this formative period in Canada's nationhood. Canada's development into a nation was not just tied to its ability to sign the armistice at the end of the First World War, or pass the Statute of Westminster, but to its ability to capture individuals, and indeed ideology, in the sovereign ban that defined it. Repression and political violence have a central place in Canada's transition from colony to nation, and law was central to this process. Canadians understood themselves as "Canadian," as part of a liberal society because of who was excluded from it. In sum, if communists were not the *homo sacer* of their era, they would need to be invented.

This book also reveals how culture was an important factor in determining how the state identified and interpreted its targets and underpinned the intelligence cycle. Moreover, it demonstrates that the targets of the state, such as Communists, had more freedom from Moscow to direct party policy. Even during the party's notorious Third Period, CPC members wanted to cooperate with moderate leftists on common goals, such as repealing Section 98. Certain transnational–immigrant activists who became leaders in the CPC were radicalized in Canada and identified with a region or a people rather than a country or state. Section 98 played a key role in sanctioning the state's ability to deport them for their political beliefs. The movement to repeal Section 98, led by the Canadian Labor Defense League, a Communist-backed group, also gave rise to Canada's early civil rights movement.

Another important theme of Section 98's creation and use was the role of fear in history.[28] Fear played an important role in Section 98's creation and the normalizing of emergency measures. While assessing the emotional state of historical actors can be difficult, if not impossible in certain instances, there was plenty of documentary evidence in the House of Commons and Senate by way of parliamentary debates (a place where emotions were often heightened) involving Section 98's creation and the many attempts at its repeal. These debates, and authorities' public statements about communism and its followers, provide us with a window into how fear factored into the decision to create and maintain emergency law in peacetime. While fear of revolt and revolution played a role in Section 98's creation, its continued existence was tied to preserving feelings of safety and security. The law kept Canadians feeling protected and safe.

This battle over what security was, over whether Canadian society was more secure with or without Section 98, also reveals how security functioned as an ideological project in that it can be understood as an idea, a third-order object much like "the state," as Abrams has argued. Like "the state," it is not a quantifiable thing but something that can be constituted, communicated, and imposed to "legitimate the illegitimate."[29] In the case of Section 98, greater powers for the state and authorities to judge individuals' politics were the illegitimate actions that needed legitimizing. In essence, security can be understood as an idea, one that shifts over time and is also contested. Law plays a central role in understanding security as ideology. Section 98 in and of itself did not make Canadian society secure. Lawmakers had to *believe* that it did. They had to believe that there was a foreign threat and that law and repression could halt it and produce a secure society, just as those opposed to Section 98 believed a secure society was one without repression, without Section 98, and therefore contested the idea that exceptional laws produced security.

This formative period of repression against communists also becomes important for understanding the ongoing targeting of leftists into the Cold War post-1945. Rather than viewing such targeting as merely an obsession of the RCMP and as Canada's obligation to its Cold War partners, we can also understand it as a *necessary function* in the maintenance of Canadian sovereignty and identity. This targeting was possible because of the sovereign ban and exclusion of subjects on the basis of political ideology, an exclusion that began in the interwar period with Section 98. McKay has argued that liberal order necessitates the creation of "officially demarcated 'exceptional spaces'" where its challengers are targeted with "precision and punished with implacable enthusiasm" and that these measures date back to the eighteenth century.[30] My contention is that with the creation of Section 98, these "spaces" became a state of being, not bound or limited by an officially declared emergency state.[31]

My use of the theories of *homo sacer* and the state of exception in a historical study are not without controversy. If Agamben is correct that the state of exception is an integral part of the logic of sovereignty dating back to Ancient Greece, should that not be the focus of the book? Is interwar Canada that unique, with the state of exception predating it by so long and existing in so many other countries? Can we really regard interwar Canada as existing outside the juridical order, with Prime Minister Bennett acting as dictator and communists being freely killed by their prison guards or police? Does Agamben not reduce history to, in essence, a philosophical equation?

These are valid concerns, but they are applicable to many theoretical frameworks. Similar reductionist charges could be made about viewing history as progressing along a Marxist materialist dialectic or as a Gramscian struggle for elites to achieve and maintain cultural hegemony. An Agamben theoretical framework does not ignore the complexities of history any more than any other theoretical framework, and further, it complements other approaches. My use of Agamben is not solely to demonstrate how emergency measures became normalized in Canada, as they have in many countries, but to reveal how that process affected the identity and political society of Canada through a process of nation-building. Further to the point about the uniqueness of Canada and whether it was really a state of exception, I maintain an interpretation of Agamben in which the state of exception is an integral part of the logic of sovereignty predating the Canadian state but does not negate the uniqueness of the Canadian situation or experience. The state of exception is a constant, always underlying function of any state, but this does not mean it operates or is resisted in every country and in every time period in exactly the same way. This also does not mean that Canada existed as a totalitarian regime in the interwar period, with communists the equivalent of the Jews of Auschwitz (what Agamben sees as a complete or total state of exception).[32] The point is that it is ultimately up to the state to decide our status, and this status can change at any time. Canada in the 1930s was just as much a state of exception as Canada in 2015. Differences exist when the state of exception moves from being "behind the curtain" to taking centre stage when a state of emergency is officially declared by the government, such as during the First World War with the implementation of the War Measures Act. Prior to 1918, when emergency measures were used, the curtain was pulled closed once the emergency ended.

What we witness in the interwar period in Canada are the moments unique to Canada when the curtain was left slightly ajar with the creation of Section 98 after the WMA powers were to end. Not everything was moved back out of sight when the emergency ended; some important emergency powers remained and became normal. The WMA preceded and succeeded Section 98 to be sure, but the important element here is that with Section 98 some of those WMA powers could now be used in peacetime *without* a formal declaration of emergency. The state of exception became a little more "open," a little more a part of society than it had previously, and the state began reducing subjects to *homo sacer* in peacetime, as much as required, to carry out its security goals, from denying communist immigrants the protection of *habeas corpus*, to protecting police officers that attacked and killed suspected communists, to restricting free speech or outlawing political parties. Communists were *homo sacer* in the interwar period as much as was necessary to complete the Canadian state's attempt at purging them and their ideas from society. At the same time we can observe how these forces were resisted and challenged and the effect of them on the processes of creating a Canadian nation and liberal state. Section 98 then stands as a significant moment in a long-standing battle of the state gradually implementing, and people resisting, the creation of a complete or total state of exception. It is a battle that has continued to the present. This study on Section 98, within an Agamben framework, turns our attention to a more structuralist or essentialist view of power. We need to understand the ill-liberalism at the root of liberal society if we are to have any hope of understanding, as Jessica Whyte puts it, how the state of exception represents the "reef on which the revolutions of our century have become shipwrecked."[33]

A brief note on terminology: I use the term "state" not in an effort to mask agency, but when engaging in broad analysis and in reference to, as Alan Greer and Ian Radforth state, "a number of institutions which together constitute its [the state's] reality, and which interact with other parts called the state system."[34] Keeping this definition in mind, I use the term "authorities" as a shorthand reference for those individuals who were members of state institutions and charged with protecting the state, for example: immigration officers, politicians, police, and Crown attorneys. I have chosen to forgo use of the term "radical" to refer to individuals who sought to challenge the political and economic status quo because the word has become associated with the international conflict against terrorism; it has become connected to movements and individuals engaged in acts of violence against state actors and civilians – quite unlike the actions of those who advocated for social change in the interwar period. Instead, I have chosen to use the term "activist" to refer to those individuals agitating for social change through front-line activities such as strikes and protests. I use the term "leftists" to refer to those on the political left, and when I need to distinguish between leftists, I use adjectives such as "moderate leftists" on the one hand and, on the other, "radical leftists" to describe those on the far left, such as communists who believed in revolution but did not actively engage in violent acts against the Canadian state or people. "Radical" is used when discussing authorities' perceptions of activists. I use "progressives" and "leftists" interchangeably. I also use "state of emergency" and "state of exception" interchangeably. I capitalize "Communist" when referring to individuals tied to the CPC or believed to be by the authorities, and I use a lower-case "c" when referring to communists in a broader sense, such as individuals who were part of a movement and not directly linked to the CPC. State authorities often saw no difference between nonparty and official Communist Party members. I also use the historical spelling of the name of the Canadian Labor Defense League.

This work serves as an important and necessary study in the seemingly never-ending heightened security climate post-9/11. By reexamining Section 98, we can historicize the increasing normalization of emergency measures that occurred after 9/11 with the creation of laws such as the Patriot Act in the United States and

Canada's anti-terrorism bill, which amended numerous laws. This re-examination allows us to witness how violence, repression, and exclusion played an important part in how Canadians eventually understood their nation to be a liberal-democratic state. This understanding became possible when Section 98 enabled the "permanence of the temporary."[35]

1

For the Protection of People and the State

The First World War was an important moment in Canadian history. Canadians won the battle of Vimy Ridge and earned the right to sign the armistice. The historical literature has often portrayed this moment as being one when Canada came into its own as a nation-state, due in large part to its wartime sacrifices.[1] But the war led to other changes as well. Prime Minister Robert Borden, a firm believer in a noninterventionist form of government, adjusted his stance over the course of the war. The problems that arose during the war, whether economic, labour, or social, led the government to incrementally increase its level of encroachment on many aspects of Canadian life. The war altered society and the state's relationship to it.[2]

A crucial and understudied element of the war's drastic changes to Canadian life is the way the state of emergency and wartime powers of the War Measures Act (WMA) became a permanent feature of Canadian life, as well as the effect of this. The result was that political violence and repression played an important role in nation-building. The government could use exceptional laws to exclude unwanted subjects on the basis of their political ideology during war or peace. Following the end of the First World War, a wartime measure designed to deal with the labour revolt (1917–1925) entered the Criminal Code as Section 98. The consensus of the historical literature is that Section 98 was a "reactionary law." By "reactionary" I mean immediately reactive to the circumstances of the day as a way to deal with the revolt.[3] But this approach fails to explain why, if it was meant to deal with a short-term crisis, did Section 98 remain a law after the end of the labour revolt?

Section 98 was a deliberate and planned attempt by the government to devise a long-term solution to left-wing activism. That it was not a reactionary law does not discount the role of emotion or fear in its creation; conversely, the role of emotion in its creation should not reduce it to an irrational by-product of hysteria. Its connection to emotion was complex. War stirred the deepest of emotions, from patriotism to loyalty to hatred and fear. Fear contributed to Section 98's creation, but lawmakers' need for safety and security was what helped preserve it long term. The government believed that the country's long-term security was ensured by Section 98's ability to outlaw ideologies it deemed disloyal. To achieve this, the emergency had to continue beyond the end of the revolt.

This process began with the creation of the WMA, which provided the government with the power to decide what constituted an emergency, in addition to introducing the targeting of individuals because of their political beliefs. Previous authors have argued that this repression was directed at immigrants because of their ethnicity, while others have maintained that repression was class based.[4] But left-wing activists were targeted because of both their class and their ethnicity. In the eyes of the government, class and ethnicity were linked. During the Winnipeg General Strike, Section 98 and amendments to Section 41 of the Immigration Act were a way for the government to normalize and extend emergency laws beyond the end of the WMA. How the government defined security and security threats was important in determining the legal response. The government's opposition to a perceived foreign and radical culture clouded the status of British-born activists, who have received little attention in the historical literature. Their adoption of radical leftist ideas drew attention to their status as immigrants. While not entirely regarded as foreign in the same vein as left-wing Eastern European immigrants, their adoption of leftist ideology cast them, in the opinions of some, as race traitors. The debates of the 1920s reveal how the fear of British activists among lawmakers justified the extension of emergency laws beyond the state of emergency. They could easily enter Canada, and because of their ethnicity, easily infect the domestic population with their ideas.[5]

A State of Emergency

Robert Borden's Union government was plagued by problems as Canada's involvement in the First World War dragged on. Wartime production led to a massive spike in inflation towards the end of the war. Citizens were accusing industry and the government of wartime profiteering, activists were opposing the war and capitalism, and national unity was fractured when the government created the Military

Services Act, which made conscription mandatory and contributed to violent protests in Quebec, where the act was bitterly opposed.

In hindsight, the War Measures Act of 1914 was supposed to have alleviated many of the government's ills. The act, modelled after Britain's Defence of the Realm Act, or the DORA, was designed as broad enough to help the government deal with any problem it would face over the course of the war. The act enabled the government to draft what were known as Privy Council orders or orders-in-council. It could declare an emergency and then issue decrees for war and security purposes, with no direct parliamentary oversight apart from ratification of the emergency.

Little remains in the archival records on the origins of the War Measures Act – a huge loss given the importance of the legislation to Canadian history. Much of what remains about the drafting of the act can be found in William Francis O'Connor's notes, which were prepared in the mid-1920s for Prime Minister Borden to assist him in writing his memoirs. O'Connor, a close confidant of Borden and supporter of the Conservatives, was a lawyer practising in Halifax. He later served as the presiding commissioner of the Board of Commerce from 1919 to 1920, as well as being appointed as law clerk to the Senate in 1934 by Prime Minister R.B. Bennett. At one point in 1911, O'Connor bluntly stated to Borden that he would be the best candidate for the "Roman Catholic vacancy" on the Nova Scotia Supreme Court, a suggestion to which Borden responded favourably, but for whatever reason the appointment never transpired.[6] In 1914, the government looked to O'Connor to advise it on drafting wartime legislation in a similar vein as the DORA. Previous attempts at drafting the legislation were not going well. Justice Minister Charles Doherty produced a draft, written by Toronto lawyer Zebulon Lash, which like the DORA attempted to predict what powers the government might need during the war. O'Connor did not believe the draft was an efficient one. The war was barely underway, and the draft of the bill was already three-and-a-half feet of galley proof. He suggested the government create a "blanket" act, so broad in scope that anticipation of future problems would be unnecessary. There was some fear that such a bill would never stand a chance of getting support from the opposition Liberals. O'Connor decided to send feelers out and approached Edward Mortimer Macdonald, a well-known member of the Liberals. He impressed upon Macdonald the importance of the legislation and asked if he would find out how the Liberals felt about it. Macdonald reported that after consulting with Laurier, he was told to "make absolutely sure that you omit no power that the government may need."

With the backroom blessing of the Liberals, the bill easily passed the House after briefly going to committee, and according to O'Connor, "sailed through the Senate without an adverse ripple." The new law was barely on the radar of the Canadian press. As Murray Greenwood observes, the coverage of the law in over a dozen newspapers spanned a mere 150 words.[7]

Of the few changes made to the bill, one of the most relevant to Section 98's creation was the addition of what became Section 4. Section 4 stated: "The issue of a proclamation by His majesty, or under the authority of the Governor in Council shall be conclusive evidence that war, invasion, or insurrection, real or apprehended, exists and has existed for any period of time therein stated, and of its continuance, until by the issue of a further proclamation it is declared that the war, invasion or insurrection no longer exists."[8] The WMA's Section 4 provided the government with the ability to define and set the boundaries of what constituted an emergency and how long it was to last. Unlike the DORA, which gave "His majesty in Council power to make Regulations during the *present* [emphasis mine] War for Defence of the Realm," the WMA had no end date. It was the sole power of the government to decide when the emergency would start or end. In this respect, the act conferred unprecedented powers on the government, unlike the DORA, for an undefined length of time. Further, the wording of "insurrection, real or apprehended," made it possible for the act to have a peacetime application.

Greenwood argues that the drafters of the WMA never intended to use it in peacetime. He cites contemporaries' use of language when discussing the WMA, including Borden, who referred to the WMA as a "wartime" measure in his memoirs. Canada did not have the power to declare war independent from Britain, and the government may never have viewed the WMA as having a peacetime application, but its very nature as a blanket act made this a possibility. As Martin Friedland has argued, the vagueness in the government's wording in defining a crisis, such as considering war "real or apprehended," and its ability to define the emergency situation and when it should end, made it possible that the act would function at some point in peacetime as well.[9] Case law was on the government's side. During the war the government regulated prices of certain goods and continued that practice for a short time after it ended. The *Winnipeg Free Press* bought paper from Fort Francis Pulp and Paper and brought a claim against Fort Francis Pulp after the war because it was charging more for its paper than the amount regulated by the government through an order-in-council. Fort Francis lost the case, with the WMA still in effect after the end of the war, the court declaring that the government had "considerable freedom to judge as to the sufficiency of the emergency upon which it bases its actions."

The drafters of the WMA, principally O'Connor, believed that his version of the WMA marked an improvement over the DORA. The DORA, he claimed, was amended often, whereas the WMA governed Canada during the war "from start to finish" without any amendments. He believed that his version of the WMA was the most effective type of act.[10] While the climate of war fuelled a sense of fear or insecurity, the government's attempt to improve the WMA, by making it better at dealing with threats than its British counterpart, reveals a calculated and planned response, at least before the war was really underway. The government understood exactly what type of act it was passing and the powers it would confer. More importantly, it was now only the government, only the sovereign power, that had the power to determine what was and was not an emergency and when it should end.[11] Such threats in need of containment would eventually include public displays of opposition to the war and opposition to capitalism.

When the First World War began, British nationalism was running high within English-Canadian society. Many had a heightened emotional attachment to empire, which the war would later shatter. Enlistment was initially voluntary, and many young men, mostly British immigrants, were initially eager to serve, viewing the war as a chance for adventure while doing their duty for the good of the empire. Newspapers churned out propaganda daily, encouraging everyone to do their part for the war effort. Recruitment organizations led parades to boost enlistment, donations for soldiers' families were collected, schoolchildren collected scrap metal, and women's groups made socks for soldiers overseas. Women entered the formal workforce in record numbers, ensuring industry could keep up with wartime production demands. Everyone was encouraged to do their part to fight "for democracy."[12]

Feelings of nobleness in fighting for king and country were shattered when waves of the broken bodies of young men returned to Canadian shores and the lists of dead grew enormous. The government passed numerous orders-in-council to try to keep the economy and wartime production stable and to combat dwindling morale and growing discontent with the war. Some of these measures included the creation of a press censor, the registration of all workers to deal with labour shortages, an income tax to help fund the war, and daylight saving time to reduce energy consumption. Among the new policies was the internment and registration of immigrants from enemy nations who were viewed with suspicion, many being branded as "enemy aliens."[13] After Borden was elected in 1917 with a Union government consisting of Conservatives and Liberals, conscription became mandatory with the Military Services Act. A once noninterventionist government had, by 1917, begun intervening in a whole host of areas of Canadians' lives, from the economy and industry to labour. Canadian capitalists helped serve as administrators of the government's new policies with respect to industry and labour. These new interventions, coupled with the negative stories of the horrors of the war emerging from the front, created a growing distaste among Canadians both for the war and the government.

Feelings of discontent and unrest continued to grow. Conscription in Quebec was met with violent uprisings, commonly known as the Easter Riots. The violence and opposition in Quebec was interpreted by the government as the beginning of a rebellion, and in fearing a civil war, it put down the rioters with a deployment of six thousand troops and the suspension of *habeas corpus*. The 1918 Easter Riots in Quebec City led to the passing of PC 834, which gave the government the legal authority to crush any perceived insurrections with military force and the imposition of martial law.[14] As Borden declared, "When there is an emergency . . ." the government will endeavour to "act instantly." Borden claimed the government would maintain order not only in Quebec but in "every part of Canada."[15] The quelling of the Easter Riots became a template for how the government interpreted and responded to opposition. The government viewed the rioters not as citizens expressing dissent towards government policy but as agitators seeking civil war. Any public display of opposition was treated as disloyal and was met with a violent and stern response. The Easter Riots were the first test of the government's use of heavy-handed and repressive powers free from the normal legal scrutiny that such actions would elicit in a state of normalcy. The measures succeeded brilliantly. Not only did the government effectively crush its opponents with the use of force and violence; it did so without suffering from any substantial legal challenge to its authority or its actions.

In addition to the unrest, the cost of living was sharply rising as wartime production soared, and so was the demand for goods. Trade unionism was growing, and when the government engaged in a policy of banning strikes towards the end of the war, discontent only grew. Socialists and anarchists were challenging the government and the war, as well as the economic system they believed was responsible for all the misfortune in society.[16] Many wanted to create a new society by ending capitalism. Groups such as the Industrial Workers of the World (IWW) and political parties such as the Social Democratic Party (SDP) engaged in general strikes and protests to pursue their causes. Following the October Revolution in Russia in 1917, in which the Bolsheviks overthrew the czar, many activists in Canada and other countries, including the United States and Britain, became emboldened by the Bolsheviks' success and ramped up their propaganda and protests. The government kept a close watch on the activities of leftist groups – Dominion Police and the Royal Northwest Mounted Police (RNWMP) recruited spies to keep close tabs on the labour unrest.[17] Calls from industry for the government to take action against activists began as early as 1917 and continued throughout 1918. In February, industry groups, such as the Imperial Munitions Board, were informing the government of labour disruptions caused by the IWW in logging and shipbuilding.[18] The government believed that it needed to do something to combat activists. It thought that many of them were entering Canada from the United States to avoid prosecution. They were openly flouting and challenging the legal and political authority of the government. For the government, they were being political in unacceptable ways and at an unacceptable time.

In the United States in 1917, the government went on the offensive against groups such as the IWW through new legislation called the Espionage Act. The act was meant to target individuals or groups that sought to stir up "disaffection" that could endanger the war effort. The act criminalized the distribution of "treasonable or anarchistic" material. It provided for sweeping powers over the press to target writing that "may be useful to the enemy."[19] Loyalty to the state was a defining feature of the act. Industry was putting pressure on the Canadian government to respond to leftist activists in a similar vein as the Americans were. For instance, on 22 March 1918, the Temiskaming Mine Managers' Association notified the government that mine managers were having a difficult time with activists, such as James Simpson of Toronto, who would later head the Toronto Trades and Labour Council and become mayor, and that "inflammatory" speeches were sympathetic to the Bolsheviki Socialists of Russia.[20] Police officials from across the country met in early 1918 to study the issue and sought guidance and advice from American authorities. Canadian police wanted to know what the Americans were doing to combat the problem in their country.[21]

Radical leftists, be they of the anarchist or socialist variety (politicians often believed the two were synonymous), were frequently portrayed as "dangerous foreigners" at work in Canadian society.[22] The acting chief commissioner of police, Albert J. Cawdron, called on the government to devise an order-in-council that would outlaw any meetings in a foreign language and ban foreign literature to halt leftist propaganda. The chief commissioner of the Dominion Police, Percy Sherwood, told the government in May 1918 that he received reports from industry that "alien enemies" were preparing to stir up trouble at Port Arthur and Fort William. "Finlanders" in particular, he noted, were a "disturbing element."[23] The IWW in Canada was categorized by the Dominion Police as an "invasion," and Finnish activists, many of whom were members, were regarded by some Anglo-Canadians as "anarchists."[24] In Winnipeg in May 1918, construction workers on strike were described by the business community as being unnaturalized foreigners.[25]

Fear was now beginning to run high. Fears of foreign, Bolshevik subversives operating in Canada were strong enough for Borden to turn to a trusted advisor to help devise a solution. That advisor was C.H. Cahan, a Montreal-based lawyer who was well connected with the Conservatives and had high political ambitions. As early as 1912, Justice Minister Doherty sought to hire Cahan to act as the government's counsel on a series of freight cases that were to go before the Railway Commission. At the time, Cahan felt he was too busy to accept but said he would consider something else in the future.[26] On 19 May 1918, Borden made an appeal to Cahan to investigate radicalism in Canada. He wanted to know if measures that were tried in the United States, such as the creation of the American Protective League (APL), should be adopted in Canada.[27] The APL was a voluntary organization backed by the American government. The purpose of the group was to encourage members to hunt for anyone whose loyalty was suspect and to report them to the Department of Justice. The group would resolve issues itself through physical violence and intimidation, including horsewhipping farmers who refused to donate to the Red Cross. It was known to commit murder, as it did when one American who was branded as disloyal was wrapped in an American flag and killed in the street. The group was responsible for hangings of IWW members.[28] Cahan accepted the offer. He made his first report to Justice Minister Doherty on 20 July 1919.

In his report, Cahan wrote that he had consulted with American officials about their response to radicalism. He toured many US and Canadian cities to gauge the unrest occurring across the northern half of the continent. Cahan told Doherty that he had been in touch with British intelligence operating in the United States. He concluded that he did not believe that enemy aliens, such as German immigrants, posed a significant threat to the government at the present time. Instead, Cahan was concerned with other immigrants he believed were enemies. He believed that Eastern European people were directly responsible for spreading "socialistic doctrines" in Canada. It was this material that Cahan believed was stirring up unrest. Furthermore, he said he did not believe that a group like the APL would work in Canada. In fact, he thought it would lead to more unrest. He thought such a group in Quebec would end up targeting Protestants and that in Ontario Roman Catholics would be targeted by this type of group.

Cahan believed emotions were behind much of the unrest. He believed that people were angry over food prices, the Military Services Act, and the treatment of returned soldiers, and were discontent with the way the government was running the country. He maintained that "the enthusiasm of the Canadian people in respect of the war [was] rapidly diminishing" and that the "moral purpose of the people" to sacrifice everything for the war was "sadly weakened." He thought that Canadians were getting too selfish. For example, he claimed that workers, fed up with stories of profiteering, now wanted their share of profits and that the returned soldier expected "everything." The unrest that was occurring was due to the population's weakened sense of purpose and the diminished ability of Canadians to continue the war to achieve victory. If the people were stronger, they could resist the urge to engage in strikes and other protests, and presumably by Cahan's logic, other selfish behaviour. People needed to feel connected to the war again. The solution, according to Cahan, was to reenergize the population, to reinvigorate their patriotic spirit so that they could harden their resolve to continue fighting. He believed himself up to the task and thought that extending the powers of the Dominion Police was the best way to restore the people's moral fibre. For Cahan, by stopping those responsible for the unrest, the weakened population would be restored to full strength and once again support the war effort. It is unclear whether Cahan actually believed this scheme would work or if he was setting the stage to justify a position for himself in the government. Borden was supportive of Cahan's efforts, as was Doherty, who asked Cahan to devise solutions for how to end the unrest in Canada and restore Canadians' resolve.[29]

There were some officials who, unlike Cahan, thought groups like the IWW or the SDP posed no significant threat. Chief Commissioner Percy Sherwood of the Dominion Police, after thoroughly investigating the complaints he had received about the IWW across the country, reported to Doherty that "no trace of IWW activity could be found in this country." Sherwood presented a much more moderate stance than the previous acting commissioner, Albert Cawdron. While he admitted that some IWW literature had been imported by groups such as the SDP, Sherwood did not believe the SDP "exist[ed] for any sinister purpose, but rather for the improvement of their conditions as workers and toward the securing of better pay." The admission by the chief was a rare one among law enforcement; Sherwood's counterpart, A.B. Perry, chief of the RNWMP and soon-to-be first commissioner of the Royal Canadian Mounted Police (RCMP), was much more of a hardliner when it came to leftists. Perry believed that the "pernicious doctrines of Bolshevism" were present throughout the country and that foreigners were especially vulnerable to them. Sherwood was clearly no supporter of communism or activists, but he did not believe, after collaborating with police across the country, that the IWW or SDP posed any real threat.[30]

Cahan responded to Doherty's request for a plan to deal with left-wing activists with a lengthy report. Cahan wanted to expand the qualifications for internment to include three more nationalities – Russians, Ukrainians, and Finns – as they were "thoroughly saturated" with socialist ideology. Cahan detailed how governments in other Allied countries had dealt with groups like the IWW. In Australia, the IWW was considered an unlawful organization for the duration of the war and for six months after its end. In the United States, the IWW's leadership was arrested. Cahan warned that delegates of the Russian Bolsheviks had arrived in Canada and the United States and that their spreading of propaganda had to stop. Bolsheviki, he argued, were "alien enemies." Cahan gave examples of seditious literature such as poems by Jack London, the acclaimed novelist, who had protested the war. He provided numerous examples of literature from such groups as the SDP, who called for an end to capitalism and the war. To combat the spread of socialism, he suggested banning a number of organizations immediately, including the IWW and SDP. All foreign literature should be banned and its distribution prohibited. "Drastic regulations," Cahan claimed, "should be drawn up under the War Measures Act for the purpose of preventing foreign propagandists from advocating and organizing revolution in Canada." Cahan believed that a public safety branch should be created to oversee the execution of the new measures, similar to in the United States, and that these measures and the office overseeing them should continue into peacetime. In the United States, he argued, even though the federal government was restrained by the Constitution, it recognized that "even in times of peace, [it] has found it necessary . . . to extend the authority of the Attorney General." Cahan was eager for the creation of a body in Canada similar to the US government's new Bureau of Investigation, with himself at the helm.[31]

As the government pondered Cahan's report, he continued to send more information both to Borden and Doherty to further support his claims that Bolsheviks were at work in Canada and the United States in seeking revolution. Cahan forwarded US intelligence reports that detailed how the new Soviet government sought to combat counter-revolution propaganda in the United States and Canada and to sabotage munitions in Canada and the US that were headed to Russia. The Allies at this time were actively supporting military operations led by the White Russians, who opposed the new Soviet government.[32]

The government announced its plan for dealing with left-wing activists on 24 September 1918, and it was clear that the hardliners had won, as the plan wholeheartedly endorsed Cahan's suggestions. The Public Safety Branch, with Cahan heading it up, was created. It introduced two new orders-in-council in line with Cahan's suggestions and the ordinances of other Western powers, such as Australia and the United States: PC 2381, which outlawed all foreign language papers and presses, and PC 2384, which was more substantial and broader in scope. PC 2384 linked certain ethnic groups, such as Finns and Russians, with radical leftists and banned other left-wing groups. It gave the government the ability to ban even more groups by designating any group that advocated economic or governmental change by force or violence as an unlawful organization, with force remaining undefined.[33] It outlawed the distribution of literature produced by these groups and the possession of it. In addition, the new measure had a reverse onus provision. An individual was presumed guilty of violating the law if they were a member of one of the listed groups or were in possession of any literature deemed seditious by officers.[34] As other historians have argued, PC 2384's focus was on labour and the left and allowed for the government to engage in "political policing."[35]

Cahan's recommendations were not entirely novel. Regulating the politics of immigrants (with deportation as punishment) became legal after the government passed Bill 102 on 22 March 1910, creating Section 41 of the Immigration Act. This section was nearly identical to Section 2 of the US Immigration Act of 1903, which permitted the deportation of "anarchists, or persons who believe in or advocate the overthrow by force and violence of the Government of the United States . . ." It prevented the immigration of anyone holding these views.[36] The explanatory notes from 1910 for Section 41 detail how the US government was justified in taking measures to deal with anarchists and how the Canadian version was similarly designed to prevent such persons from becoming a menace in Canada. Section 41 stated that "whenever any person other than a Canadian citizen advocates in Canada the overthrow by force or violence the government of or constituted authority" of Canada or Great Britain, that person would be liable to deportation. Anyone who caused a public disorder, attempted or created a riot, or belonged to any organization, secret or otherwise, that taught "disbelief to organized government" was eligible for deportation.[37]

These measures enabled the government to regulate what ideologies immigrants should adhere to by outlawing the expression of unwanted ones. The changes being proposed by Cahan were based on the Espionage Act and the US measures taken in 1903 against immigrants. In sum, PC 2384 extended exceptional measures initially targeted towards immigrants to the entire Canadian population during the war. All in Canada would be told what they could or could not believe in or how they should act politically to avoid being seen as foreign and disloyal by the government and targeted by the law. The nation as defined by the government was one that was loyal to Britain and the war effort and tied to capitalism. Nation-building by force was in effect. The war caused intense divisions in Canadian society, and among many, scorn for imperialism and empire.[38]

Following the creation of PC 2384, the government targeted potential Bolshevik revolutionaries, most notably the leader of the SDP, Isaac Bainbridge. He was pursued by the government, Ian Milligan has argued, because of the SDP's strong ethnic base and the SDP's widely outspoken opposition to the war and capitalism more generally.[39] Mass arrests became regular occurrences. The new laws and arrests did not find favour with members of Borden's Union government. Newton Rowell, president of the Privy Council and former Ontario Liberal leader, was not pleased with the government's actions, which were undertaken while he was in Western Canada meeting with police officials (he had the RNWMP cabinet file). While he did not have sympathy for Bolsheviks, he was opposed to outlawing political parties, like the SDP, simply because of their views. Rowell argued that there was nothing in the SDP's constitution that warranted attacking this labour party. He told Borden and Doherty that the only way to combat the SDP's ideas was to publicly debate them and that repression was not in the public interest. That the SDP had existed "for more than ten years" without being a target of the authorities left the government with no excuse, in Rowell's opinion, for banning the party.[40]

Rowell thought that by engaging in such actions instead of public debate, the government would only be uniting the progressive elements of society into insisting that freedom of speech and "freedom of thought" not be curtailed. He believed that questioning the economy should be a protected right. Thomas Crerar, a prominent Western Canadian Liberal and future Progressive Party leader, opposed heavy-handed actions, arguing that Cahan's policies were "the very negation of the first principle of democracy."[41] Cahan defended his position, sensing that his opponents would find favour with Borden and have the new laws struck down, or worse, that his job and office would be shuttered. In a letter to Minister of the Interior Arthur Meighen, Cahan tried to justify his method of dealing with activists with fear by whipping up the prospect of revolution and claiming he needed more staff and more resources to contain the problem.[42] Cahan's office did not get the resources it sought, and he subsequently resigned in January 1919; his office was disbanded. No sources remain to explain why Borden pulled the plug on Cahan's plans. We can only surmise that Borden was receptive to Cahan's critics because he felt he needed to keep his Union government united during the war and immediately following it.[43] With Borden off to Europe in the spring of 1919 for the Paris Peace Conference, and Sir Thomas White acting in his place in Canada, PC 2384 was rescinded on 2 April 1919.

The creation of the WMA and PC 2384 set important precedents for dealing with left-wing activists and how loyalty to the state could be maintained, in addition to revealing the importance the government placed on advisors. Individuals like O'Connor and Cahan wielded important influence within Borden's government and were responsible for both the WMA and PC 2384. They were opportunistic and sought to achieve important roles in government. Their influence also reveals how forces in civil society during the war could activate interests and ideas in the state to accomplish repression, as in the Winnipeg General Strike and prosecution of the strike leaders.[44]

The WMA and PC 2384 were based on laws in other Allied countries: the former modelled after the DORA in Britain and the latter based on the Espionage Act in the United States, as well as early versions of the US Immigration Act and Section 41 in Canada's 1910 Immigration Act. For the government, left-wing activists were an international threat. In the case of the WMA, its creators believed that the broader the power given to the state the better. Emotion was an important factor in PC 2384's creation. During the war emotions ran high throughout society. There were strong feelings of loyalty and patriotism for Britain and the war effort, which turned to anger and distain for empire as the war went on. Lawmakers felt a need to do better, such as when they created the WMA in an attempt to improve on Britain's DORA. People's anger with the government was problematic according to Cahan, and the government's fear of revolutionary action by foreigners was influential in creating PC 2384.[45]

Most importantly, the First World War provided the government with the ability to set the terms for what constituted an emergency. It established that in times of emergency, judging ideology was acceptable to ensure the loyalty of citizens. Such an action could be taken because it is only the sovereign that determines what the law applies to. Sovereign power exists independently of itself, located in a liminal state of potentiality. In the creation of the WMA and PC 2384, we witness an important expression of sovereign power, when the government not only demonstrated its ability to function outside of the normal confines of the law but also its ability to decide what the law applied to, in this case political ideology, and its freedom to act without parliamentary oversight. It alone reserved the power to judge and believed it needed to crush those who judged it and its actions or acted politically without its approval.[46] Those who were deemed disloyal because of their politics were abandoned by law in that they were subject to the force of the law but denied protection against it. Such individuals could be arrested or interned and were subject to the exceptional powers of the WMA. The result was that the government demonstrated by implication to citizens and immigrants alike what politics were and were not acceptable.

In addition, attacking people on the basis of political ideology was based not only on class lines – class and ethnicity were often linked when it came to the government's perception of leftists. PC 2384 banned Finnish, Russian, Eastern European, and socialist groups. Where one was born or what language one spoke could easily determine whether an individual was regarded as loyal.[47] Even those of British descent were regarded as foreign to some extent, should they make the mistake of falling in line with socialists or anarchists. For instance, in the case of Charles Watson and Harold Cheeseman, the two were arrested in Toronto on 1 January 1919 for "disseminating Bolshevik propaganda." After their arrests, they were charged with being in possession of illegal literature such as Marx's *Wage Labor and Capital*, among other titles. Watson was given a three-year sentence in Kingston Penitentiary and fined $500, and Cheeseman received six months in jail. The stiff sentence was meant as a deterrent, as the judge believed that "persons of British birth or descent above all should not forget the orderly traditions of their race. It would be a disgrace if they associated themselves with the propaganda of foreign cut-throats."[48] The court believed that Britons would be race traitors for supporting ideologies that it believed were disorderly, foreign, ruthless, and savage. These ideologies were not what British citizens should associate with.

The government felt it had to coordinate with its southern neighbour in dealing with activists – lest they seek safe haven in Canada. Canadian policy-makers' views of left-wing activists were influenced by its international allies. Threats were everywhere. With the war concluded, it would be only a matter of months before the government found itself again faced with an emergency situation at the hands of foreign activists, be they British or otherwise. Canadians needed to feel safe, and exceptional laws to deal with exceptional threats could help. While the government had exceptional powers during the war, these powers were meant to end. The labour revolt would change that.

Winnipeg

The rich, who have become rich on war profits, know that this is the price of blood . . . They live trembling at the thought of the future. They are afraid of retribution. They live in fear today and dread tomorrow. They feel deep down that there is a day of reckoning.[49]

These sentiments, expressed during the Winnipeg General Strike, illustrate the high level of discontent felt by workers during the revolt of 1919 and paint a picture of a working class interested in social change. The unrest in 1918 intensified after the war: workers' grievances still remained unresolved. Many were still working in dangerous conditions, for very long hours and low pay. Unemployment rose with the end of wartime production and an influx of returning soldiers. Labour was in full revolt in 1919; approximately 150,000 workers took part in 428 separate struggles. Kealey has estimated that in 1919 the equivalent of nearly 3.5 million days of work were lost to industrial conflicts. The Winnipeg General Strike served as the epicentre and climax of the national revolt.[50]

There are a host of studies that deal with the strike and its violent end, and so for the sake of brevity I will deal with the issues most pertinent to Section 98 and its creation in Parliament. The general strike began on 15 May 1919. Tensions between building workers and the Winnipeg Builders' Exchange were ongoing throughout the spring of 1919. Negotiations broke down when metal workers failed to secure a deal with the employers' council to have their union recognized; both groups sought support from Winnipeg's Trade and Labour Council, which called for a general strike. The result was that nearly thirty thousand workers walked off their jobs in support of their fellow workers. The scale of the strike reflected the tensions felt by workers in Canadian society. Sympathy strikes broke out across the country in Vancouver, Toronto, and Montreal. Winnipeg effectively shut down and was run by the Central Strike Committee, consisting of British-born workers such as R.B. Russell, William Ivens, R.E. Bray, A.A. Heaps, John Queen, and George Armstrong. Almost immediately, a group of business and industry leaders, called the Citizens' Committee of 1,000, led by local lawyer A.J. Andrews, opposed the strike and sought to devise an end to it by working directly with federal government representatives. Andrews, in particular, worked closely with Arthur Meighen to pressure Ottawa to enact new legislation that would permit the prosecution and deportation of those responsible for the strike – blamed on foreign Bolsheviks seeking revolution.[51]

Before the strike began, the government was searching for solutions to the unrest. It commissioned a special committee, headed by Solicitor General Hugh Guthrie, on 1 May 1919, to report on the existing sedition laws of the country. The committee consisted of both Liberal and Conservative members of the government.[52] No transcripts exist of that committee, but its findings were tabled in the House of Commons on 6 June 1919, with the strike well underway. Given the government's previous responses towards labour and leftists, the committee's findings were expected: Canada's laws should be strengthened. Cahan and his orders-in-council were gone, but there were many in the government that shared his ideas about left-wing activists.

Once again, Canada was in sync with its allies. Frustrated with the inability to easily deport and arrest anarchists and socialists, the US government responded to the demands of law enforcement and strengthened both the Espionage Act and the Immigration Act in 1918.[53] The new laws broadly expanded the definition of an anarchist to include persons who "advise, advocate, or teach, or who are members of, or affiliated with, any organization, society, or group, that advises, advocates, or teaches opposition to all organized government."[54] The UK followed suit. It extended wartime measures against immigrants into peacetime with the 1919 Aliens Restriction Act, which contained similar powers as the US measures, in addition to restricting employment for immigrants.[55] In nearly an identical fashion as its allies, the Canadian special committee made two suggestions: to amend the Immigration Act and to create a new Criminal Code section specifically relating to political offences. The changes would be made together. These two provisions would be in place during peacetime, the same as with the US and UK laws.

The first changes were made to the Immigration Act. Minister of Immigration and Colonization J.A. Calder introduced Bill 132 to amend the Immigration Act on 6 June 1919. The amendment would target "persons who advocated the overthrow of government, the destruction of property, and so on" and place them in the category of the "prohibited classes," thereby permitting deportation. The bill would strike out Section 15 of the act, which read, "Whenever any person other than a Canadian citizen advocates in Canada the overthrow" of government, etc., and amend Section 41, which would now read that "every person who by word or act in Canada seeks to overthrow by force or violence the government of or constituted authority" of Canada or Great Britain would be liable to deportation. The changes would be retroactive to May 1910. The bill was designed to target political activists who were British subjects, such as many of the leaders and participants of the Winnipeg strike.[56] The bill passed the House and Senate on 6 June in approximately twenty minutes, which, according to Meighen, "certainly beat all records." British-born, naturalized immigrants could now be legally deported.[57]

Meanwhile, the Winnipeg strike took a violent turn within days of the passing of Section 41's new amendment and was put down by the RNWMP. A.J. Andrews of the Citizens' Committee served as Crown in the case against the leaders; although he was eager for new sedition laws and deportation powers, they were not used. A number of the strike's leaders ended up being charged with seditious conspiracy and seditious libel. The new amendment to Section 41 was highly controversial, particularly its retroactive element, which allowed for statements dating back to 1910 to be used against prospective deportees. The amendment was opposed by influential British-Canadian trade union leaders such as Tom Moore. Using these new deportation measures would have been politically disastrous. Convicting the leaders under the Criminal Code served Andrews's goal of criminalizing the strike.[58]

The end of the strike did not change much for the government. The events in Winnipeg were still regarded as a budding Soviet-style revolution led by foreigners. The special committee to investigate sedition in Canada was created before the strike. The general strike reinforced the view of committee members that PC 2384 should be revived. Some were eager for changes to sedition, including Commissioner Perry, who according to Senator Robinson wanted "that Criminal Code amendment" that Guthrie introduced passed so that he could "take general action throughout Western Canada at an early date."[59] Despite Perry's eagerness, the mass action he wanted to take with what would become Section 98 would have seriously inflamed already high tensions, and the resulting trials would have exposed numerous agents the service had undercover in Western Canada.

On 10 June 1919, Hugh Guthrie moved that the House adopt the report of the special committee on sedition and seditious propaganda that was presented on 6 June. Guthrie presented the government's case, stressing that the recommendations of the committee would not target established labour groups. He denied that the committee was a response to the Winnipeg General Strike, as the *Globe* and other media had reported. Guthrie reminded the House that the committee had been assembled before the strike began. He admitted that the committee was concerned with political and labour unrest in Canada and around the world. Guthrie argued that organizations distributing dangerous propaganda were a threat to freedom and that many were openly operating in the United States, Europe, and Canada. He believed that these organizations were "not native to the soil of this free country" but were "foreign importations."[60] The government believed that without direct and swift action, foreign fighters would spread revolution beyond Winnipeg. Being in sync with Canada's allies and their response to the security threat, and not just quelling domestic unrest, was a pressing concern for the government.

Implementing these Criminal Code changes would work in conjunction with the amendments to the Immigration Act. The Criminal Code sections would target the existing foreign organizations and naturalized activists, and the changes to the Immigration Act would allow for the deportation of nonnaturalized activists. Left-wing activists, be they foreign or domestic, were targeted with the changes to the Immigration Act and Criminal Code.

Guthrie continued and stated that sedition was not well understood in Canada and that Canadians should look to England, who was more experienced with the subject. His analysis was that England and Canada had a policy of "passive inaction" in which not every soapbox orator would face charges of sedition. But, he claimed, the war had changed the world; there were now more threats to liberty from different schools of thought, and unrest existed throughout the world. Canada, along with other nations, had to face the reality of the new situation. Guthrie reminded the House that during the war censorship and other provisions existed within the orders-in-council that targeted groups of a seditious nature, but since the signing of the armistice and the softening of these powers, these radical groups were becoming more intrepid. He concluded: "I believe the time has come when action should be taken by this Parliament to put in statutory form some, at least, of the provisions which did appear in those Orders-in-Council."[61] Guthrie believed that the seriousness of the labour situation warranted the re-creation of PC 2384, but this time it would function as a permanent part of Canada's Criminal Code rather than a temporary wartime power. The government's emergency measures during the war were about to become a normal part of Canadian life because in the eyes of the government, the threat of political activism would never end. With the protection of the law, the government and the public could feel safe and security could be preserved.

Guthrie claimed that the proposed amendments to the Criminal Code would not be radical and that much of the Code would remain the same – with the exception of two "slight" changes.[62] The first dealt with unlawful associations: any organization could be unlawful if it supported any governmental or economic change in Canada by the use of force or violence. All its members would be found guilty of an offence if the association was declared unlawful, and all its property could be seized. What constituted force remained undefined. Section 2 of the report dealt with sedition and seditious offences. Guthrie recounted the history of sedition law in Canada and how an original definition of sedition was struck out of the 1892 Criminal Code draft bill, which sought to codify English criminal law in Canada. At that time the House opted to leave sedition undefined and allow its definition to fall to the common law. Despite leaving sedition undefined, the committee recommended that Section 133 of the Code, which was known as the "saving clause," be struck out. This clause protected someone from a charge of sedition if a writing or speech was done in good faith to right an injustice or if the speech or document drew attention to a mistake the Crown or government had made. Guthrie stated that this clause was "too broad" and acted as a "cloak and shield" for offenders to hide behind. Prosecutions around the country, he claimed, had failed due to the existence of the clause. The report suggested striking out the penalty section for sedition (Section 134); instead of having the penalty for the offence be a maximum of two years, the penalty provision should be one to twenty years in prison.

The committee defined a seditious publication, something the Code did not do. Guthrie stated that a charge of seditious libel could still take place but that now the Code contained a new section that would expressly state that anyone who printed, distributed, or possessed material that "advocated, advised or defended" or "taught" that force or violence be used to accomplish government or economic change would be guilty of sedition. The new section would cover circulating the material through the mail – no previous law had made it an offence to circulate material. Guthrie believed these changes would make Canada's sedition laws clearer. He brought to the House's attention that the US laws were much harsher and that the security of both Canada and the United States was at risk.[63]

In essence, what Guthrie was suggesting was the creation of a new Code section that would define a particular brand of sedition, or as Meighen decades later put it, the Communist brand.[64] These proposed changes were part of a gradual transition in the purpose of Canada's Criminal Code and the expectations of what the Code could achieve. Over the nineteenth century, the state increasingly shifted from "reactive to preemptive" in the way it dealt with political crimes. The conception of allegiance changed from what was formally a personal bond between the subject and the sovereign to loyalty to an "abstract state." With this transition came the acceptance of withdrawing one's allegiance to that state should it no longer serve the interests of the people. Within Britain and British North America there was, as Susan Binnie and Barry Wright have stated, a "growing Lockean notion that criticism of authority was a right."[65] Seditious words, libels, and conspiracies were common law offences, with legislative encroachments added in the late eighteenth and nineteenth centuries. The offences were legislatively restated in the 1892 Canadian Criminal Code, although the opportunity to set out a precise and limited modern definition of sedition was lost.

In Sir John Thompson's original bill to codify Canadian criminal law in 1892, seditious intention was defined as an intention that sought to "bring into hatred or contempt" the governing authority, to "excite" citizens into "alteration of any matters of state" by unlawful means, or to promote "disaffection" or "ill-will" between classes.[66] As Desmond Brown details, the necessity of a definition for sedition was challenged in the House. Louis Davies, for example, argues that sedition offences were intimately connected to the common law, which is "elastic and justly elastic. It is made by the prudence of the judges . . . to suit the development of the people and the constitution."[67] A defined sedition law would cripple the ability of judges to weigh each case on its own merits, which an offence such as sedition demanded, given the incredibly fine line between sedition and freedom of speech. While the concession left much in the hands of judicial discretion, the Code included a saving clause as a reference point. Section 133 stated that no one could be found guilty of sedition for lawfully criticizing the government.[68] However, as Guthrie made clear, the special committee of 1919 recommended the removal of that very clause, the effect of which would be to limit the ability of judges to distinguish between what was seditious and what was legitimate expression of free speech. Instead, the government would draw the line with the recommended amendments; there would be no reference to lawful criticism, and simple association with unlawful organizations would be deemed seditious. The special committee aimed to make a sweeping wartime measure into a permanent feature of Canadian criminal law.

At the same time the government was also defining what the threat to security was and what to do about it. The threat was the political ideology and actions of radical leftists, but because the security threat could not be linked to one individual, group, or even a specific time and place, the only way to restore security was to have an exceptional law target ideology and actions and be permanent. Canada's response had to match Canada's allies since the security threat existed everywhere. As Agamben argues, within the exceptional state, effects are governed, not causes. Rather than govern the cause of unrest, namely the contradictions within capitalism, it targeted the effects of it – leftwing activism.[69] But these effects, leftists, would exist as long as the cause existed, thus the law that targeted them had to last indefinitely. The link between time and crisis was shattered. The crisis now existed outside of time. It was permanent, unending, and the emergency law to combat it, to feel safe again, had to be the same.

The normalizing of emergency laws was not just an attempt to force order on the unruly. The fact that the government recognized that the emergency would extend indefinitely, and so would the legal response to it, meant that the government understood it could never order disorder. It could only manage it.[70] By policing the side effects of capitalism with the law, the sovereign power could manage the challenging impulses of its citizens and foreigners indefinitely and demonstrate by implication what ideologies were legal and Canadian.

Charles Murphy of the Liberal Party was the only person who opposed the committee's report. Murphy told the House that the committee was bitterly divided on the need for any reforms to Canada's sedition laws. He believed that people would take Guthrie's reforms as attacks against labour. His assessment would prove to be very accurate, but the report was concurred in by the House.[71]

On 27 June 1919, Arthur Meighen, then acting minister of justice, tabled Bill 160, which contained the suggested amendments to the Criminal Code. The amendments were bundled with other crime amendments, such as prohibitions against trespassing on militia property and the carrying of concealed weapons without a permit. The bill went into second reading on 1 July 1919. One of the first issues discussed was the concealed weapons amendment. Meighen used the opportunity to blame foreigners for firearm offences and link them to his sedition amendments. He claimed that with this legislation no alien would be able to possess a firearm and that recently there had been dangerous immigrants found with weapons. These dangerous men were "not British subjects; they [were] very often alien enemies."[72] In discussing the bill, there was some concern by members of the House about its targeting of aliens and not all British subjects. Guthrie defended Meighen, claiming that over the past few years nearly all serious violent crimes in Ontario had been caused by foreigners.

The strategy of the government was to portray foreigners as the cause of violent gun crime and to follow up these Criminal Code amendments with the changes to sedition, creating the impression that foreigners were concealing guns and preparing for revolution. Meighen was questioned as to why he did not regard British subjects as being just as dangerous, given that the government had recently passed legislation that enabled the deportation of British subjects. He said he did, but added: "there is a certain class of British subjects to whom we have extended the law . . . we have, under the stress of exceptional circumstances, seen fit to enact that law."[73] The exceptional law was the amendment to Section 41, with the "certain class" being socialist British-born activists. As Meighen stated, those British subjects who were targeted by Canada's changes to immigration were of a different class. They were radical leftists, and that class of British, in his eyes at least, was dangerous. There was sparsely any opposition to the bill, which passed its third reading.

Senator James Alexander Lougheed, Conservative government leader in the Senate, introduced Bill 160 and continued the government's strategy of linking foreigners to violence. He claimed the amendments were needed to target "unrest and disturbance" in Canada that had been brought about "chiefly by aliens."[74] Even though the new Code section was applicable to all Canadians, many still believed that it would affect only naturalized aliens because only "aliens" were "radicals." Lougheed stated that the government was aware of many foreign organizations that advocated anarchy and the "subversion of our present institutions and government." Before heeding Lougheed's call to quickly pass the bill, Senator Gideon Robertson, a labour man, wanted an explanation of what force meant in the bill when used in reference to "industrial or economic change within Canada by use of force or violence."[75] Lougheed presumed it referred to physical force. Robertson would support the bill only so long as the meaning of force was physical force. The Senate did agree to amend the bill's minimum sentence of one year and instead leave the minimum to the judge's discretion. Senator Lawrence Power of the Liberals took exception to the removal of Section 133 of the Code, the sedition saving clause, which received no debate in the House of Commons, arguing that such a clause was worth having in the Code to allow for free speech that rightfully criticized the government's actions. To strike it out, he argued, would be to "Prussianize the Canadian system."[76]

Lougheed assured Power that no one who had good intentions would be penalized and that the "latitude" of the Canadian law had allowed for the first time in history the establishment of a "Russian form of revolutionary government in one of our principal cities [Winnipeg]." Before the bill was passed for the third time, Power offered cautionary words: "It is said that hard cases make bad laws, and the unfortunate occurrences in Winnipeg and elsewhere throughout the country have naturally caused people to some extent to lose their heads, and measures . . . to deal with these revolutionaries are perhaps liable to make trouble for decent, honest, loyal people at some later date; that is all. I think we ought to be very careful that we do not pass some legislation which will interfere with the reasonable rights and liberties of our people."[77] Power's fears were disregarded, and Sections 97(a) and (b), later renamed Section 98, received royal assent on 7 July 1919 and came into effect 1 October 1919.

The new section was nearly identical to PC 2384. Three specific sections will be discussed in greater detail, as they pertain to the key trials of the interwar period: 98(1), which dealt with "unlawful organizations"; 98(3), which contained definitions of members or officers of unlawful organizations; and 98(8), which dealt with seditious actions by individuals.

Section 98(1) was designed to outlaw radical political groups "whose professed purpose" was to "bring about any governmental, industrial or economic change" by the use of "force or violence" or any group that advocated or taught such beliefs.[78] Parliament sought to target socialist or communist groups with its expanded definition of sedition in Section 98(1), but the subsection created more questions than answers. Section 98(1) contained no definition of "force." Labour groups opposed Section 98(1), fearing strikes would be classed as "forcing economic change" and unions as "unlawful organizations." Justice Metcalfe's closing remarks in the R.B. Russell trial following the Winnipeg General Strike reinforced their fears. Metcalfe considered strikes as a means of using "force" to win concessions as well as being able to inspire "terror."[79] The subsection contained no definition for "teaching" or "advocating." Did an association have to actively advise its members to commit a violent act, or did simply telling them there would be an "eventual" revolution, following Karl Marx, qualify as teaching or advocating? For instance, the CPC did indeed teach that the proletariat would overthrow the bourgeoisie in a revolution, but Marx never stipulated that the revolution would be violent, only that it would occur when conditions were "ripe." These were issues debated among CPC members and between Marxists, but Section 98(1) did not take into account such nuances. A group that embraced the general view that a revolution was necessary and inevitable was potentially unlawful under this subsection.

Subsection 3 of Section 98 made it an offence for anyone to be a member or officer of such an organization.[80] No procedures in the Code set out how a group could be classified as unlawful other than by a judicial determination in the context of a trial. This omission created the potential for an individual to be charged with being a member or officer of an unlawful organization without the organization having been previously classified as such by a lawful authority. Such was the situation that leading members of the CPC faced in their November 1931 trial.

Finally, subsection 8 extended Section 98's reach. *Any* person who ". . . prints, publishes, edits, issues, circulates, sells, or offers for sale or distribution any book, newspaper, periodical, pamphlet, picture, paper, circular, card, letter, writing, print, publication or document of any kind" that taught or advocated the use of force to accomplish governmental change, if convicted, could face imprisonment for twenty years.[81] The vagueness of the terms "force," "teaching," and "advocating" was thus extended to documents. An individual could be guilty under Section 98(8) for simply sharing an "unlawful" article in a newspaper with another person or for sharing their socialist or communist views with others if the discussion included Marx's theories on revolution. Other subsections of Section 98 were just as draconian. Section 98(2) allowed the RCMP to seize property *suspected* of belonging to an unlawful organization. Section 98(5) provided that anyone renting a hall to a group that was *later* found unlawful could be fined $5,000 and face imprisonment. 98(11) made it a "duty" of any government worker in any department to seize any book or document covered by the section and turn it over immediately to the RCMP. This made civil servants an untrained body of intelligence gatherers for the government.

Section 98 severely hampered an individual's free speech and association because the terms in the section such as "force," "teaching," and "advocating" could be broadly interpreted by judges. Moreover it facilitated convictions. Section 98(4) stipulated that to prove membership in an unlawful association, the Crown needed to establish only that a person had "attended meetings," "spoken publicly in advocacy of an unlawful organization," or "distributed literature." These actions created a rebuttable presumption that the individual was a member of an unlawful organization.[82] If an individual spoke out in support of an "unlawful organization" or attended a meeting of a group that was later found unlawful, that person would be required to prove their innocence.[83] In effect, an individual who believed in or sympathized with communism had to keep their political views secret.

The creation of Section 98 and the amendments to Section 41 created no stir out of doors among the press, and no significant protest or opposition was mounted to the new laws.[84] Canadians were indifferent. This does not mean that Canadians were widely in favour of them. Indifference does not equate to acceptance. In the absence of opinion polls, we may never know the level of support for them. More likely many Canadians did not understand the power of these laws or concern themselves with Section 98 if it did not affect them. There was scant press coverage of the new law across the country and the majority of what did appear was supportive of the government's actions. Editorials in major papers mentioned how force or violence should not be used to effect change, even if force remained undefined in the new section. As one reporter put it, "humanity needs growth not explosion."[85] The *Halifax Chronicle* cautioned that when freedom is "misinterpreted," it "degenerate[s] into license." The paper's editors argued just before Section 98 was passed that it would "be almost universally applauded" as it made its way through Parliament. Bolshevism, the paper claimed, had "infected" "our people," and this law would halt the "disseminators of social disease" because before Section 98, "we were left without protection against domestic germ-carriers and germ-breeders." While the law was unprecedented in Canada, it should be regarded as "commendable." While the Immigration Act took care of foreigners, the editors warned, immigrants were not the biggest threat. "Their British disciples are more daring and more effective than they," it warned.[86]

Outside of the Commons MPs expressed their views on the issue. Arthur Meighen regarded all sympathetic strikes as unlawful and disruptive, and he called the Winnipeg General Strike a "usurpation" of government authority. While he claimed he supported collective bargaining, he viewed unions and striking as "perpetual Bolshevism." Labour disruption of this type was a sign of treasonous activity.[87] The Prime Minister shared these views when he wrote in his diary that the

Winnipeg strikers had created a revolutionary plot to overthrow the government and create a Soviet-style one. His views on the strike intimate why PC 2384 needed to be re-created. In an address to labour in the *Ottawa Citizen* in 1919, he claimed that strikes and lockouts were "almost as destructive as war itself" and that "a constant recurrence of lockouts or strikes" would make it difficult for the country to return to a state of normalcy.[88] Leftist activism was equated with disorder and disruption. Senator Captain C.G. Power of Quebec stated during the passing of Section 41's amendment and Section 98 that "the truth is, if you look at the names of the persons who are leading in these demonstrations, they are not foreign names; they are all British and American."[89] Power went on to say in an interview, "If the free air of Canada does not suit the undesirables, let us deport them. Let us deport them whether they are from the slums of Warsaw, or the Ghetto of Rome, or whether they are the scourings of Whitechapel or the dock rats of Liverpool."[90] The new laws would keep Canadians feeling safe and secure from the social disease that socialism had brought. Leftists, British or otherwise, were portrayed as the lowest element of society, equated with disease and the wrecking of British institutions and values. These views of leftists and their political actions provide insight into what lawmakers thought about themselves. If socialists were a disease, foreign and unlawful, then capitalism, parliamentary democracy, and Britishness were the cure. They were normal and Canadian.

One of the most outspoken critics of the government's changes to sedition was the Toronto Trades and Labour Council, which repeatedly petitioned the House throughout the 1920s to repeal Sections 98 and 41. The Council's lawyer J.G. O'Donoghue, in an interview with the *Star*, commented on the situation facing labour in 1919 during the trials of the Winnipeg strike leaders: "If labour does nothing" in response to the convictions of the strike leaders, he said, "then labour is an ass, because its rights have been taken away." He argued that changes to the sedition laws were a threat to everyone and were a relic of the "old ascendancy and autocratic days."[91]

The creation of Section 98 was integral to the process of normalizing emergency measures, which gave the government the power to use exceptional legal measures against people on the basis of their ideology, similar to PC 2384 during the war. The plans for its creation began before the Winnipeg General Strike. Using the new amendments to the Criminal Code and Immigration Act against the Winnipeg strikers would have inflamed tensions, but this does not explain why these new laws were not used. While the authorities were sensitive to avoiding further hostilities with workers, they were still willing to use violent and deadly means to quell unrest, regardless of how workers would interpret such actions. The fact that the government did not rush through Section 98's creation once the strike escalated, even though it could have as it did with the Section 41 amendments, suggests that Section 98 was always intended to be used *later*. The government viewed the threat of left-wing activism as unending and international, and the plans to normalize emergency measures had much to do with Canada's place in an Anglo-American alliance that was opposed to radical leftists.

Fear was important in the creation of these laws, as was the desire to manage unrest. Politicians feared what could happen if Canada did nothing. The law would manage this anxiety. By creating new laws, the government believed it could protect people from the radical, un-British ways of foreign Communists and anarchists and the race traitors that were British radical leftists who had abandoned "civilized" British methods for the actions of the foreign "cut-throats." Lawmakers expressed faith in the safety and security that law would provide. It could never stamp out disorder or rectify the measures within capitalism that continually gave rise to its opponents; the law would manage these tendencies indefinitely. It would demonstrate long term, on the basis of what was illegal, what politics Canadians should believe in. The law would play a long-term role in nation-building. The creation of Section 98 was tied to the government's search for order and safety in the immediate post-war period.

A critical step had been taken by the government in the ability for an emergency measure to become normalized. PC 2384 had transitioned from being a wartime power to a peacetime one. It could now exist and be used without the need to formally declare an emergency. Time was no longer an issue. It was now part of Canada's Criminal Code that detailed the laws of the land in war or peace. Throughout Section 98's transition from bill to law, the threat posed by British activists was invoked by officials to justify extending emergency measures into peacetime. These views would continue into the 1920s, a period of relative calm, to continue the process of integrating the emergency and the norm.

A State of Potentiality

Throughout the 1920s the labour revolt was never far from the minds of lawmakers. Even though it was now firmly in Canada's past, the debates of the 1920s reveal that MPs and senators alike believed that British activists still posed a threat to Canada because of the rise of

Communist agitation in Britain and Canadian labour disruptions, such as the large-scale BESCO strikes in Nova Scotia in 1923. Debates, as Jérôme Ouelett and Frédéric Roussel-Beaulieu have argued, are important sources for revealing public concerns and opposing attitudes, and they provide a wealth of information about policy issues. The 1920s debates in the House and Senate reveal the tensions surrounding the rights of British activists and their place as citizens; many MPs believed that political ideology rather than place of birth determined nationality. For some, a British subject was no different than a foreign Bolshevik if a supporter of socialism. This was a contested claim, with some believing that British-born activists should be treated differently than other immigrants. These debates demonstrate how conceptions of citizenship and its obligations were unstable and reveal as much about lawmakers as what they thought about their enemies.[92] They also illustrate how lawmakers' need for safety and security was satisfied by keeping Section 98 and Section 41's 1919 amendment.[93] Parliament members thought that the threat of revolution continually hung in the air; the potential was always there for another Winnipeg or worse. Only the law could protect them.

In the summer of 1920, one year after Section 41's amendment and Section 98's creation, Bill X2 was introduced to the Senate by the minister of labour, Gideon Robertson. The bill aimed to amend Section 41 of the Immigration Act to protect British subjects from deportation after they had acquired naturalization. A.B. Crosby began the debate in the Senate and argued against the bill. He claimed that labour was not concerned with this bill, and curiously, as a senator, felt himself "as close to the workingman as anyone . . . truly and sincerely of the working classes." Section 41's amendment was necessary because, as Crosby stated, "God knows what would have happened if it had not gone through." He argued that the people who were truly responsible for the creation of this legislation were not workers. They were "agitators" who had come to Canada seeking revolution, even if they were from Britain.[94]

Senator W.H. Sharpe echoed the sentiment of Crosby, stating that as the law stood, the "honest labourer or the good citizen" had nothing to be afraid of.[95] Sharpe stressed that only one year ago, leaders of the Winnipeg General Strike wanted to turn the parliament buildings of Winnipeg into the seat of power for a Soviet government and that radical leftists were not only confined to Western Canada. They were now scattered among average Canadians in Toronto and in every major city. Sharpe believed Canada should follow the US lead by deporting "reds" like the United States had done with anarchist Emma Goldman. "If the law was good enough last year," he argued, "it is good enough for me this year."[96] Senator G.G. Foster claimed that Winnipeg had fallen to the "red hand of rebellion, anarchy, and revolt." He believed that other major urban centres were being corrupted by the same ideological poison. If Section 41 was amended, there would be no protection for Canada's major cities.[97]

In committee, Senator George Bradbury argued that an emergency may have necessitated the creation of the 1919 amendment but that it had now surely passed.[98] The minister of labour attempted to clear up matters by repeating the reasons for its introduction and reiterating what had transpired in the House during the summer of 1919. Robertson claimed that the amendments to the Immigration Act were designed to target foreign agitators in the country because Section 98 did not exist yet. Robertson read out Section 98 and argued that with this section in the Code, Section 41 of the Immigration Act could be amended to its pre-1919 state. Robertson claimed the amendment was "un-British" and unconstitutional because it denied British subjects a trial before being deported.[99] While Robertson had no issue with other immigrants being deported without a trial, a British subject should not be met with the same fate. Civilized countries did not deny the right to a trial. At least if British subjects were charged and convicted under Section 98, they would face a criminal trial and then could face deportation. His argument was unconvincing to the Senate; the bill was rejected in committee.

Robinson used Section 98 to justify amending what he felt was the un-British legislation of Section 41 permitting the deportation of British subjects for their political views without trial. The rights of the British subject were tied to Magna Carta and the natural law brought forth by Hobbes, Locke, and Adam Smith. The British were symbolic of progress for legislators. Robinson believed British subjects were denied the legal protections that many legislators thought central to British history, identity, and ethnicity. The judging of the political views of a British subject by the immigration department and deporting them without trial were unsettling for some lawmakers. While it had been perfectly acceptable to deport immigrants not from the mother country for their political beliefs and without a trial, the issue was not as clear-cut for British activists. For politicians, the idea of justice was central to British identity. The memory of Winnipeg underlay the discussion; it was now a symbol for the violent revolution that could await Canada if the 1919 amendments were removed.

Following the 1921 election win of Mackenzie King's Liberals and the introduction of the Labour Party and Progressive Party to the House of Commons, J.S. Woodsworth, of the Manitoba Independent Labour Party, was eager to repeal Section 98 and amend Section 41. Woodsworth had some experience with sedition, as he had been charged with seditious libel during the Winnipeg General Strike for reciting a Bible verse. He had first-hand knowledge of how easily the new laws could be misused. The former Methodist minister turned social activist and politician had a long history of working to aid immigrant communities in Winnipeg and labour in general. He viewed the legislative changes of 1919 as an affront to democratic values. His political thoughts on liberty were influenced by John Stuart Mill. He believed, as McNaught puts it, that there was an "organic relationship between civil liberty and social good."[100] His first effort to repeal the laws took place in 1922 when he tabled Bills 16 and 17, which were designed to repeal the changes made to the Immigration Act and to repeal Section 98. On 10 April 1922, Ernest Lapointe of the Liberals and Prime Minister Mackenzie King both suggested that Woodsworth's bills be discussed in a special committee. Woodsworth, being new to the House and unfamiliar with its procedures, agreed. He later felt that the Liberals' suggestion was designed to sidetrack the bills, which ultimately failed to pass.[101]

Woodsworth often claimed that Section 98 targeted labour, and his beliefs were somewhat justified given that force was never defined in Section 98. While lawmakers could not reasonably list all the ways force could be interpreted, the labour movement feared that leaving the definition entirely up to judicial discretion invited judges hostile to labour to regard labour actions, such as strikes, as "force." In the 1920 report on the proceedings of the Trades and Labour Congress of Canada, J.G. O'Donoghue, its legal counsel, outlined how the section could be used against labour groups and used Judge Metcalfe's charge to the jury in the sedition trial of R.B. Russell, one of the Winnipeg strike leaders in 1919, to prove his point. In his charge, Metcalfe stated that strikes forced employers to settle a dispute and that "Russell's definition [of a strike] given in the box" was "force, force, force."[102]

The report detailed how a court was justified in using the "natural or dictionary sense" to define force. Judge Metcalfe believed terrorism in Russell's case could be incited "without hitting a man over the head. You can incite terror of starvation; you can incite terror of thirst [through strikes]."[103] For the Trades and Labour Council, the sedition trials of the strike leaders in Winnipeg in 1919 drove home just how easily Section 98 could be applied to strike activity.

Arthur Meighen defended Section 98 and Section 41. At one point, he sarcastically claimed that many people would like to believe that Section 98 and Section 41's amendment were passed only because of the insecurity and chaotic "atmosphere of the time." He believed that many people had an arrogant view of the past and that it was all too easy to claim that everyone had been deceived by this atmosphere into rashly creating the chaos the laws sought to prevent.[104] For Meighen, the climate of the period was not a factor in the creation of Section 98. Section 98 and Section 41 were not reactionary laws.

Woodsworth remained undeterred by the failure of 1922, and in 1923 he brought forth another bill to repeal Section 98 and reinsert Section 133's safeguard clause for sedition. MPs were concerned that the bill would weaken Canada's protection from radical leftists. Debate continued over who was and was not a Canadian citizen. The Immigration Act stated that a Canadian citizen was a person born in Canada or a British subject who had acquired domicile after five years.[105] Liberal member Charles Stewart refused to believe that Section 41 enabled the deportation of naturalized British subjects. John Baxter of the Conservatives argued that the act must be confined to the term "Canadian citizen" because one could not turn Canadians out of their own country; one should be able to deport only immigrants who had acquired citizenship through naturalization, essentially by cancelling their naturalization. Samuel Jacobs, a Liberal, argued that that would produce a "citizen without a country."[106] Members agreed that the Immigration Act should no longer target British subjects if they had acquired naturalization, and even Meighen agreed that the climate of unrest had passed but that immigrants from other countries should still face the threat of deportation.[107] Woodsworth attacked the act as a whole for unfairly seeking to deport people without trial because of their political views. Woodsworth wanted the principles of justice – central to British identity – extended to include all immigrants. The House passed the bill and sent it to the Senate. The Senate had no interest in debating the changes the House proposed to Section 41; they were rejected outright. As for Woodsworth's attempt to repeal Section 98, it never made it to second reading before the session of Parliament ended.

If fear of revolution during the Winnipeg General Strike contributed to Section 98's creation and Section 41's amendment, a need for safety and security kept it from being removed. By keeping the laws as they were, politicians believed Canadians were safer. As long as the laws were there, Canadians would be secure. These laws provided "protection," as one senator claimed. The belief in the protective power of law is important for understanding the process by which emergency measures become accepted as normal. Fear too played multiple roles. While fear and insecurity played a part in the creation of these laws, fear of what could happen if they were removed kept them on the books. These laws provided politicians with a feeling that as long as Canadians had these laws, they would be safe and secure from the threats the laws targeted. Law, by its mere existence, eased fears and contributed to acceptance and normalization of the exceptional. Security, as an idea, was law.

For Canadian senators, the threat of radical British leftists was still present, but the debates also demonstrated that not everyone believed that radical British leftists posed a threat or that they should be considered the same as other immigrant activists. There were several reasons that senators may have rejected the House's bill. Following 1919, the RCMP informed the government that British activists were an ongoing threat to Canada. Since its formation after the labour revolt, the service regularly spied on anyone suspected of Communist activity. An RCMP security bulletin, dated 2 September 1920, noted that foreign agitators believed that "English-speaking" workers were ready for revolt and that "recent events in Great Britain such as the 'hands off Russia' agitation and the threat of a general strike by the Triple Alliance [were] encouraging the seditious minded." Indeed, the RCMP noted that "the promptitude with which revolutionary actions in England provoke[d]" activists in Canada was increasing and that Canadian leftists were increasingly relying on the English rather than the American revolutionary presses.[108] With the RCMP confirming that British reds were influencing Canadian activists, it was not surprising that some in Parliament were not keen on altering Section 41. The British reds had an advantage that some foreign activists did not: they could speak English and help influence Anglo-Canadians to join their cause.

The UK's repression of communists occurred during the 1920s and made headlines in Canada. In 1921, similar to the US and Canada, the UK was taking measures to up the legal penalties for sedition and trying to stamp out seditious publications.[109] In September 1925, UK authorities aimed to seize activists and deport aliens. Scotland Yard was reportedly looking for reds of British nationality who were working for Moscow.[110] On 25 October 1925, the headlines in Canada focused on the arrest of prominent leaders of the Communist Party of Great Britain (CPGB).[111] With all these sensational stories making the front page of Canadian papers, it was little wonder that a Conservative Senate would have blocked any attempt to undo the 1919 legislation.

There was ample evidence in the minds of some MPs that British activists were still at work fomenting discord within Canada. In March 1924, Woodsworth made an impassioned speech in the House detailing the treatment of Nova Scotia miners by police and their employer, the British Empire Steel Corporation (BESCO). J.B. McLachlan, secretary of the Mine Workers of Nova Scotia and Communist Party of Canada member, was an active leader in the negotiations and a British "radical" (born in Scotland). As David Frank reveals, McLachlan pushed for a campaign of "working with your coat on," a policy that amounted to striking on the job by reducing the output of the mine. But McLachlan's CPC membership and vocal opposition to capitalism and militant labour activities soon drew the ire of the authorities, as did the decision of the workers to strike. Ottawa and the province sent military troops just before the strike occurred on 30 June and set up tents and machine gun posts on BESCO property. At 7:30 p.m., under the command of Colonel Eric McDonald, the provincial police rode into a crowd of striking workers, attacking anyone who came into their path. When McLachlan sent out a letter to the workers, condemning the government and the police action, he was charged with publishing false news when his letter mysteriously found its way to the *Halifax Chronicle*. The political actions that authorities did not approve of were treated as insurgencies that had to end, even with military force and police violence, to prevent another emergency situation like 1919.[112]

With the re-election of Mackenzie King and the Liberals in 1926, Section 98 and Section 41 would receive much more attention by the government. Elected to another minority government, the Liberals depended on the cooperation of the Progressive Party to stay in power. The Liberals had to seriously consider repealing the laws to secure the support of the Progressives, or the government could fall. At the start of the first session, R.B. Bennett of the Conservatives went on the attack, accusing the Liberals of making deals with the opposition parties to stay in power even though the Conservatives had won more seats. The deal included sincere efforts to amend the Immigration Act and Criminal Code. Bennett referred to the government as a "majority of three."[113]

The Liberals planned on introducing two bills before the summer, Bill 153, which called for the repeal of Section 98, and Bill 91, which would undo the 1919 changes to Section 41. On 31 May 1926, the Liberals introduced Bill 153. Ernest Lapointe, the Minister of Justice, introduced the bill as seeking to undo changes made to the Criminal Code that were put in place so that certain portions of the War

Measures Act could continue to deal with unrest. Lapointe stated that the Trades and Labour Congress had asked every year that these changes be removed, as they feared they would be unfairly used to target labour. Lapointe argued that there were enough protections in the Code to deal with sedition and that Section 98 should be repealed. He stressed that the Section was a copy of the United States law on sedition and that the British method of dealing with sedition in the common law was a better one. It was the more civilized way.[114]

Before Bill 153 proceeded further, Bill 91 was debated on 2 June. Familiar arguments from the previous debates were introduced again, but this time Ambrose Bury of the Conservatives wanted to discuss Bill 153 together with Bill 91. Bury's argument was that if Bill 153 and Bill 91 were both passed, one could no longer be deported or charged for being a member of an unlawful association or for advocating or defending governmental change by force. Seditious foreigners, he maintained, would be protected if both bills passed.[115] Lapointe argued that an immigrant could be found guilty under another section of the Code if engaged in seditious activity and subsequently deported. Woodsworth reiterated the need for a jury trial for deportation, but Meighen scoffed at Woodsworth's suggestion, saying no one had ever had the right to a jury trial for deportation in Canada.[116] The House went into recess. The final vote would have to come after debate on the repeal of Section 98.

On 4 June, debate commenced on Bill 153's repeal of Section 98. Woodsworth pointed out that a simple bystander listening to a speech from a member of a presumed unlawful association could be found guilty under Section 98, as the individual would be required to prove their innocence. Horatio Hocken of the Conservatives attacked the arguments of Lapointe and Woodsworth by introducing the spectre of communism into the debate. He argued: "Soviet emissaries are found not only in Great Britain, but in this country, in the United States, in China . . . all over the world, and when this Dominion may be made the special object of their attack nobody can tell."[117] H.H. Stevens, a Conservative, agreed with his fellow party member, arguing that Section 98 was designed to prevent the "wrecking" of Canada's democracy.[118] The section was worthless to the "ordinary citizen" but was necessary to combat the threat of evil that foreign cutthroats may be planning – in the form of revolution or insurrection. He was emphatic that such laws protected average people.[119] The only way for that protection to remain was for these laws to exist indefinitely. The bill passed its third reading and the House adjourned at two minutes to midnight.

On 7 June, debate resumed on Bill 91's amendment of Section 41 of the Immigration Act. Bury, again, introduced the need to keep Section 41 as it was because of the repeal of Section 98, which had just passed in the House. R.B. Bennett offered a defence of Section 41, arguing that it covered offences not contained in the Criminal Code, but neglected to mention the existing sedition laws beyond Section 98. Bennett claimed that Toronto had become the central hub for communist propaganda and that Toronto groups were distributing the material across the country. With Section 98 repealed, Section 41 must remain as it was.[120] Even though it was the Immigration Act amendment that was being debated, the discussion returned to focus on Section 98. Thomas Cantley, a Conservative, argued that since the law had not been used, what was the harm in keeping it on the books, just in case? Besides, he thought there was never a time when Sections 98 and 41 were more needed.[121] The emergency of the revolt still lingered. People could live with the emergency provided they had emergency law if they needed it.

The view of many Conservative members was summed up by Edmond Ryckman. Ultimately, there was no good reason for Canada to want to invite activists over from Britain, which if the laws were removed would be what Canada would be doing. He maintained, "A Clydeside ship man, who probably does not act as he should and has been subject to the law in England, or a cockney from Limehouse, is not entitled upon his landing on these shores to the same standing [of] a Canadian citizen."[122] If Canada removed these laws, which many believed necessary to protect Canada from foreign agitators, these types would flood in because they were already not welcome in the home country of Britain. Many argued it would be a step back in terms of security and progress to allow these individuals to be regarded as the same as Canadian citizens. Regardless of the opposition, the dissenters were a minority, and the bill passed its third reading.[123]

The bills were now in the hands of the Senate, which debated Bill 91 on 15 June. In his description of Bill 91, Raoul Dandurand made continual references to Bill 153. Senator Foster claimed that once they started wiping out one bill, they would remove another and end up with nothing.[124] On division, Bill 91 failed to go to second reading. On 17 June, Bill 153 was debated in committee by the Senate. Dandurand reiterated how Section 98 was "exceptional legislation, made because of the exceptional times through which [they] were passing" and was thus no longer necessary.[125] Senator Beaubien disagreed, arguing that "socialistic principles" were being spread, particularly in places such as Montreal, and that even a "good liberal paper" such as the *Winnipeg Free Press* was reporting their spread throughout Canada.[126] Senator Griesbach brought up the issue of the prosecution of the CPGB members and questioned why Canada should lessen its sedition legislation when Great Britain had tightened its laws to deal with Communists in the UK.[127] The Communists in Canada, Senator Beaubien argued, not only threatened the East Coast in Cape Breton but the "free and breezy west" and even Montreal.[128] The Senate defeated the bill. Even the attempt to reinsert the sedition saving clause back into Section 133 was rejected for fear of weakening the other sections.[129] Conservative senators still felt that British and other foreign activists posed a threat. They agreed with Conservative House member Thomas Church that Canada should follow Australia's lead in battling activists, and quoting the Australian prime minister, Church stated, "We will make this a white man's country. It does not matter whether the anarchist comes from Europe or the British Isles, he will be deported."[130] Whiteness, along with citizenship, was questioned because of one's political beliefs. For some, the British activist occupied a space in which they were not a citizen and yet not a foreigner.

The continuation of emergency powers was a central theme of the debates, and so was the issue of who should be protected from deportation, particularly if the individual was British. As sociologist T.H. Marshall has argued in his classic study on citizenship, citizenship may be classified as legal, political, or social. One person may have civil duties to undertake in order to be classed as a citizen, while social status may entitle another person to citizenship. Citizenship can therefore be acquired or denied to segments of society.[131] While being a British subject entitled a person to citizenship in the empire, some Canadian lawmakers wanted a conception of citizenship that denied individuals the right to citizenship in Canada on the basis of political beliefs. Their citizenship should be undone if they expressed the beliefs of, and by extension subscribed to, a foreign seditious ideology.[132] But such views were not wholeheartedly endorsed; House members opposed British subjects being treated the same as other foreign activists. As Ferguson notes, for British immigrants these debates revealed how "their international status was unclear, their rights abroad uncertain, and their identity decidedly unstable."[133] This situation was glaringly apparent, as House members were conflicted about what to do with British activists and what rights they had as citizens. Were they civilized British subjects and entitled to the rights such membership ensured, or were they uncivilized agitators because of their ideology?

Fear and the need for safety and security played an important role in normalizing emergency measures. As long as the laws were kept in place, they could protect Canadians simply by existing. Politicians believed they knew Canadians would be safe with these laws but that no one could foresee the danger if they were repealed. Repeal of these laws would invite radical British leftists to Canada. The debates also reveal much about the politicians and the context of the period on the basis of how politicians conceptualized their enemies. Political challenges were only legitimate when they occurred in Parliament, but Parliament was a place where white, propertied British men were welcomed. Strikes and protests and political activity outside this realm, political options that were available to immigrant women and men, the unemployed, working class, and ethnic minorities, were regarded by many parliamentarians as signs of communism or terrorism and a threat to the safety and security of Canada's British institutions and heritage. They were not civilized political actions as authorities understood such things. Strikes were forms of force to produce change and terror that harkened back to a premodern time that did not have laws, order, or parliamentary institutions. These were the political actions of a minority of "foreign radicals," and as such they were viewed by authorities as illegitimate and even illegal. In some ways, authorities needed radical leftists to define themselves. By understanding what Canadians were not (in their opinion) and outlawing the expression of these political views, they helped shape the political identity of the country.

What the government ultimately accomplished with Section 98 was the divorcing of time from the concept of a security crisis. Before Section 98, even just years before, a security crisis was a moment in time where security, as defined by lawmakers, could be restored by the temporary use of exceptional legal means. The creation of Section 98 destroyed this concept. Now a security crisis, in this case the threat of communism, could be everywhere. As a result, the law had to continue to operate in the same way to oppose it. The curtain had not completely closed on the emergency powers used during wartime. It had been left slightly ajar.

Repression against leftists shaped the identity of the nation. Section 98 was not a reactionary law; its creation was central to the process of normalizing emergency measures and nation-building through repression. Such a process began with the government's ability to define and declare an emergency with the WMA. This power led to the creation of PC 2384 because the government believed that the spread of radical leftist ideology was an emergency that required emergency measures. Loyalty was secured by pre-emptively striking out against any activity that could lead to treasonous action, and its definition was synonymous with the way authorities defined security during the war – loyalty was security. International influences were important to Section 98's creation. Lawmakers linked class and ethnicity in creating PC 2384. With such broad powers the government could exclude individuals from the protection of law on the basis of their ideology and target them with repressive laws demonstrating to the rest of the population which politics would be tolerated in Canada and which would not.

PC 2384 was a necessary first step towards engaging in nation-building through repression, but it was limited to the war. These powers had to be normalized and extended beyond the emergency to continue, hence Section 98's creation. Law would manage the agitating leftists long term. As the debates in the House of Commons and Senate of the 1920s reveal, politicians continued to fear that British activists posed a threat to Canadian society, and as a result, Section 98 and the amendment to Section 41 needed to live on to keep people feeling safe and secure. Law was now security. While the War Measures Act enshrined in law the state's ability to implement the state of exception and predated and survived Section 98, Section 98 was the means by which some of those emergency measures could function outside a declared state of emergency. The government could now manage the unruly elements of society indefinitely in peacetime with Section 98. When the Great Depression arrived in the 1930s, so did a vocal and militant Communist Party of Canada, which started advocating for the unemployed. Many in Parliament likely believed they were right. The emergency of 1919 had never really ended.

2

Defining Suspects

The onset of the Great Depression gripped the country in turmoil. The dust bowl dried up crops in the West, grain prices plummeted, and the staggering rise in the number of unemployed left many wondering if the world as they knew it was finished. Many were claiming to have the solution to end the depression stalking the country, from the Social Credit Party of William Aberhart to the Canadian Nationalist Party to the Communist Party of Canada (CPC). The 1930s were a time when "the politics of chaos" was the norm.[1] Like the First World War, the Great Depression was a time of heightened emotions, from dismay to fear and anxiety. In 1930, the Conservative Party, led by R.B. Bennett, swept into power, forming a majority government that promised to end the Depression and restore Canadians' faith in their country.

The government, along with many Canadians, viewed the CPC as representative of a foreign and alien culture that threatened to destroy the country and its cultural heritage. In this categorization of the CPC, we can observe how both English- and French-Canadian authorities interpreted the nation according to what individuals or ideologies should be barred from joining it. Cultural perceptions of communists played an important role in maintaining the use of emergency powers outside of a declared emergency. As long as Canadians were threatened by the potential for a foreign enemy to attack, an exceptional wartime law would be needed to keep the threat at bay. Culture defined the enemy and also helped define security.

The CPC had its own view of the Canadian nation. It viewed itself as leading the way towards a socialist, gender equal, multi-ethnic Canadian republic. Previous authors have argued that the CPC, while consisting primarily of foreign members, wanted new Anglo and French members only during Moscow's Third Period and that some members were hostile towards the party's immigrant base.[2] In contributing to revisionist literature on the CPC, I contend that party members were conflicted about the obligations of the CPC with respect to foreign members and worked to accommodate them while seeking new Anglo and French recruits. Key to how the CPC dealt with its ethnic base was how the nation was understood within communist thought.

The historical literature has viewed the arrest of CPC leaders in 1931 as reflective of the state's war on communism during the Depression and the intelligence cycle as successful for authorities in that the Royal Canadian Mounted Police (RCMP) succeeded in gathering and analysing intelligence to act on a threat.[3] But the reasons for the CPC's prosecution were more complex; cultural views and fears of the foreign unknown enemy shaped how the state interpreted and responded to the CPC. The intelligence cycle was underpinned by culture. The party was also willing to act outside of established legal and political structures. It took its message directly to the people and acted political in the streets through strikes and protests and battles with police. The CPC was perceived by authorities as a direct threat to their power because of its ideology, its view of the Canadian nation, and its political actions.[4]

The CPC and the National Question

Many authors have detailed the CPC's early history, and so I will revisit only the most pertinent details for the sake of brevity. The CPC was created out of an amalgamation of like-minded leftist groups that took place over several years, with the earliest version of a Canadian Communist party existing in secret in 1919.[5] Following the successful 1917 Russian Revolution and the creation of the Communist International (CI), the CI openly supported the creation of Communist parties throughout the globe. The Canadian version originated in 1921 near Guelph, Ontario. From its inception, the CPC had accepted the discipline of the CI, as Ian Angus argues, "as binding upon all delegates present and . . . its entire membership, without any reservations."[6]

The party heavily invested itself in industrial unions and industries, and it attracted a large foreign-born membership. Immigrants with some experience in their homelands with socialism or communism helped provide necessary leadership roles within the party. Language branches were always a central component of the party; it supported the foreign-born membership and encouraged recruitment in working-class immigrant communities.[7] The relationship with these branches would become strained as the CPC shifted its policies in the late 1920s to suit the CI.

During 1928, Joseph Stalin moved to take control of the Soviet Union and eliminate his rivals. Stalin and Nicolai Bukharin (a prominent Bolshevik theorist who fell victim to Stalin's purges in the 1930s) argued that capitalism had entered the "Third Period," which was its last phase. Its end was approaching. National parties were required to adhere to a policy of strict discipline in preparation for capitalism's demise. At the Sixth Congress of the CI in Moscow, the CI changed its policies so that all international parties were to adhere to the principles of the Third Period, which entailed (in the name of resistance to fascism) fighting with social democrats and other labour groups and contesting them whenever possible. These groups were seen as not being real revolutionaries in that they stalled the collapse of capitalism by seeking to work with other capitalist parties in preserving the capitalist state and reforming it – which the Third Period hardliners believed was impossible. Third Period ideology viewed social democrats as "social fascists" for their perceived devotion to the capitalist state.

Moscow and the CPC were obsessed with having workers view the CPC as leaders of the labour movement rather than their social democrat rivals. Within Canada, the newly formed Workers' Unity League (WUL), which was affiliated with Moscow's Red International of Labour Unions and largely controlled by the CPC, would help to create revolutionary unions. By 1929, the CPC had adopted Moscow's new line and was purging itself of members who opposed the Stalin line, such as former leaders Maurice Spector and Jack Macdonald.[8]

National parties across the globe were strongly tied to Moscow, but there is no agreement as to how subservient they were.[9] What is significant is that by 1929, when the party leadership had agreed to follow Stalin's new line, with Tim Buck as the new leader, the CPC called for a ramped-up public campaign that sought to bring the class battle out into the open streets in cities across the country, to organize and lead the unorganized, including the unemployed, and to create new revolutionary unions that would contest more moderate labour unions and eventually form the backbone of a new workers' army. Communists were not opposed to acting politically in whatever way they saw fit. While they did not advocate that anyone should try to overthrow the government, the ideology of communism promoted the idea that one day if the population willed change, revolution would bring it. But more than this, Communists challenged sovereign power by being political outside of Parliament and outside of culturally accepted norms. They fought for free speech in the streets, publicly condemned the government and monarch, and pushed for the creation of policies that provided protection to their most marginalized supporters. This was in addition to leading marches where violence with police happened often.[10]

The Third Period demands of the CI clashed with the reality of party recruitment in Canada. While the party certainly needed its ethnic base, it desperately needed Anglo and French members in order to appeal to the Canadian masses. The ethnic conflicts taking place within the CPC demonstrated just how different the CPC's view of a Canadian nation was from mainstream Canadian society and how the party struggled to implement Moscow's policy given the importance of immigrants to the CPC.

Under pressure from the CI in Moscow to incorporate more Anglo-Saxons into the CPC, Tim Buck noted in a CPC meeting that "the language of Canada (outside Quebec) is English, while our Party is 90% foreign."[11] Historian Ivan Avakumovic argues that for Anglo-Saxons who came into contact with Communists, the heavy foreign makeup of the party made it look like a movement composed of ethnic aliens.[12] Party meeting minutes and CI directives throughout the Third Period frequently stressed the importance of acquiring more Anglo-Saxon and French-Canadian members. As suggested by an attempt in 1931 to recruit members in south Winnipeg, the CPC was frequently frustrated in such campaigns.[13] By 1934, the party viewed itself as one that was isolated from the majority of workers, except immigrants.[14] A party resolution dictated that the solution was to overcome the "lopsided development" of the party by recruiting at least 150 Canadian-born workers in Anglo areas of the city.[15] The top party brass made their concern with the failure of the CPC to recruit Anglo-Saxons quite clear during elections. In one instance, Buck claimed, "For a couple of months I was overwhelmed with invitations for supper to Ukrainian and Jewish comrades to meet other Ukrainian and Jewish comrades. I have yet to meet an Englishman at one of these suppers."[16]

Buck was not alone in his frustration. The CI frequently voiced its displeasure with the party's inability to secure more Anglo-Saxon members. Without them, the CI opined, the CPC would not reflect the composition of the working class in Canada.[17] The party devoted more resources to studying why the party was failing to register among Anglo-Saxon voters.[18] Relations with ethnic groups in the party, such as the Ukrainians, were strained on more than one occasion. Indeed, Ukrainians in the party considered themselves "Ukrainian

Communists." A similar view was expressed by members of other ethnic groups who blended their culture with their political lives, such as Finns, Yiddish-speaking Jews, Poles, Germans, and Croatians.[19] At times, the Anglo CPC leadership and its Ukrainian and Finnish critics would take their disputes all the way to Moscow.

The language used by some Anglo party members occasionally contained strands of resentment and hatred when discussing the large ethnic makeup of the CPC. The minutes from one meeting show that "some comrades believed that if some immigrants left the party," it would be a "better party."[20] Appearances mattered. If the CPC was to appeal to Anglo-Saxon or Canadian-born residents, it had to look the part. Rather than valuing its many minority members, the party sometimes viewed its foreign members negatively, as elements undermining its attractiveness to the Anglo-Saxon majority.

The failure to secure more domestic-born workers was not solely due to the party having an Anglo/French-centric view. Party members struggled to implement Moscow's directives. The large number of linguistic minorities within the party posed practical problems for the CPC – financially and logistically. In February 1926, the Ukrainian Labour-Farmer Temple Association (ULFTA) had made it known to the CPC that it desired a youth group of its own, to which it could teach politics and the Ukrainian culture, in addition to running ethnic-based magazines. The party was initially opposed to the idea, not because it was afraid it would dissuade Anglo-Saxon youth from joining the party, but because it feared that Ukrainian youth would leave the party's Young Communist League in favour of this new group. The party was concerned about who would finance the ethnic magazines. After much debate, the youth group was permitted to go ahead, but its publications were not funded by the party.[21]

The diverse ethnic groups within the CPC made translation a real problem for a cash-starved organization. A meeting in September 1926 discussed the difficulties of managing so many diverse groups of immigrants. Conducting business in numerous languages was viewed as a major problem, and the party attempted to reorganize its membership along language lines as opposed to regions which, it was hoped, would decrease the number of languages and hence translators. Despite the problems with organizing and communication, the party acknowledged that it had to make "whatever concessions" were necessary because it could not afford to lose any support among its foreign members.[22]

Evidence that the party feared it was losing control of ethnic members appeared frequently in party documents. On 14 March 1926, the CPC expressed a desire for an increase in "Canadian content" in the Finnish paper *Vapaus*. The party thought it would make the paper more relevant to English readers and make supervision of the paper's content easier for party leaders. The motion was opposed by the Finns, who viewed the action as an unwanted Anglo-Saxon incursion into a Finnish paper. In the same meeting, the CPC discussed the request of its Finnish and Jewish members for more sporting organizations. The central concern of the party was that it would lose control of these social groups if the sporting groups were created.[23]

Under Third Period conditions, such debates intensified. The drive for a monolithic party, combating social fascists and locked in life-or-death struggles, pushed ethnic minorities to the margins – paradoxically, the very nativism of the state's repressive campaign against the party meant the CPC could not really transform itself into an all-Canadian party. The CPC's turn towards the new line of the Third Period exacerbated tensions in 1929–30 between the Finnish, Ukrainian, Jewish, and Anglo-Saxon leadership, resulting in the purging of members from these often semi-autonomous groups.[24]

The CI was called to resolve conflicts between groups and frequently had to remind leaders of the role of ethnicity in the Third Period. In a letter from the Executive Committee of the Communist International, the CI wrote that the party had to fight sectarianism and "narrow nationalism" and recruit only "committed communists."[25] The party and the CI were concerned that the various ethnic groups established would become social subgroups detracting from party politics. But the CPC leadership and the CI did not recognize the importance of these social gatherings for ethnic groups. Indeed, as Ian Radforth, Carmela Patrias, and Ruth Frager have demonstrated, left-wing groups of Finns, Jews, and others viewed themselves as living the revolution in their daily lives, and the plays, concerts, and other activities that took place in their ethnic halls served both cultural and political purposes.[26]

Support for the unemployed demonstrated the party's support for ethnic diversity. The party regularly challenged ideas of racial hierarchy, and demonstrations provided opportunities for foreign and British workers to accomplish symbolic unity. While ethnic disputes were not entirely solved, Anglos were joining the party because of its support for the unemployed. Between 1929 and 1934 it saw an increase in Anglo members from 5 to 25 per cent.[27]

Alongside such Third Period disciplining of the often rebellious language groups, one must set a new emphasis on the nation. At a meeting with foreign workers' delegations in 1927, Stalin outlined the Communist position on the national question. When asked how Russia differed from capitalist countries in its treatment of minorities, Stalin replied that in capitalist states "second class nationalities" were created because of nationalist oppression. He believed that in the Soviet Union, national inequalities and oppression were eliminated. He claimed that self-determination of nations led to different nationalities voluntarily uniting into one federated state. He viewed self-determination as a policy of "national equality."[28] A loyal Communist validated the nation and encouraged its self-determination.

These ideas of self-determination with respect to socialism had shifted over time. Prior to 1917, self-determination for national minorities was of paramount importance in solving the national question. After 1918, Stalin still supported self-determination, but only if it could "be subordinated to the principles of socialism." Stalin believed that through socialism the problem of "backwardness" could be overcome because "these peoples [national minorities in Russia] . . . were mistrustful of the Russians, and were deeply influenced by religion." The immediate task of Soviet power, then, was to improve these peoples' economic condition, to provide educational facilities, to attract as far as possible the local intelligentsia, and to conduct socialist propaganda in the local language. Through these efforts, national minorities would move to a "higher stage" of socialism.[29] An example of Stalin's argument in the Canadian context would be the Francophone population, whose oppressors were the Anglo population, both in a class and ethnic sense. Helping the French Canadians achieve national self-determination, while still under socialism, would liberate them. Indeed, the CI had instructed the CPC to further draw out the French-Anglo tensions to win over more French-Canadian workers to the party.[30]

For Stalin, national equality would result from the removal of bourgeois oppressors.[31] The national question, as Stalin iterated in 1913, would be resolved by ". . . fighting for the right of nations to self-determination." He further stated that "the aim of Social-Democracy is to put an end to the policy of national oppression." Capitalist states, he claimed, fanned the flames of nationalist divisions to exploit them. Class-conscious workers could never truly rally around the "national" flag of capitalists.[32]

Self-determination and national autonomy, or cultural-national autonomy, were not equal concepts. For instance, Stalin argued that supporting only cultural autonomy encouraged separatism within a state. Cultural autonomy was not real political power. It was illusory and served only to divide people along national lines, placing emphasis on cultural differences, and thereby encouraging war and division. Workers and bourgeoisie, despite any shared national culture, were culturally different because of their class. Cultural autonomy in capitalist states divided the proletariat along national lines and ensured their continued enslavement by the bourgeoisie.[33] Stalin argued that only self-determination, in the political sense, would ensure true national liberation. Ethnic minorities living in a land dominated by one nation must have access to equal rights to ensure their self-determination. Regional autonomy was viewed by Moscow as a central component of self-determination. Moreover, class would serve to bind diverse groups of nationalities in their quest for self-determination.

International solidarity would allow people of different nationalities to assist each other in national self-determination movements as well as in achieving class equality. For many Ukrainians, Finns, Jews, and other national minorities, the Soviets held out a promise of national liberation within a new social and political order. The Soviet Union could provide a way for these national groups to fulfil their goals of self-determination and autonomy while remaining a part of the communist movement. Stalin's theories and the reality that faced national minorities who wanted self-determination were quite different. There are far too many examples of how Stalin violently sought to achieve his version of "national equality." But while these promises were brutally and violently betrayed by Stalin, this should not detract from the widespread belief in them in the early to mid-1930s. Indeed, part of the allure to the CPC for many leftist immigrants was the promise of cultural autonomy. Some of the largest language groups in the CPC, such as the Finns to take one example, predated the party, and groups like the Finnish Organization of Canada (FOC) and the ULFTA were not just creatures of the party, which is why the leadership of the groups clashed with CPC leaders. The CPC was unique in its attempt to coordinate and bring together these groups, though not without conflict and opposition in some cases as the party turned increasingly towards Stalin's Third Period line.[34]

On 22 January 1931, the CPC made clear its views with respect to immigrants. The minutes of a politbureau meeting state that many immigrant workers were involved in unskilled work or were unemployed and were the lowest paid and most exploited of the proletariat. The minutes addressed the national question, stating ". . . one of the most important needs for mobilizing the workers IS THE UNITY OF THE NATIVE AND FOREIGN BORN WORKERS WITHOUT WHICH NO REAL MASS CLASS STRUGGLE IS POSSIBLE."[35]

As much as the party wanted to increase Anglo-Saxon membership, it greatly desired unity between native-born members and the foreign-born. Ethnic divisions would serve only to fracture the party and allow the state to unify workers under its nation. A patriotic immigrant, devoted to the Canadian nation, would be obliged to sacrifice their national self-determination, and forced to assimilate into the capitalist nation, resulting in national and class oppression.[36] The meeting minutes outline the need to build the ethnic press in Canada. Language organizations would possibly serve as the bridge between immigrants and the CPC. Providing immigrant workers with sport and cultural activities was important, although the party believed it could not risk letting these leisure activities "become an aim in themselves."[37] The CPC could not risk engaging in cultural-autonomy policies alone, which could result in division or separatism, thereby splitting the party along national lines.

The CPC had positioned itself as a radical political alternative within Canadian society by 1929. It simultaneously welcomed ethnic diversity within the party and marginalized it by seeking more Anglo-Saxons and French Canadians, all the while stressing that although immigrants were welcome, culture was subordinate to socialism. The CPC was, implicitly, imagining a socialist, post-British, nonracialized nation.

The CPC took a radical stance in advocating for equality between men and women. The CPC's position was based on its understanding of the "Soviet woman." Women were emancipated under Soviet law and, like their male counterparts, could work in any position. Though the sexes were officially equal, women held few posts in the CI and none in its upper echelons. Still, communism offered advantages to Canadian women. In Canada, women were legally declared persons only in 1929. Women in the civil service had to resign their positions if they married. The CPC did its best to publicize the role of women in Soviet life and in the communist movement at large. During International Women's Day celebrations, the CPC made demands in marches for unemployment insurance for all workers, sought the creation of day-care facilities, paid maternity leave, an end to discriminatory treatment of married women workers, and the creation of school meal programs and clothing for children of unemployed workers. There were no groups other than the CPC calling for such changes, and for a number of women, the CPC held out promises of utopia.[38]

The party did try to put some of its beliefs into practice by following Moscow's lead and creating a women's department, the Women's Labour League (WLL), within the party. Headed by Florence Custance in 1922, the league was instrumental in helping bring together women in different ethnic groups. In 1924, the WLL published its own paper, the *Women Worker*; the paper recognized oppression against women in the workplace and at home.[39] Several women occupied important roles in the party, most notably Becky Buhay, Jeanne Corbin, and Annie Buller. But while the party claimed to support the place of women in the party, its Third Period turn wanted to bring women's groups under party control. Custance, who died in 1929, was posthumously accused of taking a "right deviation." Women's groups were increasingly viewed by the CI as pursuing separatist agendas when the real struggle, according to the CI, was the class struggle. The family increasingly held more importance to the Soviets, and the party and the CI scorned homosexuality or any other "unconventional" unions. While marriage was expected to be between equals, as Levesque states, "equality referred more to wages than the laundry."[40]

Despite the Third Period demands, women continued to play crucial roles in the CPC and the movement. Only the CPC had made such explicit and vocal demands for women's equality in Canada, the party's own limitations in this area notwithstanding. Those like Corbin or Buller, who engaged in pitched battles and occupied leading posts in the party, never had their dedication, tenacity, or courage questioned. As for women married to party members, their activism was not so easily measured, as they were often absent from official meetings and marches because they did the tasks their male counterparts abstained from, such as raising children and working in the home. For young single women, the party offered more freedom than they could find in any other group.[41] The CPC presented a radical deviation from mainstream cultural ideas about women's rights in Canada.

In addition to the CPC's promises of equality for women and attempts to bring together Anglo, French-Canadian, and immigrant workers under the banner of communism, it wanted a new relationship between Canada and Britain. In an interview with the *Star* in 1927, then party leader Jack Macdonald put forth the CPC's position towards the UK. He argued along the lines of Lenin, that imperialism worked to the detriment of the working class, bluntly stating that sovereignty for people would be obtained only with the end of imperialism. The party stood for Canadian independence from Britain, and Canada should sever its relationship with Britain and refuse to fight in British wars. Extending the argument, Macdonald proclaimed his support for "national colonial movements everywhere." When asked whether the party was actively working in Canada to support independence from Britain, he replied that it was. He claimed that even if workers achieved their goals through the parliamentary system, whether these goals would have been truly realized was questionable because "the ruling classes have always used force." Both Macdonald and former leader Maurice Spector detailed their support for the Soviet Union and strongly believed that the UK was preparing for war against the Soviets, a line frequently touted by Moscow at the time.[42]

The position taken by the former leaders was met with conflict as members struggled to find their footing in Moscow's new line. Sam Carr, a leading member of the party, had a different vision than Macdonald and claimed that the first priority should be to fight against the Canadian bourgeoisie, which, he claimed, was the principal oppressor of the Canadian working classes and held more power in Canada than their British and American counterparts in the country. By 1931, Carr's version of struggle had won out among Anglo members.[43] In spite of this, the party did continue bringing attention to what it considered imperialist actions across the globe. This propaganda was motivated by a fear that an international conflict was a threat to the Soviet Union, as the CI often claimed. The Communist paper the *Worker* drew attention to and supported mass demonstrations in Ireland for Irish independence, opposed British military actions in Yemen, supported Philippine peasant uprisings against landlords, and opposed European imperialism on the African continent and British rule in India. It is unknown how widespread support for such movements was on the ground within the party, but it regularly publicized its opposition to colonialism throughout the globe.[44]

The CPC needed to recruit the most exploited members of the working class, such as women and immigrants, into what was essentially an international communist culture or even nation. This collective movement was held together through a mixture of force and consent. Membership was voluntary, but purges were used by the leadership to ensure loyalty. It explicitly opposed what it saw as British imperialism and colonialism in Canada as well as abroad. This was the CPC's vision for a future Canada: a society that respected cultural differences, espoused equality between men and women, and was economically and politically a communist state united with other communist nations and independent of British rule, for Canada would never become a workers' republic as long as it was under the British monarchy. The communist nation would resemble a community of communities, united internationally. In joining the CPC, one entered an imagined community based on class rather than ethnicity or gender. In spite of these ideals, centralized control was still present in the movement. While members struggled to interpret and implement

Moscow's directives, they were still expected to be followed. Of particular importance was the role of revolution in communist thought. Even though Communists were fielding candidates in elections, the party believed that revolution was always a possibility. It was not afraid to support the idea that change could occur independent of Parliament if the people willed it. It frequently acted politically in ways perceived as unconventional by the authorities, such as through protests and marches in the streets. In sum, the communist movement and conception of the nation was antithetical to the dominant British model of Canada in the interwar period.

"Foreigners . . . Who Have No Interest in Our Country"

For Canadian authorities, the potential threats to the country from previous years remained as the 1920s drew to a close. The fear of a return to 1919 and the era of the British activist remained, but much more pressing was the current spread of communism in Canada, which was present in a number of ethnic communities: Finns, Ukrainians, Poles, Germans, Croatians, Hungarians, Russians, and Yiddish-speaking Jews. In its security bulletins, the RCMP monitored these communities and noted any public meetings held by "foreign-born revolutionaries."[45] CPC ideals of a socialist, post-British, nonracialized Canada that would come about through a worker-led revolution did not sit well with Canadian authorities. The RCMP's very creation was tied to monitoring leftist activity, and it was focused on communism for much of its history.[46] As early as 1921, the service trained agents to go undercover and become active members of the CPC, most notably John Leopold, alias "Jack Esselwein," who would later testify for the RCMP at the Buck et al. trial in 1931. The perception of communists was that they represented a threat to Canada's British political institutions and economy. They were a threat in need of managing.

If communism was perceived by some politicians as entering Canada during the mid-1920s, by the late 1920s and early 1930s, it was rampant. From 1928 to 1930, communism was frequently cited by politicians as the new threat that endangered the nation and made Section 98 and Section 41 all the more valuable. Throughout 1928–9, the CPC openly confronted the police, particularly in Toronto, as Communists agitated for their right to free speech by making public speeches and leading large public rallies.[47] The frequent attempts by the police to break up CPC public meetings or rallies resulted in the emergence of a free-speech campaign that involved professors at the University of Toronto.[48] These Communist speeches and public gatherings were anathema to Brigadier-General Denis C. Draper, Toronto's new police chief in 1929, who led the Toronto police in its attacks on reds. He made clear, in a speech to the Empire Club of Canada, that a good citizen was one who possessed "loyalty to the British Empire" and that a good Canadian was a citizen who was "endowed with . . . true and loyal patriotism."[49] Communists were opposed to capitalism and the government. But more important for Draper, they publicly expressed these views. For the Communists, who had no elected member in Parliament, political action and change came from actions outside of what many conservative-minded Canadians believed was acceptable. Change could come from the street. Communists were far from Draper's view of the good citizen.

Police violence against CPC members and supporters occurred in cities throughout the country, but despite the CPC successes in gaining the sympathy of some members of Canadian society, the CPC agitation failed to translate to votes at the ballot box. The government was aware of these failures. For instance, in the 1930 federal election, Richard Bedford Bennett led the Conservatives to a majority over Mackenzie King and the Liberal Party. The CPC contested nine constituencies and managed only 7,601 votes out of the total 168,540.

During the heated exchanges between police and Communists, there were three last-ditch efforts to have Section 98 repealed before the Liberals lost the election to the Conservatives. All attempts failed. The frequent attempts to repeal it had grown tiring, even for the Liberals, with Lapointe stating in 1930, "Clause 2 covers the same bill as has passed this house six times . . . This has been debated so many times that I presume I need not again give the purpose."[50] The bill received no debate and was quickly passed, but handily defeated by a Conservative-dominated Senate.

With Bennett's Conservative Party at the helm, pressure on politicians and law enforcement to prosecute the CPC continued to grow from a number of places. The authorities' attention now shifted to foreign communists, not those from the UK but from Eastern Europe. Ideas of what was truly British, and hence Canadian, were espoused by many. Industry groups across the country wanted the government to take action against Communists. In 1932, J.R. Smith of West Canadian Collieries Ltd. in Alberta wanted to know what actions the government was taking to deal with Communists. He warned the government of red penetration of the "foreign element," which was causing difficulties for his industry. Communists, he stated, might not do any harm in a community where there was a larger percentage of "English speaking people" but could certainly "inflame the minds of the foreign element."[51] The government's duty was to prevent the Communists from influencing immigrants. Writing to Prime Minister Bennett in 1930, G.L.E. Strong, of Sherwood Foresters, believed that the problem of communism was linked to immigration from Eastern and Central Europe, which was causing discontent among his workers. It was being spread only by a few "English speaking renegades." Strong thought that tightening up immigration by not allowing more distant family members of settled immigrants to immigrate might alleviate the problem.[52]

The Employers Association of Manitoba met with the Winnipeg Board of Trade and two federal ministers, W.A. Gordon, the minister of mines, and T.G. Murphy, the minister of the interior. As a result of the meeting, the association sent Justice Minister Hugh Guthrie a list of the Fish Commission recommendations, which had recently concluded in the United States. The commission looked at the penetration of communism into American society and suggested ways of containing it. The Employers Association sent the same recommendations to Bennett. The recommendations included increasing police surveillance of Communists, tightening immigration, and the suggestion that "any CP branches operating as a section of the Communist International or any part of a CP" that was "advocating the overthrow of our form of government by force or violence or affiliated with the Communist International at Moscow be declared illegal."[53] The Employers Association of Manitoba used the identical wording of Section 98 to drive its point home. Much like the Canadian business community during the Winnipeg General Strike, industry groups had an important impact on how the government dealt with communism in Canada during the Depression.

Bennett's office was flooded with letters from city councils from across the country that supported a motion originally put forth by the Sudbury city council. The motion called on the federal government to "deport undesirables and communists."[54] Again the connection was made that all Communists must necessarily be foreigners eligible for deportation. Many municipal leaders held these views. In June of 1929, in a meeting between Mayor Craig of Kingston and Mayor McBride of Toronto, Craig quipped that Toronto's Communists had made it clear that Kingston was more British than Toronto, because in Kingston, "we are all British." McBride promptly corrected him by stating, "Our stopping of Communistic meetings shows that we are truly British."[55] The repression of activists in Toronto was considered a necessary measure in protecting Toronto's Britishness.

Bennett's government took an interest in all the suggestions. Indeed, not much persuasion was needed to convince Bennett's government to take action against communism. The prime minister played an active role in intelligence matters and had no problem taking matters into his own hands. He had in his possession membership lists of Communists; these lists included people's names and home addresses. He occasionally asked people who wrote to him complaining of Communists to supply names of reds to forward to the RCMP or immigration department. In one instance, following the Buck et al. trial, a letter was sent to Bennett from a man named Nicholas Mihaychuck, protesting the imprisonment of the CPC leaders and demanding the repeal of Section 98. Bennett forwarded the man's name and information to General MacBrian of the RCMP and instructed MacBrian to cancel the man's naturalization certificate if possible (i.e., if he had one) and deport him. Bennett told MacBrian he did not like the man's "impudent tone" towards the "administration of justice."[56] Bennett supported tightening immigration to prevent more communists from entering the country. His personal role in helping to prosecute Communists was connected to his strong religious outlook and his overly controlling manner of running the government. He was ridiculed for once referring to the federal government as "my government" and for strictly controlling his cabinet ministers.[57] He rarely responded to letters about communists, except when he received a letter from someone expressing anti-communist views or from a member of the religious community.[58]

Many religious leaders shared these views. A missionary conference of the Knox Presbyterian Church on 7 May 1929 asked its members, "Is this country is going to keep British or is it going to turn foreign?" Those in attendance replied, "British for all time!" The question was posed by the Reverend Hanna of the Knox Church. It hosted a meeting that welcomed speakers from an anti-communist group called the Canadian Christian Crusade (CCC). Hanna noted that 38 different languages were being spoken in Winnipeg and that 48 per cent of the population of Saskatchewan was comprised of foreigners. If they were "properly" assimilated into British ways, they would avoid the perils of communism. "Me swear . . . me drink whiskey, me a Canadian" was the mistaken view these foreigners had of Canada, said Hanna. "We have a great task on our hands to educate, and civilize and Christianize these people," he continued.[59] Civilization was tied to Christianity and Britishness.

The Presbyterians were not the only religious group concerned with the godlessness of communism. The Catholic Church assisted the RCMP in spying when it could. The church supported the attempts of the Toronto police's red squad at cracking down on suspected reds, and RCMP surveillance records were found within Archdiocesan files. The files focused on immigrant groups such as Ukrainians and Finns who, according to church officials, sought to "implant in children atheistic, revolutionary and communistic opinions and prejudices." The children would eventually regard Russia as their own, the church feared, and scorn religion and their own government.[60] Foreigners in Toronto were corrupting the youth and children of Canada with radical ideas. In addition to its activities in Toronto, in Montreal the Catholic Church engaged in an anti-communist campaign aimed at preventing Francophone workers from joining the party.[61]

Within the communist section of his papers, Bennett kept books that were anti-communist in nature that explained communism and its dangers. This material helped form the PM's world view of communism and leftist activists.[62] Other prominent Conservatives shared these views. Ontario's attorney general, William H. Price, wrote – in regards to Buck et al.'s appeal after the 1931 trial – that "Canada's foundation rested upon Christian civilization. We have a constitution that spells liberty and peace. Communism brings not peace but a sword, and for that reason is not welcome in our midst."[63] Not only did communism threaten religious values, but by doing so it was also attacking civilization.

Price went on speaking tours denouncing communism's influence on Canada's Christian roots. At an annual meeting of the prominent Protestant organization the Orange Order, and in speeches at Knox Church in Toronto, Price detailed how the fight against communism was a fight against atheism. Communism was against the king, who obeys the law and fears God. Because it breeds atheism, Price claimed it "aims at the breaking up of the family." The individual, he argued, was central to the family and parental responsibility. Communism's focus on "the masses," he said, "wipes out the home and creates a commune." It creates "free love, as we rear our children like animals," with "the State herding the children" into groups and eliminating parental responsibility.[64] For Ontario's attorney general and the prime minister, communism's threat to Canada's religious institutions threatened their paternalistic and heteronormative view of the family. By seeking an egalitarian society, communism would cause the role of the father in the family, indeed of both parents in Price's eyes, to disappear. For Price, a family was a heterosexual married couple with children. For him and other leading Canadians who saw the family as being the central regulating body for society, communism threatened society as a whole: the state in a free-love society, without traditional marital bonds, raised animalistic children who lacked the firm and paternalistic structure the individual family unit provided. Such a state was a far cry from Price's conception of an orderly society.

Several judges, such as Emerson Coatsworth and Robert Brown, who worked on other Communist trials, believed that the values of a liberal Canada were synonymous with being British, while communism was foreign. The sacredness of property and the rights of property owners, held to be British values, were paramount. The judges agreed with Crown prosecutor Wilkins when he argued, "The Communist Party is made [up] of foreigners . . . who have no interest in our country, by that I mean they do not hold any real estate."[65]

In referring to communists, Mayor McBride of Toronto felt that "foreigners should not be allowed to come here and undermine the religious views of our young people."[66] Indeed, the atheistic element of communism, warned the *Globe*'s editors, could result in the "plant[ing of] a tree whose fruit will mean the downfall of nations."[67] At a University of Toronto debate on free speech in 1929, McBride remarked, "We are not opposed to free speech, but we are opposed to Communism because of the way it preaches sedition, blasphemy and slander." At an Orange Order meeting, McBride criticized the professors at the University of Toronto who dared believe that communists should have the right to free speech, stating, "If that is the kind of ideas the university is putting into the heads of the young men of this city, it is time we got rid of those teachers."[68]

It was not only businesses, church leaders, and politicians who shared these views about communism. Similar sentiments appeared throughout the popular press. The editorial in the *Globe* on 23 January 1931 stated that the risk of "Red free speech" and propaganda would not work on the "intelligent British born or French-Canadian." Immigrants who were unaware of British traditions were the most vulnerable to the "enemy within the gates." The police and educators' duty was to protect and help immigrants become "good British citizens" and thus believe in liberal "British" values such as the right to own property.[69] The *Mail and Empire* commented that Canada would soon be overrun by socialist peasant foreigners, that it must "remain British in its ideas and culture," and that the balance of the immigrant stock should be from places that believed in the "ideas of freedom."[70] The *Evening Telegram* in 1929 stated that "the loyalty of the British born . . . from the slums of London or Toronto is to be preferred to the mongrel internationalism of a transported Europe."[71]

Letters from the public contained similar statements. A letter signed "Common Sense" criticized the idea that any communist should have a right to free speech, saying: "Men seek to incite their fellowmen to sedition and revolution using a foreign jargon to conceal their propaganda. Are not the authorities justified in putting a stop to it? . . . Your anarchist is a far greater menace to society than your sneak thief."[72] The American Federation of Labor declared its support in fighting communism.[73] Canadian branches of the Ku Klux Klan supported the fight against communism and foreigners who played into its ideology that all non-Anglo-Saxon immigration should end.[74] For its part, the Orange Order resolved at a national meeting that the federal government should prevent the spread of communism by requiring every voter to first attest to their belief in God, their allegiance to the king, and their ability to read and write English.[75] Various ethnic organizations were eager to denounce communism, including the Ukrainian, Hungarian, Croatian, and Serbian communities.[76] Long-standing ethnic conflicts played out in the hunt for communists. In a letter to Bennett in 1931, Mike Borbowski, writing on behalf of the Welland, Ontario Polish Society, protested the abuse of Poles by Ukrainians within the Polish community, claiming the Poles were Canadian citizens while the Ukrainians were all members of Communist organizations.[77]

In formulations of good citizenship, Britishness, Christianity, property, and propriety were combined, while those who were beyond the pale of these norms were a threat and should be deported. Canada's institutions needed defending against unseen, foreign intruders, particularly in the economic climate of the times. In the House of Commons, G.B. Nicholson argued that the CPC was based in a foreign country and sought to "undermine Canadian institutions as well as those of every other country similar to ours."[78] In a letter to Prime Minister Bennett, Alberta premier John Edward Brownlee argued that deportations could help stop foreigners getting free meals at the expense of the government. There was no trouble in the province with whom Brownlee considered "our own people," such as "English and Scots."[79] Premier Tolmie, of British Columbia, believed that Communists were foreign disturbers.[80] Tolmie maintained that the situation in BC was grave and that reds with English and Scottish names were giving the public "false impressions" about communism – which was clearly foreign. Both premiers called on the government to step up prosecutions and deportations of communists.

Prime Minister Bennett agreed with his premiers about the value of deportation in protecting British subjects and preserving Canada's

British values and society. Bennett instructed Tolmie to give him the names of alleged Communists as soon as they were convicted so that he could immediately forward the names to the Department of Immigration. The government would then begin deportation proceedings.[81] Defending the state from foreigners unworthy of Canadian citizenship was of the utmost importance.

The situation was similar in Quebec, except that communism was a threat to a French and Catholic Canadian nation. Quebec's Liberal government, led by Louis-Alexandre Taschereau, violently sought to crush communism and had support from Quebec's Catholic community.[82] Fear was everywhere. Montreal's Bishop Gauthier feared communism was less interested in overthrowing capitalism than it was in condemning Catholicism. So great was this fear that all Montreal churches on 25 January 1931 condemned communism during the morning homilies. Communism was frequently damned in Henri Bourassa's Catholic newspaper *Le Devoir*.[83]

Prosecutions of prominent and low-level CPC members were frequent.[84] In 1932, Taschereau, who also served as the attorney general, asked Chief Maurice Lalonde of the province's police service to have stenographers record every speech given at public Communist meetings. Like Toronto, Montreal had its own red squad and worked with provincial police and the RCMP in tracking Communists through the use of informants. Even prominent moderate leftists such as F.R. Scott and Eugene Forsey were regarded by RCMP informants as being "communist agitators." Quebec's attempt at halting communism in the province was particularly harsh, as chapter 5 will reveal.[85]

Cultural perceptions and emotions played an important role in preserving emergency measures in peacetime. As long as Canadians feared a continual threat from a foreign danger that authorities believed could not be caught by conventional means, exceptional measures were needed to keep people feeling safe and secure. Yes, the enemy was pervasive in Canadian society, so this logic went, but people could feel safe knowing that lawmakers had the law to fight the enemy. The CPC's desires for equality between men and women or its position on capitalism were considered illegitimate because it was perceived as a band of foreign immigrants seeking to remake Canada. In many ways, the authorities needed the CPC to better understand themselves and the identity and nation of Canadians as they saw such things. For the government, the CPC reinforced what Canada was and was not. For many in English Canada, the nation was a liberal state where Britishness, property, propriety, the monarch, and Christianity were Canadian values and morals. Culture was security but also exposed threats. Communists were a backward foreign scourge that threatened British civilization. In Quebec, Communists threatened a French and Catholic nation. The Depression was about to motivate the CPC into political action. These actions convinced authorities that the Communists had to be managed.

"Foreigners, Parading the Town . . . Had a Terrifying Effect on a Lot of People"

The government recognized the CPC's ability to organize unemployed workers across the country with minimal resources. As the economic crisis deepened, the highly vocal, public agitation of the CPC for the right to preach its doctrines shifted to advocating for the right of the unemployed to receive relief.[86] The CPC was now not only asserting that it had rights, such as free speech, but also making political demands outside of the country's parliament. The unemployed provided the CPC with more potential troops, with little to lose, who could be persuaded to see the economic crisis as the result of the failure of capitalism. The CPC strategy focused on the lack of relief for the unemployed. It pressured the government to create a national, non-contributory form of unemployment insurance. Bennett's government opposed unemployment insurance – partly out of the government's ideological belief that it would not provide handouts and partly due to an inability to provide such a program because of constitutional limitations.[87]

The Depression enabled the CPC to conduct large rallies and marches of unemployed workers in cities across the country. In several Ontario cities, such as Port Arthur and Fort William (now known as Thunder Bay), Sudbury, and Cochrane, nearly one thousand unemployed workers marched through the small towns. In October 1930 in Port Arthur, both the mayor and Crown attorney pleaded to Ottawa and the attorney general of Ontario for assistance. The unemployed (who were considered Communists) had claimed during marches and parades that they would begin destroying shops and property. An RCMP detachment was sent to break up the marches. In the case of Port Arthur, raids led by the RCMP and local police were conducted of various homes and offices believed linked to the CPC.

These workers' status as both single and unemployed increased the government's anxiety. Many believed communism supported the breakup of the traditional family unit. In the eyes of the authorities, Communists were corrupting these single men and luring them away from pursuing a family and employment. For instance, the Crown attorney of Port Arthur was relieved when Mounties arrived. "If they had not been sent," he wrote, "I am perfectly sure there would have been a lot of bloodshed. You can understand that hundreds of men, almost all foreigners, parading the town, threatening to take possession of the place, had a terrifying effect on a lot of people."[88]

The invasion of foreign single men had been firmly quelled by the strong masculine Mountie presence. Cultural perceptions of communism led authorities to see the unrest as the start of a foreign, Communist-led revolt and responded to it with force. These marches were political actions by people the authorities believed had no legal authority to engage in such actions, mainly unemployed foreign "reds" or Communists. Personal letters from unemployed workers to Prime Minister Bennett during the Depression reveal that many unemployed workers simply wanted work and not a wholesale change in the political or economic system.[89] The marches were assertions of masculinity by the participants in a period of entrenched gender norms as men struggled to reclaim a lost sense of masculinity caused by their unemployment and loss of status as the breadwinner in the family.[90] The attorney general of Ontario, Colonel William Price, who was a firm believer in Communism's threat to the family, noted that it was the incident at Port Arthur that greatly motivated him to begin working on prosecuting the CPC.[91]

The RCMP assisted the government in preparing the case against the CPC and shared the government's view of it as an alien group. The government believed that a Section 98 conviction was the best way to stop the spread of this culture.[92] To secure a conviction, the authorities had to change the way they approached communism. The rallies the CPC held in Montreal, Toronto, and other areas led to some members facing charges with small jail sentences or fines, such as charges of vagrancy or unlawful assembly, and none of these directly impacted the CPC on a large scale. Section 98 provided a solution for stopping the party, but how it was used against the party had to change. For instance, in November 1929 Charlie Sims, a CPC organizer, and five supporters were the first individuals charged under Section 98 for distributing pamphlets advocating governmental change, in particular revolutionary change.

The case against the group, known as *Rex v. Emily Weir et al.*, was the first test case for Section 98. J.L. Cohen, a prominent lawyer who often assisted the CPC, was able to secure an acquittal, and the charges were dropped. In his closing remarks, the presiding judge found that "revolutionary" was too ambiguous and that regardless, the pamphlet did not fit this definition.[93] If a Section 98 conviction was to have maximum effect on the party, it would have to target the group as a whole. Police had to stop approaching the problem of communism on an individual basis. They had to stop prosecuting individuals for individual acts. Police actions had to align with their perception of communism: it was a subversive foreign group seeking revolution. Only attacking the group as a whole could stop it, and Section 98 was suited for the task.

In 1931, the federal Conservative government, along with the governments of provinces such as Ontario and Alberta and with the support of numerous municipal governments and leaders in industry and business, produced an organized and coordinated effort to have the CPC declared an unlawful organization in violation of Section 98(1) between the years 1921 and 1930 and its members arrested.

Municipal as well as provincial police, the attorney general's office, and even the postmaster were all in close communication with each other throughout 1931. Reports in Communist papers such as the *Worker* were constantly surveyed for signs of offending or illegal language.[94] Sergeant Marshall of the Toronto police reiterated the cultural assumptions that Communists were foreign subversives plotting revolution. In a letter to Draper, he wrote, "There is no way in which we can combat these people [communists] without force, as apparently the majority of Citizens do not realize how serious a matter it is, and what proportions things are getting to."[95] Only force could stop foreign revolutionaries.

Just months before the trial of Buck et al. took place in Toronto, police chiefs from across the country met with RCMP commissioner Cortlandt Starnes in the office of the Justice Minister Hugh Guthrie. While in press reports the government denied the meeting was to discuss communism, in a letter to Attorney General Price, Guthrie confirmed that communism was the major focus of the meeting:

> Dear Colonel Price,
> I desire to draw to your attention the situation which exists throughout Canada and more particularly in the Province of Ontario in regard to Communist activities . . . which I fear has gained some foothold in Canada, more particularly during the past year and a half, while unemployment has been so general.[96]

Guthrie informed Price that the RCMP had large amounts of information that would prove useful to him from years of surveillance. Guthrie stated that if Price concluded that action should be taken, the federal government and the RCMP would offer their complete cooperation, as the RCMP had undercover agents who had been working within the CPC for years.[97] Joseph Sedgwick, who worked in the attorney general's office, remembers Price telling him in a meeting, "I'm under pressure from Ottawa to take action against the Reds." Price claimed he would go ahead with prosecuting Communists so that the "boys in Ottawa" would be satisfied.[98] RCMP commissioner Starnes told Sedgwick about an agent who had agreed to testify against the CPC, later identified as Sergeant Leopold. Starnes's attempts at securing another former RCMP officer doing undercover work in the UK were unsuccessful; authorities in the UK wanted the officer to continue his work.[99]

Despite the events in Port Arthur, Price decided not to proceed with prosecution right away since despite all the information he possessed, he still felt that making the case that the party supported the use of violence against the state would prove difficult.[100] The decision was made by the authorities to prosecute the CPC because the federal government believed it should happen. What the party had done to violate the law was unclear even to the attorney general. Law was being used not because the government wanted to punish anyone who had committed a crime but because it wanted it to be used against an enemy. Justice was not the motivating factor in this case; it was the right of the state, or of the sovereign, to judge. The goal for the government and the Crown was, first and foremost, to get the CPC to a public trial. The politics of the CPC would be judged by the state so that all citizens and foreigners would understand what politics were acceptable in Canada.[101]

Information flowed into Price's office as the months followed, even on suspected Communists from the past. In a memo from Price to fellow Crown solicitor Joseph Sedgwick, Price mentioned that Major Knowles of Barrie was in charge of internment camps in Nova Scotia and Kapuskasing during the war and had a list of seventy-three Communists. Price suggested Sedgwick meet with Knowles to discuss it.[102] Indeed, Price was doing his best to accumulate as many names of Communists as possible from communities across Canada to aid in further prosecutions and deportations after the trial. Crown lawyers from Manitoba, Saskatchewan, and many other Canadian cities complied, sending Price the names and addresses of as many Communists as they could.[103] The trial garnered international attention. The American consul wanted updates on the prosecution in case the US government wanted to try prosecuting Communists.[104]

Previous works have argued that in regards to the prosecution of the CPC leadership, the intelligence cycle worked in that the authorities were successful in planning, collecting, processing, analysing, and disseminating intelligence, which led to successful arrests and prosecutions of CPC members.[105] While there is no dispute it worked, the key to understanding *how* the cycle worked and how such targets of intelligence were ever identified lies in the cultural perceptions of the period. The cycle was shaped by cultural biases and perceptions. Whom government authorities needed to target and collect intelligence on, as well as what this intelligence meant and the proper response to it, was funnelled through cultural perceptions and stereotypes.

The normalizing of exceptional powers with Section 98 enabled the government to target the CPC and take exceptional legal measures against it in peacetime. Stopping communism was now a viable option. It was the anxieties and fears in the context of an emergency and the illegitimate political actions of perceived foreigners during the Depression, combined with cultural views, that convinced the government to act against the CPC. It was its political actions, alongside its ideology and conceptions of what the Canadian nation should be, that were the most troubling for lawmakers, not because it was really engaging in revolution but because its political actions challenged sovereign power in ways the state disapproved of. The perception of what those actions meant was determined by culture. Political changes were not made on the street but in Parliament by white, propertied believers in Christianity, or so the authorities believed. If Communists continued to sow unrest, there was little to stop others from doing the same. The government had an exceptional law to combat an exceptional enemy that had pervaded society. Targeting this enemy would demonstrate to all Canadians and immigrants which politics were tolerable in Canada and which were not.

The Arrest

At 6 p.m. on the night of 11 August 1931, eighteen police officers, consisting of six RCMP members, six Ontario Provincial Police (OPP) officers, and six Toronto police officers, gathered in the hall of the OPP commissioner's office. The group waited and smoked in the hall, wondering what they were being assembled to do that night. When they were called in, Major-General Williams began the briefing: "Gentlemen we are going to strike a death blow at the Communist party – we hope." He ordered the officers to arrest the party leaders, search their headquarters and homes, and "seize every paper and every document" that could link the party members to Russia.

The arrests were to occur simultaneously, Williams explained, "to the second" if possible.[106]

The operation had a military-like feel. The strike on the targets and their headquarters would occur with to-the-second precision. Officers were sent out at 7 p.m. to arrest their targets. The CPC headquarters at 70 Lombard Street in Toronto was raided, as well as the *Worker* and WUL offices at 68A Adelaide Street. The original arrest warrant was issued for Tim Buck, A.T. Hill, Tom Ewen, John Boychuk, Sam Carr, Malcolm Bruce, and Matthew Popovich.[107] According to press reports, after the raids Toronto police announced they were in possession of evidence that proved $18,000 was forwarded to the CPC from Moscow through New York, with $11,000 going to Communists in Winnipeg. Curiously, the evidence was never produced at the Buck et al. trial. Buck was arrested at the headquarters, while Boychuk was arrested at home, both without incident. Malcolm Bruce and Sam Carr were arrested in Vancouver that same night. Despite Williams's call for precision, the raids were hardly well coordinated or executed.[108]

The same night as the raid at CPC headquarters, Detective Frank Zaneth of the RCMP went to Tim Buck's house to arrest him, not being sure where Buck was or if he had already been arrested. Zaneth, previously an undercover officer in the CPC for the RCMP, broke into Buck's house while both Buck and his wife were out, and while alone in the house seized various booklets and materials, including documents relating to Buck's membership in the CPC. The documents included meeting minutes and letterhead indicating that the CPC was a section of the CI.[109]

Two more arrests took place the following day. Police arrived at Matthew Popovich's house to arrest him on 12 August. Officer Daniel Mann and William Simpson managed to catch Popovich at home during dinner. As they entered the house, Popovich calmly put his coat on and told the officers he had expected his arrest, just not so soon. Popovich was taken into the cruiser, cautioned, arrested, and taken to the Don Jail.[110] At the CPC offices the same night, an officer had discovered party member Tomo Čačić trying to enter the WUL office. Detective John Nimmo of the Toronto police, called in to question him, asked Čačić what his position in the party was, to which Čačić replied he had none. Čačić said he was there to see the "girl that does the typing" but could not remember her name. Nimmo arrested Čačić and searched him. He found a credential that was signed by Buck that indicated that Čačić was the national organizer for the South Slav Bureau of the Party. Another one, signed by A.E. Smith, identified him as an organizer for the Canadian Labor Defense

League. Čačić made no mention of his standing in the party before he was arrested and shown the credentials by Nimmo. He was arrested because Nimmo thought he had caught a leader of the party. In reality, Čačić was a foot soldier in the wrong place at the wrong time.[111] Amos T. Hill was arrested in Cochrane by the OPP on 13 August. Despite his claim that he had been followed by police for weeks, Hill continued to take part in public speeches and meetings even on the night of 11 August, when all the other raids took place. Police had less luck in arresting Tom Ewen. George Fish of the RCMP and Detective Waterhouse of the Toronto police, finding no one home at Ewen's house, decided to break in and search it. After ransacking the residence, they camped out across the street in their cruiser, hoping to catch Ewen coming home. What they were not aware of was that Ewen had actually arrived home while the officers were ransacking his home, but he was told by his landlord not to go upstairs, and so he promptly left. The officers did find 22-year-old Mike Golinsky (known as Mike Gilmore) trying to enter Ewen's house at 3 a.m. Golinsky explained to the police that he was in town from Calgary to attend a Young Communist Conference and, having little money, was essentially camping out with Ewen for the time being. Golinsky told the officers he was a Communist. His pockets were searched, Communist material was found, and he was promptly arrested.[112] Tom Ewen eventually walked into Toronto police headquarters on 17 August, reportedly smiling as he was arrested. He turned himself in on the advice of Buck, who wanted Ewen to give himself up, presumably for propaganda purposes.[113]

All of those arrested were charged with violating Section 98 between the years 1920 and 1930, with no indication of how they had done so. Books, membership lists, and letters between party members praising the Soviet Union, in addition to Marxist literature from the Soviet Union, were used as evidence. Photos of the evidence were splashed across the pages of newspapers such as the *Evening Telegram*, accompanied by ominous headlines such as "Police Raid and Arrest in Sudden, Secret Move against Reds in Canada."[114] People may have expected to see photos of tagged weapons, cash, and other contraband, but instead they were shown stacks of books and boxes of paper. The papers implied that reds were preparing for revolution, but nothing was ever stated as to how the men had violated Section 98. The arrests were portrayed as preventative arrests. The police interpreted Section 98 as a Code section that had been designed to arrest communists for being Communists to stop them before they could start a revolution and commit a crime like treason.[115]

The only detailed description of Buck's arrest comes from Buck. He claimed that when he asked why he was being arrested, the officer replied:

> "It's not necessary, I am ordered to arrest you. You are charged under Section 98 of the Criminal Code."
>
> I [Buck] said, "Charged with what?"
>
> He said, "Well Section 98 is rather sweeping . . . you should know all about it and it's not necessary to charge you with any specific crime. You're charged with infringing the terms of Section 98 of the Criminal Code and it is not my duty to describe what those terms are."[116]

While no explanation of how the men had violated Section 98 was needed, the arrests had a Kafkaesque air about them. The breadth of Section 98 made it difficult for someone to know exactly what they had done wrong. No further answers were required by the authorities. One had to assume that one's actions over the past ten years had led to this moment. In the view of the government and the mainstream press, Section 98 was used for precisely the reason it was created, to stop subversive foreign Communists from leading an uprising. What is important is not just the actual law of Section 98, but the process, the way Section 98 was used and what this process reveals about law. The process of law can reveal the nature of it.[117] In this case, the authorities wielded Section 98 as a type of preventative arrest law. It was a means of stopping the CPC before it could commit the real crime they were worried about – treason by way of revolution. Authorities were not concerned with matters of justice or whether or not the CPC had violated the Criminal Code. This was about judgment. It was about the right of the state to use the law to publicly judge the politics of the CPC. Canadians needed to know which political ideology and actions would be accepted in Canada and which would not. That the men's arrest was about judging politics was made plainly clear when they were arrested, even though the authorities were unsure of what they had done wrong according to the law. Price did not know of any violent act they had committed, and the arresting officers had no response to the accused asking what they had done wrong: how or why had they violated Section 98? Following the arrest of the CPC members, the sovereign would now judge the politics of the group in the public spectacle of a trial.

The Communist Party of Canada sought to build its base during Moscow's Third Period by uniting domestic-born and foreign-born

Figure 2.1 The evidence of revolution: books and papers seized
during the arrest of CPC members. From the *Toronto Evening Telegram*,
12 August 1931.

workers. It presented a radical, alternative conception of the Canadian
nation. It was not seeking to do away with Canada through a Soviet-
style revolution but to dramatically alter it to an ethnically plural,
worker-led Communist state, with equality between men and women,
independence from the UK, and membership in the international
communist movement. The party sought not the destruction of Canada but a dramatic remaking of it in line with what it believed society
should look like. At the same time, with no political representation in
Parliament because it advocated for the most marginalized in society,
the CPC engaged in political action in manners it saw fit. Members
took to the streets and fought with police. The CPC vision was at odds
with much of Canadian society, which sought not a complete alteration of society in the Great Depression, but its repair.

The CPC, branded by many as being a representative of a foreign
and alien culture, came under the direct fire of a newly elected federal Conservative government that sought the party's complete anni-
hilation. Cultural perceptions and fears determined how and why the
authorities saw the CPC as a threat and how to respond. Both English
and French Canada had their own views about what the Canadian
nation was and the threat communism posed. Culture was especially
important in continuing the normalization of emergency measures
and establishing what security was and what was a threat. As long
as a foreign subversive threat lurked in the shadows that authorities

believed lay outside the realm of ordinary legal measures, exceptional legal powers would be needed to deter it or stop it. With Section 98, the government had at its disposal an exceptional law that could completely outlaw the party and stop the CPC's march to revolution. The nine accused found themselves in the spectacle of an ordinary criminal court, being tried for violating what was, in essence, a wartime emergency law.

3

The Trial

Nine accused members of the Communist Party of Canada (CPC), Tim Buck, John Boychuk, Malcolm Bruce, Sam Carr, A.T. Hill, Tomo Čačić, Tom Ewen, Mike Golinsky, and Matthew Popovich, entered Toronto's Old City Hall courthouse on 2 November 1931. The nine were indicted on three counts, the first two of being officers and members of an unlawful organization, to wit the CPC, and the third of being party to a seditious conspiracy. The 1931 trial of the CPC members, or "the Eight," as they were known, was the best-documented, largest, and best-known trial involving Section 98.[1] Previous studies have viewed the trial as an example of how the CPC threatened the established order in Canada and have stressed how the government prosecuted the CPC to stamp out communism. While the CPC did threaten the established order, it was not only because of its ideology but also because of its unconventional political actions. The CPC represented a continual threat to security. Section 98 was the only weapon that could effectively wipe out the group as a whole, and targeting their ideology was the easiest means of doing so.

No study has examined how criminal law targeted political ideology in the case of Buck et al., nor has a study delved into the broader significance of the trial in Canadian society.[2] By targeting the unlawful expressions of groups and individuals, Section 98 made it possible for the law to indirectly target political ideology. The CPC trial offers a unique window into how an emergency law (PC 2384, now Section 98) operated in a peacetime courtroom, from the challenges the Crown had in indicting the accused to evidence admission. The trial had an almost sanitizing effect on Section 98's exceptional status. Canadians' support for the trial and conviction reveals how they were becoming more comfortable living with the emergency.

Section 98 made it possible for the CPC's ideology to serve as the *actus reus* (the criminal act). The accused had not engaged in any acts of violence nor had plans for engaging in violent acts against the state. The Crown's intentions, from the indictment to the grand jury to the arguments in the trial, reveal that prosecuting ideology in order to outlaw it and stop the CPC's political actions was its ultimate goal. The government and leading Canadians viewed communism as a threat to the country's British and liberal culture. During the trial, the Crown continually invoked the fear of unrest and of communism producing a foreign-led revolution.

The defence, which recognized that the ideology of communism was the real focus of the trial, tried to counter the Crown's case by arguing that believing in Marxism was not criminal but merely represented an alternative method of understanding history. Revolution, it argued, was an inevitable historical event. The resulting conviction of the accused placed members of the CPC in a precarious position: they were all now guilty of an offence before receiving a trial. Communists became outlaws and a demonstration to all in Canada of which politics were "Canadian" and legal and which were foreign and illegal. What was most significant about the trial was not whether it was fair or not, but that law, in the service of sovereign power, provided the state with the right to judge the politics of its subjects.

Political Intentions

Norman Sommerville and Joseph Sedgwick represented the Crown, and Hugh J. Macdonald and Onie Brown represented the defendants. Tim Buck defended himself. Initially, Attorney General William Price considered the possibility of Sedgwick as the lead attorney because he had been working on the case since March 1931. Sedgwick was born in Leeds, England, and was a graduate of the University of Toronto. He still considered himself fairly new to the profession, having been called to the bar only seven years prior to the trial. He informed the attorney general's office that he could work on the case with another solicitor. Price told Deputy Attorney General Bayly that a special Crown attorney would be assigned. The more seasoned Norman Sommerville was to take on the role of leading the Crown. Sommerville, called to the bar in 1902, was originally a defence lawyer and had close ties with the federal and provincial Tories. Sedgwick was named junior counsel, and despite his hesitation in leading the case on his own, he was upset by the decision. In an interview decades after the

Figure 3.1 Communists charged under Section 98. Left to right: Matthew Popovich, Tom Ewen, A.T. Hill, John Boychuk, Michael Golinsky (charges were dropped), Sam Carr, Tomo Čačić, Tim Buck. Absent: Malcolm Bruce. From Tim Buck, *Yours in the Struggle: Reminiscences of Tim Buck* (Toronto: NC Press Limited, 1977).

trial, Sedgwick stated that he regarded his trial partner as a "second rate lawyer but a prominent Tory."[3]

The grandnephew of Prime Minister Sir John A. Macdonald, Hugh Macdonald was a graduate of Trinity College and held both an LLD and PhD. The accused were well represented with Macdonald, a lawyer with comparable experience to Sommerville. Onie Brown was a young lawyer who had just been called to the bar in 1929. Notably missing on the defence team was J.L. Cohen, who had defended many members of the CPC. An early defender of civil rights in Canada, Cohen abhorred what he viewed as state repression against communists during the Depression and the brutal tactics of the police in suppressing free speech and association. Cohen, however, was not representing the party in 1931, because of a falling out with the party leadership. Cohen opposed Section 98, which he believed pronounced "guilt by association often in a retroactive manner." Despite being offered a large retainer by the party, Cohen declined. CPC member Tom Ewen believed Cohen's new obligations were to his new client, the International Ladies' Garment Workers' Union, which often battled with the Communists during the 1920s. But according to historian Laurel Sefton MacDowell, Cohen's deteriorating relationship with the Communist leadership had more to do with his decision than his loyalty to other clients.

The party leadership wanted the trial to serve as a propaganda piece. Buck representing himself was part of this strategy. Cohen would have none of it; he was not interested in the "spectacular sort of defence" the CPC wanted and was not about to have his client tell him how to run a defence. MacDowell stated that when Cohen learned Buck was to defend himself, he "lost his temper and washed his hands of the whole thing," as well as turning away other cases from the CPC legal defence organization, the Canadian Labor Defense League.[4] Cohen referred the CPC case to Hugh Macdonald, who agreed to take it. Macdonald did his best to fight the case on legal grounds and not cater to the CPC's desires to turn the trial into a potential recruitment platform.

Justice William H. Wright was the presiding judge, known among his peers for his stern courtroom demeanour. Originally a teacher before turning to law, he spent much of his time engaged in social activities, such as being the deputy grand master of his Masonic lodge and president of the Ontario Curling Association. Wright, who was sixty-six at the time, practised out of Flesherton and Owen Sound, Ontario. In 1929, he presided over the sedition trial of another prominent CPC member, Arvo Vaara, the editor of the Finnish-language newspaper *Vapaus*, in Sudbury. Vaara was found guilty by jury after Wright displayed hostility towards communist ideology.[5]

The Buck et al. trial was extensively covered by prominent Ontario papers and to a lesser extent by newspapers in other provinces. Reporters from papers such as the *Toronto Star*, the *Globe*, the *Evening Telegram*, and the *Ottawa Citizen* sat in on the proceedings and documented testimony in their papers. The Communist paper the *Worker* closely watched the trial, with Oscar Ryan reporting, despite allegations that it and other labour papers were initially denied access to the courtroom.[6]

In October 1931, the Crown presented a copy of the indictment and depositions taken at the preliminary hearing to Chief Justice Rose. Rose requested the material in advance of the Crown's presentation to the grand jury, foreseeing problems with the indictment. The grand jury system at this time consisted of a set of jurors that would decide if a case should go to trial after being presented with the Crown's indictment and studying the evidence. If a trial was warranted, a true bill was declared and the case proceeded to trial. The grand jury system was replaced in Canada in the 1970s with a preliminary hearing overseen by a judge.

Norman Sommerville presented the indictment to Rose. The accused were charged with violating subsection 3 of Section 98 – being members of an unlawful organization – and for violating Section 133A of the Code – being part of a seditious conspiracy. When Section 98 was created, the draft that entered the Code contained an error. It stated, "Any person who acts or professes to act as an officer of any such unlawful association, *and* [emphasis mine] who shall sell, speak, write or publish anything . . ."[7] Rose argued that membership in an unlawful organization was not an offence because the first "and" in the section was conjunctive. It was only an offence to be an officer in the organization and do one of the aforementioned enumerated things. Norman Sommerville was forced to confer with the deputy attorney general of Ontario, Edward Bayly, and fellow Crown attorney of Toronto, Major Eric Norman Armour. They argued that while Rose was correct in a grammatical sense, it did not make a difference. The section would work, they argued, if the word "and" was read as a disjunctive "or." Rose was not convinced and claimed that if the Crown decided to go ahead with the indictment, he would be forced to instruct the grand jury that no crime had been committed. The Crown deferred submitting the indictment. Sommerville met with W. Stewart Edwards, the federal deputy minister of justice, who accepted Sommerville's interpretation of Section 98 and agreed to help prepare a history of Section 98 for Rose to persuade him to see things as they did.[8]

Edwards's briefing note outlined how Section 98 had been modelled on PC 2384, which used the word "or" instead of "and" throughout the relevant section. For instance, it defined a member of an unlawful association as any person who ". . . while Canada is engaged in war, shall act, or profess to act as an officer of any such unlawful organization *or* [emphasis mine] who shall sell, speak, write or publish anything as a representative or professed representative of any such unlawful organization or become or continue to be a member thereof . . ."[9] Edwards's focus was on what Parliament *intended* in drafting Section 98 rather than what was actually drafted. He claimed, "Our argument is that Parliament has clearly indicated that the least possible relationship constitutes an offence."[10] Edwards thus claimed that the grammatical error in subsection 3's construction had resulted in a "manifest absurdity or repugnance at variance with the intention of the Legislature." Parliament intended to outlaw all unlawful organizations and their activities and "the teaching or advocacy of the political doctrines of such an association." He concluded his argument with examples of cases where "and" was read as "or" and used the maxim *Salus populi est suprema lex* ("The welfare of the people shall be the supreme law of the land") to reinforce Parliament's intentions when drafting Section 98.[11] The welfare of the people was what the state decided was politically acceptable.

On 16 October, Rose heard the Crown's arguments and read the brief, but remained thoroughly unconvinced. He stated that the only way for the trial to proceed was for Parliament to alter Section 98 when the trial resumed and have the accused tried at the Spring Assizes; this was unacceptable to Sommerville. Rose claimed that even if he were wrong in his interpretation, the defence would surely raise the issue, thus leading to a protracted legal battle.[12] Joseph Sedgwick proposed a solution: the Crown could charge all the accused with being officers. Evidence could be submitted to prove the unlawfulness of the association, and following an alteration of the subsection in the next parliamentary session, "proceedings could be taken against those who [were] mere members of the association, as was always intended."[13] The goal was to ensnare the entire party and all its members with one trial, which was why the Crown did not charge the accused under subsection 8. Since there was no procedure for establishing that an organization was unlawful in advance of a prosecution, the Crown assumed that by charging the accused under subsection 3 it would have the opportunity to prove the CPC's unlawfulness in court. The indictment was revised and presented to the grand jury, and a true bill was handed down. The goal of Section 98 was to stamp out communism across the country, as the government intended the law to function exactly as PC 2384 had in 1918. Much like what Newton Rowell stated it had done with the SDP in 1918, the government wished to use Section 98 to outlaw a "political party" that "ha[d] been in existence for more than ten years without calling for any public action against it" because it opposed its "ideas." There should have been no way for the Crown to proceed with a trial given the phrasing of Section 98 – but it did.[14]

The accused were arraigned on 2 November 1931 at Toronto's Old City Hall and pleaded not guilty. Tim Buck stated he could not enter a plea because there was a motion to quash the indictment. The Crown's troubles with the indictment were not finished. Defence lawyer for the

accused, Hugh Macdonald, introduced a motion to quash the indictment, stating that the Section 98 charge of being a member of an
unlawful association was not a sufficient statement of an offence. He
argued that the real and substantive grounds of the offence lay with
the supposed unlawfulness of the CPC. Section 98 contained provisions stipulating how an association was unlawful, but there was no
indication of how the association on trial was unlawful. No such overt
act is mentioned in the indictment that would make the party fit this
designation.

Macdonald argued that the defence had no idea of what it needed to
meet because nowhere in the indictment was it detailed how the CPC
had been an unlawful organization over the past ten years. Macdonald
stated, "We are taken over a period of ten years without the faintest
indication of what is going to be brought up against us."[15] Macdonald
argued that there was no parallel to this case, as it "was the first case
that ha[d] arisen under this section."[16] There was no precedent, not
even, according to Macdonald, in the English courts. Macdonald's
argument was a simple one: how could individuals be guilty of being
officers of an unlawful association when the association itself had not
been proven unlawful?

Justice Wright argued that it should be sufficient if an offence had
been stated within the language of the Code. But Macdonald went
further and argued that even if the judge held that this count should
stand, Macdonald had a right to particulars; if the count remained as
it stood in the indictment, it would be the equivalent of indicting one
of the accused for a murder that had occurred sometime in the past
ten years. Macdonald argued that the same issue applied to the count
of seditious conspiracy; as he bluntly stated, "What was the conspiracy?"[17] Macdonald argued that this was a bigger issue than mere
language. When Sommerville offered particulars for the third count,
Wright correctly stated that it would not satisfy Macdonald, who was
arguing that the counts were "bad in law."[18] Macdonald agreed with
the judge's summary, though Wright was surprised by Macdonald's
stance, at one point commenting, "By alleging that the Communist
Party of Canada constitutes an unlawful association that is not sufficient?"[19] Macdonald maintained that the counts were indeed "bad in
law" but that counts one and two did not constitute an offence at all.
If the judge did not agree and allowed the counts to stand, then Macdonald stated he would have to see particulars. Producing them was
difficult for the Crown since the CPC had not engaged in any actual
acts that violated the Code. Macdonald then rephrased his position:
"If the association be lawful then membership in it is not a crime at

all. So that the cart is put before the horse, so to speak, in the count as it stands." How could members of an organization be tried with being part of an unlawful group without details of how this crime was committed?[20]

Macdonald cited the appeal case of Isaac Bainbridge, leader of the Social Democratic Party, who had been charged a decade earlier with seditious libel, as his reference point. The count, in addition to using the language of the Code, must set out the manner in which the crime was committed. Wright disagreed, arguing that in the case of murder, for instance, it was not necessary to state that the murder was committed by shooting or other means. Macdonald argued that the Code had not changed and that if there was nothing else stated in the counts beyond the offence, he would not know what he was expected to meet. He argued that the Crown should state exactly how the CPC had been unlawful for the past ten years. All Macdonald had in the way of particulars was a list of two hundred possible exhibits that the Crown may or may not use. He reiterated his point that the counts were far too broad for him to defend and should be quashed.

Sommerville argued that the first and second counts properly set out the offence because the Code itself defined an unlawful association. He cited Section 852 of the Code, arguing that the indictment "may be made in popular language without any technical averments . . . not essential to be proved."[21] He argued that because the nine were members of the CPC, the CPC was part of the CI, and the CI advocated sedition by intending to "incite ill will" between "his majesty's subjects," the accused were guilty of an offence. For the third count, the accused were charged with seditious conspiracy because of the CPC's ties to the CI. The Crown believed the connection would prove the party's unlawfulness. Wright agreed that the first two counts adequately outlined the details of the offence, and the Crown submitted particulars for them.[22] Macdonald was not satisfied with the Crown's particulars for the Section 98 counts, because they did not address his complaints. They merely stated that the CPC was an unlawful organization as per Section 98's subsection 1 but did not demonstrate how it was unlawful. He felt it impossible to defend his clients if he did not know what the CPC had done over the past ten years to warrant the charge against its members. The Crown was allowed to proceed without first having the CPC legally classified as unlawful.

Pleas of not guilty were entered by the accused. With the trial set to proceed, the Crown would have to prove that not only were the accused officers of the CPC but that the CPC itself was an unlawful association.[23] The nine were denied bail. Sommerville told the court that a pamphlet was being circulated, advocating for a demonstration to be held at Queen's Park to protest the trial. Macdonald knew nothing of it, but the judge agreed to deny bail and ordered the "guilty parties" to court so that they could be found in contempt. Sommerville claimed he knew where the circulars were being printed. Wright's justification for denying bail was that he did not trust that the accused would not participate in the demonstration; this was after all a "very extraordinary proceeding."[24] The Crown made good on its word and brought in Joseph Kleinstine and Bernard Meslin for contempt of court the following morning.[25] A rally, planned for the first night of the trial in Queen's Park, was broken up by Toronto police before it could get underway. Over two hundred people were quickly dispersed by the police.

Jury selection began on 3 November. The defence frequently challenged jurors. The press reported that Macdonald issued nearly ninety challenges in all. Most notably, Buck opposed the selection of Hugh Aird, son of Sir John Aird, the president of the Canadian Bank of Commerce. Twelve were finally selected from the ninety-nine called. The final twelve selected were trade workers or farmers.[26] Buck was denied permission to sit next to Hugh Macdonald; Wright claimed that it was a rule that prisoners charged with offences where the penalty was greater than five years could not leave the box. "I do not propose to depart from it," Wright stated.[27]

"A Small, Ruthless, Iron-Disciplined Group . . . with Bayonet and Rifle"

Sommerville delivered the opening address to the court. He tried to use emotions like fear and loyalty to make a connection with the jury and demonstrate that the CPC was linked to the CI and therefore should be an unlawful organization. He began by reading the jury Section 98 of the Code as well as Section 133A for the third count of seditious conspiracy. Sommerville emphasized the evil and treacherous nature of the CPC. He aimed to strike fear in the audience, stressing, "It is not argument, criticism, ideas, speeches, theories, that are here in issue, but . . . the deliberate, long continued, subtle, Moscow controlled plot to overturn, by force of arms, by violence, by bloodshed, our institutions of church and state." The CPC was not interested in the "peaceful capturing of Parliament"; this was a "small, ruthless, iron-disciplined group" that wanted to copy their Bolshevik heroes in Russia and "with bayonet and rifle" achieve the "bathing of the Country in a bath of blood."[28] He relied on war imagery to stir the deepest of emotions in his audience, such as loyalty, hatred, and fear. This was a war against Parliament by foreign fighters and subversives. Sommerville detailed how the party was constructed and how it operated. He described the tactics of the party in demonstrations that he believed were designed to "intensify the antagonisms between classes and to place the CPC as the leader" and to turn "artificial situations into civil strife and revolution." No evidence or examples of how the CPC was stirring up revolution were offered. There were no clear examples of revolutionary work that Sommerville could draw upon in his opening address. Street battles and marches could not directly link those on trial to the events. Instead he relied principally on the ideology of the CPC.[29] Sommerville claimed he would show that the CPC was a "world-wide party, of which Canada is an integral section" and that the CPC is "not a thing standing alone."[30] Sommerville's goal was to argue that the CPC's positions and theories *were* criminal acts, arguments made possible only because of Section 98. To secure a conviction under Section 98, Sommerville needed ideology to function as the *actus reus*.

Sommerville began his case by attempting to establish that the accused were officers of the party. The Crown argued that leaders in the party were officers. Its evidence was inconsistent and consisted of testimony from police officers who had arrested the accused on 11 August 1931. For instance, William Simpson, who arrested Matthew Popovich, claimed he knew Popovich and John Boychuk to be leaders in the CPC because he had witnessed them make several speeches at CPC gatherings, but during the preliminary hearings before the grand jury, he claimed he had never seen Popovich give a speech.[31] All attempts by Macdonald to challenge the admission of evidence were stymied. Two of the accused, Mike Golinsky and Tomo Čačić, were charged by police because they were suspected of being Communists. Golinsky was arrested when police found him at Tom Ewen's house, and he admitted he was a Communist when asked by officers. Tomo Čačić, who was hanging around the Workers' Unity League (WUL) office, was arrested on 12 August after officers questioned him about his membership in the party. Neither Golinsky nor Čačić were on the original arrest warrant.

Macdonald argued that Golinksy was in fact under arrest before admitting his membership in the CPC as he was not permitted to leave the presence of the arresting officers; this was confirmed by the arresting officer, George Fish. The officers' testimonies, Macdonald argued, such as those about Golinsky's statements about being a CPC member, should not be admitted. The testimonies were allowed, and

Wright prevented Macdonald from probing the issue further. When Wright asked Macdonald if he had more questions, he replied, "I would do so if I thought I was serving any good purpose by asking further questions."[32]

Court was adjourned until 10 a.m. the following day. The Crown began by presenting its star witness in the case, Sergeant John Leopold of the RCMP. As historians such as Gregory Kealey and Steve Hewitt have documented, John Leopold worked as an undercover agent for the RCMP and penetrated the CPC under the alias "Jack Esselwein." He eventually became head of the Regina branch of the party. He joined the party very early in its history, late in 1921. He was expelled by the party in May 1928. Leopold was an atypical Mountie for his time: he was an immigrant from Bohemia, now part of the Czech Republic, who had arrived in Canada in 1913. In 1914, 79 per cent of Mounties were British born. At five feet, four inches in height, Leopold was four inches shorter than the requirements for entry to the service; nor did his chest size meet the standard thirty-eight inches. In addition, he had arrived in Canada from a region considered an enemy during the First World War and was not naturalized until 1923. Still, his timing was good, joining the service in 1918, a time when it had become interested in trying to make inroads into the labour movement.

There was a strong belief in Canadian society that radical leftists and ethnicity were connected, a belief that manifested itself during the course of the CPC trial. With Leopold being able to speak six European languages, he was deemed a good fit for going undercover. Most officers of Anglo backgrounds had a difficult time trying to do secret intelligence work within the movement. This kind of intelligence gathering was frowned upon and considered in both military and police circles as being un-British because of the belief that Britishness involved a defence of civil liberties, which undercover work undermined.[33] With a foreigner engaging in such activities, there was apparently no ideological contradiction in Leopold gathering secret intelligence.

In his testimony, Leopold went over his time with the party and his duties in it. These included becoming the secretary of the Regina branch and attending party meetings and conventions. He had attended five conventions of the party since it was created in 1921. He identified nearly all the accused as having attended the same conventions, except for Golinsky and Čačić. Because of Leopold's involvement with the party, his testimony was crucial for the Crown. Leopold identified many of the accused as officers of the party. Leopold's testimony centred on the CPC's connection to the CI, a connection the Crown considered central to its case. Leopold was asked to identify the emblem of the CPC, which contained a hammer and sickle, prompting Sommerville to note that it was "a duplicate of the Moscow seal."[34] Leopold testified that some of the accused, including Buck, Hill, and Bruce, made trips to Moscow to attend congresses of the CI or for training during the years Leopold was a party member. He testified that the Young Communist League was created to indoctrinate youth into Communist ideology, that the *Worker* was an official party paper, and that Hill and Boychuk represented the Finnish and Ukrainian wings of the party. He identified Tom Ewen as head of the party's radical union organization, the WUL. His principal purpose in this early testimony was to assist the Crown in proving the details of the accused's membership in the party. Macdonald was not interested in cross-examining Leopold on the details of membership; he wanted to examine Leopold's evidence more generally at a later time.

A.E. Smith, who was head of the CPC-controlled the Canadian Labor Defense League (CLDL), was called to the stand and examined by Sedgwick as a Crown witness. He testified that Buck, Hill, Boychuk, Popovich, Ewen, Bruce, and Carr were all party leaders and part of the party's political committee. Smith claimed that he had only a general understanding that Čačić was a Communist and had seen no party membership credentials. Čačić was in possession of a CLDL pamphlet when arrested, and Smith testified that Čačić was an organizer for the CLDL, which was not on trial. Unlike many of the others on trial, Čačić was never a party leader in the CPC and had limited standing in the party. Like his coaccused Golinksy, he was not a part of the politbureau that formed the party leadership, nor did he head up any of the party's subsidiary wings or organizations.

The most damning evidence against Čačić had come from A.E. Smith. He was shown a copy of the *Canadian Labor Defender*, a periodical published by Smith's CLDL. In it there was an article on the trial with the headline "The Historical Trial of the Nine Communist Party Leaders." When asked if he thought this correct, Smith replied that he thought it was.[35] For propaganda that could benefit the party, Čačić's role as a party "leader" was sealed in court. When the Crown asked Smith about Golinsky's role in the party, he tried to retract his statement about the article being accurate. He claimed he did not know Golinsky as a member of the CPC or outside of the trial and claimed that the headline was not correct. Why Smith did not clear Čačić of being a party leader and defended Golinsky is uncertain. But since Čačić did have a previous falling-out with the party leadership over expenses for the party's low-level members,[36] it is possible that the relationship was never fully repaired.

Shifting its focus to the aims and tactics of the party to prove it was an unlawful organization, the Crown tried to introduce a booklet that it claimed was the CPC's constitution and that had been seized from Boychuk's home. Macdonald objected to its admission, arguing that a booklet found in Boychuk's residence did not qualify the Crown to claim it was the constitution of the party. He elaborated: "The booklet does not prove itself by its mere production." Macdonald tied his objection to his earlier problem with the trial proceeding: "In order to obtain a conviction under the first two counts it must be established as an independent proposition in the first instance, that the communist party is an unlawful organization, because until that is done, membership is no offence . . . the Crown cannot come in the back door."[37]

Macdonald was waiting for the Crown to produce evidence of the CPC's unlawfulness before proving his clients were members and officers of it. He believed that no offence had taken place if the accused were proven members of the CPC without the Crown first demonstrating the CPC's unlawfulness. Paradoxically, the Crown needed to first prove the accused were members of an unlawful organization to produce evidence of its unlawfulness. While Macdonald was opposed to this roundabout method of establishing guilt, there was nothing preventing the Crown from taking this route. It was in accordance with the law and Section 98. The lack of procedure in the section for establishing the unlawfulness of an organization meant that this unlawfulness could be established at trial, and the Crown's strategy was accepted by Wright.

Wright did agree with Macdonald that the constitution of an organization could not be proven in such a way. Sommerville protested, as there were no precedents to follow in proving a constitution in such a case, because no other cases had fallen under this section of the Code. He had a larger obstacle to overcome, as the issue would relate to all documents seized. Sommerville attempted to persuade Wright that he should have a case for admitting this material in regards to the seditious conspiracy count, but Wright was not allowing it. Sommerville argued that the documents seized at the organization's headquarters should be allowed into evidence. Macdonald's objection still applied; there must be evidence to prove that a document is what it stated it was.[38] But Wright disagreed. He argued that a document claiming to be a constitution of an organization, and found in the organization's headquarters, should be considered to be *prima facie* evidence.[39] The Crown submitted the evidence with the help of Sergeant Leopold.

Leopold took the stand again, and Sommerville asked him to describe the first contact he had with the party. He claimed it was a letter from Popovich, adding that he had a copy of it and could furnish it later. When asked by Sommerville about the whereabouts of the original, Leopold claimed he had destroyed it. Macdonald protested the Crown entering into evidence a copy of a letter that had been deliberately destroyed. Wright overruled him. Leopold's justification for the destruction of the letter was that in the early, underground days of the CPC, which operated as the Workers' Party of Canada, letters and documents were ordered destroyed after being read, but he had made a copy of the letter. This did not satisfy Macdonald, but he had no choice.

When asked by Sommerville what the aims of the party were when it was established, Leopold couched his answer in the language of Section 98. He claimed the CPC sought to "organize the working class of Canada for the overthrow of the existing conditions in this country" and that "by existing conditions, [he meant] the economic institutions, the state and the social order in general." When Sommerville asked how, Leopold answered, "By the application of violence and force."[40] The Crown relied on Leopold to provide another important piece of testimony concerning party finances. He claimed that some financial expenses were defrayed by the CI and that at least $3,000 had been spent in Canada to get the party started. He claimed all of the $3,000 came from the CI but that no funding had continued after 1922 since the party was supposed to be self-sufficient.[41] Sommerville was surely pleased with Leopold. He was able to further bolster the Crown's position that the CI had a direct and strong influence on the CPC, if it provided so much in the early days in the way of finances.

Leopold gave a detailed history of the transformation of the party over the years, tracing its early days as an underground party known to members as the "Z" party, the founding in 1921 of an "above ground" party (the Workers' Party), the liquidation of the "Z" party, and the formation of an "above ground only party." (The Workers' Party was renamed the CPC in 1924.) Sommerville attempted to demonstrate that the party had always followed Moscow's direction on issues such as liquidating its underground party and coming out into the open as the CPC.

Sommerville's goal was to demonstrate that the CPC knowingly viewed itself as illegal in its early days because of its support for revolution under Moscow's guidance. Sommerville began entering seized documents into evidence. Macdonald again challenged the admission of seized documents and letters on the same grounds as earlier. This time, though, Wright promptly overruled Macdonald on the grounds that anything seized at party headquarters was *prima facie* evidence of what the Crown claimed they showed. But Macdonald again illustrated the validity of his objection. Sommerville entered into evidence a document found in party headquarters from the CI that outlined the statutes of the CI, but it was dated 1920 – before the CPC had even existed. The document was taken from the library of the organization. Macdonald objected. Wright again overruled Macdonald's objection, citing that the document was *prima facie* evidence and that the CI statutes resembled resolutions similar to the party's own and would be allowed.[42]

Leopold retook the stand, and Sommerville began reading him sections from one of the earliest publications of the CPC in Canada, the *Communist*. He sought to fill his audience with fear that Communists would use violence to destroy the country. Sommerville read: "As . . . strikes grow in number and intensity, they acquire political character . . . this culminates in armed insurrection and civil war aimed directly at the destruction of the Capitalist State . . . the task of the proletariat consists of destroying the entire machinery of the bourgeois state, including all the parliamentary institutions."[43] He continued reading for some time, highlighting more ideological jargon, such as the phrase "Long live the Proletarian Revolution!" But even these passages were demonstrations of ideology, not action. Sommerville sought to equate these ideas with actions. After reading lengthier excerpts, he asked Leopold a simple question: "Was this the party you joined in the year 1921?" Leopold answered, "It is."[44]

Sommerville read from party material, including a document reporting on the Second Congress of the CI, which detailed the conditions for a party, such as the CPC, to join the CI.[45] Sommerville read all twenty-one clauses to the court. His goal with the material from the CI was to demonstrate that because of the CPC's ties to Moscow, which supported a worker-led revolution, the accused were part of a seditious conspiracy. Sommerville, at one point, read for hours, and Sedgwick took over to give him a break from reading.[46] He concluded the day with more excerpts from the CI, including speeches and addresses by the Communist theoretician Bukharin. The court was getting ready for adjournment, but before leaving, Macdonald expressed his difficulties with the trial thus far. He had a list only of exhibits for the trial and had received it only three days prior. He was told by the Crown that he would have copies of the material but had received none. He brought up the issue of bail for the accused and did manage to convince the court to grant bail. He entered into another exchange with Wright on the matter of the Crown bringing up communist theory in court; their exchange is worth citing at length:

MACDONALD: . . . all the teachings and doctrines of communism, that is
    something entirely out of the ordinary range of –
WRIGHT: I don't think it goes that wide.
MACDONALD: . . . as I understand it, that is where it will eventually
    come down.
WRIGHT: No, it is the object of this particular organization, not the
    general doctrines of communism.
MACDONALD: The general doctrines explains the objects.
WRIGHT: I don't think it is that wide at all. The Crown has to bring
    it within definition of the Criminal Code. The whole question
    is, was it unlawful, or does it fall within the prohibitive objects
    mentioned in the Code – what its affirmatives are matters not . . .
    you have to meet that.
MACDONALD: What is the Communist answer to the meaning the
    Crown puts on the expressions contained?
WRIGHT: That is quite right.
MACDONALD: That is, I assure your Lordship a very difficult question
    to meet.
WRIGHT: I am sure it is.[47]

The Crown needed only to prove that the CPC material fell within the range of Section 98, a simple task given that the propaganda of the CI and CPC repeatedly mentioned the inevitable proletarian revolt. Wright ruled that the documentary evidence and communist theory were two separate things, which Macdonald knew was not true. After all, the *Communist Manifesto* was a Crown exhibit. Broadly speaking, the general doctrines of communism did explain the objects, that is, the evidence. The ideology or theory of communism could not be carved away from the CPC; it was its sole reason for being, and thus it was on trial along with the CPC. Macdonald's only option was to argue that Marxist ideology did not seek an immediate revolution but rather sought to predict it. He needed to prove that communism was an ideology, or a theory, and not a call to arms.

Leopold was cross-examined by Macdonald on 5 November. Macdonald's strategy was to paint Leopold as more than just a police officer working undercover. He attempted to show that Leopold was at the very least a fellow traveller of communist ideology and that therefore his testimony was unreliable. Macdonald began his cross-examination by asking Leopold about the various organizations he was connected to besides the CPC, which included the Trades and Labour Council of the Saskatchewan Fair Board, of which he was a member in Regina in 1924–5. Leopold stated that he was a member of the One Big Union (OBU) in the Regina and Winnipeg district before he joined the CPC in Regina. Leopold revealed that he knew Malcolm Bruce before he was a CPC member and had asked Bruce if he wanted an invite to join the meeting Leopold was scheduled to attend.[48] Macdonald reminded Leopold of his days in the OBU before joining the CPC, in which Leopold had operated independently and was not in touch with his superiors about the CPC. Macdonald recalled his attendance and participation in the CPC-led demonstration that occurred at the American consulate in 1928 over the execution of two anarchists, Ferdinando Sacco and Bertolomeo Vanzetti, in the United States. Leopold went so far as to carry a protest banner in the march.[49] Many had believed the two men were innocent and had opposed their execution.[50]

Leopold admitted there was little difference between the underground "Z" Communist party and the open Workers' Party that existed in the early 1920s. Macdonald next pressed Leopold as to his understanding of Marxism and communist theories.[51] Wright interjected, reminding Macdonald that only certain phrases of communist theory were under trial; how the court could prosecute only certain phrases of communist theory was never made clear. When asked specifically about armed rebellion and Marxism, Leopold responded, "It is the recognition of the fact that it cannot be done otherwise."[52] Macdonald pressed him to further emphasize the communist belief in the inevitability of revolution.[53] Leopold argued that Marxism was a belief system and not an ideology that sought immediate economic or political change. Marxism was history, or put another way, a method of studying history. The CPC could make revolutionary statements because the inevitability of revolution was a belief about the way history would unfold; the accused had not actually engaged in any violence. Macdonald would return to this main line of defence when he presented his case.

In re-examining Leopold, Sommerville paid particular attention to his role in the demonstration at the American consulate for Sacco and Vanzetti. He had trouble getting responses out of Leopold, who refused to answer questions about the demonstration's purpose, until Wright led him to an answer: "Is it propaganda?" Wright asked. "It is propaganda, naturally, yes," Leopold replied. It is unclear why Leopold had difficulty answering these questions. It is possible he felt unable to provide a satisfactory answer to explain his role in the demonstration, or maybe he was more heavily invested in the movement than he wanted to admit. Leopold left the stand after having to restate that he had been hired as a regular police officer for the RCMP but was undercover. After he left, Sommerville reminded Wright that Leopold did in fact join the RNWMP in 1918. Wright agreed, but given the unusual nature of his activities, Wright wanted to make sure Leopold "could be classed as a police officer."[54] Such undercover work at this time was a rarity, and Wright felt uneasy about Leopold's double life.

The remainder of the Crown's case focused on the CPC's ties to the CI. Sommerville demonstrated how the CPC purged moderate members and toed the Moscow line in its daily activities. Its hostility towards social democrats and more moderate labour groups and its attempts to discipline its language organizations were raised as examples of the CPC's close affiliation with the CI.[55] Sommerville portrayed the CPC as a group full of aliens, one that endeavoured to replace the bourgeois and British culture with one that was foreign and communist. Troves of documents that provided examples of revolutionary language and Marx's theories of scientific materialism were read in court.

One of the last pieces of evidence for the Crown was a publication known as the Vasiliev pamphlet. Sommerville's strategy resembled that of UK authorities against the Communist Party of Great Britain when the fabricated Zinoviev letter of 1924 was used by the authorities to prove that Moscow was inciting revolution in the UK.[56] The Vasiliev pamphlet was the Crown's crucial link between the CI and the CPC; it was meant to demonstrate how the CI had directed the CPC to engage in violence. The pamphlet consisted of a series of recommendations written by B. Vasiliev of the CI that detailed how Communist organizations could assist members in revolutionary actions. Vasiliev lamented the poor fighting skills of demonstrators, noting that even when some members threw stones at police, it only demonstrated that "[their] comrades [didn't] know how to throw stones." Stating that "it is not enough to pick up a stone and throw it, but it is important that that stone should hit its target,"[57] Vasiliev recommended a regimen of stone-throwing practice for members.

Sommerville wanted to link the pamphlet to the CPC through the testimonies of police officers who had attended a demonstration in Toronto on 1 May 1931. Officer William Nursey of the Toronto police testified that the assembly that took place was unlawful because stones were thrown during the demonstration. Macdonald objected, stating that Nursey had no evidence of any Communists throwing stones, of the accused being at the demonstration, or of how the unidentified stone-thrower(s) were connected to the accused. Wright allowed the testimony.[58]

Sommerville concluded the case for the Crown by reading more excerpts on communist theory, this time from Bukharin's *ABC of Communism*.[59] In sum, the Crown sought to demonstrate how the ideology of the CPC made it an unlawful association, which was essential to secure a conviction under Section 98. The Crown's evidence rested on party documents and the testimony of Sergeant Leopold. According to the Crown, it was the CPC's support for a proletarian revolution, coupled with its close relationship to Moscow, that made the CPC unlawful and hence its members guilty of belonging to an unlawful association. The Crown wanted to connect with the emotions of the jury and tried to do so by stoking fear and patriotism in them. These were foreign agitators that threatened the British institutions of Canada. The CPC had committed no violent act, and the Crown never had to prove that it did to obtain a conviction. The Crown merely had to prove that the CPC's teachings, that is, the expression of its ideology, advocated violence. Not only was the *Communist Manifesto* evidence of the CPC's unlawfulness, but if the party became unlawful, no one could legally purchase it or other literature that contained communist teachings. As well, it would be a criminal act to attend party meetings. One could not be political if it involved communism.[60] None of this would have been possible without the normalizing of emergency laws, that is, without Section 98.

Newspapers across the country covered the trial while the emotions of the nation ran high. Sommerville wanted to use fear to question the loyalty of the accused, and the media followed his lead. Most newspapers began regular daily coverage after Leopold took the stand, while a number of Ontario papers had covered the trial from its beginning.[61] Some Toronto papers, such as the *Globe*, covered the trial in the city news section; after Leopold's testimony, the trial made front-page coverage. The idea of an RCMP spy posing as a Communist and giving secret intelligence as evidence excited the imagination of journalists and readers alike. The story had the elements of a suspenseful international thriller: a secret agent going undercover to expose an international ring of agents who wanted to overthrow the government. Newspapers across the country contained headlines such as "Policeman Acted as Red Leader," "Mountie 9 Years as Red," and "R.C.M.P. Detective Who Operated as Communist Seemed Reddest of Reds." In Winnipeg, "Communists Planned Revolt Says Counsel" was a headline story, along with Leopold's testimony. The *Gazette* played up the drama of Leopold's testimony, declaring "Reds Planned Armed Revolt." Ontario papers sensationalized the events unfolding in Toronto's Old City Hall. In the *Globe*'s three-page coverage of the trial, and under the subheading "Definitely under Moscow," the paper summarized Leopold's testimony with some embellishment. All CPC members, it claimed, had to swear an oath to Moscow to join the party. The *Globe* highlighted how the party used secret codes to communicate to members through periodicals. The paper outlined how the party adhered to the "twenty-one points" of the CI, but it paid much more attention to how members, in the early days of the party, used secret names to identify each other.

The *Star* was not much different. It outlined some segments of the trial testimony with sensational headlines claiming that a "Red Army was planned" and that the CPC "[would] take over the Machinery" of the country. The *Star* did point out that admissibility of some of the evidence came into contention during the proceedings.[62] The newspaper headlines were somewhat understandable. Stories of undercover intelligence work were uncommon, as it was a fairly new practice in policing.[63] The RCMP itself was scarcely over ten years old at this point, and tales of secret evidence and international plots made for interesting reading. The media drew on fear to connect the events in the courtroom to its readers. Fear of revolution by foreign fighters and the disloyalty of the accused splashed across the national news pulled Canadians together and focused their gaze on that Toronto courtroom.

"You Have to Play the Part"

In reporting on the events of the trial, many newspapers focused on segments that inflamed conservative British-Canadian readers. Some papers focused on testimony that discussed the CI's goal of attracting more French-Canadian workers, relying on their anti-British views to attract them to the party. The CPC's goal was, according to the *Globe*, to "foster race hostility." The *Star* reported that a "Civil War [was] urged" and that the Communists sought a "final overthrow" of capitalism. The *Gazette* reminded its readers how "Canadian Reds Look to Russia as Fatherland," and in editorials during the trial the editors supported Premier Taschereau's tough stance against communism, stating that "the Province of Quebec with its traditions of industry, of respect for constitutional government, of family devotion and religious observance, is no place in which the poison of communism should be permitted to work its social and economic mischief." The *Calgary Daily Herald* supported Leopold's undercover work and defended him. There would always be people who would scoff at this type of policing, but it was the only way to uncover subversive groups. One had to "fight the devil with fire to beat him at his own game." Similar sentiments in support of the Crown's position were expressed in papers in other provinces, such as BC and Manitoba.[64]

The *Calgary Daily Herald*'s editorial provides a window into the reservations the public had about Leopold, his evidence, and whether going undercover was an acceptable means of collecting evidence. The *Star* had attempted to come to Leopold's defence. At the end of the first week of the trial, it set out to conduct a feature interview with him, as he had become somewhat of an unlikely celebrity due to the trial. The *Star* did its best to sensationalize the interview. "Was your life ever attempted?" Leopold was asked. "I don't think so," he replied. "Not as far as I'm concerned." Leopold was not giving the interviewer, Frederick Griffin, much to work with, so Griffin pressed for more: "You did get threats, though?" "Yes," Leopold answered, "in Toronto after I was expelled from the party . . . but I ignored them."

The *Star* attempted to restore Leopold's damaged masculinity and assured the public his undercover work had not left a lasting impression. Leopold's early life as a rugged homesteader was highlighted, as was the little-known story of a time when he bunked overnight with a Moscow agent and felt scared during the night – a significant point because Leopold "was not apparently easily scared." The headline of the story made this clear. It declared that Leopold was one to "live by his wits" and a man who "ignored threats." There were suggestions circulating in the public that Leopold never wore a uniform before he testified at the CPC trial, the implication being that he was less masculine, less of a Mountie than other regular officers. The *Star* sought to rectify this, reporting that for the past three years, Leopold had been away in the North and "carrying on the traditional way of the Mounted." That should ease the public's emotions and silence accusations that he never wore the Mountie uniform except when he came to court.[65]

If there was still any doubt as to Leopold's manliness as a Mountie, the *Star* noted that Leopold had "shot every kind of big game in the

Rockies and the north." The interview even discovered that during Leopold's early days of "appearing as a harmless little radical," he used to sneak away from Regina and spend a few days "banging at the birds" much the same as a "sporting capitalist" would have done. After he had posed as a radical leftist, Leopold's role as a real Mountie was under suspicion, as was his support of capitalism. His taking a break from his undercover work, and mimicking a sporting and masculine capitalist by killing a few animals from time to time, helped the public digest Leopold's role as an undercover Mountie. Leopold did betray some of his sympathies for the activists around whom he had spent so much time. When asked, "How did you find the Communists as men?" he replied, "Just human beings . . . they don't differ from the rest of us."[66]

Star reporter Frederick Griffin continued his interview with Leopold into Saturday's edition, where it made the front page. The headline "Mountie Was Afraid He'd Talk in His Sleep to Soviet Agent" was sure to continue to draw in readers eager to read of a real-life spy drama. Leopold claimed that he could not be passive in his undercover role because he had to gain the confidence of members. He claimed he was so successful that he had garnered the trust of a Moscow organizer who was visiting Canada: "a real Russian," as the *Star* put it. Leopold outlined how he had to share a bed with this agent while the agent was touring Canada. He recounted how he feared saying too much in his sleep. He discussed how he and the Moscow representative had gotten along well. "You became bosom pals?" he was asked. "Absolutely," replied Leopold. He ate, slept, and travelled with the man to meetings. Griffin had to put Leopold's close friendship with the man back into perspective and stress that this was acting. Griffin asked, "How did you manage to make yourself show a sufficient hatred of capitalism?" "You have to play the part," Leopold explained.

The paper recounted his early days in the formation of the party until his eventual departure in 1928, when the CPC leadership discovered his double role and notified Leopold of his expulsion. "The notice was not given to you violently?" Griffin asked with surprise. "No, by mail. Very businesslike," Leopold stated. "Did you feel in danger then?" he was asked. "No, I felt quite safe," Leopold flatly stated. For a spy thriller, Leopold's story did not seem to have enough danger to it. "Did you carry a gun during your years as Comrade Esselwein?" Griffin asked. Leopold balked at the suggestion: "Oh, no, no, no, I was never armed," he replied. Griffin was clearly trying to search for just where exactly the danger in Leopold's story was, but he was coming up empty. The Communists were violent leftists, were they not? But Leopold's tales hardly portrayed a sense of danger, despite Griffin's attempts to find it.

When given another opportunity to elaborate on his role at the CPC demonstration in front of the American consulate, Leopold claimed he had been roped into it because he happened to stop by the party headquarters in Toronto just in time for the CPC march. He claimed that he had been carrying a banner for the CPC during the protest because he had taken it from the woman next to whom he had been walking after it got too heavy for her. So, as the *Star* put it, "chivalry" was Leopold's "undoing." Curiously, Leopold did not discuss his early days in the labour movement and refused to comment further about his experiences. Despite his role as a Mountie and Griffin's clear attempt to portray him as such, complete with his masculine bravado in the face of danger, Leopold still could not completely convince his interviewer of his intentions. His ethnicity and undercover role as a Communist continued to work against him. Griffin noted how this "Bohemian-born Mountie," with his "suave poker face," was intelligent. He was surprised that Leopold's motivation in the operation, in his opinion, was not the well-being of the public. He thought that Leopold did not resemble a typical police officer. Instead of ending his interview with praise for Leopold, the article ended with trepidation, telling readers that Leopold was a cold, calculating individual.[67] If Leopold could not portray the communist movement in a more menacing light, Griffin's piece implied, maybe the taint of leftist ideology remained.

Curiously lacking in its coverage of the trial was the CPC's own paper, the *Worker*. The paper had a biweekly run, but despite the huge significance of the trial for the party, no special issue or edition was drafted to provide more coverage of it. The paper ran only two editions that focused on the trial, one when it began and one when it was over. The paper had set up a "workers' jury" that weighed the evidence throughout the trial and predictably decided the accused were not guilty. The author of the article failed to note that the actual jury consisted of farmers and workers.

The press coverage of the trial reinforced the Crown's fear-laden argument that the CPC was a foreign body, subservient to Moscow, and seeking to engage in a Canadian revolution. Papers sought to deflect criticism from Sergeant Leopold and protect his status as an RCMP officer. There was scant attention paid to the actual actions of the party; the ideas of the CPC were treated as evidence enough of the guilt of the accused. Section 98 was the law, and no questioning of it appeared in the press. Even within the *Worker*, the repeal of Section 98 was never the focus. The paper simply advocated for an acquittal, and only well after the accused were convicted did the paper begin calling for Section 98's repeal.[68] Indeed, the "workers' jury" that the Communists had set up as a propaganda mechanism still tried the accused under Section 98 in their mock trial. In other words, both within the CPC's own paper and the mainstream Canadian press, the trial was portrayed as an important one, but never an illegitimate one. The *Worker* protested the authorities' prosecuting the CPC members for their ideology but did not dispute the power of the authorities to do so, at least before the members lost the trial. The trial, while highly significant in the eyes of the public, was not regarded as exceptional. Section 98 and the trial being considered normal marked a significant advancement in the acceptance of exceptional laws for dealing with communists.

"A Method of Conceiving History"

The case for the defence began on 6 November 1931, the same day the Crown's case concluded. Macdonald's task was difficult; he would have to demonstrate that communist ideology did not make the CPC an unlawful organization under Section 98. This was no easy task, given that Communists believed in a worker-led revolution. But Macdonald did have some room to manoeuvre. He knew that the party's ideas were being tried and that ideas are flexible and elastic. His strategy was to call the accused to the stand and challenge the Crown's interpretation of the documents. The defence would admit that Communists supported revolution but maintain that this was not illegal. For Communists, revolution was inevitable. Marxism, he argued, was simply a different way of interpreting history. For the defence, it was history that was on trial.

Macdonald stated that the defence would go through the Crown's evidence and "explain it and indicate that it [did] not mean what it appear[ed] to mean."[69] Wright was skeptical: "How can any witness come and say that it [a document] does not mean this or that? That is for the jury."[70] Macdonald argued that the situation before the court was "what is, in effect, a philosophic system which puts into practice the doctrines of Marx and Engels and Lenin." Wright would not allow it and claimed that the trial was not a trial based on theory, just on the evidence before the court. He did not want to get into communist theory, but it was impossible not to since every major communist publication was a court exhibit, from Lenin and Bukharin to Karl

Marx. Macdonald maintained that he needed to explain expressions and terminology. Wright agreed that if a term was unclear, it was fine for him to do so.[71] Macdonald would have to rely on Wright and the Crown having limited knowledge of communist ideology to convince the court that *all* the phrases he sought to challenge were ambiguous. Court resumed at noon on 6 November, with Tim Buck taking the stand.

Buck explained the formation of the CPC and its activities in the trade unions. Macdonald asked Buck whether violence was ever the result of CPC activities; he stated that it never was. Macdonald moved to the subject of Leopold's role in the CPC. Buck testified that he knew Leopold as an active member of the party and not just a passive one.[72] Macdonald next read the CPC constitution. Reading the phrase "revolutionary Marxism," he asked Buck to explain it. Wright interjected, stating that he ruled that the interpretation of the constitution was for the jury alone to decide. But when Macdonald argued, "Revolutionary Marxism, the expression in itself is absolutely meaningless as it stands there, to any Jury," Wright reluctantly agreed and permitted him to continue.[73] Wright questioned Buck directly: "What is the meaning of revolutionary Marxism?" With enthusiasm, Buck explained its meaning.

Buck gave a detailed history of Marxism, describing it as a philosophy, and lost much of his audience in the process.[74] He tried to simplify things: "Dialectical materialism, the law of value and surplus value and class struggle," he explained, "are the basis for Marx's philosophy." He explained that Marxist philosophy provided for an analysis of capitalism and was a means of interpreting history. He explained that when CPC members used the term "revolutionary Marxism," they were referring to a method of analysing the development of history, of the state, and of political economy.[75] When Wright asked if it was only a method of analysis, Buck replied that Marxist philosophy carried its "own conclusions" that were "revolutionary," and continued, saying it was a "method of conceiving of history." The testimony was fast becoming a discussion of history, economy, and society. Wright probed further: "Would not a short definition be, that this is an absolute change in the method of analyzing history?" Buck agreed, and Wright continued, "History, economy, and social change?" Buck added, "Just for clarity, almost absolute, with the difference: that the system that was here first, was built according to the system being our philosophy." Wright asked, "In other words evolutionary as well as revolutionary?" Buck agreed. Marxism was both.

Wright continued his discussion with Buck, getting to the heart of the issue: "What kind of a revolution is this revolutionary Marxism? Is it violent or peaceful?" Buck had a difficult time providing a simple "yes" or "no" answer. He was being asked to categorize how a future proletarian revolution would come about. His testimony in response to the question would be theoretical, but it would still be evidence. Buck tried to provide a detailed explanation of the purpose of revolutionary Marxism, but Wright wanted a "yes" or "no" answer. Buck stated that the method of revolution had never been prescribed by Marx. Revolution could be violent or peaceful; it depended, Buck said, "on the other party," the state.[76] When asked about the CI being the highest in command for the CPC, Buck did not deny it; in fact, he agreed.[77]

Macdonald questioned Buck about the Vasiliev pamphlet. Buck claimed he had never read it and that it must have come in the mail, along with numerous other pamphlets that arrived regularly from the United States.[78] Buck explained how the pamphlet had no binding authority over the CPC and was not an official document of the CI. But what did force or violence mean to the CPC? How did its interpretation connect to the historic inevitability of a Marxist revolution?[79] Macdonald debated this with Wright and its relevance to Section 98. The teachings of Marxism argued that historic inevitability meant that history would progress to a point when class warfare and conflict were inevitable. Marxism did not indirectly teach force or violence, as Wright claimed it did. It was theoretical. What words meant in the broader context of how the CPC understood history was, in Macdonald's opinion, highly relevant.[80] What the CPC taught was identical to their beliefs and intentions, and the court maintained these were not on trial, but they were.

Macdonald and Wright continued to discuss just what type of force and violence the CPC was aiming for, if any at all. They discussed the wording of Section 98, especially the use of force or violence to produce a governmental or economic change.[81] The court was concerned with the direct result of the CPC's teachings; Macdonald argued that if violence did take place in some future revolution, it would be incidental and not a direct result of the CPC's teachings.[82] Sommerville maintained that the purpose of the CPC was to destroy capitalism and all its institutions. But Macdonald countered that Marx was prophetic. The CPC in following Marxist theory was preparing for the moment when revolution would arrive. This revolution was similar to the Second Coming in Christian religious teachings. The debate continued with the Crown, defence, and judge trying to ascertain when the revolution would arrive and who would be responsible for it if and when it came. The interplay of this battle for interpretation in the courtroom reveals how they were both correct. From the standpoint of the law, such expressions did advocate force or violence to produce economic or governmental change. The expressions fit Section 98, but at the same time these were expressions of theories. This fascinating exchange reveals how this courtroom became an exceptional space; theory and law clashed in the courtroom as Marxism was held up to scrutiny by the Crown and defence to come to a conclusion about whether the expression of these ideas, and indirectly the ideas themselves, were legal or illegal in Canada.

All of these issues could have arisen only because of the ability of sovereign power to normalize exceptional laws, such as by creating Section 98, which enabled ideas to be considered criminal acts. More difficulties continued to arise for the defence. Wright ruled that Buck could speak to his own opinion only and not to the party's, but Macdonald disagreed, arguing that as party secretary Buck could speak for the CPC.[83] Macdonald pointed out that Section 98 could "cut both ways." If Buck was breaking the law for being an officer of an unlawful organization, who should speak *for* the organization if someone was found guilty of being a member of it, if not the members, or indeed the *leader*, of the organization? How could the organization speak for the membership and not the members for the organization? Wright was firm in his ruling; the party secretary could not speak for the party. Sommerville's cross-examination of Buck failed to yield much. Any attempts by Sommerville to challenge Buck on the violent nature of revolution were stymied. Buck held firm to the principle that revolution was an inevitable historic event.[84]

Tom Ewen testified next. Leader of the CPC's militant WUL, Ewen was fiercely ideological. After denying the CPC engaged in violence, Ewen denied that the Vasiliev pamphlet was binding on the CPC or that the CPC sought to engage in violence. On the question of CI influence on the CPC, Ewen denied that the CPC received orders from Moscow, insisting that it received only guidance. Ewen was unwilling to admit that the CI exerted control over the party.[85] Much to the chagrin of the defence, Ewen was eager to spar with Sommerville during his cross-examination, which continued for hours. Sensing Ewen's eagerness to extol communist ideology, Sommerville barraged Ewen with a slew of questions relating to Moscow's guidance of the CPC. He wanted to use Ewen's support for the Soviet Union to further fan emotions of patriotism and loyalty in the jury by painting him and the other accused as traitors.

He cited examples such as the CPC's dispute with the Finnish members of the party over the perceived opposition of the Finnish labour paper *Vapaus* to the new Moscow line in 1931. Sommerville accused Ewen of trying to strong-arm party members in the language groups. Finding it difficult to defend himself against Sommerville's attack, Ewen used more party propaganda in his answers. For example, on the issue of moderate unions, Ewen stated that they sought class peace, but when Sommerville replied by asking whether he believed in class peace, Ewen said no. Similarly, when Sommerville asked, "And you develop as much as resistance as possible on the part of the workers?" Ewen replied, "The maximum amount of resistance to starvation."[86] (Ewen claimed he supported a workers' defence corps.) Ewen replied in the affirmative to Wright's question: "Do you deny the right of the police to interfere with your demonstrations?"[87] For Ewen, the right of the CPC to express its politics in public superseded the authority of any law.

During the court's afternoon session, Sommerville continued questioning Ewen about the language organizations' independence from both the CPC and the CI. Sommerville argued that from time to time the CPC complained about some of the activities of the organizations to the CI. He asked about a complaint the CPC had made because Ukrainian members were singing "O Canada." Ewen claimed he did not remember the complaint, but that it was possible. But Sommerville pressed on, claiming that the CPC leadership had been offended by the Ukrainians' actions. Ewen claimed he had no recollection of this, but he could not answer why the complaints ever went to Moscow to begin with.[88] Sommerville next sought to target Ewen's loyalty. He asked if the Soviet Union was considered the "Fatherland" and if every member of the party was loyal to it. Ewen replied that loyalty to the Soviet Union was important to the party. Sommerville questioned where party members' loyalties would lie in a hypothetical war between Canada and Russia, and Ewen responded: "We advocate defence of the Soviet Union . . . No matter who the aggressor against the Soviet Union is."[89] Ewen's defence of the Soviet Union made it more difficult for Macdonald to argue that the party was not a band of foreign subversives.

A.T. Hill and Malcolm Bruce testified for the defence. Hill, a member of the Finnish Organization of Canada, and Bruce, once editor of the party's newspaper the *Worker*, both denied that the CPC engaged in violent activities or supported revolution. Bruce reinforced the defence's case, arguing that communism was an ideology and that revolution lay "in the lap of history."[90] Sommerville made little headway in his cross-examination.

After a brief questioning of Golinsky, in which he testified that he had no significant role in the party, and a brief cross-examination, the Crown withdrew the charges against him.[91] Čačić did not take the stand, and despite the Crown's flimsy evidence of his status as an officer, his charges were not withdrawn. The case for the defence was now finished.

Wright wanted to end the trial as quickly as possible and asked Buck if he wished to address the jury. Buck had no time to prepare but agreed to speak. In an impromptu speech, Buck spoke to the jury for three hours. "Communism is on trial here today," he told the jury. "If we are convicted, Canada will be the only English-speaking nation in the world in which the Communist party is illegal. The only country in the world with a democratic parliament which outlaws Communism is Japan." After numerous interjections by Wright, Buck claimed: "World revolution does not mean merely the releasing of a horde of men with beards, but a release of all the forces which join together to destroy the system of imperialist capitalism." Buck's performance of this address, later called by the CLDL his "indictment of capitalism," drew the party faithful to him. In their eyes, he was now a capable leader.[92]

Court resumed on the morning of 12 November, with both Macdonald and Sommerville addressing the jury. Macdonald went first and highlighted the extraordinary nature of the trial. "These charges are of a new and unprecedented nature, not only in this court but in any British court," Macdonald told the jury. He continued: "In any ordinary trial the accused would be charged with some certain act. There can be no crime, broadly speaking, without criminal intent . . . If men advocate a system of economics – socialism – . . . that is not a crime. That is the essence of our existence – change . . . This is simply an international body of men with similar views as of how they can best improve the lot of mankind."[93]

Section 98 was no ordinary law, and quite rightly Macdonald recognized this was no ordinary trial. What was at issue in the trial was not that imperialist capitalists were out to crush communism in Canada. It was the manner in which law was being used to influence an individual's politics through the Criminal Code. While the party and the CI wanted to use the trial for propaganda, Macdonald demonstrated throughout the trial how law was being used for political purposes. It was being used by authorities to contribute to a construct of security. Canadians would be safer with an outlawed CPC. Macdonald was faced with an insurmountable task in defending the accused; he knew he would lose, but he could at least expose the trial and

Section 98 as inconsistent with what he believed the law was supposed to be about – justice.

Sommerville addressed the jury next. Once again he conjured up his war narrative to stir emotions in the jury. The jury's duty, he argued, was "to save the state from the insidious teaching of Bolshevism."[94] Sommerville began his address by telling the jury that the literature coming from Russia was not simply academic theories and that for Buck and his comrades these documents meant real revolution. He reminded them of the secret formation of the CPC, playing up the foreign origins of the party: "Can you picture this foreigner from Latvia carrying out the orders of Moscow and meeting Buck, Popovich et al and thus organizing the CPC? Russian leadership, Russian chairman, Russian program, Russian money, and an entirely Russian conception."[95] According to this logic, the accused had aligned themselves with these foreigners and renounced their ties to Canada. There was, Sommerville stated, "but one CI, one Communist Party throughout the world," and all were members of it. Moscow called the shots. The party existed not to introduce reforms, Sommerville cautioned, but rather to exploit everyday needs as a springboard to lead workers to revolution.[96] The party in Moscow that had overthrown the czar was the same party operating in Toronto and preparing to overthrow Parliament. Sommerville outlined the authority of the state for the jury: "It is the fundamental right of every state to preserve itself against attack from within as well as without and to punish those who abuse the freedom of the land." Calling them the "guardians of the state,"[97] Sommerville warned the jury that an acquittal would sanction Moscow's teachings. He called on them to help him in his war against communism:

In the shadow of Remembrance day . . . I call upon you in the name of your own land to give me men to match my mountains, give me men to match my plains, men of courage, men of vision, men with wisdom in their brains. Give me the men on this jury . . . give me men who have devotion to the finest traditions of our race, and I'll give you the men who will say that sedition shall not stalk the land.

Then with all the intensity he could muster, Sommerville gravely warned the jury, "DO NOT FORGET THE QUESTION OF THE ALLEGIANCE OF THESE MEN TO THE FATHERLAND."[98]

The Crown's strategy throughout the trial was to invoke emotions of fear and patriotism in the jury by portraying the accused as traitors because they subscribed to a foreign and dangerous ideology and acted at the behest of Moscow. This argument was central to the Crown's ability to establish the blameworthiness of the accused, particularly for the count of seditious conspiracy, which was solely based on the CPC's connections to the CI. These activists were race traitors who betrayed their duty as good moral citizens by being loyal to the wrong patriarch, the Soviet fatherland.[99] The Crown used a war narrative to appeal to the jury members' emotions, such as their sense of loyalty and patriotic duty. With the Crown portraying itself as the masculine figure of the brave general and the jury as his brave male soldiers, the jury would push back the foreign army and protect the land and race of Canada by delivering a guilty verdict. Sommerville was no doubt eager for the trial to wrap up on Remembrance Day to add further symbolism to his argument, but he had to settle for 13 November instead.

Wright began his charge to the jury, stressing that what was important was whether the accused came under the language of the Code. In regards to Section 98, Wright stated: "Something has been said here about this being an unusual law, a harsh law, and that a jury should struggle against convicting a man for violation of an unreasonable law . . . whether it is harsh or not, it is the law . . . it is the duty of every loyal Canadian citizen to peacefully submit to the law."[100] It did not matter if the section was "unusual" or exceptional. Its history as PC 2384 or the controversy surrounding its use was not relevant to the court. Whether the law was unusual or harsh, it was the law. It was now normal, and its reputation should not impact the jury's decision.

Within two hours, the jury returned a verdict of guilty on all three counts. When court resumed on 13 November, Macdonald asked for leniency, arguing that the Eight were "political criminals, because their views on political questions [brought] them into conflict with the State."[101] In passing his sentence, Wright stated that the crimes "were of a serious nature" because of the way in which the CPC "made special appeals to those who were not born in Canada and who were not versed perhaps in the spirit of Canadianism." The Eight were not "political criminals" but had committed "a species of treason" for striking "at the very foundation of our social and governmental fabric in this country."[102] Wright recommended deportation for those who were foreign born. All but Čačić received a five-year prison sentence for the first two counts and two years for the third, with the sentences to run concurrently. Čačić's lower standing in the party was acknowledged by Wright, and he received two years for the first two counts and one year for the third. Macdonald informed him that they would appeal.

The greatest crime of the accused, as Wright indicated, was their attempt to indoctrinate the foreign born. Communism was not part of the spirit of Canadianism that foreigners had to subscribe to, which for immigrants meant not being political in the manner they saw fit, such as by joining the CPC. It was a term that seemed to imply that immigrants needed to remain passive and subservient in a liberal society. The CPC was a perceived threat to the state's hegemony, and the state had responded with Section 98.[103] Security, as the authorities defined it, had been strengthened. Wright's words highlighted not just the exceptional status of the court and Section 98 but the newly acquired status of CPC members as more than political criminals. They exemplified an entirely different class of criminal: a species of traitor. They were a scourge on society, outcasts from the social fabric. By outlawing the CPC, the criminal law helped the government judge what political ideologies were acceptable in Canada: communism was not one of them.

Many of Canada's leading papers expressed their support for the verdict, and even the *New York Times* commented on the trial. It recognized the implications of the trial in that thousands could be arrested because of the decision.[104] The trial was a strong message to the Canadian public to avoid the dangers of communism. The didactic message of the trial was not lost on the editors of the *Toronto Daily Star*, as the front-page headline on 13 November read: "Communism in Canada Is Dealt Death-Blow Today by Sentences."[105]

The Eight appealed the conviction on the following grounds: that the indictment against the accused was "bad in law," as Macdonald had outlined during the trial, that the judge refused to allow the defence to show the aims and objects of communism, that there were peaceful communist revolutions, and that the use of force and violence was a central component of communist teachings. Macdonald argued that violence or force was not the "direct result of any act of the accused or any act of the Communist Party of Canada and the evidence [did] not prove a charge within Section 98 of the Criminal Code."[106] The accused were represented at the appeal on 13 and 14 January 1932 by I.F. Hellmuth and Hugh Macdonald; Sedgwick and Sommerville represented the Crown. Chief Justices Middleton, Masten, Orde, and Grant heard the appeal and upheld the conviction under Section 98 on 19 February but struck down the seditious conspiracy charge, which was found insufficient. The court believed that the indictment was insufficiently worded, as it was not clear exactly what the conspiracy was. The Crown's bill of particulars did not resolve the problems with the indictment for the third count. According to the judges, given that the first two counts were the more serious charges, dismissing the third count would have no bearing on the sentences.[107]

The court's reason for upholding the convictions on the first two counts (those under Section 98) followed the same logic as the trial: the CPC was directly linked to the CI, and thus all the CI teachings were also those of the CPC. The CI documents that appeared during the trial were again put on record during the appeal, complete with all the mentions of "civil war," "armed rebellion," and "violent defeat of the bourgeoisie." Theories and statements from the theses and statutes of the CI were portrayed as if they described actual events that had occurred in Canada. On these grounds and Leopold's evidence, the conviction was upheld.

There was little doubt the accused would be convicted. The state had mobilized every power it could to ensure the conviction, from the use of multiple law enforcement agencies to conduct arrests and collect evidence to using an emergency law (PC 2384, which was now Section 98) to prosecute the accused. The successful use of Section 98 in peacetime shed it from its wartime origins and sanctioned its nor-malization. Section 98 was no longer an emergency law; it was just – as Wright told the jury – the law. Judging politics was now acceptable in Canada in war or peace. The law was a means of nation-building and important in constructing an idea of security.

The trial of the Eight also revealed the nature of law and power in their case. As mentioned, the significance of the trial was not whether justice was or was not served; it was the demonstration of the sover-eign's ability to judge and of the process of the law. In spite of all the reasoned and legal arguments for why the accused should never have been tried, they were and were convicted. Such an act demonstrated the nature of law in this case, which was not rule but judgment – the trial itself. The most important goal for the Crown and the government had been to bring the Communists to trial. Everything else, such as how to prosecute the case, was worked out later. Agamben states that "the ultimate end of the juridical regulation is to produce judgment; but judgment aims neither to punish nor to extol, nether to establish justice nor to prove the truth. Judgment is in itself the end."[108] With only the sovereign deciding what the law does and does not apply to, law as judgment is reflective of sovereign power. If the law is the right to try, or "tribunal right," punishment and whether an accused is guilty or innocent become irrelevant. In Kafka's *The Trial*, the char-acter of the priest reminds Joseph K., "The court wants nothing from you. It welcomes you when you come; it releases you when you go." The trial and the process were law. The trial was an end in itself and not a means to justice or any other goal. In a state where emergency is indistinguishable from normalcy, power is the trial.

Stopping the spread of communism was Section 98's principal intent, and the section's significance lies in the way it demonstrated how what was permitted during a time of war – judging politics – became acceptable in peacetime, once it entered the Criminal Code. It was only the ability of the sovereign to normalize emergency powers, specifically PC 2384 as Section 98, that allowed the state to judge the politics of the CPC, a judgment that now legally permitted the use of even more exceptional measures like deportation. The heart of the Crown's case rested on demonstrating how the ideology and, by extension, the political beliefs of the accused were criminal acts. It tried its best to stir emotions in the jury through the use of war imagery and a war narrative. The broader significance of the Buck et al. trial to Canadian society was not just whether the trial was fair or was a violation of civil liberties: it was the way in which a wartime emergency power had become a part of everyday Canadian society by becoming a part of the Criminal Code, and the way in which this emergency was used to equate ideas with criminal acts, as the trial plainly illustrated.

The Crown was successful in making its case that the CPC and its ideology expressed foreign teachings that advocated the overthrow of the government and economic system, despite the defence's claims that communist ideology was an alternative means of interpreting history and society. At the heart of the trial was the demonstration of the nature of law and power in the CPC members' case. The ability of the Crown to secure a conviction and to proceed with its case in spite of every legal obstacle it faced, and the fact that it and the government's main goal was to get the case to trial, demonstrates that the end goal of the law in this case was judgment. Within the exceptional state, power and law are the right to try.

With the CPC classed as unlawful, authorities in Canada began taking whatever exceptional measures were needed to rid the country of communism's insidious teachings, including hunting and flushing out other CPC members that had now been forced into hiding. Nation-building through the use of state repression was now underway, and it was legal as much as it was brutal.

4

Citizens of the World

Following the conviction of Buck et al., Section 98, as Justice Wright had correctly articulated in his address to the jury, achieved a transition: it was now no longer an "unusual" or "exceptional" law – it was the law. After the trial, the government engaged in one of the most widespread political deportation campaigns in Canadian history. The history of political deportation has received little attention from historians, aside from Barbara Roberts in her classic monograph *Whence They Came: Deportation from Canada 1900–1935*. This chapter aims to build on this path-breaking work by explaining the broader ramifications of deportation policy and the connections between sovereign power, political thought, and nation-building.[1] The conviction of Buck et al. was important to the state's goal of wiping out communism, not only because it outlawed the party, but because it enabled authorities to legally target the foreign roots of the CPC. Communism was viewed by many as a foreign culture and nation, and now those foreigners spreading communism could be deported.

This chapter focuses on those communists most vulnerable to the state's repression after Buck et al.'s conviction: transnational communist activists. Deportation functioned as a nation-building mechanism because it set the terms for who could be qualified as citizens, as well as being an important contributor to an ideological construction of security. If the foreign threat could be literally expunged from the country, Canadians would be safer and more secure. This measure was possible only because of the state's ability to reduce these activists to the status of *homo sacer*, a person subject to law but unable to be protected by it. Once emergency law was normalized and targets identified, judged, and convicted, they could now be reduced to *homo sacer*, a figure abandoned by law. The purpose of their reduction to this status was not to have them killed with impunity by Canadian authorities, but rather to easily dispose of them and to ensure that they had no way of interfering with the state's goal of deporting them. If other states opted to kill these *homo sacer* after their deportation, it was inconsequential to the Canadian state. Immigrant Communists were more vulnerable than domestic-born ones because they had no protections from repressive state actions like deportation. These activists often considered themselves "citizens of the world," having no country with which to identify and instead viewing themselves as members of a people, such as their ethnic group, and part of the communist movement.[2] Section 41 of the Immigration Act provided for the deportation of immigrants for their political beliefs. This law enabled the state to legally judge the politics of immigrants outside of the legal protections that citizens received. Law, in the service of sovereign power, enabled the state to reduce someone to the status of *homo sacer* on the basis of nativity and political ideology.[3]

It was transnational activists' support for communism, their belief in the unbelievable, that enabled their movement to be restricted. This new approach to the study of deportation can help us understand not only the law's role in providing democratic states with the legal ability to deport, but more importantly, how law enables the state to determine citizenship, and the legal rights it provides, on the basis of political ideology.

An examination of the case of the Halifax Ten, as they were known in the labour press, and the case of Tomo Čačić is useful for exploring these themes. The Ten were arrested in raids across Canada after the Buck et al. trial, and Čačić was the only one of the eight convicted who was eligible for deportation. Because of their high-profile status in the CPC, many of the legal documents pertaining to their cases have survived in the archives. Section 41 played an important role in controlling these immigrants' entry into citizenship, while the case files of the Ten and Čačić provide some insight into the lives of the deportees. Many of these Communists came to North America as sojourners and became radicalized while on the job, working in dangerous conditions. These facts complicate the existing historical literature that claims that the communist and socialist movement was built by leaders who arrived in Canada. Leaders in the movement could also be made in Canada. By looking at these documents, combined with writings from the Finnish, Croatian, German, and Polish labour press, we can examine the effect of deportation on these individuals, and how for some, it cost them their lives.

A "Spring Cleaning"

Once the Buck et al. trial was completed, the authorities quickly began preparations to deport immigrant members of the party.[4] The Finnish labour paper *Vapaus* and the Polish conservative paper *Gazeta Katolicka w Kanadzie* both reported that Mayor Ralph Webb of Winnipeg, a fervent anti-communist, was publicly calling on the government to take further actions against Communists and engage in a "spring cleaning."[5] Following the unsuccessful appeal of Buck et al. in February 1932, the immigration department, in cooperation with the RCMP and provincial authorities, began one of the most disturbing round-ups of the era.

Preparation for the raids began on 11 December 1931. The RCMP sent out notices to its districts across the country, informing commanding officers that the service had been contacted by the immigration department, which required assistance in arresting CPC members for deportation. Officers were reminded that they must, while planning the raids and carrying them out, maintain "absolute secrecy . . . until zero hour."[6] It is unknown how many round-ups of CPC members took place during the 1930s, because political deportations were often carried out under the guise of other reasons, such as an immigrant becoming unemployed and being in need of relief.[7]

On the night of 2 May 1932, the round-up began. This operation, the most extensive and clandestine of its kind, sought to nab some well-known leaders of language organizations in the CPC, such as Arvo Vaara, Conrad Cesinger, Dmytro Chomicki, and Ivan Sembaj – most of whom were arrested during the first week of May. Martin Pohjansalo, translator for the Finnish paper *Vapaus*, and Arvo Vaara, who was the former editor of the paper, were arrested in Sudbury by the OPP.[8] John Farkas was arrested in Oshawa, Dan Chomicki and Conrad Cesinger in Winnipeg. Ivan Sembaj was picked up in Edmonton, and Hans Kist and Gottfried Zurcher were arrested in Vancouver. In Montreal, Steve (Stefan) Worozcyt, or Worebek, of the Ukrainian Labour-Farmer Temple Association (ULFTA), was arrested and, on 19 May, Toivo, or John, Stahlberg of the Finnish Organization of Canada (FOC) was arrested. In the majority of cases, the men were arrested overnight and whisked away by train to Halifax.

According to some press reports, these raids were the second in a week. On 7 May, the *Toronto Star* reported that dozens of Finnish and British people had been secretly rounded up the week before and quickly deported, and that all were under heavy RCMP guard. No details were available as to who they were and how many there were.[9]

Others arrested were not eligible for deportation and were released, including Orton Wade, a Canadian-born citizen.[10]

Section 41

While the Halifax Ten fought their deportations, their options were limited. The Immigration Act of 1910 set out the parameters of politically based deportations in Section 41, with procedural regulations set out in Section 42. The act provided for the deportation of nonnaturalized or domiciled immigrants who were "member[s] of or affiliated with any organization entertaining or teaching disbelief in or opposition to organized government." Both groups, it stated, "shall . . . be deemed to belong to the prohibited or undesirable classes, and shall be liable to deportation." These measures were initially intended to deal with the wave of pre-war radicalism linked to socialist and anarchist groups operating in Canada and the United States, but they later proved useful to the authorities amid the rise of post-war labour unrest and during the Great Depression.[11] The wording of the section was identical to Section 98, the Criminal Code section that enabled the government to outlaw the CPC. Indeed, Section 98 was meant to take the state powers normally directed at immigrants and make them applicable to everyone – outside of a declared emergency state.[12]

Section 41 gave the government more power in dealing with foreign activists than Section 98, since no criminal court trial was required. Deportation, as Roberts remarks, "was an administrative, not a judicial matter," meaning that "prospective deports did not have the rights that they would have in a judicial process." Moreover, "the deportation process was overturned by the courts only when the Department got caught being sloppy in its procedures."[13] By abiding by regulations created by Parliament, the immigration department was safe to carry out deportations legally and free from public scrutiny. Paradoxically, to keep the country secure and to protect the rule of law, Canadian immigration officials needed laws to allow them to operate outside of the public gaze.

As mentioned earlier, Section 42 of the Immigration Act detailed the procedures for carrying out deportations. To determine if the Halifax Ten met the requirements for being deported, they appeared before a board of inquiry, which consisted of three individuals hand-picked by the department. The board acted as judge and jury in the cases. Separate deportation hearings were held for each of the ten individuals. Sergeant Leopold of the RCMP, the star witness in the Buck et al. trial, was called to the hearings to give evidence. The immigration department's reasoning for having Leopold testify in these hearings was that he could identify the CPC as an illegal organization and submit evidence collected during the trial about the deportees in order to prove their membership.[14] If they were proven to belong to the CPC, the undesirable status of the deportees under Section 41 – their advocacy or teaching of the overthrow of government by force and violence – would then be established, making them eligible for deportation. The conviction of Buck et al. under Section 98 was a crucial step towards the deportation of Communists.

Lawyers for the deportees, if they were lucky enough to have one, had few options. Deportees had no right to a jury, even though they were, in many ways, being tried for their actions and under the law were entitled to a fair trial. They could not challenge the admissibility of evidence or call witnesses to support them. They could challenge the right of the immigration department to detain them, such as by initiating a *habeas corpus* challenge, but these often failed because they had to be filed in the city where the deportee was held and the department often moved individuals to skirt these challenges. To quash a challenge, the department needed only to prove that it followed its own rules.[15] The deportees had to stand accused of an offence and be held accountable for it, but the process was an administrative matter. Immigration law was used not to ascertain if the immigrants were guilty of a crime but to judge their politics and deport them. Leopold, along with other undercover RCMP agents, testified at each of the deportees' hearings. Leopold testified that he believed all the organizations the men were affiliated with were unlawful.[16]

Lawyers for the Canadian Labor Defense League (CLDL) filed a *habeas corpus* challenge to dispute the detention of the Halifax Ten.[17] When it was rejected by Justice Carroll, the CLDL appealed to the Supreme Court of Canada. The appeal centred on the lack of particulars provided by the immigration department to the appellants. The lawyers questioned how the department could detain the men if it could not show how they were guilty of belonging to an unlawful association at the time of their arrest, only at some point in their past. But the court found that all that was required was that the allegations had been made with "reasonable certainty" in regards to the appellants' "violation of the act" (Section 41).[18] It did not matter whether the deportees were active Communists or not. The court stressed that there was "no analogy between a complaint under the Immigration Act and an indictment on a criminal charge." For instance, in a criminal case the Crown could not compel the accused to take the witness stand, while in a deportation hearing, the deportee was often the "chief witness" compelled to face the accusations of the department or face immediate deportation.[19] In sum, the department followed the laws that allowed it to carry out deportations as effortlessly as possible and deny deportees the protections found in the criminal law. These were exceptional powers, yet normal components of Canada's Immigration Act.

Section 41 was a law that enabled the government to target the politics of transnational activists outside of long-established legal principles. In many ways, it was a law designed to circumvent law. Section 41 was meant to set the boundaries of acceptable political ideology for immigrants and domestic-born Canadians alike by demonstrating the characteristics of those who did not qualify as citizens. This was possible only because of the state's ability to exercise its sovereign power to create the *homo sacer* in society. As De Genova argues, with deportation, "the whole totalizing regime of citizenship and alienage, belonging and deportability . . . is deployed against particular persons in a manner that is . . . irreversibly individualizing."[20] With Section 41, the state possessed the power to unmake and recast citizens, removing them from the social fabric on the basis of their professed political ideology. Because of their politics, they were individualized, and removed from Canadian society. They were the most susceptible to the direct power of the state, where citizenship and noncitizenship were decided at its whim.

Citizenship is not simply a status that determines who an individual's rulers are, but rather one that identifies members of the political order and the sovereign. It is the state that decides who is and is not a citizen and the qualifications to be one. In this context, citizens are identified by what political ideologies they adhere to.[21] By reducing transnational communist immigrants to the status of *homo sacer*, the state was exercising its sovereign power to set the boundaries of who should and should not be citizens on the basis of their politics. The state could now control their "bare life" as much as required to legally deport them.[22]

The Halifax Ten and Tomo Čačić

The files in the archives, coupled with accounts from newspapers, have provided a window into the identities of the deportees and the secretive deportation tactics that the Canadian government engaged in during the 1930s. Besides being high-ranking members of the party, the majority of the Halifax Ten, and Tomo Čačić, were sojourners before joining the party. Their initial intention had been to work and then return home, but they discovered communism and joined the movement in North America. These Communists identified with a region or ethnicity rather than a state.

Arvo Vaara was born in Vassan Laani, Truvan Pitaja, Finland, on 28 January 1891 and baptized Lutheran. Vaara worked as a farmhand and in construction. He arrived in Canada in December 1908 as a sojourner, never intending to stay in North America. Like many other immigrants of the period, he came to Canada to find work, often doing difficult jobs that many Canadians avoided.[23] His intention was to move back to Finland and buy his own farm. By 1924, he had settled in Sudbury, where he became the editor of the Finnish labour paper *Vapaus*, a daily published by the FOC. Vaara never identified with any one nationality. While he was born in what is today Finland, it was a part of the Russian Empire at the time of his birth and during his youth. Finnish citizenship did not exist at the time. Vaara quipped that he never actually knew what his citizenship was.[24]

Vaara became an influential CPC member because of his strong links to the Finnish community and his role in running *Vapaus*. But he often clashed with party leadership, especially during the rise of Stalin's so-called Third Period of capitalism, when Moscow demanded strict party discipline.[25] Vaara was known to the authorities. In 1928, he was convicted of seditious libel after allegedly writing an editorial in *Vapaus* criticizing the British monarchy.[26] Vaara was described as a loyal follower of the CPC, and at the age of forty, he was considered an "old hat" at leftist activism.

There are few recorded details about Vaara's private life. In an interview with the *Toronto Star*, an unnamed former Sudbury city councillor and co-worker of Vaara gave his impressions of him, stating that Vaara lived alone, rarely drank, and was never seen with women. He told the reporter that Vaara was generally a quiet individual. The *Star* reported that Vaara would probably not stay in Finland but would go to "Korea" and from there to the Soviet Union. The reporter misunderstood: the source probably meant that Vaara would travel to Karelia, a border region between Finland and the Soviet Union that attracted many unemployed Finns from Canada over the course of the 1930s.

The desire to leave Canada for Karelia developed into a type of "Karelia fever" among left-wing Finns, as historians such as Varpu Lindström have demonstrated.[27] The Soviet Union's eastern side had become the Karelia Autonomous Republic of the Soviet Union (KASSR) in 1923. Unbeknownst to communist Finns in North America, over the course of the 1930s, Stalin's forces began large-scale programs of pacifying the area by imprisoning or liquidating any perceived threats, which included Finns. Historians have estimated that thousands of Finns were executed or transferred to prison camps in the Soviet Union during this period.[28]

Conrad Cesinger was born on 25 February 1901 in Augsburg, Bavaria, in Germany. He worked in Germany in a chemical lab and possessed a college education from a technical school. He left Germany for the same reason as the other deportees – to find work. A single man, he sailed from the port of Bremen and arrived in Canada in July 1926, docking at Halifax. Cesinger travelled to Winnipeg before making his way to Saskatchewan, where he worked as a farmhand. He returned to Winnipeg in 1931. Much like Vaara, Cesinger discovered communism in Canada while working in difficult conditions. After a string of injuries, which included having his hands "frozen," Cesinger was unable to continue as a farmhand. He filed a claim with the Compensation Board against his employer, the Northwest Lumber Company, but his claim was refused.[29]

Cesinger's main task in the party was to build the popularity of the CPC among German-speaking workers. He quickly climbed the party ranks and, in 1931, was appointed to the newly minted National Party Fraction Bureau (NPFB), which was the controlling body behind the German Workers and Farmers Association (GWFA). The GWFA, much like the FOC and the ULFTA, was an ethnic association that blended politics with culture.[30] Based in Winnipeg, it was closely aligned with the CPC and run by prominent CPC members such as Jacob Penner. According to RCMP documents, Cesinger was second-in-command of the organization, behind Penner. Cesinger served as editor of the German labour paper *Deutsche Arbeiterzeitung* (*DAZ*). However, much like Vaara had resisted *Vapaus* toeing the new Moscow line, Cesinger claimed at his deportation hearing that despite his being made secretary of the NPFB, he did not support the GWFA toeing the line. He claimed there was some discussion within the GWFA to "get closer to the Communist Party" but that he opposed it becoming a wing of the CPC. It is unclear whether Cesinger made the claims to try to avoid deportation or if he really was opposed to the GWFA becoming closer to the CPC.[31]

Dmytro Chomicki (known as Dan Holmes) was one of the few whose immigration file was retained by the immigration department. The RCMP also retained its records on him. Chomicki was born in the village of Ottynia, Austria, on 3 December 1898. He arrived in Canada with his parents in 1913 when he was fifteen. After the First World War, the place of his birth became part of what is today Poland.

Chomicki, like Vaara, never thought of himself as a citizen of any country. The Austria of his birth no longer existed at the time of his application for naturalization in April 1927, which was denied, presumably because of his ties to the CPC. Baptized Catholic, he married Marion Perchal in 1921 at Holy Ghost Catholic Church in Winnipeg. Together they had one daughter, Makie. Although Chomicki started an apprenticeship in Austria as a machinist, he never completed it and worked in Winnipeg as a printer for the Workers and Farmers Publishing Association, which published *Ukrainian Labor News* and *Working Women*, among other labour papers. Chomicki was a member of the CPC and served on the District 7 Executive Bureau in Winnipeg. The RCMP considered him an important member of the ULFTA and a skilled printer, which was a valuable asset to the group.[32] While serving as secretary of the bureau, Chomicki had an important role in trying to recruit Polish immigrants. Although Chomicki did not consider himself a Pole, his language skills were an asset for the party (he identified with being Western Ukrainian).[33]

It is uncertain what success Chomicki had in his attempts to draw more Poles into the CPC. The party's Polish contingent was increasing enough that the CPC created a Polish labour paper called *Budzik*. *Budzik* began publication in 1932 and was later succeeded by the paper *Glos Pracy*.[34]

Alas, little remains in the archives on Ivan Sembaj. He was a native of Poland but, at his deportation hearing in 1932, claimed he was a citizen of the Soviet Union. He arrived in Canada in October 1923, married, and had a Canadian-born child. He briefly worked on farms in Manitoba before joining the Ukrainian Labour-Farmer Temple Association, where he was an executive member of the organization at the time of his deportation. He was a member of the Workers Benevolent Association and the CLDL. The immigration authorities regarded him as intelligent and hence dangerous. He was forty years old at the time of his deportation.[35]

That the RCMP included these four men in its round-up made sense given that they all occupied senior positions in their respective CPC language groups and that the authorities feared the Communists' attempts at drawing in immigrants to their cause.[36] The reason for the arrest of the remaining men was not so clear. Gottfried Zurcher, Stefan Worozcyt, and Hans Kist were small potatoes in the ranks of the party, though Zurcher and his spouse (who was arrested and described in mainstream media reports as "Mrs. Frederick Zurcher wife of Gottfried Zurcher") and Stefan Worozcyt were all members of the CLDL, which was known for its agitation for workers' rights.

While Hans Kist was not a CLDL member, he was a highly vocal member of the CPC.

Gottfried Zurcher was born in Switzerland. He arrived in Canada on 9 September 1927 and lived with a friend in Manitoba who had promised him farm employment. He worked as a farm labourer for ten months before becoming a welder with the Manitoba Bridge and Iron Works. He then relocated to Vancouver. Zurcher pursued full-time activities with the CLDL after 1931. He was married and thirty-two years old at the time of his arrest in 1932. His wife was also arrested and taken to Halifax. She was described in the *Worker* as head of the CLDL's Vancouver branch. She was just as much or more of a target for the authorities because of her work in the CLDL. The lack of details about her illustrates that while a number of prominent women were recognized in the communist movement, some were recognized only on the basis of their status of being married to an activist. The *Worker* mentioned her only so as to demonstrate the harshness of the state's tactics in deporting Zurcher's wife, rather than recognizing her status and participation in the movement in her own right.[37]

The deportation of Zurcher's spouse, and that of other women involved in the communist movement, reveals that women activists were treated no differently by the authorities than their male counterparts. If they were eligible for deportation, the department would see it through. However, women did face additional scrutiny by immigration authorities, broadly speaking. They were subjected to deportation for moral reasons, both in the United States and Canada. For example, women were deported for being "fallen" by having a child outside of marriage.[38]

A native of what is present-day Poland, Stefan Worozcyt arrived in Canada in 1926 to take up farm work in Western Canada. But Worozcyt skipped out on his train and instead landed in Hamilton, and later in Montreal, where he worked as a window cleaner. Worozcyt was not a particularly high-standing party member. The only evidence the immigration department had on him was that he was a member of the ULFTA, the CLDL, and the Society for Assisting the Liberation Movement in Western Ukraine. Though born in Poland, Worozcyt identified as being Western Ukrainian, not Polish. He was from the region known as Galicia in Eastern Europe. He was thirty years old and single when arrested.[39]

At the time of his deportation, Hans Kist was a recent arrival in Canada, unlike his fellow deportees. He arrived in Vancouver and sought farm work, soon joining the CPC. He was involved in strikes at Fraser Mills and in unemployment rallies in Vancouver. Kist was a member of the National Unemployed Workers Association and the Friends of the Soviet Union, both of which had ties to the CPC. Like his fellow deportees, he admitted to being a member of the CPC until it was declared unlawful. Kist was confrontational with authorities, leading the immigration department to categorize him as "saturated with communistic beliefs" and as "a thorough going troublemaker." Kist was dangerous because of his lack of respect for the law.[40]

The remaining individuals who made up the Halifax Ten were Martin Pohjansalo, John Farkas, and Toivo Stahlberg. They were arrested as a result of the fishing expedition initiated by Ontario's attorney general, William Price. In preparation for the Buck et al. trial, Price solicited the names of Communists from Crown attorneys across the country so that the Crown could act quickly against them once the group was convicted.[41] Few details of their lives remain. We do know that Martin Pohjansalo, known as Parker, was born in Finland and was single and twenty-two years old at the time of his deportation. Having arrived in Canada on 23 May 1913 as a three-year-old when his parents came to Toronto, he knew no country other than Canada. Becoming the associate editor of *Vapaus*, Pohjansalo travelled and worked closely with Vaara. Crown Attorney Wilkins of Sudbury identified him as a known Communist.[42]

John Farkas was a single worker from Hungary who was thirty years old at the time of his deportation. Having arrived in Canada on 23 July 1926, Farkas later moved to Oshawa in February 1928, after brief stints in the West looking for work. He started a grocery store on Albert Street in Oshawa's downtown core, but his idealism led to his bankruptcy; unable to turn away unemployed workers needing food, he was forced to close his store.

Farkas became a member of the CPC but had problems with the party. He was known to local police. When he was involved in a fist fight with Ed Macdonald, the unemployed organizer for the CPC in Oshawa, he was charged with disorderly conduct. Farkas cut ties with the CPC after the fight. He participated in marches for the unemployed but never spoke again at meetings. Farkas reportedly said he was "through making public demonstrations for communism." His grocery-store partner, Carney, stated that he and Farkas would frequently have debates about religion, as Carney was active in the local Greek Orthodox Church. Carney stated that despite the debates, he would not go so far as to consider Farkas an atheist (an indication that, among CPC members and supporters, religion may not have been totally absent from their lives, despite the views of the party).[43] He was a member of the CLDL, the Unemployed Workers Association, and the Hungarian Workers Club. Farkas likely came to the attention of the immigration department through various sources: he had had several encounters with the provincial police, and Crown Attorney J.A. McGibbon of Oshawa told Attorney General Price about Farkas's spreading of communist propaganda in the city.[44] The immigration department concurred with McGibbon that Farkas was a constant source of trouble in Oshawa.[45]

Toivo "John" Stahlberg was born in Finland and arrived in Quebec in 1910. He then travelled to the United States and resided there for ten years. He received his US naturalization in 1917. A blacksmith by trade, Stahlberg worked as a ticket agent for steamship companies before serving as the business manager for *Vapaus*. His residence in Canada began in October 1925 while he was still periodically travelling to the US. Stahlberg left the CPC in 1928 during the Stalinization period of the party, but stayed with *Vapaus*, presumably because he disagreed with the Third Period policies of the party at the time.[46] With the turn of *Vapaus* to the new line, it is doubtful that he would have found much freedom staying with the paper. He was a member of the FOC, a radical Communist group according to the immigration department. He was married and forty years old at the time of this arrest.[47]

Tomo Čačić's deportation case was high profile because he was the only member of the Buck et al. trial in 1931 who was eligible for deportation. His deportation was carried out one year after the Halifax Ten hearings, after completing his sentence. Sources on Čačić's life are rich because he was an avid writer. He wrote to his Canadian comrades in the Yugoslav labour press in Canada for years after being deported. His writings provide a unique first-hand account of the life of a transnational activist who was deported from Canada. Like many of the members of the Halifax Ten, Čačić was radicalized in North America after first travelling to the United States and later moving to Canada in 1925. He presumably joined the CPC in 1927. Much like members of other ethnic groups, Čačić served a useful role for the CPC as an organizer in the Croatian community. He was instrumental in creating a labour paper for Yugoslav workers entitled *Borba*. A prolific writer, many of his writings survive to the present day. Čačić described the need for *Borba*'s creation in the following way: "In the beginning [Croatian immigrants] . . . were doing seasonal jobs in mines and forestry and building roads and railroads . . . At that time there was no clubs for us, except some clubs that were organized by the Kingdom of Jugoslavia. There were no newspapers except some that were organized by Serbs. Our immigrants that were chased away from their homeland by the Kingdom did not want to hear about that paper."[48]

Čačić's Yugoslavia was a workers' state that included Croatians, not the Kingdom of Yugoslavia, which he regarded as a Serbian state under the rule of King Alexander. Čačić had worked hard in his early years at the CPC, and in his writings he displayed pride in his ability to learn English on his own and serve as editor of *Borba*. In some of his writings, he discussed the difficulties of the community in setting up a paper: "Our immigrants were mostly peasants & working class, mostly with no education or qualifications to manage a paper. The ones with education went into business. I became editor of the paper and prayed that we would do a good job."[49] The CPC provided an ideal political opportunity for him to express both his nationalist and communist ideals. While the CPC certainly did its best to subordinate its language organizations, it still continued to value them and immigrants like Čačić, Vaara, and Chomicki. The CPC was the only organization available that provided a space for the expression of their ethnicity and their politics, however conflict ridden the relationship became.

Like other deportees, Čačić had an important role in the party but was never a big fish, at least not until his arrest. He had a falling-out with the party brass when he openly criticized the party's lack of funding for lay members. In his later years, he engaged in public battles with comrades, defending his role at *Borba*. Čačić's subordinate in the early days of *Borba*, Franjo Ugrin, wrote to the Yugoslavian labour paper *Jedinstvo* in 1966 about the early years of labour radicalism among Yugoslavs living in Canada. He discussed his early work with Čačić in trying to get *Borba* started and described how the paper started to grow and expand just before the CPC leadership was arrested. He claimed that Čačić's arrest nearly "beheaded" their movement and that his arrest was a result of "his own improvidence." Petar Žapkar replaced him as the editor but was arrested shortly after and deported along with Čačić.[50] Čačić took exception to Ugrin's statements. According to Čačić, Ugrin was his "right arm" in issuing the paper, but he resented Ugrin faulting him for his own arrest. He told his interviewer that across the globe "thousands of the best revolutionaries were arrested before 1941." He claimed that in Yugoslavia, many were jailed for years or murdered. "Were they all arrested because it was their fault?" Čačić asked. He doubted that, concluding that "they were arrested because they were revolutionaries."[51]

Čačić's RCMP security file confirms that he was never a leading figure and that his arrest was because he was in the wrong place at the wrong time. His file raises questions about other elements of his interpretation of the events of 1931, which implied an official interest in quelling Yugoslav sedition. According to Čačić, after his arrest, the Yugoslav consulate in Canada "were hoping that once I was gone the paper [*Borba*] would disappear in Canada. They were mistaken, *Borba* was under new management and other newspapers began to appear."[52] Čačić's belief that he had been arrested to silence his work in the ethnic labour press and that Yugoslav officials in Canada were involved was unfounded. His arrest was not premeditated, and the RCMP was entirely unaware of his activities prior to it.

The cases of the Halifax Ten and Tomo Čačić shed light on the transnational activist during the interwar period. Much like other anarchist transnationals, those immigrants who joined the CPC viewed Canada as but one locale in an international struggle.[53] These cases also illustrate the nature of communist activism among immigrant workers: of all the members of the Halifax Ten, only one, Ivan Sembaj, confirmed that he had socialist leanings before arriving in Canada. The remainder of these individuals were sojourners who had no intention of remaining permanently in Canada but rather sought to return to their homelands, as their testimony to the immigration department revealed. They became activists in the communist movement, with several climbing the ranks within the CPC.[54] Contrary to the perception of the authorities, they were not foreign activists coming to Canada, but rather foreigners who became activists in Canada. In the Finnish community, left-wing leaders fleeing the Finnish Civil War helped to spread the communist message to fellow Finns and likely influenced some immigrants of other ethnicities, but the same cannot be said of other groups such as the Croatians, Poles, or Germans. In sum, it was North American industrial capitalism, and the inherent contradictions within it, that created many of the Halifax Ten Communists. This is not to say that socialist leaders arriving from Europe were not important to the movement in Canada or that the majority of immigrants discovered socialism in Canada. Rather, these facts complicate the view that European socialist leaders built the movement in immigrant communities in Canada. Some leaders were made in Canada, and of the leaders who did arrive from Europe, their words likely resonated with many immigrants because of the difficulties these immigrants faced in the workplace.

The Halifax Ten and Tomo Čačić were "rebels without a country."[55] They were opposed to capitalism and the modern state but were also created out of it, as capitalism created the means by which workers were thrust into a global labour market as "unprotected, and rightless proletarians."[56] They identified as being both communists and as part of their respective peoples. Their ethnic ties and class were not incompatible. Once they were established by state authorities as Communists, they were cast out of Canadian society, but where was home? Chomicki's homeland had its borders redrawn after the First World War. Vaara's Finland was not the Finland of his birth. Čačić was an enemy of the Kingdom of Yugoslavia for being a Croatian communist nationalist. Deportation served as the ultimate tool to control and regulate their freedom of movement, a freedom central to their lives in a world of mobile capital.

"Protest These Actions"

Following the arrest of the Halifax Ten and their transfer to Halifax, reaction from the ethnic community and CPC language groups was swift and strong. For instance, *Deutsche Arbeiterzeitung* (*DAZ*) reported that when Cesinger was arrested he was not allowed to contact a lawyer. The paper used the event as propaganda to issue a call to arms, stating, "Protest these actions perpetrated in democratic Canada, which eclipse even the darkest days of Tsarist Russia" and "Demand the release of Comrade Cesinger and the abducted leaders of the Canadian proletariat!"[57] *DAZ* was not the only paper calling on its community members for mass action. Similar calls to action were made in *Vapaus* and *Glos Pracy*, which claimed that shortly after the arrests, mass protests from community members took place in Winnipeg's Market Square, with thousands adopting a resolution calling for the "unconditional release of imprisoned labourers" in Halifax.[58] The CLDL initiated a campaign to focus the public's attention on the plight of the prisoners, claiming they could face death or torture if sent back to their home countries. It arranged rallies and protests to demand the release of the Halifax Ten and Čačić. The CLDL provided legal representation for the men and challenged their detention in Halifax. Although limited funds often hampered its best efforts at resistance, the CLDL published a manifesto in *Glos Pracy* and other papers calling on readers to push for the release of the men.[59]

Other ethnic labour papers detailed accounts of the torture and executions that Communist deportees faced.[60] Even the RCMP advised the government of the fate awaiting deportees sent to regions in Europe.[61] The *Worker* frequently reported on political deportations but devoted much attention to the case of the Halifax Ten, presumably because a number of the men held a higher status in the party and because of the brazenness of the operation. The paper used the deportations as propaganda, categorizing all of those arrested as leaders and claiming that the secret kidnappings were evidence of the government doing the bidding of industry. It, too, called on its readers to protest the deportations.[62]

At times, the CLDL engaged in more creative ways of protesting deportation than rallies and petitions. After the Buck et al. trial, Tomo Čačić, when mentioned alongside his comrades, was suddenly one of the CPC leaders.[63] The play *Eight Men Speak* was an agitprop performance dramatizing the trial and imprisonment of the eight defendants in Buck et al. The performers played the roles of the eight convicted and spoke directly to the audience, informing them of their hardships in prison. Čačić's character served a useful purpose in not only protesting his prison conditions but deportations in general. In act 4, the characters introduce him, and he speaks to the audience. His character tells the audience of his imprisonment and life in jail, and then his captors "devise a new torture. They order me deported to fascist Jugo Slavia. They know it means my certain death . . . Workers, you can put an end to this! (*He points through the bars to the audience.*)" All the characters then turn to the audience and point: "Will you? (*pause*)."[64]

The play, as well as Čačić's coverage in the Communist press as a CPC leader, served to draw attention to Čačić's plight and the deportations in general. It demonstrated how Čačić's recent celebrity status in the party was only due to his arrest along with those of the other top party officials. His previous work had received little to no attention. Čačić, as symbol, served to bring the plight of immigrant Communists to people's attention, but at the expense of the accomplishments of the real Čačić.

While the secretive nature of the arrests sparked outrage in the House of Commons and in some of the mainstream press, it is doubtful that any of it affected the government's efforts to halt the deportations.[65] As this case reveals, the immigration department merely took greater steps to ensure a strong legal case. As Roberts suggests, it is doubtful that many citizens truly realized how deportations of immigrant activists were such a perversion of legal principles during this period.[66]

Citizens without a Country?

Tracing what happened to the deportees after leaving Canada reinforces how deportation provided the state with the power to rule over a deportee's life and body and demonstrates the very real effect that the use of emergency measures and deportation had on people's lives. While information on what happened to all members of the Halifax

Figure 4.1 Cover of Oscar Ryan's pamphlet *Deported!* which protested the deportation of the Halifax Ten. From Oscar Ryan, *Deported! The Struggle against Deportations and for the Defense of the Foreign-Born Workers: The Case of Ten Prisoners in Halifax, of the Thousands Who Face Deportation* (Toronto: Canadian Labor Defense League, 1931).

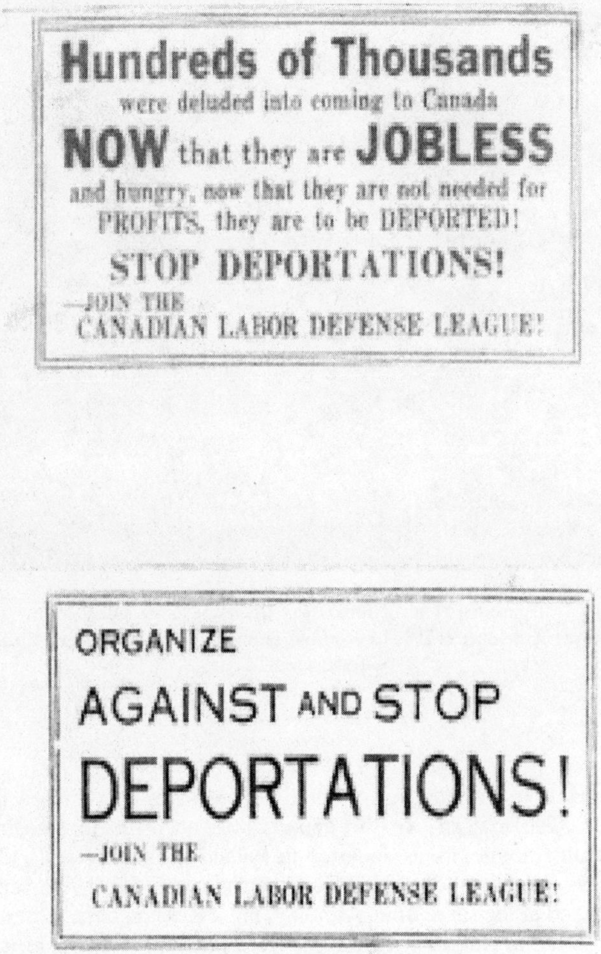

Figure 4.2 Stickers that members of the CLDL stuck to posts and buildings during a protest in front of the Department of Immigration and Colonization office in November 1932. From Library and Archives Canada, RG76, vol. 738, file 513057.

Figure 4.3 Photo of Tomo Čačić when first incarcerated,
the only member of the Buck et al. to be deported. From Library and Archives Canada, RG73,
vol. 579, file 2663.

Ten remains incomplete, grim details about some of the men have emerged. The majority of the deportations occurred in December 1932. Dan Chomicki was deported to Poland in January of 1933, as was Steve Worozcyt. Gottfried Zurcher and his spouse were sent to Switzerland at the same time. Although not a Russian citizen, Sembaj was deported to Russia in July 1933, the delay due to the inability of the immigration department to secure a passport for him. The *Toronto Star* reported that the department had a difficult time deporting him because he was a "man without a country."[67] (There had been passport delays for some of the other men as well.)

An active Communist in Canada, Hans Kist presumably continued to participate in the movement when he returned to Germany. *DAZ* reported that Kist was taken into custody by Nazi authorities and placed in a concentration camp. While in the camp, his torturers continually placed cement blocks on his legs, effectively crushing them. He is presumed to have died from massive hemorrhaging. The *Toronto Star* reported that the Nazi authorities were seeking from Canadian officials the deportation of other German Communists.[68] In the ensuing years, Kist's immigration file was purged from Canadian archival records. *DAZ* noted that Kist had left behind a wife and child in Vancouver. His obituary in the paper stated, "Now another worker's life has fallen victim to the capitalist terror. The day of reckoning will come."[69] While *DAZ* mourned the death of a comrade, it also used the occasion to drive home the threats that deportees faced.

Ivan Sembaj maintained his ties with his Ukrainian comrades in Canada after his deportation. However, Sembaj and other prominent Ukrainian leftists were not included in Stalin's communism. Upon his arrival in Russia, Sembaj was arrested and placed in Stalin's Gulag. He presumably died in custody. In a sad act of betrayal, some of Sembaj's colleagues in Canada wrote in the ethnic press that Sembaj must have betrayed the communist movement and gone the way of Trotsky by becoming an "enemy agent."[70]

As he had been naturalized in the United States, Toivo Stahlberg was deported there, although it is unclear where he ended up later. Stahlberg's letters to his comrades contained the usual anticapitalist cries found in other communist propaganda, in addition to providing insights about how anti-communist Finns assisted the Canadian government. In a 1933 letter to *Vapaus*, Stahlberg detailed how "military commander Mr. Helmberg," of the White Finnish forces, "acted as a witness in the case against comrades Vaara and Parker" and how he suspected that the White Finns in Montreal, supporters of the Finish monarchy, had tracked his movements within Montreal, facilitating his arrest.[71]

The fates of Arvo Vaara, one of the most prominent deported CPC members, and Martin Pohjansalo were first reported in *Vapaus* shortly after their deportation. Vaara and Pohjansalo managed to get a postcard out shortly after they left Canada on 17 December 1932. *Vapaus* included the text of Vaara's card in an article dated 5 January 1933. Vaara mentioned that they were due to arrive in England on 23 December and were hoping for "a chance to change the destination of [their] trip, which [he had heard was] Helsinki." Adding that they had not "suffered from seasickness," he signed off: "Proletarian greetings to all of Canada's workers, A. Vaara."[72] The next update came on 17 March 1933, when *Vapaus* stated that the two men were in the Soviet Union. The Soviet International Red Aid (IRA), a type of international version of the CLDL, was known to assist deportees facing deportation to countries hostile to communism. The group presumably assisted the pair with their escape. Updates on the two ceased for decades. The only mention of their possible fate came from an editorial in 1958 entitled "Let's Stick to the Facts Please," in which *Vapaus*'s editors tried to counter earlier claims made by its rival social-democratic paper, *Vapaa Sana*, which claimed that the dreams that many Finns had of Soviet Karelia were false. It said: "Thousands of Finnish-Canadians went there . . . The communist Okhrana picked them up one by one . . . sending some of them to be shot straight away, and others to be exiled to prison camps in different parts of Russia."[73] In a chilling description, *Vapaa Sana* recounted the horrors of Stalin's purge of Soviet Karelia. Close friends of Vaara mentioned that he probably would have travelled to Soviet Karelia after being deported. For its part, *Vapaus* defended its position that while it was perfectly willing to discuss Stalin's crimes, these were "lies." It accused *Vapaa Sana* of spreading propaganda. *Vapaus* believed it was the same kind of misinformation *Sana* had been pushing for years, such as when it claimed that others had perished under similar conditions: "Arvo Vaara, Hilja Kratz, Martin Parker and many others have been 'liquidated' in Soviet-Carelia [sic] – although it is known facts that Arvo Vaara died an old man from natural causes, Hilja Kratz is at the moment well-off somewhere in a nursing home in Moscow, and that Martin Parker (Pohjansalo) is in some responsible office, most likely, also in Moscow. Just to mention a few."[74]

Vapaus's claims that Vaara "died an old man" and that Pohjansalo was working in some unnamed responsible office sounded implausible. More likely, Vaara and Pohjansalo were both executed along with thousands of others, presumably because their socialism and nationalism were not acceptable to Stalin.

Things were not so grim for the others who were deported. Not much is known about what happened to Conrad Cesinger after he landed in Germany. The RCMP continued to keep watch over the ethnic press in Canada well into the Cold War. The RCMP noted that in the anti-Nazi German paper *Volksteinne*, an article had appeared in the August 1947 issue with the headline "Conrad Cesinger Is in Germany." It reported that Cesinger managed to continue his international fight in the communist movement and that he was working with the German socialist party to help rebuild Germany after the fall of the Nazis.[75] Cesinger wrote to his fellow comrades from East Germany following the war. His letter details the devastation Germany suffered and the plight of refugees. He lamented that people were talking about rebuilding cities ravaged by bombs but forgetting about the "human wrecks" who "struggle[d] for their bare existence." He provided a chilling description of Germany's descent into Nazism and the destruction of the country for Canadian readers:

> Millions of people were on the move, fleeing from a fate that had already caught up with them. And thousands ended their own lives when the dawn heralded the coming of a new day. The Witches' Sabbath was over, the glamour faded. You can experience a catastrophe, but describing one is impossible . . . a flood may have disastrous consequences, and the panic spreading in the wake of a fire in a cinema doesn't bear thinking about; but to imagine the ground dropping away from under a nation of 60 million people is, to the human mind, inconceivable.[76]

In spite of the devastation, Cesinger described the attempts to rebuild by "the people . . . tormented by the Nazis" as hope in the chaos. These were the people, he wrote, who "were the ones spat upon as subhuman beings and stateless folk."[77] Cesinger played an active role in the Socialist Unity Party of Germany. His activism that had begun in Canada continued in war-torn Germany. He had found a new purpose in rebuilding the war-torn nation of his birth and continued his support for a renewal of the country in line with his activism.

Dan Chomicki survived his return. In Poland, he took up arms against fascism in Europe by joining the Polish Liberation Army while Poland was occupied by the Nazis. When the Nazis were driven out by the incoming Red Army, Chomicki was rewarded for his efforts, the Soviets claiming that he had been instrumental in winning key battles against the Nazis. He was promoted to colonel and awarded the Order of the Red Army for gallantry.[78]

Despite Chomicki's successes in Europe, Canada was never far from his mind. He wrote to his friends in Canada through a number of Ukrainian labour papers. In one letter in 1946, he described being visited by a Canadian-Ukrainian delegation that was surveying liberated Poland. Ever the proponent of communist ideology, Chomicki praised Canadian Communists for taking Stalin's new line: "You see, the situation was such that we were ready to unite with the devil himself as long as it would help us defeat Hitlerism and achieve true democracy." He told readers: "You shall see me soon in the film that will be shown at the Polish labour hall [in Winnipeg] when the delegation returns to Canada. Convey my best greetings to our parents and tell them that I hope to see them soon."[79] Chomicki made several attempts to visit his parents. Following the war, a number of Polish veterans were welcomed into Canada by the government. Chomicki approached the chargé d'affaires for a six-week visa to enter Canada, but no response from Canada was received in Warsaw. His spouse, Marie Ann Chomicki, wrote to Mackenzie King in 1947 to plead that Chomicki be allowed to enter Canada.[80] But her letter fell on deaf ears. For as much as the Liberals may have protested the deportations in the House when they were taking place, once in power they offered no help to the Chomicki family. External Affairs referred the issue to the RCMP, whose response was hardly surprising: no special consideration should be given. As L.H. Nicholson, assistant director of criminal investigation for the RCMP, noted, "this man [was] a communist." Nicholson added that the party or Ukrainian Communists might use Chomicki's visit as an attempt to stir up propaganda.[81]

Marie and her daughter were reunited with Chomicki in Poland, but he still made attempts to return to Canada. In 1952, he became head of the immigration department in Warsaw and planned to try to join the Polish Legation in Ottawa. External Affairs and the RCMP both ensured that no visa was granted to Chomicki. Marie and her daughter returned to Canada after Chomciki's death on 27 July 1957.[82] Prominent CPC member Leslie Morris honoured him in the labour paper the *Canadian Forward* and recalled how he had joined the Workers' Party with Chomicki in 1921. He recounted how Chomicki loved Canada dearly and "possessed a quiet bravery which stood him in good stead during the lonely years of village exile." Morris concluded the obituary: "The memory of this dear friend will remain with us, as well his story of police brutality in the Hungry Thirties."[83] Chomicki died in Poland still trying to find a way to return to the country he considered home.

Tomo Čačić continued to fight for the international communist movement after his deportation in 1933. With the aid of UK Communists who had been contacted by the CLDL, Čačić made a daring escape from his train car, which was to take him to Yugoslavia. From there, he made his way to the Soviet Union and wrote home to friends, praising Stalin's Soviet Union. Curiously, despite the praise, at the first opportunity Čačić left the Soviet Union and never again wrote as fondly of it as he had while he was there. It is possible that Čačić's brand of communism did not fit with Stalin's but that he knew enough to not say otherwise while in the Soviet Union. After the outbreak of the Spanish Civil War, Čačić left for Spain in March 1937 and joined the International Brigade for the defence of Republican Spain. It is presumed that he enlisted on his own accord. He was joined by several of his Canadian comrades, who were all from his Croatian hometown. During 1937–8, Čačić became captain in charge of a company fighting deep in enemy territory near Villanueva de Córdoba. Čačić stayed in the conflict until its conclusion and fought in Northern Catalonia until he was forced to flee with five hundred thousand others into France, where he then entered a concentration camp not far from Saint-Cyprien.[84] The RCMP continued to gather intelligence on Čačić, much like it did for Chomicki and Cesinger, from the ethnic labour press in Canada. Judging from the RCMP file, the service's officers took whatever information they acquired from translated papers at face value. Translators did not provide word-by-word translations but often summarized information they thought pertinent. The service so heavily relied on the press reports that it closed its file on Čačić when, in 1942, *Novosti*, a *Borba* successor, wrongly announced his death in Spain.[85]

According to Čačić, the concentration camp conditions were difficult to bear. He wrote to the ethnic paper *Slobodna Misao* (another successor to *Borba*) in 1940: "Although the workers are in good humour I can't wait to get out of this province because it rains 345 days a year. The weather here is miserable and changing almost 24 hours a day." The paper *Slobodna Misao* was known for its Croatian separatist sentiments as well as for being a Communist-controlled paper. The paper claimed in an article entitled "Croats and the War in Spain" that Republican victory in Spain would mean that "the international situation [would] favour the liberation struggle of the Croatian people."[86] Fascist influences were present in Croatia and were ultranationalist in nature, but Communist Croatians were deeply nationalistic as well. Čačić would have shared the paper's vision of a future proletarian-led state of Yugoslavia where nations, such as Croatia, were self-determining and retained their regional autonomy.

Years later, writing in 1958, Čačić described his condition in the camp as brutal. People slept outside with no protection from the elements, and meals were "100 grams of bread and cabbage a day," with people waiting in line for hours for water.[87] Čačić claimed that several of his wounded friends had died in the camp. He had harsh words for the French government: "Not one leading capitalist regime in the world was as brutal as the French. They are real barbarians." He found it surprising that even though France was "occupied by Germans and both times Russia, England and America saved them," they had no qualms after the Second World War about "starting wars in their colonies that were fighting for their freedom."[88]

Čačić left the camp in 1941 and began working in a mine in northern France until he became aware of Hitler's invasion of Yugoslavia. He crossed through occupied France (without a visa or passport) and entered Nazi Germany. He worked in the construction industry until he could secure a fake passport and entered Nazi-occupied Yugoslavia in January 1942. Čačić claimed that at this time he "was suffering from tuberculosis" and thus not really "capable of joining the Partisan war" (he writes: "I did not look like a man but as a dead body"). But "afraid to go home or to the hospital," he had no choice but "to go into the Partisan army."[89] Because Čačić could not risk being detected by officials for fear of being imprisoned or killed, he joined the Yugoslav Partisans instead of recuperating.[90] He joined for personal nationalist sentiments but also as a means of survival. He wrote: "In the army I had light duties, lectured in the front lines of war, later I was sent to do field work and I was responsible for West Lika and one area of the Croatian coast (Primorje) where I was an organizer of the Partisan group and transferred people & material from the island to the inland of the country. In October of 1943 I was injured in the right leg and sent to Italy for treatment and my leg was amputated above the knee and I was treated for TB."[91] He returned to Yugoslavia at war's end in 1945, retired at the age of fifty-four, and worked for twenty more years organizing workers' councils and living off a modest pension. He was no doubt proud to witness the formation of a Communist state he had had a hand in creating, one that was strongly nationalist and not under Stalin's rule.[92]

Čačić was frequently celebrated in Canada's ethnic labour press, specifically the Yugoslav papers. In 1961, he was referred to as "a genuine revolutionary" and a "pioneer of the revolutionary press in Canada." In his later years, the RCMP referred to him as the "notorious Tom Čačić."[93] Čačić died on 10 September 1969. On 19 September 1969, *Jedinstvo* printed the following:

> Tomo Čačić died on Tuesday in Višnjevac near Osijek at the age of 73 . . . It seemed as if the distance between Yugoslavia and those faraway metropolises of America, prairies of the Soviet Union and combat fields of Spain actually meant nothing at all to him. Until today, despite his age of 73, he never considered giving up as an option.[94]

Čačić, like the members of the Halifax Ten, was deeply dedicated to his communist beliefs and rarely shied away from conflict. Revolution was part of the class struggle, and when it materialized, these transnational activists joined the battle, notwithstanding its location, even if the price of fighting was their lives. They saw little conflict in taking up the independence movements that were linked to their people or region while still remaining devoted Communists and part of their own communist nation of sorts. They viewed conflicts such as the Spanish Civil War as another front in an international war. These activists may not have had a country or state to call their own, but they were not without a people.

The effect of normalizing emergency measures on immigrant members of the CPC was profound. Deportation enabled the government to define the qualities and boundaries of citizenship, including what kind of political ideology citizens should subscribe to if they were to belong in Canada. It also contributed to ideas of security. For state authorities, the physical removal of communists from the country would make Canada safer. Such nation-building was possible because of the state's ability to use law to judge politics and reduce transnational activists to the status of *homo sacer*. These immigrants defined themselves as being part of a people and the communist movement rather than as part of a place, and as a result, the state could isolate them outside the legal protections granted to citizens. As *homo sacer*, they had no legal right to challenge this isolation.

Section 41 was the main immigration law that maintained their status as noncitizens because of their communist politics. Section 98 also had an important role in these deportations. Evidence seized in the raids against the CPC in August 1931 was crucial to demonstrating the deportees' links to the CPC and its subsidiary organizations. The testimony from RCMP officers such as Sergeant Leopold gave the deportation hearings an air of legitimacy, even if these hearings did not afford deportees anywhere near the same legal rights as a criminal trial. Although the government continued in its quest to purge Canada of foreign activists, the majority of the Halifax Ten had discovered communism in Canada. They became Communists because of the working conditions on the job, which were dangerous, underpaid, and demeaning.

Even within the Canadian communist movement, there were divisions that could not be reconciled, as some, including Sembaj, Vaara, and Pohjansalo, discovered. What they believed their movement to be was not what Stalin dictated it was. For good or for ill, these immigrants struggled abroad to see their movement realized. Canada was just one of the many fronts in what they thought was an international struggle. During the process, they continued to see themselves not as stateless beings but, as Arvo Vaara claimed, as "citizens of the world."[95] While these immigrants engaged in their individual battles overseas, the Canadian government continued its struggle against communism at home, and at an ever-accelerating pace.

5

Outlaws

During the 1930s, the government policy of deporting foreign-born Communists occurred alongside a general campaign of repression against all communists, both real and suspected. The mid-1930s served as fertile ground for left-wing activism. The Depression kept unemployment high, and the authorities continued to use law enforcement to disrupt demonstrations, protests, and strikes. Section 98 was a means of combating communism, but its success was mixed. The CPC was driven underground, but it was not completely eliminated. The goal of the authorities was to label the CPC's subsidiary organizations as unlawful, or at the very least, have leading members of these groups sent to jail. Section 98 was one tool in the legal arsenal, but more could be made.

Previous studies of the period have focused on specific repressive events, repression in specific provinces, or repression as it related to RCMP surveillance.[1] Section 98, and the continued normalizing of emergency measures, was central to the repression of the period. Industry leaders and prominent citizens across the country kept pressure on the government to crush the forces of unrest that communism bred, but the CPC resisted this offensive. By hunting communists, the authorities continued targeting the effects of the unemployment and inequality produced by capitalism rather than these injustices themselves. Communists and radical leftists continued to exist. Lawmakers continued to persist in their belief that law could protect Canadians and keep them safe, and more exceptional laws, even more far-reaching than Section 98, were created.

Once policy-makers had agreed that an emergency law could be used in peacetime, more were easily created. In addition, police ramped up the violence against activists. The trial of Arthur "Slim"

Evans, and of lesser-known activists, demonstrates how Section 98 was used in a multitude of ways by law enforcement, from intimidating hall owners to facilitating frequent searches of persons and property. The state had the right to judge people's politics, and the police treated communists and suspected Communists as being outside of law, beating them indiscriminately, or in some cases, killing them. The murder of Montreal's Nicholas Zynchuck reveals how the state could kill a suspected Communist and not be guilty of homicide. Section 98 became an instrument of terror, and it certainly sparked feelings of terror in those who experienced its effects. Police violence and brutal crackdowns were now part of what constituted security.

Defending the Need for "Unusual Legislation," and the CPC Response

The federal government continued repressing Communists and fellow travellers through the use of the criminal law following the Buck et al. trial. There was support for this strategy from like-minded individuals in industry and in provincial and municipal governments. For instance, in March 1933, the City of Prince Albert Police Committee informed Prime Minister Bennett that it had adopted the 23 December 1932 resolution passed by Vancouver's Board of Police Commissioners. The resolution sought a tightening of the Immigration Act, as well as more deportations, which would stop enabling Communist agitators to remain in Canada.[2] The Princeton Board of Trade thought the foreign element was dangerous in Canada, and it too wanted more deportations. Conservative elements in ethnic communities denounced communism, such as the Ukrainian Sporting Association on 18 June 1933.[3] Winnipeg mayor Ralph Webb, instrumental in pushing the fight against the CPC in 1931, continued the pressure on the federal government following the Buck trial. Manitoba had still not pursued action against Communists with Section 98, and Webb vented his frustrations with the federal government. Writing to H.H. Stevens, minister of trade and commerce, he stated that the "situation was getting serious in Winnipeg" and questioned how long the government would allow Communist groups to continue operating.[4]

Bennett was receptive to the anti-communist letters and information. He continued to forward any intelligence he received and gave people advice on what to do about communists in their area. He kept tabs on any information his ministers received, such as a letter Immigration Minister Gordon received in April 1932 from lawyer J.C. MacCorkindale of Toronto. MacCorkindale had been told by one Joe

Gallagher that Communists were planning parades where they would wear returned badges similar to ones worn by the Canadian Legion. MacCorkindale worried about the effect on the public if the demonstration became disorderly. He offered his aid in breaking up the organization that wanted to lead the march. Doing so, he believed, would return the "majority of the rank and file . . . back to proper Conservative lines of thinking." It is not known whether Bennett took him up on the offer.[5]

Bennett continued to do his part in combating communism. For instance, he kept in close touch with J.R. Smith of West Canadian Collieries Ltd. in Blairmore, Alberta, asking him to advise him of Communist movements. Smith told Bennett late in 1932 that reds were active in strikes and among the unemployed and that the government needed to prevent further penetration of red influence, particularly within the city government, where the reds had a majority and thus had the "foreign element" under their control.[6] Bennett encouraged citizens in other provinces, including Quebec, to press the attorney general of the province to pursue Section 98 charges against Communist groups.[7] Bennett continued his attempts to gather intelligence. For example, after he received a letter from Alec Lockwood, in Manitoba, in which Lockwood wrote that agitators were mostly of "foreign birth," Bennett asked him to contact the attorney general and asked for the names of suspected Communists "in confidence" so that he could try to have them deported. He congratulated Lockwood for his "fine sense of public duty as a citizen of Canada." The prime minister was more than eager to try to deport suspected Communists, even if done under the nose of the provincial authorities.[8]

Other fellow Conservatives, such as Hugh Guthrie and Ontario attorney general Colonel William Price, did their best to spread the message about the evils of communism and defend Section 98. Price gave a number of speeches at conservative organizations, such as at the annual Orange Order celebration in Kingston in 1932, the Women's Canadian Club, and Knox Church in Toronto at the behest of the Canadian Christian Crusade, a prominent anti-communist group in the area. He gave a guest lecture at a summer school for the Young Conservatives Association in 1933 in which he defended Section 98. He told his young audience how Canada had had a "foretaste of revolution" with the Winnipeg General Strike in 1919. He equated Section 98 with similar legislation from other countries, such as Britain's Defence of the Realm Act, arguing that "the passing of unusual legislation to meet the needs of perilous times is one of the duties of government." Section 98, he argued, ensured that Canada was protected from the violent overthrow of the government, for "communism or fascism are foreign to Canada." Section 98, he claimed, was designed to ensure a peaceful progression of governments. Section 98 was civilized. Its opponents were not.[9]

At his other speaking engagements, Price spread the message that it was communism that was pulling people away from Christianity, that its purpose was the breaking up of the family, and that "our civilization is based on Christian teachings." Section 98 was a tool to help preserve a Christian, paternal, and capitalist version of the family – a civilized family in his view. Communism, as mentioned in chapter 2, threatened the masculine, hetero norms of the family in which leading government officials believed. Anxieties about how communism threatened the family played out during the unemployment marches in 1931, when predominately single unemployed men marched in the streets of numerous towns, and in how relief was distributed: single men were ineligible for relief. The government's strategy for dealing with the Depression was not only about improving the economic situation; it was about maintaining a particular construction of the family. Men with families were eligible for relief to keep the unit together, while single, unemployed men were treated as potential threats. [10]

Ethnicity was another factor in the government's evaluation of who was wrecking Canada's democracy and threatening its interpretation of security. When Price addressed the annual meeting of the Liberal-Conservative Association of Toronto, with the prime minister in attendance, he posed this question to his audience in regards to foreigners: "Why let them ruin the country?" He answered it by reminding people that "any leader today must do things for the state even if it hurts his party" and that no actions could be taken "that wound in any way the state."[11] The state had to be protected at all costs, even if it meant taking unpopular or antidemocratic actions.

The normalization of emergency powers continued as Canada approached the 1930s. In 1927, Mackenzie King's government made significant changes to the War Measures Act (WMA). It removed Sections 2 and 5 from the WMA, two sections that specifically referenced war. "War" in the short title of the act was now equated with "emergency," and evidence of insurrections (which included war) moved into Section 2 under the subtitle "Evidence of War." The new long title, "An Act to Confer Certain Powers upon the Governor in Council in the Event of War, Invasion, or Insurrection," cemented the act as a broad emergency power more powerful than the British Emergency Powers Act of 1920.[12]

The Unemployment and Farm Relief Act of 1931 stipulated that relief for the unemployed was a local matter, but provided the government with the ability to spend as much as it needed and gave it the power to lend money to provinces or municipalities should they find themselves in need. Bennett claimed that the government needed greater power to deal with threats to law and order. The formal title of the act was "An Act to Confer Certain Powers upon the Governor in Council in Respect to Unemployment and Farm Relief, and the Maintenance of Peace, Order and Good Government in Canada." The preamble stated that the act would give the government "the powers necessary to insure the speedy and unhampered prosecution" of administering relief and "the maintenance of peace, order and good government."[13] The act never stipulated what these broad powers were or the measures they would take, but Bennett's introduction of the bill in the House left little doubt. He claimed that his government needed broad discretionary powers to combat groups that spread "their pernicious political doctrines" and that his government would "free this country from those who ha[d] proved themselves unworthy of Canadian citizenship," that is, communists.

Mackenzie King countered by holding up a copy of the War Measures Act and claimed that his "right hon. friend [was] asking for precisely the same powers" outside of a state of war. The irony was rich given the changes King's government had made to the WMA just four years earlier. Bennett was unwavering: "This is a land of freedom . . . where men may think what they will and say what they will, as long as they do not attack the foundations upon which our civilization has been built."[14] Bennett combined the emergency economic measures with powers he claimed the government needed to combat communists. These broad powers were designed for use in peacetime to manage the threat communists posed. While the act was set to expire in March 1932, it served as an important signal that open expression of dissent would not be tolerated. Bennett had effectively given law enforcement the government's blessing to engage in a widespread crackdown against left-wing activists.[15]

The government's belief that the Great Depression was an exceptional period provided it with another opportunity to normalize emergency measures to deal with anyone threatening "peace, order, and good government." Lawmakers saw the aforementioned as the cornerstones of an ordered and secure society. Authorities were permitted to use whatever powers were necessary. The act provided a broad mandate for the type of measures the government could use against anyone threatening these ideals. These measures were broader in their scope than Section 98 ever was. It was getting easier for emergency laws to function as normal ones, and the act set the tone for the repression that followed.

Not surprisingly, anyone who sought Section 98's removal was regarded as a threat to civilization and disloyal, and this perspective was reflected in the debates of the period, with J.S. Woodsworth and other progressive members being regularly accused of being unpatriotic for seeking Section 98's repeal.[16] Because no other law could "touch communism," Bennett scoffed at the idea of repealing Section 98.[17] The Communist agitation of the day, Conservatives claimed, proved Section 98's necessity.[18] It was now not only normal but necessary. The Conservative Party was not alone in its assessment of the evils of communism. Not only did numerous press outlets and law enforcement back the government's actions against Communists, as previous chapters have revealed, but many in the legal establishment supported the government. The *Canadian Bar Review*, for instance, remarked in regards to the Buck trial that the jury had "launched a movement against the Communist International." It further claimed, "More than that, we may now begin to contemplate the failure of the attempt to Russianize this planet into the worst of all possible worlds."[19] Even though the government had support for its tough stance on communism, the CI and the CPC sought to counter the offensive.

The Illegal CPC

In the fall of 1931, just before the Buck trial began, the party and the Communist International (CI) began preparing for the possibility that the party would be outlawed. The CPC ramped up its propaganda machine just before the trial, instructing the Canadian Labor Defense League (CLDL) to start a defence fund and begin mobilizing to agitate against Section 98 and deportations. The party leadership expressed its frustration with the lack of publicity the trial was receiving, which the leaders deemed was partly the fault of members. In October 1931, the CPC leadership admitted there was a lack of money available for fighting legal cases and that members were putting local cases ahead of the case involving the CPC leadership. The party executive classified it as a failure to "understand the seriousness" of the Buck trial.[20]

The CI advanced its own theories besides the finding of illegality for why the trial had been a failure for the party. It argued that the party had been caught unprepared: it had insufficient organizational strength, and a "deep-rooted legalism" accounted for serious mistakes during the trial. The members' defence was based on the theory of the "automatic collapse" of capitalism and failed to portray the CPC as the organizational instrumental in its collapse; the defence should have focused less on defending the inevitability of revolution and more on using the "court to explain the party program to the broad masses."[21] According to the CI, there was no point in having a CPC, at least as per the testimony of the CPC leadership during the trial, in which they argued that revolution would come automatically. The CI warned that this argument was folly, as the bourgeoisie would never voluntarily surrender its power. The members' failure, according to the CI, was that they were too focused on defending themselves and, by extension, the party. The propaganda message was especially important to the CI, and the failure of the members to push it was the result of "right opportunism" within the party.[22]

While the CI chided party members for not using the trial as a valuable outlet for propaganda, it still believed that the party could survive. It had lost few members and still had an underground recruitment campaign. The CI correctly recognized that the party was illegal only in Ontario. A strategy was needed for members in other provinces, as it would be "erroneous to imagine that the decision of the Ontario court [did] not affect the position in other provinces." In other words, other provinces would try to copy Ontario's strategy, and the party should assume this would happen. The question was now: How could the party survive, still be political, and resist the offence in such a repressive climate?

Public meetings were stopped immediately, but the party message itself would not be hidden; it would be disseminated through other legal forms.[23] The strategies for operating in a state of illegality or semi-legality were sent to all party districts in October 1931, before the verdict in the Buck trial was issued. The strategy involved holding underground leadership committees, having only small party groups, keeping no membership records, only referring to members by numbers, holding party meetings in homes, and keeping organizers known to police away from demonstrations. In addition, a reserve list of party secretaries would be created, party "secrets" would be held at secret locations, and locations for printing would change often. If a member was arrested, they would deny membership; if members were charged under Section 98, the cases would be fought individually and not as a group. Members were dissuaded from travelling in groups. The strategy included the creation of a counter-intelligence unit and the creation of a theory paper on illegality. Members were encouraged to continue participating in elections.[24]

The strategy for maintaining party operations in a state of semi-illegality worked because despite the authorities' best efforts, no other CPC-controlled group was ever found guilty under Section 98. Ironically, the authorities' legal offensive against the party in 1931 made it more difficult to stop and contain the CPC. The trial of 1931 had the effect of scattering the party into the wind. CPC members joined other legal organizations, enabling the CPC to continue being political. Section 98 contributed to the growth of communism and made it more difficult to contain.

The CLDL's advocacy for Section 98's repeal was having an effect on how authorities charged individuals with violating Section 98. A letter from Joseph Sedgwick to Colonel Price details the government strategy for dealing with Communists. As chapters 1 and 2 outline, state authorities often viewed communism as a foreign, imported culture linked to immigrant activists. Immigrant members of communities, such as the Finns, Ukrainians, and Yiddish-speaking Jews, and immigrants from Eastern Europe nations like Poland and the former Yugoslavia were often considered more susceptible to communism. Many of the CPC's members were from these communities. Authorities equally despised the British Communist, who was viewed as being corrupted by a foreign and dangerous culture. Indeed, the Anglo-Saxon Communist was the state's main concern after the deportation of foreign CPC members in 1932. Explaining that he had contacted the RCMP and Bennett about the issue, Sedgwick reported that he did not believe that "foreign agitators" posed much of a threat anymore.[25] He thought that the government should not worry, "within limits," as the Communists did a good job attracting opposition, adding: "I do not think it possible for them to convert our Anglo-Saxon stock." Sedgwick's letter was frank in its assessment. Immigrants from the listed countries were traditionally the focus of the government, as these countries were where it thought communism originated. Anglo-Saxons were described as superior and able to resist the influence of Communists, unlike some immigrants.[26]

Sedgwick advised Price that for language groups and other subsidiaries of the CPC, Section 98 should be "disregarded." Prosecutions should take place "only where there is actual violence, sedition or any other breach of the established and uncontroversial law." Sedgwick's letter revealed that Section 98 would now be used selectively since the controversy surrounding it was growing. While foreign-born Communists did not represent the threat that they once had, Sedgwick believed that Bennett "was absolutely right" when he claimed that the CPC "was now the CLDL" and that future prosecutions against prominent Communists should be "against [A.E.] Smith and the other Anglo-Saxons or English-speaking foreigners in charge of the CLDL, and against *The Worker*." If authorities pursued a Section 98 charge, the RCMP may have enough evidence for a conviction. He concluded his letter by restating that the "influence of propaganda among the foreign born, while annoying, [was] not dangerous." The government's deportation campaign against foreign-born activists, from Sedgwick and Bennett's perspective, worked, and the focus was now on Anglo-Saxon leaders. For despite their assumed ethnic superiority, it was presumed that Anglo-Saxon Communists and "English speaking foreigners" posed a risk to Canada's Anglo-Saxon stock.[27]

Feelings of vengeance were a factor in Bennett's targeting of Smith and the CLDL. Responding to the mayor of Verdun in Quebec, who congratulated Bennett for removing A.E. Smith from his office during a meeting (in November 1933) when Smith advocated for the release of the Eight, an end to deportations, and Section 98's repeal, Bennett wrote that it was time to stop "Smith and his followers" from spreading "propaganda of gross misrepresentation" and to prevent liberty from "degenerat[ing] into license."[28] Bennett, a devout Methodist, despised Smith, presumably because of Smith's past as a Methodist minister. Bennett viewed Smith as a traitor to his former profession or, worse, to God. Bennett replied to a letter from J.A. Miller, who complained about a sermon at an American United Church by a pastor who knew Smith. He responded by saying, "If he knows Smith, he should know his history . . . everyone of the old officials of the Church know the type of man he is."[29]

The government's focus for the remainder of Bennett's term in office was on Anglo-Saxon Communists and those groups affiliated with the CPC. Section 98 was now reserved for exceptional cases. The RCMP thought that one particularly "dangerous" Anglo-Saxon operating in BC was the next big CPC fish Section 98 could ensnare. He was known by his nickname, Slim Evans.

"An Extreme Radical"

In April 1932, Arthur "Slim" Evans came under the focus of the RCMP. Born on 24 April 1890 in Toronto, Evans moved west at an early age, seeking work as a carpenter. He had a history with the RCMP, having been convicted of stealing union funds while working for the United Mine Workers of America in Alberta. At the time of his arrest, Evans was working as an organizer for the Workers' Unity League (WUL) and was active across the West. The RCMP

thought that his previous conviction would prove an embarrassment
for any local union leaders that wanted his help in organizing workers, but this was not the case. The RCMP regarded him as an "extreme
radical." Constable N.E. Macfarlane described Evans and the Unity
League as "making the only worthwhile progress towards organization" in BC among needle tradesmen and longshoremen.[30]

Evans's RCMP file remains heavily redacted. Intelligence on
Evans often came from other workers who acted as informants for the
RCMP but were active in organizing unions themselves. Their motives
were competitive because providing information to the RCMP could
hamper the competition that the WUL was posing to other unions.
For instance, Evans successfully persuaded the Fishermen's Union
to adopt the radical position of no negotiation or arbitration. The
Lumber Workers Industrial Union was adopting the militant WUL's
models, much to the chagrin of other groups such as the American
Federation of Labor.[31]

Evans left Vancouver to attend a conference on the unemployed in
Ottawa and on his way back to BC went on a speaking tour throughout the West on behalf of the National Unemployed Workers Association, a subsidiary of the WUL. He gave numerous speeches supporting
striking workers. Vancouver city police notified the RCMP that if
Evans returned to Vancouver, they would arrest him on a charge of
vagrancy for his being a general nuisance. The RCMP was eager to
stop Evans and was forced to admit that his speaking abilities left
him in "in a class by himself," as one informant put it.[32] The attorney
general of BC took a keen interest in Evans. He was investigating
communism in the province and thought Evans was the reason it was
spreading. The question for the authorities was how to silence him.
He was careful to spread the communist message in his speeches,
but he denied his membership in the CPC. The authorities' opportunity would come when Evans's organizing skills were called upon by
Tulameen coal mine workers in Princeton, BC, in September 1932.

The workers sought the WUL's assistance to help them win back
a 10 per cent wage cut the company refused to restore.[33] The WUL
notified Evans and suggested he include Princeton in his itinerary.
Evans held several meetings in November where he denounced the
government, the mine managers and owners, and the actions of the
provincial police and RCMP in breaking up strikes. In one meeting,
the RCMP reported, Evans said that change could not be done by
way of the ballot box and that workers had to fight to make gains,
but not damage property as workers needed infrastructure intact after
capitalism was overthrown. He denied being a member of the CPC

but stated that he believed in their message. Evans stated that he was amazed that all that stood between what workers needed was some storefront glass and that instead of singing "God Save the King," they should sing "God Save Our Class" and "To Hell with the King."[34] The situation in Princeton was tense, and the mine manager, George Murray, and several other loyal employees attended Evans's meetings and warned him to leave town. Witnesses reported that while police frequently stood watch over the meetings, none were present when Murray and his entourage arrived one night to attend an Evans speech. It is hardly surprising that local authorities despised Evans. At one meeting he reportedly pointed at the police at the back of the hall and said, "Just because those two yellow legs are standing at the back don't let them stop you from voicing your opinions or speaking your piece." At another Princeton meeting, he reportedly walked up to a police officer and offered advice on how the police could curb his activities: "Make sure your gun is loaded, look down the barrel, and pull the trigger."

Evans and other workers claimed that the police worked closely with the local Klu Klux Klan to assist them in intimidating the workers not to strike, and some strikers like John Beronich said they had been badly beaten by Klan members. Witnesses stated that Murray visited the homes of employees that spoke out against him and beat them. Evans, along with four others, was arrested on 7 December, four days after the strike took a violent turn. Some witnessed police ride into strikers on horseback and club pedestrians and anyone in sight, including a fourteen-year-old boy.[35] One man, Eli Djakovick, claimed he had been beaten so badly that he suffered permanent hearing loss. The strike and Evans organizing were political actions that would not be tolerated.

The RCMP was unsure of what charge to lay against Evans. Much like the Buck et al. trial, Evans's arrest had more to do with the authorities exercising their right to judge his politics than his breaking a law. They arrested him without knowing what law to charge him with violating. They wanted to put Evans away in prison for as long as possible, and they wanted to use him to snag other CPC-allied groups. Section 98 offered the best solution because it would take him out of the Communist organizing job, potentially for years, and give the Crown the chance to snag groups linked to him. In the RCMP reports on Evans, S.T. Wood pondered whether it might be possible to use Evans as a link to the WUL and Mine Workers' Union of Canada to get both organizations banned. Crown attorney H. Bullock-Webster, who tried the case against him, was in agreement with charging Evans with violating Section 98(1) and asked the RCMP for any evidence it had seized from local raids in Vancouver so that the Crown could make the connection between Evans and the CPC. The Crown would then link him to other groups, and their unlawfulness would be established.[36] The *Worker* reported that initially all the men arrested with Evans had been charged with violating Section 98. It later reported that only Evans was being held for violating Section 98.

The reports reflected a change in the Crown's strategy. Evans was initially charged with being a member of an unlawful organization, the CPC. But the Crown abandoned the idea of linking him to the CPC or WUL because proving the connection would have been extremely difficult; there was no direct evidence. His charges were later changed to violating Section 98(8) for giving speeches in November of 1932. The Crown alleged that he advocated and taught that the economic and governmental system should be changed by force.[37] After initially denying him bail, it granted it on 29 January 1933.

Though the mine owners eventually gave in to the strikers' demands on 17 December, the situation was still volatile for much of 1933. The police used Section 98 to strike fear into the community and intimidate them. Former strikers had their houses raided frequently by police with search warrants, granted under Section 98(6), looking for seditious literature. Several hall owners were warned by police that they could face charges under Section 98 if they continued renting their halls for any union or worker-led meetings. Evans claimed that he had been searched three times over the corresponding months and that every location he visited had been searched by police for evidence. He said that on 28 April 1933, he was kidnapped by approximately twenty-five armed men and taken to Coyle, seventy-five miles from Princeton, and placed on a train to Vancouver. He claimed that the men included two police constables and the president of the Board of Trade, P. Gregory, who told Evans that if he returned to Princeton he would do so at his own risk. Evans exited the train at his first opportunity and took the first one back to Princeton.

The men were charged with kidnapping, but at their trial, witnesses for the accused stated that they had all had tea together and that Evans voluntarily accepted the paid train ticket bought by a citizens' "volunteer committee." The judge dismissed the charges. Evans's trial was originally scheduled to begin on 12 June 1933, but he submitted an affidavit of prejudice in the selection of the jury on the grounds that it was not representative of all the electoral districts in the area, as was earlier stipulated. He claimed the continual police harassment hampered his ability to formulate a defence. The trial was pushed back to September.[38]

Evans's trial began on 11 September 1933 in Vernon, BC, in the Superior Court of British Columbia, with Justice W.A. Macdonald presiding. His trial provides a window into how an individual Section 98 case was handled by the court in contrast to the group prosecution of the CPC. In addition, the trial reveals how the word "force" in Section 98 was interpreted by judges.

The trial began with a request from Evans's lawyer, Gordon Grant. Evans wanted to examine and cross-examine witnesses with his lawyer answering questions of law and suggesting questions to Evans for his cross-examinations. While the judge pondered the request, he did not allow it. Evans could sit with his counsel instead of in the prisoner's box, but he had to conduct his own defence, if that was what he wanted. However, Macdonald provided Evans with quite a bit of leeway during the trial and sometimes helped him formulate questions so that he could avoid asking leading ones, which he was prone to doing. Evans could still rely on Grant for advice when court was not in session and to present legal challenges such as requesting a dismissal.[39]

The Crown's case against him consisted of officer testimony and was designed, like the Buck et al. trial, to create a climate of fear because Evans was whipping up unrest and disorder. Numerous officers testified that at meetings with coal miners, Evans stated that while he was not a member of the CPC, he agreed with their platform and thought capitalism around the world should fall. Evans's statements at organizing meetings were the main evidence against him.[40] Similar speeches were made on two other occasions in November of 1932. Evans managed to have officers admit that he was a menace to the community and business because of his organizing.[41] In one exchange in which Evans cross-examined officer Corporal Thompson, Thompson claimed Evans's instructions to workers to be "militant," which was the equivalent to asking them to engage in violence since that was how Thompson interpreted the meaning of "militant." In addition, Thompson claimed, "The audience must be taken into consideration . . . an audience of men that barely understand English, hearing terms like that, are affected thereby." According to Thompson, foreign workers might run to their dictionaries to look up "militant" and realize that it means using "force," in which case Evans's speeches could easily inflame the minds of malleable foreigners. Evans retorted by asking Thompson if he had ever thought to look up the word himself. Thompson claimed he had not.[42]

Throughout this cross-examination, Evans tried to demonstrate that police repression was used against the strikers. He confronted

Thompson about threatening hall owners with Section 98. Thompson admitted that hall owners had been read the penalties of Section 98(5) but claimed that officers had not forced any halls to ban meetings from taking place and had given only "advice." He acknowledged that several halls had closed.[43] But Evans's admirable defence of the miners and his exposing of police brutality in halting the strike did little in addressing the charges against him.[44]

At the heart of the case against him was the interpretation of the word "force." What force was Evans advocating? He tried to demonstrate that force could be interpreted in several ways. At the opening of the case for the defence, his counsel presented a motion calling for a dismissal on account of there having been no crime committed. Grant argued that even if Evans was telling people that the workers would take over the government, he never said when nor advocated that they do it. Grant contended that this was a matter of opinion or "prophecy." This was not teaching or advocating the use of force to produce economic or governmental change. Grant stated that had Evans told the workers at the meetings to "go out and use force to obtain communism," only then would he have committed a Section 98 offence.[45]

These arguments had no sway with the court. Section 98, according to the trial judge, was created "to stop the teaching of communism in Canada." Evans was more interested in exposing police misconduct than addressing the charges. His defence consisted of calling witnesses of the police use of force during the strike to testify, along with several others who had witnessed his speeches and did not believe he advocated the overthrow of the government. The vast majority of his witnesses reiterated the events of the strike and the police crackdown against the miners.[46] In addressing the jury, Justice Macdonald repeated Justice Wright's comments about Section 98 in the Buck et al. trial. He reminded the jury that in regards to Section 98, "Whether that be good law, or bad law, it does not concern you . . . that is the law of the land." He then quoted Justice Wright's explanation from the Buck et al. trial that Section 98 was exceptional, but it was the law. It was normal.[47] Evans was convicted on all counts and received a one-year prison sentence.

Evans's appeal was heard in February 1934 in the BC Court of Appeal before five justices, Justice M.A. MacDonald presiding. Grant represented him and argued that no evidence of guilt had been produced at the trial. He claimed that the statements his client had uttered did not constitute an advocacy of force and that any law-abiding citizen could have uttered them and not be found guilty of violating

Section 98. But the judges argued that Evans's statement to the strikers, "Then we will have to fight," constituted an advocacy of force. Grant argued that when the judge had stated that Section 98 was created to stop the spread of communism, he influenced the jury. MacDonald dismissed the claim, arguing that no objection was made at trial and that the "trial judge merely stated his opinion." Justice McPhillips summed up the sentiments of the judges when he claimed that Evans's "vituperation" of the police demonstrated that he thought "all those in authority should be subverted . . . It was all a means to an end of getting rid of the authority of the government." His appeal was dismissed on 6 March, and the judges ruled that his sentence would begin on that day, even though Evans had been in custody since his conviction in September 1933. This had the effect of adding six months to his sentence.[48]

Much like at the Buck et al. trial, Section 98 enabled the Crown to claim that the advocacy of certain ideas was a criminal act. No evidence demonstrated that Evans had taught or encouraged anyone to use force to overthrow the government. His utterances in favour of force were directed at the miners in attendance at the meeting; they had to fight to defend their position by striking, an intolerable political action for the authorities. The broad reach of Section 98 was such that innocuous statements were construed by judges to mean that Evans was advocating that people engage in armed rebellion against the government. The section was used to curb organizing activities and silence union supporters, actions that the authorities believed created a safer and more secure society.

Evans's case demonstrated how without actually charging an individual, the authorities used Section 98 as a form of intimidation to break up or prevent public meetings and to continually provide police with the legal authority to search for seditious material. It enabled sovereign power to judge individuals, and their politics, without a trial. If the authorities suspected individuals were Communists or supporters, Section 98 provided the legal means to use repression to demonstrate what politics were unacceptable for Canadians.

The law provided police with the ability to inspire feelings of terror in the population by giving them the legal authority to continue to harass and intimidate suspected "reds." In addition, Evans's case revealed how the CI advised members to deny CPC membership, which many did when confronted.[49] But the strategy had no effect on the ability of the authorities to prosecute someone for violating Section 98, as judges had a large degree of leeway in their interpretation of the word "force" in the section. The authorities reserved their use of Section 98 for prominent CPC members so as to avoid controversy, and as a means of intimidating others, such as hall owners.

The Other Cases

Throughout the 1930s and before Section 98's 1936 repeal, more Section 98 charges took place, as did protests against it amid widespread unemployment. Clashes between police and strikers/protesters occurred across the country. Large-scale arrests were becoming commonplace. During some of the larger clashes with police, it was not unheard of for fifty or more persons to be arrested at one time. These arrests were occurring in nearly every province across the country.[50] No doubt Bennett's anti-communist fervour increased as the unrest continued, and so did his fear of it. Bennett surprised his fellow Conservatives with how far he was willing to prepare for revolution. In 1932, the WUL organized a demonstration of the unemployed and held a conference in Ottawa. A delegation was sent to meet Bennett, but he agreed to meet only on the steps of Parliament. He had a strong message for the group. An armoured car patrolled the grounds along with two armed RCMP detachments, while a third mounted detachment lay hidden but at the ready. This deployment was arranged to meet a delegation of twelve workers armed with a petition. After a heated exchange of ideologies, the men walked away in an anticlimactic fashion. The conservative *Ottawa Journal* described this charade as un-British and decried it, saying, "This Chicago-like flaunting of fire-arms . . . smacks more of fascism than of Canadian constitutional authority."[51] Bennett seemed to want to barricade Parliament for the revolution that never came.

Documented cases of Section 98 from within this tense climate remain difficult to trace because many provincial archives purged their trial transcripts from the 1930s. The best source of evidence of Section 98 prosecutions is the radical labour press. Mainstream press outlets reported only on large, well-known cases like Buck et al. and to some extent the Evans trial. But papers such as the CPC's the *Worker* went to great lengths to keep track of Section 98's use against the paper's friends and allies. These stories contained their fair share of anticapitalist rhetoric, but the reporting does not seem questionable or inaccurate when stories that appeared in the *Worker*, such as those from the Buck et al. trial, are compared to mainstream papers.

The *Worker* reported on three Section 98 cases in 1932. The first involved Steve Koslov in Montreal. Koslov was charged with violating subsection 3 of Section 98 in the summer of 1932 while distributing antideportation leaflets on behalf of the CLDL. Koslov was searched by police, who found a button with the words "Build the revolutionary movement." Presumably, the unlawful organization he was a member of was the CLDL. At his trial on 21 June, the Crown attempted to link Koslov and his button to the leaflets he was distributing and the CLDL, which the defence argued had nothing to do with his charges. The defence argued that the button was not displayed or worn, as Section 98 required; it was found in Koslov's pocket. On 28 June, Koslov was acquitted. The judge agreed with the defence, reasoning that Koslov was not wearing the button as Section 98 required. The wording of Section 98 enabled Koslov to escape conviction.[52]

Another Section 98 case involved George Kellog. The story in the *Worker* described the pretrial hearing. Kellog was unemployed and arrested under Section 98 for distributing leaflets protesting the Bennett government's relief camps for single, unemployed men. W. Ogden, an organizer for an ex-servicemen's organization who worked undercover as a police agent, was the star witness for the Crown. But the judge failed to find enough evidence for the case to proceed, and Kellog was released.[53]

A case involving Section 98 appeared in Port Arthur on 8 December 1932. The *Worker* reported that Slim Whalen, an immigrant of unknown origins living at 81 Cumberland, Port Arthur, had been ordered deported after being convicted of "registering at a hotel under a false name." His property was reportedly seized under Section 98. Apparently, the CLDL lawyer representing Whalen angered the judge when he suggested that if a "London banker" had registered under the wrong name, no one would have noticed. The judge allegedly claimed that he had never been so disrespected in his thirty-five years as a judge. Trial records for this period from Port Arthur could not be located. It is not known why Whalen's property was seized under Section 98 nor what the initial charge against him was. Nor could his deportation be confirmed. "Slim Whalen" was a nickname.[54]

Several cases of Section 98 and acts of police repression against activists did garner more attention and coverage, both in the *Worker* and in mainstream papers such as the *Toronto Star* and the *Globe*. On 12 January 1933, at a meeting of unemployed workers that was designed to organize an Ontario hunger march to protest relief conditions, the Toronto police's red squad entered the meeting and arrested everyone in attendance – forty-five people in all. Two individuals, George Beatty and James Baker, were reportedly charged with violating Section 98, but court records could not be located to confirm whether they were actually tried under Section 98. The case may have been similar to the case against those arrested alongside Evans, where the Crown opted to try the accused with violating a lesser offence so as to increase the likelihood of a conviction. It was a common tactic at the time. For instance, in December 1932, the WUL helped organize an Alberta hunger march, attended by several thousand supporters, which was violently broken up by police. Murdoch Clarke and Roy Berlando, well-known members of the Mine Workers' Union of Canada and the WUL, were part of the organizing team. They, along with twenty-five others, were convicted of unlawful assembly, although the authorities originally hinted at proceeding under Section 98 for all of those charged.[55]

While on a speaking tour advocating for the release of Buck et al., David Chalmers, a prominent Communist from the Montreal area, was stopped in Port Colborne, Ontario, for reportedly using communist phrases such as "turning imperialist war into civil war." The chief of police was present at the meeting and arrested Chalmers for violating Section 98. The only evidence that was produced came from a local news reporter. Joseph Sedgwick attended a pretrial hearing and detailed the events in a letter to Edward Bayly, the deputy attorney general. Sedgwick stated that Chalmers's lawyer had asked for a dismissal in exchange for Chalmers agreeing to not return to Port Colborne. The Crown attorney, T.D. Cowper, and the police were both satisfied with this, as there was little hope of getting a conviction. Nothing was found on Chalmers linking him to the CPC (he was presumably charged with violating subsection 3), and Chalmers's speech actually decried the use of violence or force. The case was discharged by the attending magistrate, and Sedgwick believed this was the best outcome possible, given the circumstances.[56]

Two cases of Section 98 that garnered more attention than most were the cases of *Rex v. Derry* and *Rex v. Feigelman*. Trial transcripts for these cases were among those purged by both the Ontario and Montreal archives. What remains are scattered accounts of the cases in the press and their trial dockets confirming that the Crown sought a Section 98 conviction. Joe Derry (Dyvoyck) was an active and leading member of the Young Communist League (YCL), a CPC-controlled group that was designed for Communist youth. After giving a speech in York County, Ontario, protesting the arrival of a Japanese naval squadron in Victoria, BC, Derry was arrested by Toronto police on 6 April for violating subsection 3 of Section 98, that is, for being a member of an unlawful organization, the YCL. The Crown's goal was to have this subsidiary of the CPC outlawed. D. Goldstick represented Derry at his preliminary hearing and argued that during the

Buck trial, Mike Golinsky, a member of the YCL, had had his charges dismissed because he had argued that the YCL was not considered an unlawful organization. The judge did not agree, arguing that the Crown dismissed charges against Golinsky because it had insufficient evidence to link him to the CPC, not the YCL. The Crown's case with Derry centred on linking the YCL to the CPC. The Crown presented copies of the CLDL publication the *Canadian Labor Defender*, the *USSR in Construction*, the *Masses Song Book*, and other periodicals available for purchase from newsstands as evidence. Other evidence against Derry consisted of membership cards for the Workers Sports Association, as well as cartoons and drawings seized from his home. One young witness who testified for the Crown apparently claimed that he had signed an affidavit for police only because of police intimidation. Toronto police detectives testified for the Crown.[57] The case did not go to trial until late in 1934, which allowed Derry, while out on bail, to travel the country on a speaking tour with the CLDL, which was organized under the name the "Joe Derry Defense Committee."

Derry travelled to Ottawa, Timmins, and Cochrane, Ontario, in addition to Montreal and Verdun, denouncing Section 98 and demanding the release of Arthur Evans and Tim Buck et al.[58] The charges against Derry afforded him a bigger audience and more recognition than he would have otherwise ever received. He was now a victim of the Canadian state's repression. When the case went to trial in December 1934, the presiding judge, Justice O'Connell, claimed that the Crown had failed to produce any evidence proving Joe Derry was a member of an unlawful association. The Crown's apparent hodgepodge assembly of publicly available documents and testimony of police officers was nowhere near what was available during the Buck et al. trial, and without a Leopold type of undercover officer's testimony, the linkages between the YCL and CPC that the Crown provided were too thin. Derry was acquitted of the charges.[59]

The case of *Rex v. Feigelman* occurred among a general backdrop of censorship and an intense offensive against communism in Quebec, which reached its highest point in 1933–4. In January of 1933, Premier Taschereau ramped up the campaign against Communists after opposition leader Maurice Duplessis wrongfully accused them of burning down Saint-Jacques Church. In the eyes of the government, Communists were a clear and present danger to Quebec's French and Catholic way of life. They were a threat to security, which was equated with the status quo. In April, Deputy Attorney General Charles Lanctôt met with Superintendent Frederick J. Mead of Montreal's RCMP detachment, urging the service to seize seditious publications without a warrant.

Mead explained that the federal RCMP would be able to use such powers only in an emergency, such as a revolution, and that Quebec was not experiencing one. In addition to a broad campaign against Communists, Lanctôt wanted Bella Gordon's band of Communists prosecuted, but noted that they were "very active and very cautious, and had for [a] lawyer the Jew Garber," referring to CLDL lawyer Michael Garber.[60]

Taschereau's government found a way around the need to declare an emergency to seize seditious material without a warrant. Bill 28 was introduced in January 1934 and dramatically upped the ante in the Quebec government's battle with Communists. The bill would provide police with unprecedented censorship powers and was designed to curtail protests and the sale and distribution of radical literature. Louis-Athanase David, provincial secretary in Taschereau's government, stated publicly that the bill was directly aimed at Communist activities in the province.[61] The CLDL and WUL were both highly active in Quebec, agitating against police repression and the repeal of Section 98, along with protesting the government's lack of unemployment relief. Much like in other provinces, protests and strikes were being met with violent responses from police, with some of the largest clashes occurring in Rouyn at the Noranda Mines. Seventy-seven people were arrested on 11 December 1933 as strikers clashed with police on the road to the logging camps. The most notable of the arrests were of prominent CLDL and WUL organizers such as Harry Raketti, Jeanne Corbin, Annie Evanik, and Jerry Donahue.[62]

Bill 28 was opposed by progressives in the province, such as F.R. Scott and the Emergency Committee for the Protection of Civil Liberties, a group of liberal-minded citizens which hastily came together after Bill 28 passed Quebec's Lower House in January 1934. The bill passed as the Certain Meetings and Advertising Act, better known as the David Bill, having been named after Louis-Athanase David.[63] Its key points read as follows:

3. No person shall distribute or cause to be distributed, post up or cause to be posted up, or otherwise made public, a circular in a city or town, unless such circular shall have been submitted to and been approved by the chief of police . . . approval contemplated by section 3 shall not be granted if the printer, maker or author of the circular is not domiciled in this Province . . . every person who commits any infringement of this act shall be liable, in addition to the costs, to a fine not exceeding one hundred dollars . . . any member of the Provincial or municipal police may seize and confiscate,

in any place whatsoever, any circular distributed, posted up or otherwise made public.[64]

The new law borrowed heavily from Section 98 by targeting public meetings and the spread of literature to curb communist ideology. But it was more drastic in the way it expanded police powers and limited free expression. Unlike Section 98, which targeted individuals or groups for attending meetings of an unlawful organization or for distributing literature, this bill required circulars be pre-approved by police before they became public. A circular was required to state the printer's name and where the office was located. The bill was much more powerful than Section 98. Police could seize any radical publications *anywhere* in the province, even those that were for sale at newsstands or located in someone's home. A trial did not have to take place for the authorities to decide whether the material was advocating force or violence. If it was not pre-approved by the police, it had no right to be made public. The law was designed to be more efficient in targeting disloyal actions than Section 98. While an individual could face a fine for contravening the act, they could also face criminal charges. The new law set the stage for even more arrests and conflict in Montreal.

Montreal police initiated their own crackdown on the press before the law came into effect, using the old censorship powers of Section 98. On 13 January 1934, Saul Feigelman and his sister found themselves face to face with Section 98. Saul Feigelman, a Montreal art student, and his sister operated a small bookstore named the Hidden Bookshop in Montreal's downtown core. Supportive of the kind of radical leftist politics that the CLDL espoused, they sold *La Vie Ouvrière* out of their store, along with other titles sympathetic to the Communist cause and titles that espoused an individual's right to civil liberties.

Police entered the shop while Feigelman's sister, Ann, was working and charged the pair with violating Section 98 for having activist literature on the premises. Under orders from Chief Louis Jargaille, police seized large quantities of books, newspapers, and other periodicals. When one of the attending constables, Constable Forget, was asked by the owners why the material was being taken, he replied, "We are seizing all seditious literature under Section 98 of the Criminal Code." When asked why fictional stories by acclaimed novelist E.P. Openheim were being seized, he reportedly replied, "I don't read." Feigelman and his sister appeared in court on 16 January. Feigelman reported that other vendors had appeared and pleaded guilty to Section 98 charges and received suspended sentences. This was confirmed by reports in the *Worker* in May 1934. Both Feigelman and his sister pleaded not guilty. Following the charge, he was expelled from his art school and his case was remanded until 17 October. The family's store was only open half-days because of their frequent court appearances. Justice Loranger heard the case in the fall session of the King's Bench. Feigelman was found guilty and sentenced to one month in jail, while his sister received a suspended sentence.[65] No transcript exists of the trial; only trial dockets remain, but Justice Loranger's charge to the jury was read to the Commons by J.S. Woodsworth during the passage of Section 98's repeal bill in 1936.

Loranger's charge offers a glimpse into how the Quebec court perceived communism and Section 98. Beyond Loranger's obvious anti-communism, he noted that Canada was Christian and that communism's godless ways would not be tolerated, particularly when spread to impressionable youth. Loranger stressed that the purpose of Section 98 was to protect "[their] people," French Canadians, from Communists. He could not understand how Feigelman's sister could have kept such seditious material out in the open. It was likely because she had no idea it was illegal. Many other vendors thought the same when they pleaded guilty to violating Section 98.[66] Such was the power of Section 98. Material that was legal after the Buck et al. trial could suddenly and without warning be judged when it suited the authorities.

Feigelman expressed his feelings about his arrest in an article published in the *Worker*. He wrote that he was back from his one-month vacation (prison), where he had been sent "not as a Communist, not as a revolutionist, but because [he] dared to sell the press of the French-Canadian working class." Feigelman wrote that he often laughed while in prison, claiming that the "boss class" would not arrest the publishers of the papers because that would violate the freedom of the press. Instead, he claimed, "the art of intimidation" was being practised, as "news dealers" were "frightened" into pleading guilty in exchange for being released on suspended sentences and promises of "never to display the paper on their stands. Thus in a quiet manner the newspaper would become illegal; there would be no jury trials, no publicity and no hue and cry about the attack on free press." But Taschereau's plan, he claimed, had backfired. He wrote that he and his sister were fighting the attack on the freedom of the press and that if they won, it would be a victory for publications like *La Vie Ouvrière*, and if not, the issue would be raised by the public. Feigelman saw his case as a dire warning for all Canadians and in particular for "members of [his] own race, the Jewish workers in Quebec, particularly those belonging to the Canadian Jewish Congress or to the Zionist organizations."[67] Feigelman was correct in that his case did become publicized: it was described in the House of Commons, and the RCMP kept tabs on the Feigelman case as it worked its way through the legal system.[68]

The attack on Montreal's press vendors continued throughout 1934 while Feigelman's case was working its way through the courts. Once the David Bill came into effect on 30 April, authorities wasted little time. On 1 May 1934, Montreal police raided the offices of the popular labour paper *La Vie Ouvrière* and confiscated the entire 1 May edition of the paper. Several days earlier, the offices of the CLDL in Quebec were raided, and copies of the May issue of the *Labor Defender* were confiscated. The new law made it much easier for the authorities to engage in broad-based censorship. However, the raids had little effect on the activist movement in the city; *La Vie Ouvrière* reported that sales had jumped by 50 per cent since the police raid, and the paper held a funding drive to meet the increased demand.[69] How many vendors faced Section 98 charges in addition to violating the David Bill is uncertain, given the lack of transcripts from this era.

Women were particularly active in the front lines of the Communist ranks and as a result faced repression with the same brutality as their male counterparts. Many nameless women fought on the front lines of May Day marches, free-speech campaigns, and antiwar demonstrations against police. In August 1934, during a strike in the garment industry in Montreal, eleven of the twelve people arrested were women.[70] The first Section 98 case was against a female activist, Emily Weir. Well known to the authorities were some of the most notable female members of the CPC, such as Becky Buhay, Jean Corbin, and Annie Buller. Buller's criminal trial, during the trials of activists from the Estevan coal miners' strike in 1931, reveals how the treatment of women activists was just as brutal as that of men, if not worse because of their gender. Buller's trial attracted much attention for several reasons, including her strong skills as an orator, the severity of the riot, and the fact that she was a woman. Not only was Buller being prosecuted entirely by men, but, as Endicott observes, women faced "all-male juries, male judges, male newspaper editors, male prosecuting attorneys," and she was a member of the WUL and CPC, groups that, while officially advocating for equality, were male dominated. Moreover, she was married and a mother as well as a leading union organizer, demonstrating that it was not just single young women who were vocal activists. Given the lengths the RCMP took to secure convictions in the trial, including fabricating evidence, her conviction was assured.

Worth noting is Justice Hector Macdonald's remarks during sentencing. He claimed that Buller was "more guilty than any of those who used physical force [in the riot]" because she had "used, or rather abused" her "fatal gift of eloquence . . . to stir up the feelings of the workers against the employers and as between class and class." The jury recommended leniency for Buller, possibly because of her gender, and because she was not at the riot. Macdonald believed that it was only because of Buller's gender that the jury asked for leniency. He argued that because women sought equality with men, they should receive equal responsibility, and so he sentenced her to one year's hard labour and $500 in fines.[71] While claiming to have given Buller a sentence equal to that of a man, Macdonald never saw past Buller's gender. The sentence was harsher, not equal as the judge claimed, given that no witnesses could put Buller at the riot and that the jury asked for leniency. Buller's persuasive charms, or fatal gift, made her more dangerous. Not only were her politics judged, but so was her morality because of her gender. Her belief in equality brought a stiff sentence for her limited involvement, and she was not alone. Other female activists experienced similar fates (such as Sophie Sheinin, a leader in the National Unemployed Workers Association). Buller suffered at the hands of authorities who went to extra lengths to punish female activists for transgressing the gender role they believed women should play.

The statistics available for this period reinforce the severity of the repression that was taking place during Bennett's years in office. The Canadian government's campaign against perceived radical activity and against real and suspected Communists increased once the Great Depression was under way; the peak of unemployment was approximately 30 per cent in 1933.[72] After Buck et al., the Canadian government increased the frequency and severity of its repressive activities. The CLDL claimed that in 1931 approximately 720 people were arrested, with 155 being convicted for what it claimed were working-class activities. This was a marked increase from the previous year, when it claimed approximately 200 persons were arrested. These numbers included arrests for unlawful assembly, rioting, sedition, Section 98, assault, vagrancy, and disorderly conduct, among other transgressions; the Section 98 numbers represented a fraction of those numbers. In 1932, the CLDL claimed that 839 had been arrested and 195 convicted. In 1933, the uptick in arrests continued.

The group reported 1,167 arrests that year, although these numbers included those charged with assault, vagrancy, and disorderly conduct, among other crimes, an increase of 17 per cent from the previous year. The number of arrests grew: the first four months of 1934 saw 463 arrests.[73]

The CLDL's numbers could have been inflated, but the group had an accurate account of whether repression was increasing after the Buck et al. trial because it defended the bulk of those charged. Its estimates do not seem inflated when compared to figures obtained by more moderate leftists. In 1933, F.R. Scott attempted to find out how many arrests and convictions were occurring in the 1930s. According to official statistics from the Dominion Bureau of Statistics, the number of crimes for sedition before 1931 would have been so low that they would have been included in the miscellaneous category. The statistician who replied to Scott's query claimed that 1932 witnessed a great increase, to the point that the crime now needed its own category. Statistics for 1932 were not available at the time of Scott's request, but the bureau did state that in 1928 there were 119 charges for rioting and unlawful assembly and 103 convictions. Those numbers increased in 1930 to 201 charges and 169 convictions. In 1931, there were 206 charges and 168 convictions.[74] The CLDL's numbers included far more categories, but if the Bureau of Statistics' number of convictions for just the category of rioting and unlawful assembly is any indication, the CLDL was *underestimating* just how many were being arrested and convicted for what it deemed working-class political activities.

Section 98 provided fertile ground for the normalization of more exceptional laws. It played an important role in the repression of the period and in ensuring Bennett's goal of preserving "peace, order and good government." Repression was security. Whether law enforcement chose to prosecute individuals under different sections of the Criminal Code in the 1930s does not diminish the fact that Section 98's creation reinforced the government's belief that it *had the right* to judge politics to maintain loyalty. It is impossible to speculate on the impact of the repression of the 1930s without Section 98, but it is certain that Section 98 had a role to play in the repression that took place, whether directly or indirectly. The effect of Section 98 on the repression of the period was profound. In addition to laying the foundations for new repressive laws, it was used in a multitude of ways, from legalizing the deportation of Communist immigrants to providing the authorities with the legal sanction to engage in frequent and repeated searches of persons and places, shutter public meetings, and institute large-scale censorship. It gave the police the belief that in attacking communists, even with violence, they were doing so legally. With the police targeting activists and their supporters in such heavy-handed ways, many had good reason to fear the police and Section 98. For them, it was Section 98 and the police that produced unrest and insecurity.

When authorities became accustomed to using exceptional measures, they were no longer exceptional – they were necessary. After Buck et al., communists became criminals, with no trial needed. While domestic-born communists still had the right to a trial to determine if they were Communists, police often judged communists on the spot and used Section 98, or similar laws modelled on it, to intimidate, or even physically attack, suspected Communists. The verdicts of trials were not as significant as the right of the sovereign to try an individual because of their political beliefs, demonstrating to all Canadians and foreigners what politics were and were not acceptable in Canada. Nation-building was being practised through repression.

Once the government began with Section 98 the process of normalizing the emergency, the ability to detach the security threat from a specific threat or moment in time, more laws followed. The WMA was amended to have a peacetime application, and the Unemployment and Farm Relief Act gave the government the legal tools it needed to use whatever measures it needed. Quebec's David Bill built on Section 98, making censorship easier. While repression was tied to the country's unemployment situation, it is debatable that the repression against Communists and their supporters during the 1930s would have reached the heights it did, had the CPC not been officially categorized and declared an unlawful organization. Indeed, as Judy Fudge and Eric Tucker have stated, even though the number of known Section 98 prosecutions was small, Section 98 and Buck et al.'s conviction "further legitimized the crackdown [against Communists], at least in the eyes of politicians, law enforcement officials, and judges."[75]

No one knows how many times Section 98 was used or how many people pleaded guilty. Hugh Guthrie admitted during a speech he made before the Calgary Bar Association in 1933 that Section 98 was proving effective during protests resulting from the unemployment situation in the country.[76] It was managing disorder and providing security. Plea deals were common, as the Chalmers case illustrates. The broad reach of Section 98 was best summed up by

Norman Keys when in 1933 he wrote in the *Fortnightly Law Journal* that the limits of Section 98 were "measured by a policeman's helmet."[77]

The Murder of an Immigrant: Nicholas Zynchuck

The state repression of the 1930s increased in 1933, particularly in Montreal as Premier Taschereau launched his aggressive campaign against communism. If the Buck et al. trial was the start of the repression against Communists and fellow travellers during the Great Depression's exceptional state, the case of Nicholas Zynchuck in Montreal represented the depths of it. His case demonstrates how ethnicity and culture helped influence who was (and was not) a Communist.

On the afternoon of 6 March 1933, Montreal police were called to 3962 Saint Dominique Street in Montreal's downtown core. Saint Dominique contained a number of townhome complexes, many of which were rented to Polish immigrants, mainly Yiddish speakers, working in nearby factories and shops. On this afternoon, police walked in on an eviction, the history of which dated back to the previous Friday. John Wlostizosk was a Polish immigrant who had been renting 3962 with his wife. Wlostizosk had fallen on difficult times and become unemployed, probably because of the broken leg he was nursing at the time of his eviction. He was two months in arrears on his rent and was ordered to pay immediately or be forced to leave. Wlostizosk could not pay, and the next day a court-ordered bailiff and his assistants attempted to evict the family, claiming that they had an order to do so from the Supreme Court. They were unsuccessful, and Mrs Wlostizosk reported that she was thrown to the ground by the men and had her clothing torn.

The majority of the witnesses stated that the bailiff returned at 2:30 p.m. on 7 March; he and his assistants reportedly forced their way into the home and pulled Wlostizosk out of his bed, dragging him outside. Wlostizosk's wife, while screaming, clung to the bed sheets as her husband was dragged out of the home, and she was then pushed down the stairs. Her screams drew neighbours from all around, and soon a crowd of several hundred emerged, urging the couple to stand their ground and not leave.[78] When constables Joseph Zappa, Paul Couchey, and Victor Jette of the Montreal police arrived at the scene (later joined by Constable A. Cloutier), they found an angry mob, the bailiff's truck half-loaded with furniture and clothing from the home, a screaming Mrs Wlostizosk standing on the steps to the house, and a

half-clothed John Wlostizosk leaning against the house to keep himself up. At this point, Nicholas Zynchuck, a Polish immigrant, former
Canadian Pacific Railway worker, and a border at 3962, arrived home.
He reportedly ran up to the house searching for his clothes. When told
by bystanders that the items were in the truck, he entered it but found
nothing of his inside. He reportedly then grabbed one of the bai-
liffs by the arm, saying, "I want my clothes." The bailiff replied that
he could not have them because everything in the house was being
seized. When Zynchuck made for the house again, he was blocked by
the three constables. The crowd, which had grown to approximately
two thousand, began removing furniture and items from the truck to
prevent them from being taken.[79]

From this point on, the eyewitness accounts differ drastically.
Three witnesses and the officers claimed that they saw Zynchuck
grab a bar of some sort (reportedly an iron bedpost) from the truck
and begin swinging it at the officers, slightly grazing one of them.
As he turned to attack the bailiff's assistant, Constable Joseph
Zappa fired his revolver, hitting Zynchuck in the back mid-swing.[80]
Fourteen others claimed that Zynchuck had no bar.[81] Yetta Rotter,
of 3972 Saint Dominique, gave her account to the *Toronto Star* the
morning after the shooting, and it was corroborated by the majority of the witnesses. Zynchuck, she said, "just asked them [the
police] to let him get his clothes. Then someone said 'shoot him,'
and the constable pulled out his gun and fired" as Zynchuck turned
to leave.[82] On the morning of 7 March, Constable Zappa, seated at
the back of police station no. 12, was interviewed by his superiors,
who included Assistant Inspector A. Brodeur, with a *Star* reporter
present. In the interview, which formed the basis for the official
police report, Zappa claimed he had shot Zynchuck because he,
Zappa, "was mad." "Why didn't you shoot over the man's head?"
his superiors asked. The constable grinned and shrugged his shoul-
ders: "He's a communist." When Zappa was asked if he was excited
at the time, he replied, "No."[83]

Assistant Inspector Brodeur announced a half-hour later that the
shooting was "justified under the circumstances though regrettable."
The public had to understand, he explained, that this section of the
city was "a hot-bed of communism." Police actions may not have
been just, but the police did what was necessary for security. René
Clouette, the attending bailiff charged with evicting the family, told
reporters an account that differed from that of the other witnesses. He
claimed he went to the house on the afternoon of 6 March with about
a dozen assistants but found men in the home who were adamant that

the furniture not be taken, and so he returned with about fifty assistants and began loading furniture into a truck. He claimed that one of the tenants, John Wlostizosk, entered the scene, walking in on his own accord but with crutches. Clouette denied the witness accounts that he and others had dragged Wlostizosk out of bed by his feet and pushed his wife down the stairs of the home. The shooting occurred, he explained, as the mob began taking things out of the truck that he and his men were loading.[84]

Led by Deputy Coroner Dr Pierre Herbert, a coroner's inquiry with jury was ordered on 8 March to investigate Zynchuck's death. Antoine Senecal and Albert Berthiaume conducted the case for the police, and Michael Garber, retained by the CLDL, cross-examined witnesses. The scene in Montreal was tense. Police were dispatched throughout the city to quell outbursts of protests following the shooting. One hundred "communists" were reportedly dispersed from Viger Square. The courtroom itself was under heavy police guard, and a number of officers were armed with tear gas should protesters threaten the court. The first witness examined was Adolph Sasnofvska of 4370 Saint Dominique Street. He testified that Zynchuck was a Ukrainian born in Poland who had come to Canada five years earlier and who worked as a labourer. He was thirty-seven years old at the time of his death. Sasnofvska's description of Zynchuck's ethnicity reveals that he was an immigrant of Polish citizenship but that he identified as being Ukrainian. He was presumably born in the former Eastern Galicia. René Clouette, the bailiff charged with evicting Wlostizosk, told the inquiry the same version he had earlier provided to the media. His assistants gave a sensational account of Zynchuck grabbing a bedpost, letting out a cry in his native Ukrainian, and then charging the house in a crazed, barbarian-style attack, swinging the bedpost wildly.[85]

Zappa was called to the stand but did not want to testify. The coroner told him that he was not obligated to do so, but one of the jurors stood up to say that the jury wanted him to give evidence. A five-minute recess was called. After conferring with Senecal and Berthiaume, who represented the police, Zappa gave his account of what happened. He claimed that the crowd was getting difficult to control and that some people started taking furniture out of the truck. One of the people removing furniture darted towards him with a six-foot iron bar. The man began swinging the pole as he approached Zappa. After taking one swing at Zappa and missing, Zappa claimed that the man turned to swing at the bailiff, and as he swung, Zappa shot at his leg but his gun "kicked up" and the man "was shot in the back." "I was afraid for my own life," he stated, and that all he could do was fire in the man's direction to protect himself.

Under cross-examination, Garber asked Zappa if Zynchuck first asked to enter the house. Zappa replied that he did not, stating that Zynchuck got the bar from the truck, tried to hit him but missed, and took another swing at Bertrand the bailiff before being shot. Garber asked Zappa why he did not fire a warning shot in the air. Zappa replied that he had already threatened to do so, but it had no effect on the crowd. He claimed that no one ordered him to shoot. Garber asked, "Did you tell the reporter of the *Star* that you were mad when you shot?" Zappa replied, "Mad? Mad? Well I was not very happy." Garber continued, asking, "Were you asked by the *Star* reporter why you did not shoot over the man's head?" Zappa replied that the reporter had just asked his name and left. He also claimed he had never told Zynchuck to move or he would shoot. Zappa's account was implausible.[86]

Witness testimony contradicted the scene painted by the bailiff and officers. Robert Dubareau, a passer-by who lived on Saint Catherine, claimed he saw Zappa shoot Zynchuck and that there was no iron bar in Zynchuck's hands or any swinging of a bar by Zynchuck. Another witness, Mrs Rotter, said the same thing. The papers did not detail the accounts of other witnesses that contradicted the officers' claims or note whether there had been other any other witnesses.

Inconsistencies in the bailiff and Zappa's testimonies went unaddressed. The press reported that some of Garber's questioning had been stopped; Garber was likely not allowed to question much of the evidence. The evidence that raised the most doubt about Zappa's version of events was the autopsy report. Curiously, the autopsy report was entered into evidence, but it is not clear if anyone discussed it further in court. The report, read into the record by Dr Rosario Fontaine, stated that the bullet entered Zynchuck from the right side of the back and travelled right to left, tearing through a kidney before finally resting in his spine. Zynchuck was shot at a maximum distance of four to five feet (with one paper reporting that the autopsy report stated that he had been shot at a distance of eighteen inches). This meant it was impossible for Zynchuck to have cleared a minimum six-foot space around him with an iron bar. The report matched eyewitness accounts the morning after the shooting that stated that Zappa had shot Zynchuck as he turned his back to the officer. He was shot in the back on the right side, and the bullet travelled from right to left, which could have occurred if Zynchuck, facing Zappa, had begun turning to the left to leave, exposing the right side to Zappa's revolver.[87] Either way, the bulk of the evidence raised questions about the officers' version of events, but to no effect. In a closing statement to the jury, Deputy Coroner Herbert reminded the public: "We have never had any problem with the French-Canadians, and it is always the foreigners who start such trouble. When four constables are faced with 500 angered foreigners their lives are in danger . . . I hope that this will be a lesson for other foreigners who attempt to resist the police."[88] Zynchuck's death would teach the foreign communists how they should behave and respond to police. The jury reached a decision in less than a minute and cleared Zappa of any misconduct.

That the coroner's inquiry failed to satisfy the Saint Dominique community was obvious from the way the community rallied behind their fallen member with one of the largest funeral processions the city of Montreal had ever seen. Fifteen to twenty thousand people marched from Verdun to the funeral parlour of William Ray at Arcade Street at 12:30 p.m. on 11 March. Some of those walking in the long columns of marchers hummed "The Internationale," and CLDL musicians played for the marchers. Labour leaders made speeches reminding those in attendance of how Zynchuck was killed. The real culprit, some speakers claimed, was Bennett and his policies, while others said Zynchuck was killed because of private property. Some speakers insisted that the lives of workers were just as valuable as those of the "bosses." WUL representatives spoke at the funeral. Zynchuck's death brought the community out in the tens of thousands, but it is doubtful that everyone was there to hear the CLDL or WUL use Zynchuck's funeral as a means for spreading propaganda. Indeed, there was serious doubt as to whether Zynchuck was ever a Communist or that he had belonged to the CLDL, the WUL, or any other labour organization. The Reverend R.G. Katsunoff of the Church of All Nations spoke at Zynchuck's funeral and stated that he knew Zynchuck as a member of the Ukrainian Greek Catholic Church who had no relatives and belonged to no Communist organizations.[89] Some members of the CLDL and other Communist organizations went beyond condemning his death and used Zynchuck's funeral as a platform to preach political propaganda. They tried to paint Zynchuck as a Communist killed for being a Communist when he was actually killed because he was foreign born and because he was *presumed* a Communist on account of his ethnicity, class, and where he lived. Shortly after the funeral procession was underway, Montreal police sent an even stronger message to the foreign community as a reprisal for Zappa's inquiry and to prevent Communists from using his death as a spectacle for recruitment.

As the steady line of marchers quietly carried on down the street, some holding signs condemning the death of Zynchuck, plain-clothes officers entered the crowd, and so did eight hundred mounted officers who were lying in wait for the marchers. Officers charged into the funeral procession dispersing people, punching and clubbing any who did not move quickly enough. Witnesses described the scene as chaotic; droves of people fled in terror, fearing for their lives and safety. The crowd spilt into groups of fifty, and even passers-by – not part of the march – were caught in the cross hairs of police. A woman on her way home who could not move fast enough for the officers was pushed into a snowdrift. Witnesses watched in shock and horror as marchers were knocked to the ground and, when they did not get up quickly enough, faced even more punches and kicks. One man was passed from officer to officer, who kicked or punched him for the length of a city block. Others witnessed a man beaten badly by police as he walked; he stopped walking to try to recuperate, only to have officers deliver a punishing blow from behind, knocking him unconscious to the ground, where he was left.

Neither young nor old were spared the fury of the police. Nor were the reporters: Henry Prysky of the *Gazette*, and son of Detective Sergeant Felix Prysky of the homicide department, was beaten by police even after he identified himself as a reporter. Mounted officers mowed over marchers, forcing them into the streets, where other officers forced them back onto the sidewalk. According to witnesses, the mourners never retaliated. They were determined to keep the march from turning into a riot or violent protest. Statements from witnesses, to the dismay of both the CLDL and Montreal police, affirmed that the vast majority of people at the funeral were there for Zynchuck and not in support of any Communist politics. The Verdun Workers Association, who led the procession, denounced some press suggestions of Communist activity, citing that 35 per cent of their members had served in the Great War and strongly denouncing suggestions that their loyalty should be questioned.

The mourners' non-resistance did not deter police. One machinist, as the *Herald* described him, was walking along the street when police began clearing it. "Suddenly I was tripped," he said, "and thrown into a snow bank. While I lay there two other men bent over me and struck me in the face." The man claimed that police never asked him a single question before the beating started. A mile from the march, witnesses reported that a woman walking with a toddler was pushed by police for not walking fast enough and that when she protested, she and her toddler were forced into a snow bank.[90] Police had deemed the funeral a political action by Communists and a security threat. They decided – they judged in the moment – what was and was not legal and what to do to stop it.

Montreal residents felt outrage and condemned the events at the funeral. The *Herald*, in an editorial, denounced the actions of police and stated that "the actions of the police force on Saturday were a blot on the honour of the force . . . Had they been agents of Moscow they could not have served the cause of violence better."[91] The *Star*, as well as the *Gazette*, was equally critical of the police for attacking the funeral. Besides reporting the attack on its own reporter, the *Gazette* detailed a bizarre scene in which two plain-clothes officers, each "taking the other for a communist," got into a fight. They were eventually separated by officers who recognized them. One officer lost some teeth in the scuffle, but he was dissuaded by other police from taking out an arrest warrant on the other officer. The two reportedly shook hands, and police refused to release their names.[92]

The violence at Zynchuck's funeral prompted a strong response from community groups. Protests began immediately after the funeral. In one instance, 225 youth protested the death of Zynchuck and the events of the funeral at the Youth Forum on Drummond Street. Some of the most outspoken criticism of police actions, ironically, came from Christian churches and ministers who claimed that it was the police, and not the Communists, who were behaving in an *un-British* manner. On 13 March, members of the Protestant Ministerial Association voted in the majority to appoint a committee that could represent Protestant churches, as well as a diverse segment of prominent citizens, to press for a judicial investigation into the events of the eviction at Saint Dominique Street and Zynchuck's funeral. The committee was separate from religious institutions but provided them with some representation.[93]

Called the Citizens' Committee, the group consisted of prominent community members such as ministers, lawyers, and academics, including Professor F.R. Scott and law professor Warwick Chipman, a prominent member of the bar in Montreal. The committee heard evidence from ministers such as the Reverend Katsunoff, who spoke at Zynchuck's funeral and now reiterated his claims that Zynchuck was no Communist. He described the funeral and the events leading up to it after Zynchuck was shot. Wanting to give Zynchuck a funeral, he explained, were a dozen representatives of different societies, such as various Ukrainian and Polish groups. Katsunoff explained that a Greek-Catholic priest was approached to conduct the funeral but that he was asked too late and could not do it in time. He claimed that the police kept one of Zynchuck's closest friends detained for hours and compelled him to sign Zynchuck's body over to them to stop a funeral from being held. Montreal police recognized that a funeral for Zynchuck could become a spectacle for the Communists. Katsunoff recalled how police tried to storm the funeral parlour in an effort to get Zynchuck's body, but people jammed the entrance to the parlour and stood watch until a funeral was arranged. Katsunoff told the committee that the funeral march was orderly until someone blew a whistle. Someone shouted, "Come on boys," and plain-clothes officers jumped into the crowd. A banner held by one of the marchers that read "Shot in the back" was grabbed by police as they entered the crowd from all directions, beating the crowd as they entered. Katsunoff was sure that the two plain-clothes men that he had spoken to "smelt of some kind of liquor." The committee heard that several witnesses of Zynchuck's death claimed that they could swear under oath that they saw him shot as he turned his back to Zappa in an effort to leave. It was later reported that Zynchuck's grave site was purchased by an unnamed sympathetic citizen of Montreal who had never personally met Zynchuck.[94]

The committee refrained from deciding anything and instead took a wait-and-see approach until further official inquiries were completed. Following the publicity that the committee meeting generated, Montreal deputy chief Charles Barnes, who oversaw the police response to the funeral march, commented on the funeral, stating that he had seen "no trouble anywhere" and witnessed no violence, as the crowd was easily dispersed. Despite Barnes's attempt at damage control, a new inquiry into Zynchuck's death was about to be called.[95]

On 14 March, Joe Batula, a former fellow officer of Zynchuck's in the Polish army, filed a complaint against Zappa in the death of Zynchuck so that an arrest warrant could be issued against him for manslaughter. Michael Garber and another lawyer retained by the CLDL, Oscar Gagnon, represented Batula. Justice Victor Cusson agreed to issue a prewarrant inquiry to investigate whether a warrant should be issued for Zappa's arrest. He set the date of the hearing for 21 March. Gagnon explained that a hearing was needed because all the evidence at the coroner's inquest "was designed to exculpate the constable" and that they had had "no chance to present [their] evidence."[96] Gagnon's statement confirms that the evidence of witnesses that could contradict Zappa and his fellow officers was suppressed during the coroner's inquiry.

Zynchuck's death and funeral spurred progressives into action and solidarity. In addition to the frequent protests throughout the city, writers in the *Canadian Forum* claimed that these events symbolized the illiberal state of Quebec. Zynchuck's death and funeral became the source of inspiration for a variety of poems, stories, and plays, including a play entitled *Eviction* performed by the Workers' Experimental Theatre. Poet Dorothy Livesay wrote a poem entitled "An Immigrant (Nick Zynchuck)" and a story, "Zynchuck's Funeral." As mentioned earlier, F.R. Scott was instrumental in forming an ad hoc group to protest the events and suggest reform. He had been outraged by witnessing a labourer who had been standing near the street during the funeral suddenly be knocked to the ground by a "ferocious punch to the jaw" from a man later identified as a plain-clothes police officer. The CLDL temporarily united with the Trades and Labour Congress and the Montreal Labour Party to protest Zynchuck's death and the funeral violence. They had support from the Protestant Ministerial Association, the Montreal Women's Club, the Delorimier Liberal Reform Club, the League for Social Reconstruction, and the Montreal United Church's Committee on Social and Economic Research.[97]

The hearing began on 21 March. Oscar Gagnon of the CLDL stressed from the outset that this was not a trial, just an inquiry to decide whether an arrest warrant should be issued, and thus a hearing of evidence *ex parte* as per article 655 of the Criminal Code was sufficient to issue the warrant. In an unexpected move, Justice Cusson allowed *both* sides to present evidence, including witnesses called by Zappa's counsel, Philippe Monette. Berthiaume was permitted to represent the police. Variations of Zynchuck's death were told to the court in English, Polish, and Yiddish. The courtroom was initially restricted to the public, but by midmorning the judge had lifted the restrictions, and it became filled to capacity.[98]

The bailiff Clouette retold his version of events. But the majority of the witnesses in this hearing told a different story than the one told by Zappa, his fellow constables, and the bailiff and his assistants during the coroner's inquiry. These witnesses described how Zynchuck was shot in the back by Zappa as he turned to leave. Several witnesses claimed that the bailiff's assistants shouted at the officers to shoot Zynchuck. Papers reported that Zappa's counsel, Mr Monette, was very aggressive in his cross-examination of witnesses, leading Garber to ask the judge why cross-examination should even be allowed, as this was not a trial. The judge claimed he wanted all the facts before making his decision. The defence gave their interpretation next. It followed the same story as told by the witnesses during the coroner's inquest. The autopsy report was read into evidence again by Dr Rosario Fontaine, who claimed that on the basis of the hole in Zynchuck's jacket, the shot might have been fired from a distance of four or five feet but not less than eighteen inches. Witnesses for Zappa claimed that the crowd was advancing until Zappa fired his gun.[99]

On 24 March, Judge Cusson announced that he had decided not to issue a warrant for Zappa's arrest, citing that riot conditions had prompted Zappa to shoot, as Zynchuck was part of a crowd of thirty or more persons who were advancing on the officers. Whether Zynchuck was armed or not was inconsequential to the judge; "killing one or more," he stated, there being no other way to suppress the riot, constituted a "justifiable homicide." Exceptional measures were necessary. Curiously, Zappa's evidence, given on the day of the judge's decision, contained mention that the crowd was advancing on him, and yet, even after the coroner's report, Zappa claimed that Zynchuck was "six, eight, nine" feet from him when he shot.

The CLDL lawyers did not agree with the judge's finding, stating that it was significant that no iron bar was produced as evidence. When Cusson asked the lawyers what Zappa was to have done beyond shooting, Garber replied, "I believe that he'd have to read the Riot Act before shooting." The judge was taken aback, asking, "Do you believe that a Montreal jury – or a jury anywhere – (you are a lawyer of reputation, Mr. Garber, and I appreciate you highly) but do you believe that any jury would find Constable Zappa guilty?" The judge insisted on an answer from Garber, who replied, "It might happen. There might be a jury that would find him guilty of manslaughter." Cusson disagreed, stating that he had had no hesitation in refusing the warrant – "none." The CLDL made one last plea to Premier Taschereau, but it fell on deaf ears. The Citizens' Committee did not seek to further fan any flames: the legal process had run its course. The committee recommended that police not send plain-clothes officers to break up crowds in the future, something the police force said it would consider. Joseph Zappa was completely exonerated.[100]

The case of Nicholas Zynchuck shows the depth of the repression against Communists and anyone presumed of being one. For law enforcement, communists were automatically guilty of an offence and violence had become part of the construct of security. Members could never publicly admit that they were CPC members or even publicly state that they believed in the same ideology without exposing themselves to the possibility of a Section 98 charge. But the most significant danger to Canadian society was how individuals were classified as being Communists.

In light of the fact that many CPC members would simply deny membership, the Communist was not easy to spot. Some markers could potentially give one away, as in the case of Zynchuck, an Eastern European immigrant who worked as a labourer and lived in an area with a concentrated number of suspected Communists. In the eyes of law enforcement, communists were emblematic of what Foucault terms the "dangerous individual." Foucault argues that such a category of person was created over the course of the nineteenth century as *Homo penalis* shifted to *Homo criminalis* or, in other words, as the Benthamite idea of legal sanction against what a person *did* shifted to one of sanction against what a person *is*. Such a distinction came into acceptance because the law, and legal psychiatry in particular, demanded more about individuals. It was not enough for an individual to admit to a criminal action. More was demanded by the courts and society about the accused as an individual. Crimes were no longer just actions that people did; they instead came to define what a person was. Crimes were the product of criminals, of dangerous individuals who had to be weeded out of society.[101] This view was embodied by the authorities in their approach against communists. For them, these people did not just support Communists or share the ideas of communism; they *were* Communists and hence dangerous. Communism was not just a part of one's identity – it was *the* identity. Zynchuck was killed by Zappa because, as Zappa stated, "he was a communist." Only after was it discovered that Zappa had not killed a Communist, as he had thought, but a man who wanted to retrieve what few belongings he had before they were lost to him.

The role of police violence against communists throughout the Depression, starkly illustrated in the events of Zynchuck's death and funeral, is important because of how it relates to sovereign power, the state of exception, and security as an idea. As Walter Benjamin demonstrates in "Critique of Violence," police have broad discretionary power. Police violence, for Benjamin, has a "law-preserving" function. It occupies an anomic space in that it does not fit neatly into debates about whether violent means are justified to achieve a just end. This is because for Benjamin, police violence is not "reasoned" but "fate-imposed." Police can involve themselves in a situation "for security reasons ... where no legal situation exists." The police escort "the citizen as a brutal encumbrance through a life regulated by ordinances, or simply supervis[e] him [or her]." As Foucault argues, the police lack an *essence* when discipline is internalized throughout society. Instead, they become in a metaphysical way ever-present everywhere through the eyes of regular citizens. In this regard, the police, as Benjamin states, serve as a "ghostly presence in the life of civilised states."[102]

The ability of police to judge issues of public order and security on a daily basis creates an area of indistinction between "violence" and "right" in an identical fashion to that of sovereign power, which is both ruled by law and able to suspend law, with only the sovereign possessing the power to kill and not be guilty of homicide.[103] Thus Zynchuck's death at the hands of Zappa was fate-imposed violence because no legal situation had existed. Montreal police were responsible for resolving the situation as they saw fit in the moment, and their cultural perceptions about who was and was not a threat guided their actions. The indiscriminate violence that the police unleashed upon the tens of thousands of marchers at Zynchuck's funeral, in broad daylight in downtown Montreal, was undertaken in a zone of indistinction, where police decided what action to take in the immediacy of the moment and where violence against communists had become acceptable in the construction of security.

This was the case during the violent clashes of the 1930s, when police on horseback rode into strikers. During these violent clashes, police acted out of necessity. Arendt argues that state violence can be interpreted as occurring because of a loss of control or a loss of power. In such cases, state authorities can perceive their actions as necessary. She states that "sheer violence comes into play when power is being lost."[104] Police were lawfully able to administer brutal levels of violence because it was they who determined, in the absence of a legal situation, how much force to use and whether it was acceptable in the fate of the moment against Communists or dangerous individuals.

These presumed necessary police actions were integral to the creation of a zone of indistinction because necessity creates law for itself.[105] Zappa's final exoneration by Justice Cusson reinforces how the police violence Zappa used against Zynchuck was an acceptable, law-preserving function, or in Cusson's oxymoronic phrase, justifiable homicide.[106] By using violence and repression against Communists or anyone believed to be one, repression functioned in the service of nation-building and security. Dissenters were forcefully dealt with by police. This was possible only because exceptional measures necessary for dealing with the emergency of communism that authorities believed threatened Canadian society were normalized with Section 98.

The violence of the repression also stoked feelings of terror and fear in the population. Whether it was police threatening hall owners with closure, continually and randomly searching people and property, beating strikers (including youth) to the point of hearing loss, or attacking mourners violently at a funeral because they may have believed in the wrong type of politics, Section 98 and nation-building through repression invoked, and indeed relied on, fear and terror. The police, both a symbolic and a real mechanism of sovereign power in the lives of citizens, could even murder a presumed Communist and not be guilty of homicide.[107]

The state-sanctioned repression of communists during the 1930s was possible because of how the government and law enforcement believed that exceptional powers could be used and created during the Depression. The government continued the process of normalizing emergency measures by creating new ones and using Section 98. The section was one of the government's most potent weapons to combat leftist activism. Expressions of communism were criminalized because of it, and it gave legal sanction for police to engage in violence against communists to achieve security. Violence contributed to constructing security. The government continued spreading the belief that communism was a foreign culture. The CPC, under direction from the CI, devised a method for continuing their propaganda even as repression against members and fellow travellers continued.

During the repression that followed the Buck et al. trial, Section 98 was used in various ways, such as when Evans and other activists were charged with violating it. It was a means to strike fear into people and terrify them if they supported Communist activists, from continual searches of property to stamping out the left-wing press. It was the death of Nichols Zynchuck that symbolized everything wrong with Section 98; people innocent of any crime, even political ones, could have their fate decided on the spot, with the limits of their guilt measured by the "size of a police officer's helmet." Violence and murder were legal only if conducted by the sovereign power, and they were exercised in the case of Zynchuck and the violent clashes police engaged in with activists. The government had established with Section 98 its right to judge the politics of Canadians and to nation-build through repression. It had also created more laws along the same lines with no issue. Section 98's endgame was approaching as its opponents became more organized and more vocal in their opposition to it. It would take a riot of historical proportions, new Section 98 arrests, and the mass support for a then-novel concept, civil rights, to finally rein in its power, at least temporarily.

6

Judgment

Opposition to Section 98 emerged from trades and labour councils shortly after it was created. But its opponents had little support from other leftists because it had never been used. Following Buck et al. in 1931, many on the left were awakened to the dangers of Section 98 and mobilized on a massive scale to oppose it. For many progressives, Section 98 symbolized terror and state repression and spurred the re-conception of what rights citizens were entitled to and which ones should be protected. No longer were only property rights sacrosanct; growing numbers of Canadians now believed that civil rights were in need of protection. Progressives argued that if the government had the power to engage in repression, Canadians were entitled to protection. In contrast to those who supported Section 98, progressives put forth a different idea of security: they believed Canadians' safety would be better secured once Section 98 was gone and that its repeal would be an important step in protecting Canadians' civil liberties.

Previous studies on the history of human rights in Canada have maintained that an early rights movement began in the mid-1930s with the creation of the first civil liberties groups. These were tied to progressives such as F.R. Scott and the League for Social Reconstruction. Because the Canadian Labor Defense League (CLDL) was concerned only about workers' rights, its efforts are often regarded as a precursor to this rights movement.[1] Yet it was the CLDL that ended up leading the first and largest, at that point in time, broad-based rights movement. It was the CLDL's efforts that spurred other progressives to join the movement it had launched. Canada's rights movement was initially influenced by the CLDL, which sought to protect the rights it felt workers were denied because of Section 98, such as the rights to free speech and assembly. In an ironic twist of fate, it was the exclusion of communists by way of the sovereign ban that gave rise to Canada's civil rights movement; it was thus a movement that needed the exclusion in order to exist. Canadians needed the exclusion of communists in order to envision a liberal society that protected civil liberties, a liberal-democratic Canada that safeguarded civil rights. The exception proved the rule.

From a strategic standpoint, repealing Section 98 was critical for the CLDL's survival, and while it had the initial support of the Communist International (CI), the CI had failed to anticipate just how liberal the CLDL would become. This chapter contributes to the growing body of literature demonstrating that Communists did have more autonomy from the CI than previously believed.[2] The CLDL strategy of trying to unite with other leftists, before Moscow's turn to a "united front" against fascism, was effective in broadening support for the repeal of Section 98 by attracting moderate progressives and respected thinkers such as Frank Underhill and F.R. Scott. Key to resisting Section 98 was the ability of CPC supporters to do what they did best: act politically in the manner they saw fit, regardless of whether their actions were tolerated by the authorities. But this time they aligned themselves with broad segments of society, challenging the ability of the state to define the security threat as being caused by a minority of foreign agitators.

Bennett's government was determined to continue using Section 98 to halt unacceptable political actions, such as in the case of the On-to-Ottawa Trek, which was a political action designed to improve the plight of the unemployed and also repeal Section 98. Even with little evidence, the authorities tried to paint the strike organizers as members of an unlawful organization. The election of the Liberal government of Mackenzie King led to Section 98's repeal in 1936, but the repeal also led to a strengthening of Canada's sedition laws.

The CLDL and the Making of Liberal Communists

J.S. Woodsworth and other progressive members of the House, as well as the Trades and Labour Congress, opposed Section 98 from its inception. So too did Mackenzie King's government, even though Liberal and Conservative senators voted against Section 98's repeal. It is unknown whether the Liberals genuinely supported Section 98's repeal or passed bills to keep their minority government knowing the bills would fail in the Senate (King promised House progressives that the Liberals would put forth bills to repeal Section 98). Those most directly affected by Section 98, the Communists, did not actively seek its repeal until Buck et al. were charged with violating it in the summer of 1931. When the CPC turned its attention to Section 98, it did so through its subsidiary group, the CLDL, which led the effort to repeal the law and demand the protection of workers' civil rights – a novel concept at the time.

When it was created in 1925, the CLDL was designed to function as a temporary body to provide immediate aid to striking members of the newly minted Mine Workers' Union of Canada in the Drumheller-Wayne minefields of Alberta. In September of 1925, the initiative to establish a permanent body was taken by Tim Buck in cooperation with Moscow's group, the International Red Aid (IRA). The IRA was a body established by the Soviets to provide assistance to Communists around the globe, both to support their revolutionary efforts and to aid members and their families who faced jail or persecution. The CI advised the CPC to establish such a body in Canada as early as 1924. The CLDL was modelled on the IRA and the International Labour Defense (ILD), created by the Communist Party of the United States of America in June 1925.[3]

While the group's creation was heavily influenced by the Communists, its founding committee was diverse. The group was unsuccessful at preventing convictions in the case of the miners, but it did manage to raise $4,000 in support of them and their families.[4] The CLDL disbanded its provisional committee after holding its first convention on 27 October 1927. Within two years, the group had established fifty-two branches with a total of approximately three thousand dues-paying members. The group's constitution, established at its first convention, stated that the CLDL's main purpose was to "unite all forces" into a broad national body that would defend and provide support for workers prosecuted for their "activities within the Labor Movement," irrespective of their "political or industrial affiliations, race, colour, or nationality."[5] Its mandate included providing aid to families of arrested workers, providing legal defence and funds for arrested workers, advocating for the "repeal of anti-working class laws," and defending foreign-born workers against "persecution, unwarranted deportation and exclusion." The CLDL was the only group at the time whose explicit purpose was to defend workers who faced the brunt of state repression and to provide aid to foreign workers facing deportation. It welcomed workers of all ideological leanings as members.[6]

The group provided legal aid to workers during the late 1920s and into 1930, so much so that by February 1930 the group had a deficit of $2,500, most of it owed as lawyer fees, the lion's share to lawyer

J.L. Cohen. The CI tried to structure the direction of the CLDL. Large recruitment and funding drives were held in March and June of 1931. As much as the CLDL was designed as a group appealing to all workers, the CPC leadership stressed the importance of foreign-born members to the CLDL. The party brass believed that the support of the CPC's language organizations was critical for the CLDL, as was the issue of deportation.[7] According to the CPC leadership, the CLDL's antideportation stance directly affected its existence because it needed the support of the CPC's ethnic base.

While few women rose to leadership positions in the CLDL as Jeanne Corbin and Becky Buhay did, the group attracted more women to its ranks than other CPC-affiliated groups. The list of delegates from its 1930 congress included thirteen women whose recorded occupation was "housewife" and who were from women's groups such as the Ladies Auxiliary of the Canadian Labor Defense League.[8]

The CPC tried to steer the CLDL away from legal defences. It wanted the group to mobilize workers against international fascism and support "class war prisoners," stop the practice of paying fines for workers, and provide legal defence only to select cases, especially "important political cases," without defining what those were.[9]

Once Buck et al. were convicted, the CLDL ramped up its efforts to have Section 98 repealed. The headline in the CPC paper the *Worker* on 21 November 1931 stated: "Mobilize for the Repeal of Section 98." The issue called for all workers to oppose Section 98 and to attend an upcoming conference organized by the CLDL. The paper claimed that "no strikers" and "NO LABOUR ORGANIZATION" were safe from prosecution.[10] It linked Section 98 to the group's continued opposition to political deportations and used the repeal of Section 98 to advocate for the release of Buck et al. The CLDL's strategy for repealing the law involved increasing the public's awareness by distributing pamphlets and holding conventions. It wanted to expand the CLDL and build partnerships with as many groups as possible, including other labour organizations and parties. In addition to rallies and protests, it flooded Parliament with protest resolutions and petitions.

By July of 1933, the CLDL had gone to extraordinary lengths to organize and advocate for Section 98's repeal. The group reported that five million pieces of literature, mostly pamphlets and manifestos, had been distributed – two million of them in the first half of 1933. The group printed one booklet and three pamphlets on the trial of the Eight, which together had a circulation of sixty thousand.[11] Meetings and conventions calling for Section 98's repeal were advertised in the *Worker* nearly every month from 1932 to 1935. The group managed to organize a nationwide petition with approximately two hundred thousand signatures from individuals in 814 different cities and presented it to Mackenzie King, J.S. Woodsworth, and Prime Minister Bennett.[12] In the same year, the CLDL secured fifty thousand endorsements from Ontario workers in support of Section 98's repeal and printed fifty thousand protest place cards. Protest resolutions were routinely sent to Hugh Guthrie, William Price, and R.B. Bennett. It is little wonder that the government's focus shifted to trying to stop the CLDL in 1933 and 1934.

Led by A.E. Smith, a delegation of workers from a number of locales met with the minister of labour on 22 February 1933 to demand Section 98's repeal, Buck et al.'s release, and an end to deportations. They were rebuffed, but the CLDL made an impression on the government. In February 1933, Guthrie admitted to the House that he was sufficiently aware of the CLDL. He even assumed the league must be getting funds from somewhere because he was learning of "the activities of this association through petitions from every quarter of this dominion," adding: "I am not overstating the case when I say that I have hundreds and hundreds of them. I have now ceased to acknowledge receipt of them." He noted that "there [did] not appear a single Anglo-Saxon or French Canadian name" on the long petitions, only the "names of foreigners, unpronounceable names for the most part." He reiterated his point that because of the CLDL, Section 98 was more necessary than ever. He grudgingly admitted that the CLDL had built a huge movement against Section 98 and had even obtained the support of the churches.[13]

The authorities did not really believe that the CLDL was run by immigrants. They knew it was being led by Anglo-Saxon Communists, and this concerned them. Since Buck et al.'s conviction, the majority of the CLDL's new members were Anglo-Saxon. The group grew rapidly, and the CI took notice. From July 1931 to October of 1932, the group grew from 5,000 affiliated members to 14,360. From November of 1931 to August of 1932, forty repeal conferences were held in Ottawa, Toronto, Hamilton, Calgary, Winnipeg, Vancouver, Regina, Montreal, Glace Bay, and Sudbury.[14] On the whole, the demonstrations were not large, but the delegates represented many workers. In February of 1933, for example, 876 different bodies sent resolutions to the government representing 171,315 workers and farmers; 243 resolutions came from trade union locales representing 88,902 workers. The CLDL was still undertaking its legal defences, which continued the financial crisis for the group. Its growth was remarkable: from a few hundred members in its early days to 16,471 by July of

1933, 7,023 of them hailing from the British Isles. Beyond sales of literature, it was the CLDL's membership that kept the group alive. In 1932, the *Labor Defender* went from a run of 1,500 to 6,500. The following year saw an increase in dues payments by 50 per cent at a time when 70 per cent of the CLDL's membership was unemployed.[15] The CLDL was being supported by those with the least means in Canada. After Buck et al.'s conviction, the group achieved what the CPC prior to 1931 could not: it grew at a quick rate, was able to draw in support from outside Communist ranks and, most importantly, recruited Anglo-Saxons. The irony of the CLDL's success cannot be overstated. Without Section 98, none of it would have been possible.

The CLDL built support for its repeal campaign among workers by framing Section 98 as reflective of capitalism's flaws and as a weapon of the state to whip up emotions of fear and terror in people. For instance, in circulars calling for Section 98's repeal, the group argued that Section 98 was "capitalist legislation designed to suppress the workers' movement" and prevent people from protesting against poverty and war.[16] CLDL repeal conferences stressed that by repealing Section 98, workers' rights of "free speech, free assembly and freedom of organization" would be ensured.[17] The CLDL sent letters to all trade unions and all workers' and farmers' organizations, encouraging them to participate in an eastern congress against Section 98. In the letters, A.E. Smith mentioned the imprisonment of Buck et al. and the recent charges against Joe Derry and Arthur Evans, the number of arrests over the past six months for working-class activism, and that Section 98 was "the most formidable expression, of this rise in terror."[18] Echoing throughout the pamphlets and CLDL conferences was that Section 98 represented the pinnacle of repression and capitalist cruelty. The arrest of Joe Derry was an attack not just against youth but against working-class youth who tried to protest their conditions by organizing opposition.[19]

The CLDL stressed that Section 98 targeted not just individuals, but organizations, and if Derry's group, the YCL, could be targeted by authorities, so could every group in the labour movement. Section 98 was the authorities' way of maintaining, according to the CLDL, the state's policies of starving the unemployed.[20] The CLDL claimed that it was everyone's duty to protect the values of "democratic and constitutional criticism," which Section 98 denied.[21] For the CLDL, the removal of Section 98 would pave the way for workers to demand immediate reforms, including improvement of their living conditions and an end to unemployment and possibly even capitalism itself. For the CLDL, the removal of Section 98 was security. The section was, as Smith described it, the highest expression of the government's "terror." To beat it, the group would have to confront the fear and terror it brought. Removing Section 98 was the only way to truly usher in a more progressive society that respected civil rights and protected workers' security as the CLDL understood it.

The CLDL succeeded in acting politically by agitating and organizing tens of thousands for the repeal of Section 98 because it drew attention to its broad impact (any organization faced a potential charge) and framed it as more than a law. For the CLDL, Section 98 was symbolic of state terror and the means by which the government silenced opposition. During the worst years of the Depression, such claims resonated among the tens of thousands of unemployed youth in Canada who were the bulk of the CLDL's members and main source of its funding.

Cooperation and Conflict: The CLDL, the CCF, and the CI

The CLDL spread its views of Section 98 to other progressives and wanted their cooperation to build a widespread movement to repeal it. Repealing Section 98 meant ending unjust deportations and releasing Buck et al., but the CLDL also hoped to pull more progressives into the Communist ranks. The call for cooperation came much earlier than the Soviet Union's official policy change to a "united front" against fascism in 1935. A.E. Smith made such an offer to J.S. Woodsworth before Buck et al. were charged on 22 April 1931. The two had a prior relationship working as Methodist ministers within the social gospel movement. Smith wanted Woodsworth to step up his attacks against Conservatives in the House of Commons and sharpen the class divisions between Bennett and the rest of the population. He claimed he did not agree with the vicious verbal attacks that CPC members had levied against social democrats, even though Smith continued the attacks in the 1930s.[22] Woodsworth appreciated the letter, but declined the offer.[23] But the CLDL would not give up on the message of cooperation.

In 1932–3, the Co-operative Commonwealth Federation (CCF) was formed following two conventions, one in Calgary in 1932 and the other in Regina in 1933. The CCF was a loose federation of farmers, labourers, and socialists. Prominent early members included the Ginger Group – a group of progressive MPs united in their views and who sat apart from the mainstream parties in the House. With Woodsworth as the leader of the new federation, the group had support from the League for Social Reconstruction (LSR), a group led by intellectuals, with members such as F.R. Scott, Frank Underhill, and Eugene Forsey, among others. The LSR, Scott and Underhill specifically, were responsible for drafting the *Regina Manifesto*, which was the CCF's founding document, and presented at the group's Regina convention in 1933. Motivated by the seriousness of the Depression, the CCF's aims were to reform capitalism into a socialist state, which they believed would put the interests of the people first. They viewed themselves as having the solution to the problems of the modern economy and that this solution was through socialist reform.[24]

The CLDL moved swiftly to make a connection with the group even though the organizations disagreed on how to create a new socialist state, with the CCF seeking one through democracy and reform and the Communists through revolution. Despite the difference, the CLDL approached the CCF to join forces in 1933 against Section 98, secure a release of the Eight, and stop unjustified deportations. The CLDL proposed a joint conference with an equal number of delegates from the CCF and CLDL to discuss building a united front in support of these goals. The CLDL's invitation indicated that it was open to any suggestions from the CCF on the issues. Woodsworth replied in the negative, and for good reason, for despite Smith and the CLDL's calls for cooperation, social democrats were still being branded by Communists as traitors to the working class, dupes, and "social fascists" in traditional Third Period inflammatory style. Becky Buhay of the CLDL responded to Woodsworth's rejection, claiming that the CLDL would go directly to the CCF membership in the absence of support from Woodsworth.[25] The strategy was effective.

Several events in the 1930s fuelled the CLDL's efforts at cooperation with progressives. In 1932, while the Eight were incarcerated, a riot broke out in Kingston Penitentiary in which 450 inmates protested their conditions. Buck was charged with inciting to riot, and nine months were added to his sentence after his trial in 1932. An unknown guard fired seven shots into Buck's cell seven days after the riot occurred. Smith and the CLDL were incensed and accused the government of trying to assassinate Buck. In the House, Guthrie claimed that the shots were intended only to frighten Buck.[26]

Smith led another delegation to Ottawa to meet Bennett and protest what Smith called the "frame up" against him. He demanded Section 98's repeal and an investigation into the shooting. Bennett shot down both requests and furiously ordered Smith out of his office.[27] As a result of Smith's repeated claims that the government was responsible for the shooting, and Bennett's hatred of him, Smith was charged with sedition early in 1934. He was acquitted, and the broad support he received from the public included CCF members, even though Smith continued to publicly blame Woodsworth for misrepresenting workers. Woodsworth forbade any cooperation with Communists, but as Smith put it, "CCF clubs sent delegates to our defense conferences."[28] Given the similarities in ideology and goals, it was difficult for some CCF members to see the rationale of the CCF leadership's heavy-handed rejection of Communist calls for cooperation. With the Soviet Union officially promoting cooperation in 1935, things got worse for the CCF in 1936. CCF members in Ontario, led by Ben H. Spence, invited Communists to support them at a May Day celebration. Spence and three others were expelled from the CCF, as were four CCF Ontario Clubs. The frequent Communist efforts at cooperation pushed Woodsworth and the CCF leadership to tighten party discipline.[29]

While the efforts of the CLDL to cooperate with CCF members are well documented, how the CI viewed these attempts at cooperation during its Third Period policy of class against class is not. Many historians have avoided discussion of how the CLDL fit in relation to the CI not only during the Third Period, but during the united front or "Popular Front against Fascism."[30] That the CLDL called for cooperation before Moscow's turn to a popular front strategy strongly reveals the independence from the CI that Communist members and groups could exert. Circumstances facing the CPC in Canada, such as the presence of Section 98 and Buck et al.'s conviction, forced the CLDL to function differently than other CPC-backed organizations such as the Workers' Unity League (WUL). Similar to the WUL, the CLDL was by the time of the Third Period a Communist-led group that was by no means exempt from Third Period ideology. But in spite of Smith's claims that social democrats were not acting in labour's best interest, they were still encouraged to join the CLDL, in a clear attempt to boost the membership of the league. Such a call would have provoked tension with Moscow during the Third Period, particularly if the "social fascist" new members did not become card-carrying Communists. The CLDL claimed to support all workers *regardless of political affiliation* or ethnicity. Its constitution gave it an obligation to defend its members, and its membership far outstripped that of the CPC. These facts, coupled with the CLDL taking up legal cases in which dozens of workers were arrested (such as when Murdoch Clarke and Roy Berlando were arrested with twenty-five others in an Alberta hunger march) or in which it tried to right a moral wrong (such as in the case of Zynchuck, who was *not* a

CLDL member) meant that the CLDL likely legally defended those "social fascists" the CI so despised or even workers with no political affiliation. Yet despite the CLDL's claims of support for all workers, there is little evidence that the group engaged in widespread efforts to help defend indigenous peoples in Canada or, indeed, engaged in any broad campaigns to defend the rights of racial minorities beyond its calls to end deportations. Still, it worked tirelessly to defend many workers in a legal system in which they otherwise had no means of defence, much to the group's financial detriment. It was starved for cash and nearly bankrupt by 1930 because of the large number of legal cases it took on.

By engaging in the bourgeois legal system that it opposed, and by working side by side with liberal lawyers, it simultaneously, albeit indirectly, sanctioned that which it opposed, a liberal state and its laws. By relying heavily on the support of foreign-born workers and defending them, the CLDL went against the grain of the policies of the CPC leadership with respect to the CPC's aims to recruit more Anglo-Saxon and French-Canadian workers. The CLDL was one of the Communist-led organizations, the WUL being the other significant one, that the CI would have little choice but to tolerate if it wanted to spread the Communist message in Canada after the CPC was found unlawful in November 1931.

Following Buck et al.'s conviction, the CI offered its input on the problems facing the CPC. It thought that the CPC conducted a defence that was *too* legal in 1931 and expressed its dissatisfaction with the CLDL's early efforts at repealing Section 98. In 1932, well before the united front policy of the Soviet Union was underway, the CI felt that the CLDL was blurring class lines and that its attempts at cooperation with social democrats and other leftists benefitted only trade unions. Even though the CI was not impressed with the CLDL's strategy, the CI admitted that the movement could strengthen the party.[31] Still, in spite of its many successes, the CI continued to take issue with the league's message and tactics even as it admitted that the CLDL was doing the most for communism in Canada, ironically by defending workers' legal rights. The CI admitted in 1934 that the CLDL's "struggle against terror" appeared now as "the spearhead of the whole movement."

This is not to say that the CLDL operated in a state of complete independence from the wishes of the CI, but that the realities facing the group's survival were paramount. The CI was willing to have the CLDL continue its efforts at cooperation, provided it could interpret the CLDL's actions as trying to absorb CCF members and lead the labour movement rather than as advocating for the protection of liberal freedoms, even if its constitution and actions revealed otherwise. However, the CI still believed that the CLDL was "confus[ing] the masses" and making too many opportunistic mistakes, in that it was not "assimilating" new members from the CCF.[32] The CI doubted a mass movement to repeal Section 98 would be successful. It thought that there were too many contradictions among the bourgeoisie and that members of the government had been anxious to appear democratic to appease the public. The CI argued that partnership with moderate leftists was folly because if everyone from progressives and liberals was opposed to Section 98, it could result in workers thinking that the moderates, not the Communists, represented them. The CI maintained that it was the party that should be leading the movement for the repeal of Section 98 and that the identity of the party should not be "submerged."[33]

Even though it was not meeting Moscow's standards, the CLDL continued to seek partnerships by calling on all workers to join the fight against repression and Section 98's repeal. By 1934, the CI believed that the group had "failed to improve organization" and still had not assimilated new CCF members.[34] Part of the reason for this belief may have been the changes made to the CLDL's constitution in 1932. Still committing itself to the defence of *all* workers as it did in 1927, the CLDL now included a surprising addition in its list of aims for the organization; in addition to legal defence and fighting deportation, the group expanded its purpose to include the "fight for the right of free speech, free press, freedom of organization and assembly for the workers, and for the right to strike and picket, and defend themselves."[35] In this way, the story of the CLDL contributes to a growing literature on individuals and groups of leftists that sought to defend the rights of workers, women, and racial minorities.[36] The CLDL was a group conflicted by what was expected of it. Supporting individual freedom was at odds with the CI's goals of assimilating workers into the communist movement. It tried to live up to the CI's expectations but had to grapple with the reality facing its members and the threats posed by Section 98 and state repression. Assimilation of CCFers was not the main goal (even if it was the CI's); winning the fight against repression and freeing the CPC leadership were more important to the CLDL. Indeed, the CI argued that the CLDL's position on Section 98 was far "too liberal."[37] The irony was rich; as early as 1931–2, it was the Communist-led CLDL that began a mass campaign in Canada to fight for the liberal rights of workers. A broad chorus of voices supporting Section 98's repeal was necessary to remove it. CCF members, its leadership, and even its intellectuals could agree that Section 98 had to go.

Communist Liberals

Francis Reginald Scott was one of the leading voices from Canada's intellectual community who bitterly opposed Section 98 and the repression of the 1930s. A law professor at Montreal's McGill University, a poet, and one of the early leaders in Canada's civil rights movement, Scott grew into his socialism. His father was an Anglican archdeacon in Montreal and exposed him to the social gospel movement, a brand of Christianity that promoted societal change and social action to create a heaven on earth. He attended Oxford as a Rhodes Scholar and was influenced by the British Fabians and by the writings of J.S. Woodsworth. Such a background shaped the young poet into a socialist who sought to place, as he wrote in 1933, "human welfare above property rights."[38]

Scott was one of the founding members of the League for Social Reconstruction (LSR). Spurred by the devastating unemployment and poverty during the Depression and the state repression against progressives, the group sought a transformation of Canadian society in which the state would take the lead in securing the general well-being of society, from providing national health care to ensuring and protecting individual freedoms. Theses reformers believed that these reforms were necessary to fix the problems of society. Scott and the group were often regarded by the RCMP as Communists for their social-democratic beliefs.[39] The LSR played a leading role in the formation of the CCF, with F.R. Scott and Frank Underhill in particular being responsible for the drafting of the CCF's founding document, the *Regina Manifesto*.[40]

Central to the LSR's conception of the state role in protecting individual freedoms was the elimination of Section 98. But for Scott and other leading members of the CCF, the repeal of Section 98 was not about capitalists seeking to silence calls for reform or even revolution, as the Communists believed. For these progressives, Section 98 was anathema to liberal democracy. The law, and the repression linked to it, was un-British and antidemocratic, the antithesis of the kind of law a state should have. For both the LSR and CCF, reform of society was the goal, and much like the Communists, who believed that socialism was the harbinger of the new modern society, Section 98 had no place in the group's vision of a newly reformed Canada. The protection of civil rights became a part of what Scott and other progressives believed a democratic state had to do. For Scott and others such as Underhill, protecting civil rights played a key role in how they understood security. As Eric Adams writes, this period was a crucial one in the evolution of the concept of rights in Canada, with Scott playing an important role. Prior to the 1930s, rights that were protected by the state were mostly property rights, but for Scott, civil rights such as freedom of speech and assembly were necessary and essential to constitutional law in a democracy.[41] Section 98 and its repeal were important in launching this change in thinking.

Progressives' view that Section 98 (and the deportations linked to it) stood opposite British justice and traditions appears in the debates to repeal Section 98 and Section 41 during the 1920s. J.S. Woodsworth argued that British justice demanded that a person receive a trial before being deported, as deportation was akin to judging someone guilty of an offence. He argued that Section 98 was in violation of proud British values like freedom of speech and referred to moments where revolution was acceptable, such as during England's Glorious Revolution of 1688. There were times when people needed to be political in unconventional ways. The British-history-based imagery continued into the 1936 debates for Section 98's repeal, when Woodsworth read from an article stating: "No nation ever became truly great save by successful sedition and revolution . . . The signature of King John was placed to the Magna Charta, wrenched from him by the nobles; revolution led King Charles to the block; the corn law riots – these were crimes against the law and seditious, but no one hangs his head in shame because of them."[42] Woodsworth explained that R.B. Graham, KC, a magistrate in his riding, read this when he proposed a toast to England during the annual Saint George's Day dinner, complete with music by the regimental band of the Princess Patricia's Canadian Light Infantry. For Woodsworth, what made England truly great was the way in which turmoil changed the country for the better and how its legal institutions' treatment of sedition was both progressive and modern.

Scott and other progressives shared these ideas. Scott publicly denounced Section 98 after the trial of Buck et al. He was passionate in his condemnation, even though his societal status could have easily led him to retreat into a less controversial and more comfortable life. Scott published an article in the *Queen's Quarterly* in 1931 about the trial that urged Canadians to ask themselves "what our traditions of freedom of speech and association really mean, if anything." He remarked how the Communist Party was a legitimate political party in nations across Europe, including Britain. He observed that with the Buck et al. verdict, Canada had aligned itself with "Italy, Japan, Poland and some of the more reactionary Balkan states," but that only Canada claimed to be a democracy.[43] Scott detailed the extraordinary powers of Section 98 and argued that there was no "particular incident, no attempt at rebellion which move[d] the police to make the arrests" of Buck et al.[44]

In regards to whether the party sought change by unlawful means, Scott pointed out that it was "not difficult by ordinary legislation to destroy Canadian institutions." Nova Scotia, he noted by way of example, had recently abolished the Legislative Council by legal means. Deportees suspected of "'red' activities" were tried before boards of inquiry, which were "not composed of judges" and held "secret trials." He continued: "This is as dictatorial and contrary to Canadian traditions as anything could be, yet it is apparently legal." These were not the actions of a British democratic society but of an uncivilized totalitarian one. Scott agreed with the defence in the Buck trial, remarking that revolutions do not come about because "parties make them," but because society changes. They are thus a "part of the logic of history, which Communists cannot prevent or create any more than capitalists can." The Communist Party, he concluded, was thus on trial for something that it had not advocated or taught, since it did not "advocate the inevitable."[45]

Following the publication of his essay, Scott gave public lectures on free speech and continued to write articles denouncing Section 98 and the deportations linked to it. For Scott, the deportation hearings for deportees like the Halifax Ten were a series of secret trials that were anathema to democracy.[46] Yet Scott was unwilling to join the CLDL or link himself to the group. Like other CCF members, he was a firm proponent and supporter of parliamentary democracy; as Walter Young explains, the CCF's "liberalism kept them from being communists while their socialism prevented them from being liberals."[47] Scott fit this description, although in the early years of the CLDL's repeal campaign he did lend some support.

In 1932, Scott published an article in *Canadian Forum* entitled "Not Guilty," which he permitted the CLDL to reprint as a pamphlet. In a heavily sardonic and sarcastic style, Scott chided everything from Prime Minister Bennett's handling of the Depression and the Senate to the verdict in the case of the Toronto Communists, but he focused heavily on Section 98. He wrote: "It was apparently invented by the state of New York, and it suited so well the famous American methods of repressing crime that we thought we had better copy it . . . Our parlour Bolsheviks had better understand what they are in for

. . . has any Canadian bookseller ever sold a copy of the Communist Manifesto? Twenty years for him. Has any Canadian professor taught a class of students in political science that there are occasions when revolution is morally justifiable? Clap him in gaol with the Communists."[48] The article mocked Parliament's creation of Section 98, ridiculing what Scott perceived as Parliament's belief that the British law Canada inherited was somehow inferior because it lacked Section 98. The article was reprinted in the Communist paper the *Worker*, and the party heralded Scott's condemnation of Section 98 as brilliant.

Still, any initial aid that Scott lent to the CLDL in its repeal aims, like the right to reprint the aforementioned articles, was very modest. Not only did his liberalism conflict with the CLDL, but he resented Communists attacking social democrats like Woodsworth and himself. For instance, when approached in 1936 by Jack King, who was both a CLDL and CCF member, on the creation of a civil liberties organization, Scott responded by warning him against any kind of partnership with the Communists.[49] While Scott and other progressives were wary of cooperation with Communists, others such as Alfred Stiernotte, an engineer based out of the University of Alberta and member of the LSR's Calgary branch, believed that some cooperation was acceptable, given the need for a broad-based civil liberties organization.

Stiernotte was not opposed to working with Communists to safeguard freedoms such as freedom of speech and assembly, which Section 98 curtailed. But Scott and others, among them Underhill, were not interested in aligning the LSR with a group that Liberals or Conservatives could not get behind. There were divisions, as Lambertson mentions, with classical liberals who supported protection of freedoms but not the growth of the welfare state. While Underhill supported Stiernotte's proposal, he felt it would be too difficult for the LSR to get involved. "If you can find the leadership somewhere," he wrote, "a great many of us would serve in the ranks. The leadership is at present being provided by the CLDL, who are doing very good work, as far as I can observe, but there isn't much use for the despised bourgeoisie trying to work along with the communists." The CLDL, he thought, would have little interest in protecting the rights of the bourgeoisie.[50] It is possible that this lack of interest was because the CLDL believed that the bourgeoisie needed little help protecting their rights and certainly did not face the same hardships as working-class individuals, immigrant workers, or the unemployed. Stiernotte went on to form the Canadian Civil Liberties Protective Association (CCLPA), Canada's first civil liberties association.[51]

The group was short-lived, but Scott and other progressives did support organizations that had ties with, or were working with, other Communists during particular moments of crisis, such as the Zynchuck affair and the formation of the Emergency Committee for the Protection of Civil Liberties, which opposed Quebec's David Bill. Others, such as R.L. Calder, a Crown prosecutor and First World War veteran, had, like many others in this period, shifted to the left because of the state's repressive actions. He eventually left the Liberal Party and ran for the CCF in 1939. Calder strongly believed in "our British heritage of freedom," and for him, working with Communists was not out of the question.[52] The degree of separation between moderate progressives and Communists involved in the protection of civil liberties was not immense. While the communist message of protecting workers' rights to seek reform or even revolution was at times difficult to reconcile with moderate progressives' view that the state's violation of freedoms was not in keeping with British traditions, both groups could agree that repression and Section 98 needed to end in order for rights to be protected. The *Regina Manifesto* included the removal of Section 98 as one of its principal goals.

Section 11 of Underhill's original draft stated that the CCF stood for a "revival and maintenance" of what were once established "individual rights in British countries, the rights of freedom of speech and assembly." In language similar to CLDL pamphlets, the section continued, stating that Canada had seen a rise in "Fascist tendencies among all government authorities. The lawless and brutal conduct of the police in breaking up public meetings and in dealing with prisoners . . . whose pol-social [*sic*] views they do not approve must cease." The CCF claimed Section 98 was created "as an instrument of oppression against working class leaders." The final draft differed little from the original.[53]

To many progressives, Section 98 was a blight on Canada's democracy. Moreover, like the CLDL, moderate progressives viewed Section 98 as symbolic of the state repression of the period, an instrument of oppression designed to invoke feelings of terror. The CLDL's messages were resonating; no one could feel safe as long as Section 98 remained. These progressives viewed themselves as upholding British traditions and liberty by attempting to remove Section 98, in stark contrast to more conservative elements and the Bennett government, which believed they were protecting British traditions *with* Section 98. For progressives, Section 98 threatened people's security by limiting their civil rights.

The success of the CLDL in surviving the state's attempts to crush it throughout the repeal movement had much to do with its ability to continue acting politically outside of Parliament and uniting with moderates. This occurred in a variety of ways, from organizing petitions and rallies to participating in protests, conferences, and marches. By Communists uniting with non-Communists, the repeal movement became less about a minority of foreign activists trying to change the law and more about "Canadians" wanting it removed. The support of moderate leftists had a legitimizing effect on the CLDL's repeal efforts.

In many ways, progressives and more radical leftists beat back Section 98 by violating it. They were advocating political change by "force," that is, acting outside of Parliament to demand political change, refusing to abandon the issue of repealing Section 98, and compelling the government to carry out their demands. "Force," after all, was left undefined in the section and could mean more than using violence. One last major political act would force the government to engage in one last major response to quell unrest when a band of unemployed young men clashed with police in Regina in the summer of 1935.

"A Law unto Themselves"

Amid the growing chorus of opponents to Section 98, it would be used one last time along with more repression to quell an unconventional political action. The On-to-Ottawa Trek leaders, Arthur Evans, George Black, Ivan Bell, Ernest Edwards, and Jack Cosgrove, were the last known individuals charged with violating Section 98. In the summer of 1935, they were charged with being members of an unlawful organization, the Relief Camp Workers' Union (RCWU). In the case of Cosgrove, he was charged with being a member of the WUL, and in the case of Evans, the CPC. Halting the trek was the Bennett government's last stand against illegitimate political actions, and the Conservatives were soundly defeated in the federal election in the fall of 1935. As much as the trek was about unemployment and the relief camp system, it was also about the repeal of Section 98, as the trekkers adopted the repeal of it as part of their demands. The Depression and the Regina Riot played an important role in Mackenzie King's Liberal campaign of "King or Chaos." The Regina Riot and the preliminary trial that followed illustrated the exceptional measures Bennett was prepared to use against anything that remotely smacked of communism.

The origins of the On-to-Ottawa Trek dated back to 1932. Bennett, as mentioned in chapter 2, had tenaciously clung to the idea that hard work, sacrifice, and perseverance would break the Depression and that relief only encouraged idleness. But even Bennett was forced to admit that borrowing and economic stimulus were needed.[54] However, this still did not solve the massive unemployment problem, as single unemployed men were not eligible for local relief and were frequently drifting from town to town via the top of freight cars or "riding the rods" in search of work.

As many previous authors have argued, the On-to-Ottawa Trek was perceived as a problem by Bennett and others, such as RCMP commissioner James MacBrien, because they viewed the unemployed as potential foot soldiers in the communist cause and because the CPC actively worked to organize and engage them in protests through subsidiary organizations such as the WUL and the Single Men's Unemployed Association.[55] MacBrien was quoted in 1932 at a veterans' celebration as saying that if Canada was rid of communists, "there would be no unemployment or unrest." Bennett certainly feared a revolt. He increased the RCMP by three hundred members and also spent an additional $250,000 on riot gear in December of 1931. It was in this context that Canada's unemployment relief camps were created.[56]

My examination of the trek and the lead-up to it will be brief. The camps housed single unemployed men who were ineligible for relief and were abysmal failures. Men were paid a menial twenty cents a day and, as one camp member recalled, "it was just the right size to be insulting."[57] The policy created exactly what Bennett hoped to avoid. While the men's survival was at least assured because they were fed and housed, the insulting payments led many of them to view their conditions as little better than prisons or quasi-concentration camps. Communists wasted little time in organizing them.

The RCWU was in operation in 1933 under the auspices of the WUL. The Communist organizers promoted the idea that the camps were slave camps and called the men the "royal twenty centers," reminding them of their state-funded daily salary.[58] As Waiser notes, the agitation was successful in that over the four-year period of the camps' existence, "there were 359 strikes, demonstrations, and disturbances, while 17,391 men or 10 per cent of the total camp population were discharged for disciplinary reasons."[59] This militancy exploded in 1935 when the RCWU called in veteran organizer Arthur Evans to lead a strike involving camp workers in British Columbia on 5 April. Evans had already been campaigning for better conditions for camp workers and organized a conference in March of 1935 that saw RCWU districts support seven demands, including raises and a work-and-wages program, the right to vote for camp members, an end to the Department of National Defence's control of the camps, and the repeal of Section 98. As much as the trek was about the camp system and unemployment, it was also a political act against Section 98, designed to force Ottawa to listen to the trekkers and repeal the law.

Strikers from various camps in BC converged on Vancouver in April. After spending two months in Vancouver, with none of their demands met, the men confronted the issue of what to do next. The group decided to take their concerns to Ottawa.[60] The trekkers had public support in nearly every city where they stopped. Whether because of their youth (some were as young as sixteen) or the public sympathy felt for a generation of young men lost to the Depression, people donated food and other items. However, not everyone was welcoming to the trekkers. From its inception, the trek was feared by officials such as Gary McGeer, mayor of Vancouver, who claimed it was a Communist movement that was "openly flouting constituted authority."[61]

RCMP commissioner MacBrien was eager to put an end to the strike. The federal government was also eager to intervene and halt the trek but needed a reason to do so because government members had claimed that it would not intervene unless a province requested aid. The RCMP informed the government that the strike needed to end because, as RCMP assistant commissioner S.T. Wood put it, it was "clearly a revolutionary movement."[62] The federal government decided to end the trek. On 11 June, MacBrien advised Wood not to let it continue beyond Regina. Wood advised local police and Mounties in the area to be ready for trouble but not to carry a loaded sidearm or ammunition, because the Communists often sought to provoke police. In the House, Guthrie claimed that the trek contained Communist elements and that "law and order" needed to be upheld. Saskatchewan Liberal premier Jim Gardiner had a rocky relationship with the Bennett government and protested its decision to stop the trek in his province. Bennett claimed that the railways had asked for assistance to stop the illegal use of their trains – a thinly veiled excuse to justify the overstepping of the federal government's jurisdiction. Government officials met with trek leaders, but with no resolution in sight, the stage was set for a violent end to the trek.[63] Given the authorities' uneasiness about previous marches of unemployed single men, with thousands of them now marching across the country and asserting their own masculine identities in trying to protect their respectability and dignity, the federal government felt compelled to act. It could not allow this challenge to authority to go unchecked.

On 25 June, MacBrien told Wood that the Trek would be stopped by any means necessary and that the government would institute a state of emergency to halt it. The news was good for Wood, who regarded the trekkers as "carrying out the policy of the Communist party."[64] But Ottawa had no plan to declare an emergency; as far as can be determined, MacBrien was acting on his own. On 27 June, several trekkers, including Jack Cosgrove, Ivan Bell, and Ernest Edwards, attempted to leave the province by truck despite rumours that the RCMP had set up a roadblock and were turning back trucks. With the group under surveillance, Wood wired MacBrien, telling him the government had to declare an emergency. MacBrien ordered Wood to proceed with any arrests and seizures he saw fit to carry out and said the government would back him. Wood advised the province of the situation. The RCMP now believed itself to have emergency powers that it had actually given to itself.[65]

Cosgrove, Bell, and Edwards were arrested as they tried to leave the province. On the night of 1 July, Dominion Day, the authorities brought the trek to a violent end at Market Square at 8 p.m. as the trek leaders addressed a crowd of trekkers and citizens with children present. The RCMP swooped in as the leaders finished speeches at the square, storming the crowd and breaking up the peaceful gathering. After clearing the square, officers were met by hordes of strikers who threw every object available at the officers. Hundreds were injured. Detective Millar of the Saskatchewan police was killed in the melee when someone smashed a two-by-four across his head. Police retaliated after learning about Millar, indiscriminately clubbing and beating anyone found on the street. When trekkers had several officers cornered and were throwing missiles at them, police fired warning shots and Wood gave the order for every officer to have ammunition. Waiser describes the police that evening as being "a law unto themselves." When several other officers were caught by trekkers throwing rocks, Staff Inspector McDougall of the Regina police ordered his men to spread out and fire at will with no warning. Several trekkers were hit and retreated. Surprisingly, none of the trekkers died in the onslaught. Wood reported to MacBrien the following morning that the riot was quelled with no shots fired. He was apparently unaware of the scale of the melee that ensued after Evans and the other leaders were arrested.[66]

The RCMP and local police launched their offensive believing they had emergency powers, and they did. The RCMP gave *itself* emergency powers (believing the official declaration was an eventual formality) to quash the trek, and their actions were defended by and sanctioned by the government following the riot. Given the exceptional state, an exceptional law was used. Even though many in the public opposed Section 98 and its use, the trek leaders were charged with violating Section 98 for being members of an unlawful organization, the Relief Camp Workers' Union. Cosgrove was charged with being a member of the WUL and Evans of the CPC. The Crown targeted all three organizations for being unlawful. Sergeant Leopold was brought into Regina just before the riot to help Crown prosecutors build their case. Although Ottawa was convinced that the trek was revolutionary in its character and leadership, the CI files are almost silent on the trekkers and their movement. Initially, the Communist leadership did not support the trekkers leaving Vancouver and thought it a foolish venture.[67]

While the government was using force and exceptional laws like Section 98 to quash the trek, the CI was fixated on making sure that Communist candidates were prepared to face their CCF rivals in the coming federal election. Indeed, in a twenty-page document on Canada, only one brief paragraph mentioned the trek. One page in particular was scornful of the rebellious ways of Canadian members. "Some comrades develop a bad attitude towards party discipline," the CI lamented; they gave "lip-service" to it, believing that discipline belonged only in the "constitution" of the party, but discipline was important according to the CI. It was party discipline, after all, that the CI believed could help Communist candidates win elections against the CCF.[68] The violence by police against the trekkers was the Bennett government's last demonstration of repression as a form of nation-building and last major attempt at enforcing their idea of security, which centred around crushing communism by any and all means. The government permitted force and violence to be used to crush a political action it had decided was linked to communism. Canadians were meant to take notice about which politics and actions were permitted and which were not.

The preliminary hearing of *Rex v. Ivan Bell, George Black, John Cowan Cosgrove, Arthur H. Evans, Ernest Edwards and Matthew Shaw* began on 19 July 1935 with Walter B. Scott, police magistrate, presiding. H.E. Sampson appeared on behalf of the attorney general, and F.B. Bagshaw and E.C. Leslie appeared on behalf of the minister of justice. The hearing was delayed by several days, as Bagshaw and Leslie wanted Matthew Shaw, who had left the province, brought back to stand trial with the others, even though Sampson did not believe there was enough evidence to convict him. Tom H. Newlove defended the accused.[69] The Crown intended to prove that the

Relief Camp Workers' Union was an unlawful organization because of its connection to the Workers' Unity League, which was affiliated with the CPC. The degrees of separation were many, to say the least, because even if the RCWU was affiliated with the CPC, affiliation alone was no crime, even under Section 98. The Crown had to prove that the RCWU shared the same beliefs as the CPC, which was not an easy thing to do, as the trekkers had developed a reputation for being against violence. But in many ways, the trek was doing exactly what the government charged it with doing, trying to force political change, except not by violent means. The trekkers wanted political action taken on their unemployment situation and their living standards, as well as for the repeal of Section 98. They were being judged for being political in ways the government did not approve of.

The Crown's evidence came from uniformed and undercover RCMP officers who had penetrated the camps and from the local police. Additional evidence came from workers employed on the exhibition grounds that had housed the trekkers in Regina. Witnesses identified items within the exhibition grounds, such as makeshift clubs and iron pipes. The Crown intended to show that the trekkers were preparing to engage in violence at the behest of the leadership. The difficulty for the Crown was that none of the evidence could connect the leaders to the Communists.[70]

Part of the Crown's case relied on trying to prove the RCWU's connection to the CPC and again, like in the Buck et al. trial, stoking fears of revolution because of the connection. One way the Crown lawyers tried to do this was through Arthur Evans, whose ties to the CPC were well known by the authorities even if they were never proven in court. Newlove was worried about evidence that linked Evans to the CPC because he thought that Evans should be tried separately from the other accused. He believed that if evidence was entered against Evans, and his ties to the CPC demonstrated, it would negatively affect the case against the other men. But his attempts to halt the admission of such evidence failed. The evidence that concerned him was about an incident that occurred after Evans and the trek leaders met with the prime minister. Evans was enraged after his meeting with Bennett and his cabinet and the flat refusal of the government to negotiate any of the trekkers' demands. Acting as a sacrificial lamb to save his fellow trekkers from jail (and presumably anticipating where Cosgrove et al.'s Section 98 charges would lead), Evans declared at a trek meeting that because he was a member of the Communist Party, he knew Cosgrove and the others were not members. He claimed that Section 98 was an unfair law by which individuals had to prove their innocence.[71]

Other evidence came from relief camp worker pamphlets, including one dated 20 July 1934, a year before the riot took place. Newlove protested, arguing that there was no evidence to show the men were members back then, but Leslie replied that this was the same kind of evidence used in the Buck trial. Newlove countered that Buck, in conducting his own defence, "had not the legal training to object to it," adding: "Evidence of something that transpired at a time when these men are not being charged with being members of an unlawful association, is not admissible to prove that the association is unlawful now." He elaborated: "The evidence went through in that case [Buck et al.] because [they] admitted that they were members of the Communist party, and also admitted apparently that that was still the existing thesis and tactics and policy of the Communist party . . . if they had not, I don't think that evidence should have gone in at all."[72] Newlove argued that no one could assume that past policies were still relevant to a group presently on trial for violating Section 98, and said that if the Crown tried to use evidence of past CPC policies, such as with Leopold's testimony, he would oppose it. Undercover officers gave evidence that the group was revolutionary, but could not explain why.[73]

The Crown called its expert witnesses to testify on the afternoon of 30 July. Inspector George Fish of the RCMP took the stand. He was the man responsible for the search of the WUL secretary Tom Ewen's home in 1931, and when Fish was about to produce a letter found in Ewen's home, Newlove objected, claiming that evidence from 1931 was not relevant. The Crown claimed that the RCWU was unlawful because of acts it had committed and its association with the WUL. Leslie claimed that the defence needed to prove that what applied in 1931 did not apply now.[74] Newlove disagreed, arguing, "There is some document, no matter what it purports to stand for, that was seized in 1931 – surely that is no evidence that that association is unlawful in 1935 – and particularly when you consider that this document was there and apparently has never been acted upon." For emphasis, he noted that there was no such a thing as a Relief Camp Workers' Union in 1931.[75] When Scott asked Newlove if he could simply show that there was no longer a connection between the group in 1931 and now, Newlove retorted, "Why should I have to? . . . Even under Section 98, [the Crown] must prove that the accused, by their actions, or words, or something, indicated that they were members of an unlawful association." He then added: "Would you be prepared to say that Great Britain was prepared to make a declaration of war now because . . . it [did] in 1914?"[76]

. Scott allowed the evidence, noting Newlove's objection. That afternoon, testimony came from the Crown's best-known expert, Sergeant John Leopold of the RCMP. The Crown decided to tap the well one more time in an attempt to use the evidence that had worked so well in 1931 and in deporting foreign-born activists. Leopold recounted his history in the CPC and testified that the WUL was affiliated with the Red International of Labour Unions (RILU) and did the bidding of the CI. The RILU was a group created in response to Communists getting kicked out of established unions such as those belonging to the American Federation of Labor (AFL). According to Leopold, this dual union movement would create revolutionary unions and the WUL was the centre of such unions in Canada.[77] Much like in the Buck et al. case, CI documents were read in court that contained Communist jargon about the workers overthrowing the bourgeoisie as well as references to the RILU. The Crown's goal was ambitious, as it wanted to prove that the WUL was affiliated with the CPC and hence the CI, and then that because the RCWU was affiliated with the WUL, it must share the same ideology of the CPC and WUL and hence be unlawful.

Leopold was cross-examined by Newlove, who wanted to make things more personal and uncomfortable for him. As Steve Hewitt notes, Leopold struggled with alcoholism while undercover and following the Buck trial.[78] After reviewing Leopold's history in the party, Newlove confronted him on his alcoholism and asked him if he had been drinking heavily in Regina, which Leopold did not completely deny. He claimed he didn't know and didn't think so. Newlove continued: "Weren't you drunk fairly regularly?" Leopold said he hadn't been, but when Newlove asked him whether he had been gambling on the wheat market, Leopold admitted that he had been "dabbling." In addition to painting Leopold as an active member of the party, like Macdonald had tried to do years earlier, Newlove attacked his credibility by portraying him as a drunk who gambled away other people's money, whether from associates or the RCMP.[79] Newlove asked Leopold to replay the events of the past several years and tried to make him look like a man who had betrayed people he knew well, both at the Buck trial and during the deportation hearings in 1932. Newlove's most successful line of questioning was about to end Leopold's usefulness for Crown lawyers in deporting and prosecuting Communists.

He asked Leopold if he could swear that the Workers' Unity League was currently affiliated with the Red International of Labour Unions. Leopold responded that it was in 1931. That was not good enough for Newlove. He aggressively pressed on: "Are you prepared to swear that it is now?" Leopold stumbled and tried to stick to his earlier answer: "I couldn't swear that it is now, but it was in 1931." Newlove would not let Leopold skirt the question and repeatedly asked it until he could force Leopold to relent. He finally did and answered, "I am not prepared to swear it is affiliated, but it has connections." Newlove was not finished with Leopold. In an attempt to quash Leopold's usefulness in linking Canadian groups to Moscow, he questioned if Leopold could swear now that the WUL took orders from the Red International of Labour Unions. This time there was not much fight left in him. Newlove needed to ask the question only once before Leopold answered, "No, I am not prepared to swear now." For the Crown, the well had run dry as far as Leopold was concerned. He had no knowledge of the communist movement outside of his own experiences prior to 1931. Years after Buck et al., Newlove demonstrated how Leopold's usefulness had its limits. With Leopold's testimony complete, the Crown ended its case.[80]

The Crown agreed to withdraw the case against Bell, citing that it had insufficient evidence against him. All of the men except Cosgrove and Evans would be tried for being members of an unlawful association, the RCWU; Cosgrove would be tried for being a member of the WUL and Evans of the CPC. Newlove agreed to allow the evidence detailing Evans's and Cosgrove's memberships in their respective organizations that had been produced in the preliminary hearing to be used at trial. Police magistrate Walter Scott believed there was enough evidence against the accused to proceed to a trial.[81]

No evidence was ever produced to directly link the RCWU to the CPC. Instead the Crown relied on dubious linkages between the RCWU and other groups, hoping to eventually make connections to Moscow organizations. The crucial enemy for the Crown was time. They had no undercover officer in Communist circles who was near any leaders as Leopold was in 1931. Despite the fact that there was no direct evidence to link the RCWU to Moscow and prove it advocated violence, the case would proceed to a trial. The government was determined to use exceptional means and laws to crush any hint of communism. It could not allow the trek, an unsanctioned political act it viewed as against the law, as an affront to security, to go unchecked. The RCMP's raid that provoked the Regina Riot was defended by the federal government, even though the service had given itself the power to crush the strike using any means necessary. Wood was even prepared to use force after the riot had the government of Saskatchewan not aided in disbanding the trekkers and sent them out of the province. He believed his men should have been armed with machine guns.[82] While the Crown and the RCMP were certainly aware of the scant evidence against the accused, they proceeded with the case anyway.

The government was determined, as long as Bennett could cling to office, to crush his opponents' ability to be political in ways he opposed. Arthur Evans began speaking out about the events of the strike while on bail and was supported by local progressives and citizens who were upset by the events of the riot. He distributed pamphlets that claimed that the federal government was behind the end of the trek. Bennett personally contacted Tom Newlove, telling him that Evans's claims in the pamphlets about the federal government were untrue. Newlove apparently disagreed and believed Evans's and the locals' versions of events. Bennett contended that the provincial law society might have something to say about the issue, and Newlove subsequently resigned as the trekkers' defence counsel.[83] The government had no qualms about intimidating anyone trying to assist the trekkers. The Bennett government's use of exceptional means to deal with anything remotely related to communism finally ended on 14 October 1935 when Mackenzie King's Liberal Party swept into office, winning 70 per cent of seats. It was the largest majority government in Canadian history up to that point.

A Fine "Piece of Political Comedy"

On 3 March 1936, the Section 98 case against the trek leaders was withdrawn, the Crown citing a lack of evidence. While there is little doubt that the Crown lacked evidence, the timing was important. It followed the closing statements of the Regina Riot inquiry, which cast some doubt on RCMP actions and testimony.[84] More importantly, the Bennett government lost the election. While there is no evidence to prove that the new federal government was involved in the withdrawal of charges, it is likely that the Liberals, after campaigning on repealing Section 98, would not have wanted a high-profile Section 98 trial to occur so soon after taking office and may have had some influence in having the provincial authorities withdraw charges.

King offered no new or grand ideas during the campaign or following it. The message was a simple one: "King or Chaos," a slogan that fit the mood of the time. Although Bennett's government did not cause the Depression, it did not help end it much either. Its restrictive trade policies and lack of dedicated support for the unemployed only made the Bennett government seem hopelessly out of touch with the plight of the common citizen. Moreover, the state-sanctioned repression of the period did not help Bennett's government at election time.

He tried to campaign on a law-and-order platform, but it was difficult to convince the electorate of his claims amid the labour and social unrest. One in five voters sent a more radical candidate to Parliament, often from the ranks of the Social Credit Party or CCF, with the Communists still unable to secure an electoral win. The turn to less conventional parties was a sign not only of regional tensions but of people's mistrust in the traditional parties. But King believed that people wanted a return to a more secure and safer option, and it was only the Liberal Party that had national support at this time.[85] His instincts were correct.

Part of King's platform was the repeal of Section 98, a nod to the growing chorus of opposition to the law. On 2 August 1935, King outlined his views on Section 98 during a radio address. He told his audience that the Liberal Party believed that "the excuse of the present crisis" had led to the violation of individual rights. "Liberalism," he reminded people, stood for "the British principle of FREE SPEECH and FREE ASSOCIATION," and the Liberals would defend it by repealing Section 98 and "end[ing] the present practice of arbitrary deportations." He added, "The Liberal party will give no quarter to Communism in Canada. Those who advocate the overthrow, by force, of our existing institutions, are enemies of society, and should be so regarded."[86]

Ever the conciliator, King tried to appeal to the broad campaign calling for Section 98's repeal by arguing that Section 98 did not protect but instead trampled on British principles and justice. He also appealed to those fearful of communism and its growth by reassuring them that Section 98 would not be needed to prevent communism, for which he had no sympathy.

The Liberal government's solution, which was designed to appeal to these two groups, was to repeal the bulk of Section 98's most offensive and contentious elements while preserving its core, namely its ability to set the terms for what political expressions were not acceptable. The solution was presented in a series of memos to King by Deputy Minister of Justice W. Stewart Edwards. Section 98 would be repealed, but Section 133, the sedition section, would be amended. Edwards began work on devising a suitable substitute for Section 98 with the minister of justice, Ernest Lapointe. In his letters to Lapointe, Edwards claimed that the goal was to remove Section 98's "so-called objectionable" elements but still maintain the Code's ability to target Communists. Edwards and Lapointe outlined how other Code sections could preserve much of Section 98, such as Section 134, which dealt with seditious libel.[87] The goal was to amend the Code sufficiently so that elements of Section 98 that targeted communism were retained and only those subsections of Section 98 that overlapped with other Code sections were repealed.

Edwards presented King with a summary of the changes to Section 133, which included adding a new subsection, subsection 4, which contained a new term called "seditious intention." Seditious words would be defined as words that expressed a seditious intention. Without limiting the generality of the definition, the new subsection stated that a seditious intention was presumed where "*any person publishes or circulates any writing in which it is advocated, or teaches or advocates, the use, without the authority of law, of force as a means of accomplishing any governmental change* [emphasis mine]." This single change was an important one because when combined with other sections, such as Section 134, it preserved the core of Section 98's subsection 8.[88] It allowed the government to still target the expression of unwanted political ideologies such as communism. Edwards noted that he had made sure Section 133's new subsection 4 resolved the "and/or" problem of Section 98's subsection 3. He wrote, "The presence of this conjunctive embarrassed us in the Toronto prosecution and it does not, I think, properly express what Parliament intended."[89]

To reassure King that much of Section 98's powers to target communism would not be lost, Edwards provided him with a side-by-side comparison of the new Section 133 subsection with Section 98(3). Edwards stated that the new Section 133 subsection did away with the "unlawful organization" term but that there was no cause for worry. If the authorities regarded a group as being unlawful, it could be found to be part of a seditious conspiracy, and individuals could be prosecuted if they expressed a "seditious intention" contrary to the new Section 133(4). Section 98(3), the subsection pertaining to "members" or "officers" of an unlawful organization, would disappear completely as it would have no purpose, as would Section 98(5), which targeted hall owners who rented a hall to an unlawful organization. Edwards reminded King that the authorities could still search an individual or organization's property with warrants, negating the need for Section 98's subsection 6.

Section 98(8) was preserved with both Section 133's amendment and the existing Section 134. Force was still undefined in Section 133, but Edwards did not feel a more constrictive definition was needed, because of the addition to the section of the words "without the authority of law."[90] The Liberals wanted to reduce the penalty for seditious offences, outlined in Section 134, from twenty years to two. Section 98's subsections 10 and 11, on the importation of material and on the duty of government employees to seize it, respectively, would be removed with the changes.[91]

The Code revisions were designed to maintain the state's ability to target ideology. King's radio address, and the notes of Edwards and Lapointe, illustrate that the government never had any intention to do away with the state's ability to judge the terms of political expression. With the new amendments, only the most contentious aspects of Section 98 would be removed, such as the seizure of imported materials, or subsection 5, which targeted hall owners. The government still retained the power to prosecute Communists, and while it wanted to reintroduce the sedition saving clause that allowed for legitimate grievances to be aired against it, all of these were changes that applied only to the Criminal Code. The government always retained the power to invoke the War Measures Act to manage disorder.

Bill 96's second reading began on 19 June 1936. Ernest Lapointe opened the debate, stating that the repeal of Section 98 had "been recommended by a tremendous majority of the electorate of Canada." "It was an issue everywhere," he added, including in his own province, where it was the main topic of the campaign. He reviewed Section 98's history and highlighted how the section was identical to PC 2384. Lapointe stressed that the calls for repeal came from all directions in Canadian society, not just activists. He argued that Liberals believed it was "dangerous to perpetuate in peace time enactments which are war time measures and designed to meet special emergencies . . . which exists [sic] in time of war." "The danger," he added, "is mainly in the precedent which it creates . . . [for] if we can put aside the ordinary rules of law on a matter of this kind, why not put them aside on other matters as well?"[92] The Liberals believed that the special powers of Section 98 created a dangerous precedent, but the state had already had the power to "put aside the ordinary rules of law," such as during the creation of PC 2384 and Section 98, or Section 41 in 1910 with respect to immigrants.

Lapointe spelled out why Section 98 violated the rule of law, inadvertently demonstrating how the section set a new precedent: it allowed searches of persons or property on mere suspicion of wrongdoing and placed guilt on an individual for merely attending a meeting of an unlawful organization or renting a hall to one. After his vigorous attack on the illiberal nature of Section 98, he explained why he "propose[d] to add a few words to Section 133": "It is merely to make it clearer that nobody can by words or writing preach the use of force to bring about governmental changes."[93] He argued that fighting communism should be done by argument and should not rely on the

"Criminal Code as Section 98 had not prevented communism in any way," hence there was no reason to keep it.[94] Despite Lapointe's defence of liberty, the Liberals' motivation for the adding of "a few words" to Section 133 was the same as the Union government's when it created Section 98 in 1919: to make things clearer for the people and courts in regards to sedition. Repealing Section 98 by adding to Section 133 demonstrated the ongoing process of normalizing emergency measures, which permitted nation-building through the use of the criminal law for judging politics in peacetime. Section 98 was the precedent. The Liberals' ideas of security were not much different from those of their predecessors. Security was still equated with stamping out communism and ensuring that the state had the legal right to judge one's politics. Once PC 2384 became accepted as part of the Criminal Code in peacetime, it was easier to take the emergency measures that were normalized and reorder them in different ways, such as by adding "a few words" to a different Code section. Lapointe could amend the Code to retain the crux of Section 98 with no need for a special committee like that created in 1919.

J.S. Woodsworth questioned the new Section 133 amendments, which was not surprising because he was an outspoken opponent of Section 98 and had tried for years to get it repealed. Though he did praise the Liberals for repealing it, he could not help but point out what Lapointe was doing, stating, "What he [Lapointe] gives with one hand he partly takes away with the other," and asking the House, "If we had sufficient protection [against sedition], as he said, in the Criminal Code, I ask him why it is necessary to strengthen the Criminal Code at this time." Woodsworth argued that the revisions were too broad and too sweeping as they stood, as many historical works, including English ones, had defended the right to use force against tyrannical governments. He thought it strange that the Liberals were proposing this addition to sedition law, especially given that the prime minister was the grandson of William Lyon Mackenzie.[95]

Conservative C.H. Cahan, the original drafter of PC 2384, came to the defence of Lapointe. He recounted the history of PC 2384, created to combat seditious literature being printed in Canada, and its role in combating seditious organizations operating in both Canada and the United States. He disagreed with Section 98 providing the RCMP with the authority to seize property but believed that subsections 1 and 8 should be preserved. "Now what the minister has done, in order to camouflage what purports to be a complete repeal of Section 98," said Cahan, "is to make an addition to Section 133 dealing with sedition. Let us consider the matter fairly."[96] Cahan felt that Lapointe's amendment should be broader but conceded that as long as advocacy of force to produce governmental change was still criminalized, he did not care what section it was in as long as it was clear enough that no magistrate would have to sift "through a thousand cases" to "ascertain what the law of sedition really is." For one of the creators of Section 98, the Liberals' bill had its shortcomings but was otherwise acceptable.

There were dissenters who did not believe repealing Section 98 was a good idea. Characteristic of many of Section 98's supporters, Herbert Wilton, a Conservative member representing Hamilton West, claimed that the threat of communism could not be understated. Communists were teaching their children "to have no respect for the law and order" and "advocating everything that is disrespectful to the social structure." "They come out of their places like rats out of holes in the middle of the night" to distribute propaganda, he added, and that those were the individuals that Section 98 targeted. "No law abiding, self-respecting Canadian citizen need fear Section 98," he stressed.[97] For Wilton and other like-minded Section 98 supporters, Communists sowed mayhem and were a danger to security; only by keeping Section 98 could chaos be controlled. Canadians needed the law, many argued, to feel safe.

R.B. Bennett shared these sentiments. Bennett spoke at length in defence of the section, arguing that "national liberty is dependent upon the restraint of individual liberty." The laws that "restrain individual liberty" were not "enacted" for the "law abiding citizen but as restraints upon citizens who would convert liberty into licence." Bennett made it known for the first time that he was not in favour of the RCMP's power to seize property but that the seizure of property was found in many other laws, such as those applying to gaming houses. He claimed that Section 98's other subsections were innocuous and that reasonable citizens would not want Section 98 removed but amended. He invoked fear, warning his audience, "In these days is it desirable to repeal that section?" Bennett believed that if people actually "understood" the section, they would want it modified, not repealed.[98]

In committee, the bill was slightly amended, with the words "within Canada" added to the end of Section 133(4): it was no longer an offence for a person to claim force should be used to remove a government outside of Canada. The bill was read a third time and passed later that afternoon.

The debates surrounding Section 98 revealed how the hard work of the CLDL, the CCF, and others such as the LSR had paid off. The central reason for repealing Section 98 was that it was believed to violate citizens' rights, whether freedom of speech or association or property. While some Conservative members believed that individual rights should be curtailed for the good of the whole, the discussion within the House still centred on how best to protect the rights of Canadians and how Section 98 did or did not do that. The repeal movement was able to have the issue of protecting civil liberties become a campaign issue, compelling all parties to debate and find the best means of doing that. More than one MP pointed out that the Liberals' repeal of Section 98 was a half measure. Subsection 4 of Section 133 ensured that a broad law affecting the politics of Canadians would still remain in the Code.

The Senate debated Bill 96 the next day, on 20 June. Following Senator Raoul Dandurand's introduction of the bill, the similarities between subsection 4 and Section 98 were immediately pounced on by one of Section 98's original creators, Senator Arthur Meighen. Meighen first attacked the notion that Section 98 was draconian and targeted political ideology. He highlighted why Section 98's previous repeal bills had never passed the Senate – "No such Bill as this affecting Section 98 was ever presented here" – and stated that he would support this bill because while it repealed Section 98, it restored the crux of it. Meighen did not believe, though, that the revised Section 133 would have as much teeth as Section 98. He ended his comments about the bill with an attack on the Liberals: "The denunciation of it [Section 98] and the promise to repeal were only means to an end – an electoral end – and now we are given this repeal and this restoration, which are perhaps as fine a piece of political comedy as this century has seen."[99]

Dandurand did not challenge any of Meighen's claims, and others, such as one of Bennett's last appointed Conservative senators, Senator John Haig, joined Meighen's attacks. Haig claimed that the current bill made "the law more comprehensive than it was before" because it said that "intention is presumed against the accused." He was puzzled as to why the government claimed that because it had amended Section 133, it was going to repeal Section 98. "Under this clause [Section 133, subsection 4]," he claimed, "any person accused of seditious intention will have thrown upon him the onus of proving his innocence." He added that he did not oppose it at all but just thought the whole exercise was hypocritical.[100]

Dandurand's only defence for the Liberals was that he was not one of the Liberals campaigning on this issue in the last election. Of all the attacks by the Conservatives, there was no defence offered by Liberal senators. Senator George Gordon of the Conservatives offered an explanation that went unchallenged, stating that the minister of justice "knew that without it [subsection 4] no honest senator would vote for the repeal of Section 98."[101] There was truth to the statement since the Conservatives had held a majority in the Senate since the end of the war.[102] Meighen did not oppose the bill but thought the draftsmanship faulty.[103] The bill passed its third reading on 20 June 1936.

The new subsection did not actually go further than Section 98, as the Conservative senators claimed. But in many ways, as Liberal members spelled out in memos to King, the amendment to Section 133 was similar to Section 98 as it could be combined with other measures already in the Code to achieve a similar effect. The new subsection was an attempt by the Liberals to placate the Senate and other hardliners while ensuring an election promise was kept by repealing Section 98. To back the bill, the Conservative senators needed to reassure themselves that the new subsection would be just as effective in the courts, if not more so, than Section 98. Many of the comparisons between Section 133 and Section 98 were political attacks designed to portray Liberals as disingenuous in claiming that they had repealed Section 98. But these comparisons were mostly correct. King did not want to be portrayed as being soft on communism, and the Liberals would rather have been accused of being duplicitous than be seen as giving sanction and safe haven to communism.

While Section 98 was retained in some fashion after its repeal, the success of the repeal movement was substantial. Leftists of all stripes were able to temporarily agree on one crucial point: that Section 98 needed to go and people's civil rights should be protected. Leftists of all stripes challenged the idea that security, provided through Section 98, was protecting democratic society. In their eyes, it was destroying it. Rather than feeling safe, people felt terror with Section 98 because the state was engaging in nation-building through repression. Section 98's repeal was a strong demonstration of the power of collective organizing and of acting political in whatever way people chose. The strength of the repeal movement to change the political climate of the time and force Section 98 into the shadows reveals how broad-based organizing, within an exceptional period, kept a space open for public engagement and action, forcing the government to acknowledge the public's power. It demonstrated that the normalization of emergency measures, and as a result nation-building, was a process that could be disrupted and challenged. Fear of societal turmoil brought Section 98 into existence, but many feared the turmoil that Section 98 created and felt they would be safer without it.

Despite the power of the movement, it made a crucial mistake. By reducing state repression to Section 98, by having the section become a symbol of repression, the movement's win against the state did not cut very deep. The repeal movement focused on a law, on a symbol of repression, and not the power that created the law and that repression. It did not end the state's ability to judge people's politics. As long as the state continued to retain the ability to wield emergency measures in peacetime or otherwise and exclude individuals, nation-building by way of repression would continue, as would the further normalization of repressive laws. In an ironic twist, the repeal movement ultimately set in motion Canada's civil rights movement, and by doing so, Section 98 and the exclusion of communists from Canada's political identity advanced the creation of a liberal society in Canada and shaped Canadians' understanding of their nation as a liberal-democratic country that should respect civil rights. By way of the sovereign ban, executed through the exclusion of communists, Canadians defined themselves as a country that should tolerate the civil rights of people, though the ability to exclude communists was still possible with Section 133's amendment. Canadians needed communists: they needed to repress them to understand themselves as part of a liberal society.

The remnants of Section 98 in the current Criminal Code serve as an artefact, existing as what Agamben calls the "memory of the original exclusion," when communists were excluded from Canadian society, as well as revealing their "capture" by Canadian sovereignty. The section's presence in the Code serves as a constant reminder of the qualifications for exclusion and acceptance.

The repeal of Section 98 was hailed in newspapers across the country, even in those that previously saw no issue with Buck et al.'s conviction, a strong indication that the progressives did manage to change the opinion of the country with respect to civil rights. The *Winnipeg Free Press* denounced Meighen's claims that the repeal was a fake. It viewed Section 98's repeal as the final "liquidation" of the general strike, as it had taken "seventeen years to heal the wounds inflicted on the public mind."[104] The *Montreal Gazette*, like other more conservative-minded papers such as the *Globe* and the *Mail and Empire*, was more cautious about Section 98's repeal, claiming that it would only embolden Communists. The *Globe* feared that the repeal had "led the agitators to believe they [could] carry on their work without danger," though it did remind its readers that law and order had not fallen by the wayside because of it.[105]

If the CPC was not emboldened, its members were certainly jubilant. The CPC celebrated and paid little attention to the revision of Section 133, probably because the unlawful organization component of Section 98 was removed and so there was hope that a legal CPC would return. Buck quickly wrote to Lapointe asking him to overturn his conviction, but his request was denied. Nonetheless, Buck and company staged a demonstration at Queen's Park and burned Section 98 in effigy: a large book with "98" written on it.[106] The *Star* thought it disingenuous of the Conservatives to pretend that "the section was a credible one" or to "obscure the fact that it had its origin in a war time order-in-council."[107] The *Toronto Telegram* noted, "Section 98 has been killed, but its spirit goes marching on."[108] In the ethnic labour press, the reception to Section 98's repeal was mixed. For instance, both *Vapaus* and *Glos Pracy* acknowledged that Section 133 was amended but claimed that the greater victory that should be celebrated was Section 98's repeal. The German labour press was more critical, claiming that in repealing Section 98, the government had replaced it with "another law that would have a similar effect as Section 98." The paper referred to this as a "liberal manoeuvre." Both Sections 133 and 98, they claimed, should be repealed.[109]

Section 98's lasting effect on the CLDL and its leader, A.E. Smith, was more dramatic. The CLDL's attempts to defend civil rights in Canada inadvertently changed the group and Smith's view of it. Smith and the CLDL broadened their outlook. They were no longer concerned only with workers' rights but saw themselves as defenders of civil rights for all Canadians. For instance, within the records of the CLDL are A.E. Smith's notes for a speech he gave on civil liberties in 1939. In them, he quotes from John Stuart Mill, believing that rights were not natural but social and were rooted in the struggles of those who fought and "often died for liberty." He called on workers to be "rid of fear," for "the worth of a state is to be found after all, in the worth of the individuals which compose it." Reject "intolerance," he claimed, at all costs. "Social rights," he argued, "belong to you and me, not because we are rich or poor, wise or foolish – white or black; not because of our opinions or our prestige . . . not because of our social position – BUT BECAUSE WE ARE HUMAN BEINGS." After Section 98's repeal, Smith and the CLDL viewed themselves in the same light as other defenders and fighters of civil liberties and as part of that history. Their fight continued into the Second World War to protest the government's use of the War Measures Act. The reasons behind their struggle, and their opposition to Section 98, were captured in a note from 1940 found in Smith's records that claimed that in a democracy, "the most important aspect . . . IS THE FREEDOM OF THE MIND."[110]

Section 98's repeal movement was instrumental in the creation of a civil rights movement in Canada. Woodsworth's early attempts to put forth bills to repeal Section 98 in the House of Commons in the 1920s were the earliest efforts at repeal. It was not until the law was used against the CPC that a broad-based movement developed; this was due to the intense and sustained efforts of the CLDL. Their efforts at cooperation with other progressive groups, even if their actions were not entirely approved by the CI, were instrumental in bringing about the repeal of Section 98 and bringing the protection of individual rights into the mainstream. Progressives found like-minded allies in the CCF and in intellectuals, such as those who had formed the LSR. From across the spectrum, they viewed Section 98 as a symbol of state repression that needed to be removed to safeguard the rights of Canadians in a democracy. Canadians' security was tied to Section 98's removal. The repeal movement could survive the violence of sovereign power because it was broadly organized. It was no longer just CPC members and supporters acting politically, but a broad swathe of society. The state could not define the security threat as being the result of a minority of foreign agitators; the movement was too broad now. The repeal movement had success in engaging in political acts the authorities opposed, such as the On-to-Ottawa Trek, which was not only about unemployment and the camps but about repealing Section 98.

In spite of the demands for Section 98's repeal across the country, the federal government continued its attack on anything remotely tied to communism. The government's failed prosecution of the trek leaders for violating Section 98 had revealed how its end was in sight. However, even though Mackenzie King's government repealed Section 98, its repeal was a half measure. The government never rescinded the WMA and its ability to create such laws to begin with. Section 98's repeal resulted in Section 133's amendment. The Criminal Code still provided the government with the ability to judge Canadians' politics and indirectly regulate their ideological adherence. Security was still linked to the state's right to legally judge politics. Nation-building by way of repression could continue as long as the state's power to exclude remained, something it could do only with exceptional laws. Section 133's subsection 4 is still with Canadians in the current Criminal Code.[111] Whether it will ever be used again, and whether it could withstand a Charter challenge, is debatable, which speaks to the power that the repeal movement was able to wield. It serves as both a memory and a reminder of what one should believe or not believe in a liberal society. It was, and remains, an exceptional law.

Conclusion:
Towards a Real State of Exception

Why was Section 98 created? It was created by the authorities to indefinitely manage the disorderly or disruptive effects that capitalism produced, mainly in the activism of leftists, whom the government used to shape the political identity of the nation through exclusion. The creation of Section 98 was possible because of the illusory boundary between the exception and the norm, and its creation shattered the linkages between crisis and time because the law had to replicate the ongoing nature of the new security threat to combat it. Fear was an important factor in Section 98's creation and its use. The experience of Section 98 demonstrates how security can function as ideology in that the people's belief in security, in the law's ability to protect, was of central importance to the authorities' ability to have people believe security could be achieved. After Section 98, the emergency or crisis could exist all the time and everywhere, exposing the ability of sovereign power and law to judge people's politics and exercise its right to define the political identity of the nation and its subjects through the sovereign ban. Repression played an important role in shaping the Canadian nation, and the law was integral to legitimizing, sanctioning, and normalizing this repression.

Such nation-building and ideas of security were contingent on people's view of the nation, be it of a white British capitalist nation or a nation consisting of a French and English partnership but with Catholicism as a strong influence on identity. It was a nation in line with such views that needed to be built and kept secure. Only by normalizing the abnormal (the emergency law) and by having the normal (the state that existed before the normalized emergency law) become the abnormal could the authorities legally turn communists (immigrant ones in particular) into *homo sacer* and engage in nation-building via

222

the repression of them. Many Canadians interpreted Canada as a liberal, democratic state because of the sovereign ban and the power to exclude. The process of exclusion may have begun with Section 98, but it continued long after it was repealed.

The War Measures Act (WMA) and the ability of the government to create a state of exception, or state of emergency, gave lawmakers the power to police the loyalty of citizens and immigrants. When the government created PC 2384 in September 1918, it took measures, contained in the 1910 Immigration Act, designed to repress immigrant activists and applied them to the entire population. During the war, leftist organizations were outlawed, as was the expression of unwanted and dangerous ideologies such as communism and anarchism. Loyalty was linked to ideas of security. It was the labour revolt following the war that led the government to believe that the powers it had given itself during the war should be maintained indefinitely. The government carefully studied other nations' sedition legislation, deportation policies, and wartime emergency powers, such as the United States' 1917 Espionage Act and Great Britain's 1914 Defence of the Realm Act, and sought to craft a more effective version of these laws. It was in lockstep with its international partners in combating unwanted leftist ideologies. Section 98 was not a reactionary law. It was created not to order disorder but to manage it long term. Fear influenced its creation, but a desire to ensure feelings of safety and security kept it in existence. After Section 98, the emergency powers dealing with the regulation of politics remained on stage – the curtain having been left slightly ajar.

With the start of the Great Depression, many people called on the government to outlaw the Communist Party of Canada and deport Communists who were perceived as foreign; these calls fell on sympathetic ears. Bennett's government believed that communists represented a foreign and alien culture. Cultural views helped define threats to the nation and security, which were equated with the cultural status quo. Competing interpretations of the nation influenced why the CPC needed to be outlawed. The intelligence cycle, the process of planning, collecting, processing, analysing, and disseminating intelligence, was underpinned by culture. Culture determined how the state saw its targets. The CPC was a radical alternative to mainstream politics, as it envisioned a multi-ethnic, socialist-republic nation. It did not seek to do away with Canada, but to remake it. Worse, the party represented the oppressed of society and spoke for them not in Parliament – but in the street. With no political representation, it represented itself by acting politically in whatever way it could.

Further, the party faced internal strife about how best to implement Moscow's directives while dealing with the realities facing the party on the ground.

That Section 98 contributed to the regulation of Canadians' politics is plainly illustrated in the case of *Rex v. Buck et al.*, wherein the heart of the Crown's case rested on demonstrating how the ideology of the accused was the criminal act. The Crown centred its case on proving that CPC members were agents of Moscow who planned to overthrow Parliament. It relied for evidence on party literature, such as the *Communist Manifesto*, rather than actual plans or acts of violence. The defence countered that Marxism was a means of interpreting history, and it was this interpretation that the Crown sought to outlaw. The trial laid bare the power of the sovereign and the law to judge. In the face of every legal challenge the Crown faced, the CPC members were still convicted. The trial was not about justice; it was about the power to judge and manage the effect of unrest while not addressing the causes of it.

The conviction of the Eight provided law enforcement with the legal authority to arrest anyone who could be tied to the CPC, but for immigrant members of the party, no trials needed to take place. After the trial, communists were *homo sacer*, as much as was necessary to carry out the state's goal of deporting and purging them from society. The government viewed the removal of Communists from the country as necessary for establishing its view of security and the nation. Many of these immigrants had no homeland or country to identify with but considered themselves part of a people and of the communist movement more broadly. They were denied the same legal protections as citizens but were vulnerable to laws such as Section 41 of the Immigration Act (1910) and to the new unlawful status of the CPC. The cases of the Halifax Ten and Tomo Čačić demonstrate that transnational activists could be made in Canada and not just abroad. They could be sojourners, as Čačić and many of the Halifax Ten were, who joined the communist movement in Canada because of unsafe and often degrading working conditions, a number of them becoming leaders in the movement.

The trials of Arthur Evans and others reveal the broad reach of Section 98, the exclusionary status communists now occupied, and how the state used repression to forcefully engage in nation-building. Violence against communists became necessary for security. Section 98 was used in a number of ways, such as by intimidating hall owners or justifying repeated searches of persons or property. For progressives, it was a means of invoking feelings of terror in people and came to symbolize the state's repressive policies. The murder of Nicholas Zynchuck and the brutality of Montreal police at his funeral reveal how the state could use violence against those it perceived as threats, even killing them, and not be guilty of homicide. The murder reinforced the urgent need for the repeal of Section 98, which the Canadian Labor Defense League (CLDL) had advocated for since Buck et al.'s conviction.

The CLDL led a widespread campaign to repeal Section 98 and defend workers' rights. CLDL activists sought cooperation with other moderate leftists, such as those in the Co-operative Commonwealth Federation and the League for Social Reconstruction, before the CI's official turn to a united front policy against fascism. It was this mass movement led by the CLDL to repeal Section 98 that spurred the creation of an early civil rights movement in Canada and hindered the state's ability to define the crisis as being the result of foreign activists. The need for the continuance of emergency measures was directly challenged. The removal of Section 98 and the protection of civil liberties were what progressives believed established security. The Bennett government's sanction of the RCMP's use of force to end the On-to-Ottawa Trek and the subsequent arrests of its leadership reveal the lengths the government would go to to crush communism. Despite the obstacles facing the progressive voices in the country, they managed to force the government to repeal Section 98 through broad-based organizing. The Liberals' election win led to Section 98's repeal, and the repeal represented a significant step in the ability of progressive forces to unite in order to temporarily halt the state's ability to open the curtain further on emergency measures. But the state's folding of Section 98 into other Code sections preserved important elements of the exceptional law. In addition, progressives conceptualized what Canada was by what they felt it should not be doing: excluding on the basis of politics. Yet it was the exclusion of the communists that made this interpretation of Canadian identity possible – the exception defined the rule. Ultimately, the process that began in 1919 lives on. Section 98's presence in the current Code serves as a memory of the original exclusion of communists and a reminder of what ideas are and are not Canadian.

All of this is not to say that Section 98's repeal was a complete failure but rather that the victory of repeal has to be tempered by an understanding of how the state was able to retain the bulk of its most significant powers. We need to understand both the successes and failures of the repeal movement. The movement did represent a type of emergency brake being applied to the steady march of using

emergency powers in peacetime and should be interpreted as a significant achievement for civil rights in Canada (along with other notable victories such as the right for collective bargaining, which was
won in the 1940s), but this victory needs to be weighed against the
state's ability to retain the bulk of Section 98's core elements and its
continued reliance on emergency powers to deny liberties, such as
with the creation of the Padlock Act, internment and forced relocation
during the Second World War, the Kellock–Taschereau Commission,
the Cold War spying regime, and the current anti-terror laws.

Indeed, almost immediately following Section 98's repeal and
Section 133's amendment, copycat laws were created. One of the
best-known examples is Quebec's "Act Respecting Communistic
Propaganda," known as the Padlock Act. Created by Maurice Duplessis's Union Nationale government, the law was expressly designed
to combat communism in the province. The province possibly had
federal backers for its new law. Hugh Guthrie advised Bennett that
communism in Quebec was on the rise and in May 1935 provided the
PM's office with a report on Communist activities. The report was
subsequently forwarded to His Eminence the Cardinal Archbishop of
Quebec.[1] Whether Bennett's government sensed an election loss and
the repeal of Section 98 or it simply felt the need to share intelligence
with Quebec authorities is uncertain. Certainly, officials in the church
and government needed no extra incentive to want to outlaw communism in the province, but the report from the federal government
would have, at the very least, made the passing of the Padlock Act
more justifiable in their eyes.

The similarities between the Padlock Act and Section 98 are
numerous and were summarized by F.R. Scott and the newly minted
Canadian Civil Liberties Union in their many protests against the
law.[2] For instance, Section 3 of the law made it an offence to "possess
or occupy a house within the Province, to use it or allow anyone to
make use of it to propagate Communism or Bolshevism." Section 12
made it an offence to "print, to publish, in any manner whatsoever,
or to distribute in the Province any newspaper, periodical, pamphlet,
circular, document or writing whatsoever, propagating, or tend-
ing to propagate communism or bolshevism." The debt of gratitude
the Padlock Act owed to Section 98 is readily apparent in just these
two examples. Duplessis's government would have viewed the law
as an improvement over Section 98. For instance, the Padlock Act's
Section 3 combined Section 98's subsections 1 and 5, but was more
explicit and extended their reach. Not only could Quebec authorities
shut down any hall, but they could shutter any private dwelling where

communism was preached, and the act explicitly named communism. There was no need for beating around the bush. The law dispensed with the messy business of a criminal court trial to prove communism's unlawfulness. No discussion of it was permitted – anywhere.[3]

Section 98's influence continued to be felt beyond Quebec and the 1930s. During the Second World War, its influence appeared in regulation 62 of the Defence of Canada Regulations, added on 4 January 1940 by the minister of justice by order-in-council. It stated that any officer of an organization who committed the offence of disaffection would make each officer of that organization guilty of an offence, as well as any future member.[4]

Section 98 proved useful to the government of Pierre Trudeau during the October Crisis of 1970. Sections 3 and 4 of the Public Order Regulations of 1970, issued by the Trudeau government during the October Crisis, used the wording of Section 98 to outlaw the Front de Libération du Québec (FLQ) across the country. Section 3 stated, "The group of persons or association known as Le Front de Libération du Québec and any successor group or successor association of the said Le Front de Libération du Québec or any group of persons or association that advocates the use of force or the commission of crime as a means of or as an aid in accomplishing governmental change within Canada is declared to be an unlawful association."[5] Currently, the sedition section of the Criminal Code, Section 59 subsection 4(a) and (b) stipulates that "every one shall be presumed to have a seditious intention who (a) teaches or advocates (b) publishes or circulates any writing that advocates, the use, without the authority of law, of force as a means of accomplishing a governmental change within Canada." "Force" remains undefined in the Criminal Code in this section. The lack of a definition and reliance on judicial interpretation was one of the main contentions progressives had with Section 98.

Bill C-51, or the Anti-Terrorism Act, 2015, was passed in the House of Commons on 6 May 2015 and in the Senate on 9 June. Its broad powers, which include criminalizing ideas linked to terrorism, giving Canada's intelligence agencies more power and targeting anyone seeking to "undermine the security of Canada," which includes, in subsection B of the "Interpretation" section, "changing or unduly influencing a government in Canada by force or unlawful means." "Force" is once again left broad and undefined, accompanied now by the new vague phrase "unduly influencing," in this newest incantation of Section 98.[6]

The broader significance of this study is multifaceted and far-reaching, particularly in today's heightened security climate. Section 98 marked a moment in Canada's history when the government began using the state of exception as a "paradigm of governance." Exceptional powers were normalized, resulting in the state's ability to engage in nation-building through repression because the targets of repression legally became outcasts of society. It was a process that was ongoing and extended beyond Section 98's repeal. This book enables historians to re-examine repressive events in Canadian history and see them not as disconnected anomalies in a liberal society, but as the continuation of a process that started with Section 98. Section 98 began a long-standing battle of the state gradually implementing, and people resisting, the creation of a complete or total state of exception – a condition that can be viewed as an integral component of state formation and the formation of a liberal society. Future research can offer a revised look at a number of laws and events, from the Padlock Act, to the Gouzenko Affair and the Kellock–Taschereau Commission, to the October Crisis, to the continued use of deportation in the late twentieth century and into the present, all of which can be linked and understood not just as moments when civil liberties were violated, but as important moments when the state continued the march towards normalizing more emergency measures, though at times these steps were challenged. These events can be connected, understood as being part of an ongoing practice. An analysis of security, what it has meant and how it has changed over time, can demonstrate how the law shifts alongside how threats are perceived. More research into how security itself functions as an ideological project could offer new interpretations of moments of heightened security in Canada's past, such as the Cold War, to take just one example. We must grapple in future research with the concept of security, what it has meant to people, how it has been expressed, how it functions as ideology, if we are to find a means of resolving the state's ability to "legitimate the illegitimate." The nature of past security crises determined the nature of the responses, but the effects of these responses have been cumulative. What kind of state, then, is Canada, and other nations like it, such as the United States and Britain, gradually becoming? If we see the state of exception as part of the construction of a liberal society, then what is the endgame? A new focus on present-day Canada could lead to interpreting Canada less as an "insecurity state" and more as a developing "emergency state" as the government continues to increasingly rely on and seek to normalize emergency measures to defend against challenges to Canada's identity and politics.

This study has important connections to the present. The 2001 "anti-terrorism" amendments to numerous Canadian laws, the events of Toronto's G20 riots, the Edward Snowden revelations, and the Anti-Terrorism Act of 2015 continue the trend that began with Section 98. Within all these examples, emergency measures were used during a non-emergency state. The powers that the government granted to law enforcement following 9/11 and in 2015 bear resemblance to 1919 in that these powers rely on the belief that the threats facing the country will be present indefinitely.[7] While some of these powers have been overturned by Charter challenges, many have not, and the government has revived a number of lapsed powers, such as preventive arrests and forcing individuals, even if they have not been charged with an offence, to testify at secret hearings or risk being jailed for up to a year. These measures have become part of Canada's laws during peacetime.

During the G20 riots in Toronto in 2010, the Executive Council of Ontario issued an order-in-council to provide security forces with increased powers of arrest. No debate took place, and there was no formal declaration of an emergency – none was needed. Toronto police told the public that the increased powers, originally created during the Second World War to protect strategic buildings, provided police with the power to arrest anyone within five metres of the security fence surrounding the G20 summit. Police detained people outside the fence, citing the new powers. Yet the increased powers applied only to the interior of the fence. When media asked Toronto police chief Bill Blair if police had the power to detain people on the outside of the fence, Blair smiled and claimed, "No, but I was trying to keep criminals out." Much like in the Zynchuck affair, the police operated in an area of indistinction between violence and right where, as Benjamin states, no legal situation existed. No formal federal inquiry was ever called to investigate the arrest of over nine hundred people, the largest mass arrest in Canadian history up to that point to time. Only two years later, the record for the largest mass arrest would be broken again during the Quebec student protests in 2012, when over 2,500 were arrested.[8]

The Edward Snowden affair reveals the ongoing normalization of emergency powers. Snowden, an employee of a security firm contracted by the US National Security Agency (NSA), revealed a massive surveillance program undertaken by Western powers following 9/11 and directed at civilian communications. The Communications Security Establishment (CSE), Canada's signals intelligence agency, reportedly participated in assisting the NSA with surveillance.[9] The Snowden affair reveals how an activity, signals intelligence, originally developed and used during a state of war to intercept enemy communications, most notably during the First and Second World War, has drastically expanded since then to become a normal function of states during peacetime and directed at the general population. The state of exception has increasingly become a useful and too-convenient tool for governments. On 9 December 2014, the US Senate released a scathing report that documents the role of the Central Intelligence Agency (CIA) in the torture of terrorist suspects since 9/11. It documents how prisoners in Guantanamo Bay and other secret prisons were deprived of sleep for weeks, subjected to "rectal rehydration," isolated for weeks in darkness, and forced to use a diaper to defecate, and how some were waterboarded (a torture technique that simulates drowning) – one prisoner was waterboarded 183 times. Some faced torture to the point where they were psychologically unresponsive. No individuals were charged, because all of it was legal. None of the prisoners were protected by the Geneva Conventions. They existed outside the law. The depth of Canada's role has yet to be uncovered, though Canada has been implicated in condoning the use of torture against terror suspects through rendition programs.[10]

These events reveal a systemic issue in governance. While the focus of this study has been on left-wing activists, the ability of Western states such as Canada to normalize exceptional measures is by no means a left or right issue. It is a problem rooted in the mechanisms of sovereign power and integral to the formation of states.[11] Nor have communists been the only ones with *homo sacer* status within Canada. Exclusion being used to define inclusion has occurred countless times in Canadian history and continues today, including with Canada's indigenous population and other racial and ethnic minorities.

The repression during the interwar period was as flagrant as it was brutal. I contend that a different and more nuanced interpretation of the Canadian state is required. Instead of understanding Western states such as Canada, the United States, and Britain as liberal-democratic states, we can complicate this view and interpret them as states that *practise* liberal democracy. This suggested interpretation would acknowledge that a liberal-democratic state is not an absolute concept, but rather a fluid and organic ideal in a constant state of flux, while acknowledging that all states share in the logic of sovereignty independent of their professed ideological leanings. If liberalism is inseparable from ill-liberalism, and if repression is a necessary component of state formation and nation-building, then we must wrestle with the perhaps uncomfortable reality that liberal order as it exists in a state structure, such as Canada, is rooted in the exception and the sovereign ban, as the state must continue the practice of reserving its right to force individuals of its choosing to be "free" as well as its power to exclude the "unworthy."

This study on Section 98 has historicized the use of emergency powers in peacetime. September 11, and the terrorism that continued in the world after this event, did not fundamentally change the world with respect to governments' uses of emergency measures in peacetime, whether in Canada or in other nations such as the United States.[12] The event accelerated a process that began much earlier with Section 98.

Future studies must grapple not only with the state's power to grant and protect rights, but with its legal ability to take them away. Western societies still look to the state to protect rights, but the state is also the same body that can remove them. This does not mean that removing or suspending rights is easy or happens often, but there is currently no legal barrier, no legal protection that cannot be legally undone. This book has raised serious issues around being political in Canada. How do people be political, and who gets to be political? The spaces for political action and engagement are increasingly shrinking as political actions not sanctioned by the state (such as strikes or sit-ins) become labelled as illegal and legislated to stop, or worse, are designated as acts of terrorism. Further, what political actions are available to immigrants in a seemingly shrinking environment for political action? The power of the state to make citizens and interpret threats still remains a pressing issue around the globe, even when no political actions are occurring. Most recently, the government of the Dominican Republic gave the state the power to strip citizenship of anyone of Haitian descent, even if they were born in the Republic, making them instantly eligible for deportation. While Stephen Harper was prime minister of Canada, the Canadian government made deportation an easier process in certain cases, by enabling the state to remove citizenship from dual citizens if charged with a terrorism offence (including those born in Canada) and by once again enshrining a minister with broad powers for deciding the fate of a deportee. The subsequent Liberal government of Justin Trudeau promised to reverse the Conservative changes to the Citizenship Act. While it removed the more contentious elements of the law, such as the stripping of citizenship for terrorism offences, it has continued to use the other elements of the law (such as the removal of citizenship acquired under false pretences) to revoke citizenship at an even greater rate than the Harper government. Even if this practice stops, there is nothing preventing new laws even more restrictive than past ones from being created. Preventative arrest is also in the Criminal Code of Canada. No emergency needs to be declared for police to arrest someone on the belief that they might commit an offence.[13]

While this work contends that security can be understood as an ideological project, this is not to suggest that security is somehow fictional, nor that threats to people are fictional. Threats are very real, but we must scrutinize the response to threats to understand the evolving relationship between security, law, and society. Since 9/11, terrorist threats to civilians and state officials and infrastructure, be they from groups or lone individuals, have increasingly been regarded not only as heinous crimes but also as *acts of war*, and have be met with warlike security responses by states. These responses have included locking down entire major urban cities with no declared state of emergency, invoking a seemingly ongoing state of emergency (as France did in the wake of the Charlie Hebdo attacks), authorizing assassinations by drones (as the United States has done), and instituting widespread surveillance – and the list goes on. I am not insinuating that anyone, such as intelligence agencies or law enforcement, should be "blamed" for these actions; they are but a part of contemporary society and culture, as are governments. This book is intended to identify a serious issue in society through a historical study (and the ramifications of it) – an issue to which there is presently no easy fix. The "march" towards an emergency state that society appears to be on is one that all parties have to find a way out of. The "war on terror," a phrase that many, including US president Barack Obama, thought ridiculous given it was a declared war on a tactic or even noun, is alive and well.[14] We must interpret security not as some universal construct that lies outside of historical, political, sociocultural, and economic forces but rather as part of and shaped by all those elements if we are to understand the processes, public support, and mechanisms behind states of emergency and their acceptance.

Ultimately, what made Section 98 significant was not just whether trials involving it were fair or whether abuses stemming from it were violations of civil liberties or even how often it was used. It was the start of an ongoing process of implementing a total state of exception and of engaging in nation-building through repression, an important and necessary component in the formation of a liberal society in Canada.[15] This work reminds us how during the interwar period, a formative period for Canada's sovereignty and national identity, political repression and violence were part of Canada's national formation. Unity was, as Ernest Renan stated many years ago, "brutally established."

A Real State of Exception

Walter Benjamin theorized, at the height of Nazi terror, and before he took his own life to escape repatriation into Nazi hands, that the only way to combat the state of exception was to create "a real state of emergency."[16] What did he mean? What was a real state of emergency? Agamben theorizes that Benjamin ultimately had the final say of sorts with his rival theorist Carl Schmitt. By using the word "real," Benjamin appears to distinguish between his version of the state of exception and Schmitt's, which Benjamin believed was a fictitious one – not that it did not exist (it was very real for its victims during the Nazi terror) but that its revoking of civil liberties and the state's encroachment into the lives of citizens, as de la Durantaye states, "seemed to be based on a juridical fiction that was at the same time a fiction of justice." Benjamin, then, was trying to speak truth to a lie, the lie that the state of emergency was and needed to be "the rule."

But if it is not the rule and instead a lie, what would a real state of emergency look like if it were possible? We can only theorize, and no one has theorized such a state completely, but some have speculated. One of Benjamin and Agamben's great contributions to solving the dilemma of the state of exception, and the logic of sovereignty as being rooted in the ban, is that the answer to it must come not from utopian dreams of paradise but from the problem itself.

If a place where life becomes law is a place of darkness and ultimate domination (the emergency state we are becoming and discussed in this book), the inverse, where *law becomes life*, might offer hope. In such a state, one could freely think and act, and life would have free reign. All notions of sacrality would be gone. If human beings are, as Agamben theorizes, not destined to complete any historical mission, if "the life that begins on earth after the last day" when the state of exception in which we live ends "is simply human life," if we have no "task" to meet, if we are living always in a state of potentiality, then we are always free, free to commit horrors, yes, but free to change things and bring about a more equitable society.[17] Such a transformative or evolutionary change is not likely to occur for generations, if at all. A real state of emergency may not be an easy task, but as long as we continue to retain our freedom of mind, which A.E. Smith believed was so important for humanity, we can still imagine, still theorize, still dream, and still hope, with a chance for life to live free. It can change.

Appendix 1

Excerpt from the 1910 Immigration Act

41. Whenever any person other than a Canadian citizen Duty of officers to send complaint to Minister concerning certain acts of undesirable classes. advocates in Canada the overthrow by force or violence of the government of Great Britain or Canada, or other British dominion, colony, possession or dependency, or the overthrow by force or violence of constituted law and authority, or the assassination of any official of the Government of Great Britain or Canada or other British dominion, colony, possession or dependency, or of any foreign government, or shall by word or act create or attempt to create riot or public disorder in Canada, or shall by common repute belong to or be suspected of belonging to any secret society or organization which extorts money from, or in any way attempts to control, any resident of Canada by force or threat of bodily harm, or by blackmail; such person for the purposes of this Act shall be considered and classed as an undesirable immigrant; and it shall be the duty of any officer becoming cognizant thereof, and the duty of the clerk, secretary or other official of any municipality in Canada wherein such person may be, to forthwith send a written complaint thereof to the Minister or Superintendent of Immigration, giving full particulars.

42. Upon receiving a complaint from any officer, or from any Investigation of complaints concerning undesirable classes. clerk or secretary or other official of a municipality, whether directly or through the Superintendent of Immigration, against any person alleged to belong to any prohibited or undesirable class, the Minister may order such person to be taken into custody and detained at an immigrant station for examination and an investigation of the facts alleged in the said complaint to be made by a Board of Inquiry or by an officer acting as such. Such Board of Inquiry or officer shall have the same

235

powers and privileges, and shall follow the same procedure, as if the person against whom complaint is made were being examined before landing as provided in section 33 of this Act; and similarly the person against whom complaint is made shall have the same rights and privileges as he would have if seeking to land in Canada.

2. If upon investigation of the facts such Board of Inquiry or examining officer is satisfied that such person belongs to any of the prohibited or undesirable classes mentioned in sections 40 and 41 of this Act, such person shall be deported forthwith, as provided for in section 33 of this Act, subject, however, to such right of appeal as he may have to the Minister.

Deportation in such cases.

219   3.

16   Chap. **27.**   *Immigration.*   9-10 Edw. VII.

Order to leave Canada.

3. The Governor in Council may, at any time, order any such person found by a Board of Inquiry or examining officer to belong to any of the undesirable classes referred to in section 41 of this Act to leave Canada within a specified period. Such order may be in the form D in the schedule to this Act, and shall be in force as soon as it is served upon such person, or is left for him by any officer at the last known place of abode or address of such person.

Penalty for rejected or deported person remaining in or re-entering Canada.

4. Any person rejected or deported under this Act who enters or remains in or returns to Canada after such rejection or deportation without a permit under this Act or other lawful excuse, or who refuses or neglects to leave Canada when ordered so to do by the Governor in Council as provided for in this section, shall be guilty of an offence against this Act, and may forthwith be arrested by any officer and be deported on an order from the Minister or the Superintendent of Immigration, or may be prosecuted for such offence, and shall be liable, on conviction, to two years imprisonment, and immediately after expiry of any sentence imposed for such offence, may be again deported or ordered to leave Canada under this section.

Deportation of head of family.

Deportation of dependent member of family.

Cost of deportation.

5. In any case where deportation of the head of a family is ordered, all dependent members of the family may be deported at the same time. And in any case where deportation of a dependent member of a family is ordered on account of having become a public charge, and in the opinion of the Minister such circumstance is due to wilful neglect or non-support by the head or other members of the family morally bound to support such dependent members, then all members of the family may be deported at the same time. Such deportation shall be at the cost of the persons so deported; and if that be not possible then the cost of such deportation shall be paid by the Department of the Interior.

Appendix 2

Section 98 of the Criminal Code of Canada, Revised Statutes of Canada, 1927, ch. 36

1. Any association, organization, society or corporation, whose professed purpose or one of whose purposes is to bring about any governmental, industrial or economic change within Canada by use of force, violence, terrorism, or physical injury to person or property, or by threats of such injury, or which teaches, advocates, advises or defends the use of force, violence, terrorism, or physical injury to person or property, or threats of such injury, in order to accomplish such change, or for any other purpose, or which shall by any means prosecute or pursue such purpose or professed purpose, or shall so teach, advocate, advise or defend, shall be an unlawful association.

2. Any property, real or personal, belonging or suspected to belong to an unlawful association, or held or suspected to be held by any person for or on behalf thereof may, without warrant, be seized or taken possession of by any person thereunto authorized by the Commissioner of the Royal Canadian Mounted Police, and may thereupon be forfeited to His Majesty.

3. Any person who acts or professes to act as an officer of any such unlawful association, and who shall sell, speak, write or publish anything as the representative or professed representative of any such unlawful association, or become and continue to be a member thereof, or wear, carry or cause to be displayed upon or about his person or elsewhere, any badge, insignia, emblem, banner, motto, pennant, card, button or other device whatsoever, indicat-

ing or intended to show or suggest that he is a member of or in any wise associated with any such unlawful association, or who shall contribute anything as dues or otherwise, to it or to any one for it, or who shall solicit subscriptions or contributions for it, shall be guilty of an offence and liable to imprisonment for not more than twenty years.

4. In any prosecution under this section, if it be proved that the person charged has:

   a) attended meetings of an unlawful association; or,
   b) spoken publicly in advocacy of an unlawful association; or,
   c) distributed literature of an unlawful association by circulation through the Post Office mails of Canada, or otherwise; it shall be presumed, in the absence of proof to the contrary, that he is a member of such unlawful association.

5. Any owner, lessee, agent or superintendent of any building, room, premises or place, who knowingly permits therein any meeting of an unlawful association or any subsidiary association or branch or committee thereof, or any assemblage of persons who teach, advocate, advise or defend the use, without authority of the law, of force, violence or physical injury to person or property, or threats of such injury, shall be guilty of an offence under this section and shall be liable to a fine of not more than five thousand dollars or to imprisonment for not more than five years, or to both fine and imprisonment.

6. If any judge of any superior or county court, police or stipendiary magistrate, or any justice of the peace, is satisfied by information on oath that there is reasonable ground for suspecting that any contravention of this section has been or is about to be committed, he may issue a search warrant under his hand, authorizing any peace officer, police officer, or constable with such assistance as he may require, to enter at any time any premises or place mentioned in the warrant, and to search such premises or place, and every person found therein, and to seize and carry away any books, periodicals, pamphlets, pictures, papers, circulars, cards, letters, writings, prints, hand bills, posters, publications or documents which are found on or in such premise or place, or in the possession of any person therein at the time of such search, and the same, when seized may be carried away and may be forfeited to His Majesty.

7. Where, by this section, it is provided that any property may be forfeited to His Majesty, the forfeiture may be adjudged or

declared by any judge of any superior or county court, or by any police or stipendiary magistrate, or by any justice of the peace, in a summary manner, and by the procedure provided by Part XV of this Act, in so far as applicable, or subject to such adaptations as may be necessary to meet the circumstances of the case.

8. Any person who prints, publishes, edits, issues, circulates, sells, or offers for sale or distribution any book, newspaper, periodical, pamphlet, picture, paper, circular, card, letter, writing, print, publication or document any kind, in which it is taught, advocated, advised or defended or who shall in any manner teach, advocate, or advise or defend the use, without authority of law, of force, violence, terrorism or physical injury to person or property, or threats of such injury, as a means of accomplishing any governmental, industrial or economic change, or otherwise, shall be guilty of an offence and liable to imprisonment for not more than twenty years.

9. Any person who circulates or attempts to circulate or distribute any book, newspaper, periodical, pamphlet, picture, paper, circular, card, letter, writing, print, publication, or document of any kind, as described in this section by mailing the same or causing the same to be mailed or posted, in any Post Office, letter box, or other mail receptacle in Canada, shall be guilty of an offence, and shall be liable to imprisonment for not more than twenty years.

10. Any person who imports into Canada from any other country, or attempts to import by or through any means whatsoever, any book, newspaper, periodical, pamphlet, picture, paper, circular, card, letter, writing, print, publication or document of any kind as described in this section, shall be guilty of an offence and shall be liable to imprisonment for not more than twenty years.

11. It shall be the duty of every person in the employment of His Majesty in respect of His Government of Canada, either in the Post Office Department, or in any other Department to seize and take possession, of any book, newspaper, periodical, pamphlet, picture, paper, circular, card, letter, writing, print, publication or document, as mentioned in this section, upon discovery of the same in the Post Office mails of Canada or in or upon any station, wharf, yard, car, truck, motor or other vehicle, steam boat or other vessel upon which the same may be found and when so seized and taken, without delay to transmit the same, together with the envelopes, coverings and wrappings attached thereto, to the Commissioner of the Royal Canadian Mounted Police.

Appendix 3

Excerpt from Memorandum for the Prime Minister Re: Bill 73: An Act to Amend Section 98 of the Criminal Code, 12 June 1936

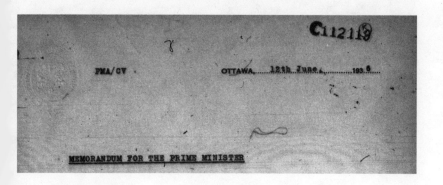

Re: Bill to amend the Criminal Code

The following is a comparative statement
with respect to section 98 and the proposed new subsection
(4) to section 133:

Section 98	Section 133 (4)
1) Makes any organization whose purpose is to bring about governmental, industrial or economic change by use of force, or which teaches or defends such use of force or threats of injury for such change, an unlawful association.	No similar provision, but such an organization might be evidence of a seditious conspiracy with respect to any governmental change advocated by use of unlawful force under section 134 and is not affected by the proposed amendment.
2) Provides that any property, real or personal, belonging to suspected to belong to an unlawful association or held or suspected to be held by any person on behalf thereof may be seized, without warrant, if authorized by the Commissioner of the R.C.M.P. and forfeited to His Majesty.	No similar provision and any writing, prints or documents which it is desired to seize for the purpose of evidence would in the ordinary case be done under the authority of a search warrant except, of course, if such document were in the possession of the person arrested while committing an offence.
3) Provides that any person who acts or professes to act as an officer of an unlawful association and who sells, speaks or publishes anything as representative of such association, or who becomes a member thereof, or wears or carries or displays any badge, etc., indicating that he is such a member or associated therewith, or who contributes anything as dues or otherwise to it or solicits subscriptions shall be guilty of an offence and liable to imprisonment for not more than twenty years.	No similar provision

C 112120

-2-

(4) Provides that it shall be prima facie evidence that a person charged is a member of an unlawful association if it is proved that he attends meetings of such an association, speaks publicly in advocacy thereof or distributes literature thereof by circulation through the mail or otherwise.

No similar provision - evidence required would be in accordance with the ordinary rules of evidence.

(5) Provides that any owner, lessee, agent or superintendent of any building, room, etc., who knowingly permits therein any meeting of such association or subsidiary or branch thereof, or any assemblage of persons who teach, defend, etc., the use without the authority of law, of force, violence, etc., to person or property shall be guilty of an offence and liable to a fine of not more than $5,000.00 or to imprisonment for not more than five years or to both.

No similar provision

(6) Provides for the issue by any judge, magistrate or justice of the peace of a search warrant authorizing any peace officer, etc., with assistance, to enter at any time any premises mentioned in the warrant and to search the same and every person found therein and to seize and carry away documents, etc., and when so taken may be forfeited to His Majesty.

The remarks with respect to subsection (2) are applicable here and in addition the ordinary search warrant can only be executed in the day time, unless special authority to the contrary is granted, and the authority to search does not include that of searching persons.

(7) Provides for the procedure in the case of forfeiture.

There is no specific provision for forfeiture in the ordinary procedure with respect to seizure of this class of goods but same may be detained for certain purposes, such as appeal, and would probably remain indefinitely in the records of the court.

(8) Provides that any person who prints, publishes, edits, circulates, sells, etc., any book, pamphlet, picture, writing, print or document of any kind, etc.,

The proposed amendment would make a person liable to imprisonment for two years under section 134 who publishes, or circulates any writing, γ

-3-

C112121

in which is taught, advocated, advised or defended, or which in any manner teaches, advocate, advise or defend the use without lawful authority of force, violence, terrorism or physical injury to person or property or threats of, such injury as means of accomplishing any governmental, industrial or economic change or otherwise shall be guilty of an offence and liable to imprisonment for not more than twenty years.

print or document in which is advocated, or who teaches or advocates the use, without the authority of law, of force as a means of accomplishing any governmental change. This amendment does not apply to the defence of the use of force or the threats of injury as a means of accomplishing any governmental, industrial or economic change, nor does the proposed amendment apply in any way to industrial or economic change.

(9) Provides that any person who circulates or distributes any document, etc., as described in this section, by mailing the same in the post office shall be liable to imprisonment for not more than twenty years.

No similar specific provision but, of course, the circulation of a document advocating the use of force, without the authority of law, to accomplish a governmental change is prohibited and the penalty for breach thereof is not more than two years imprisonment.

(10) Provides that any person who imports from any other country, or attempts to so import any document, etc., as described in this section shall be liable to imprisonment for not more than twenty years.

No similar provision

(11) Provides that it shall be the duty of every person in the employment of the Government of Canada to seize and take possession of any such document upon discovery of same in the mails of Canada or upon any station, wharf, yard, etc., and when so seized to be transmitted to the Commissioner of the R.C.M.P.

No similar provision.

W Stuart Edwards

Notes

Introduction

1. Justin Ling, "Canada Considers 'Preventative Detention' in Wake of Ottawa Attack," *Guardian*, 23 October 2014.
2. Tobi Cohen, "Controversial Anti-Terror Bill Passes, Allowing Preventative Arrests, Secret Hearings," *National Post*, 25 April 2013; Thomas Walkhom, "Canada's Opposition Must Be Ready to Oppose When Necessary," *Toronto Star*, 24 October 2014; Ian McKay, "The Liberal Order Framework: A Prospectus for a Reconnaissance of Canadian History," *Canadian Historical Review* 81, no. 4 (December 2000): 616–78.
3. Gordon to Bennett, 14 June 1932, R.B. Bennett Papers, Library and Archives Canada, 49366–72; James Struthers, *No Fault of Their Own: Unemployment and the Canadian Welfare State 1914–1941* (Toronto: University of Toronto Press, 1983), 52–3.
4. Bill Waiser, *All Hell Can't Stop Us: The On-to-Ottawa Trek and Regina Riot* (Calgary: Fifth House, 2003), 21; Lita-Rose Betcherman, *The Little Band: The Clashes between the Communists and the Political and Legal Establishment in Canada, 1928–1932* (Ottawa: Deneau Publishers, 1982), 2; Craig Heron and Myer Siemiatycki, "The Great War, the State, and Working-Class Canada," in *The Workers' Revolt in Canada, 1917–1925*, ed. Craig Heron (Toronto: University of Toronto Press, 1998), 35; Barbara Roberts, "Shovelling Out the Mutinous: Political Deportation from Canada Before 1936," *Labour/Le Travail* 18 (Fall 1986): 90.
5. Barbara Roberts, *Whence They Came: Deportation from Canada 1900–1935* (Ottawa: University of Ottawa Press, 1988), 22.
6. Such actions can also be understood as a process of "permanent exceptionalism," as expressed by Leo Panitch and Donald Swartz in *The*

Assault on Trade Union Freedoms: From Consent to Coercion, 3rd ed. (Toronto: Garamond Press, 2003).

7. See, for instance, Agamben's discussion of time and the state of exception in Giorgio Agamben, "For a Theory of Destituent Power," *Chronos* 10, 16 November 2013.

8. Douglas Hay, "Civilians Tried in Military Courts: Quebec, 1759–64," and Jean-Marie Fecteau and Hay, "'Government by Will and Pleasure Instead of Law': Military Justice and the Legal System in Quebec, 1775–83," in *Canadian State Trials*, vol. 1, ed. Murray Greenwood and Barry Wright (Toronto: University of Toronto Press, 1996); Douglas Hay, "Tradition, Judges and Civil Liberties in Canada," *Osgoode Hall Law Journal* 41, no. 2/3 (Summer/Fall 2003): 319–22; W. Wesley Pue, "The War on Terror: Constitutional Governance in a Permanent State of Warfare?" *Osgoode Hall Law Journal* 41 (2003): 267–92; Murray Greenwood and Barry Wright, eds., *Canadian State Trials*, vol. 2 (Toronto: University of Toronto Press, 2002); Barry Wright and Susan Binnie, eds., *Canadian State Trials*, vol. 3 (Toronto: University of Toronto Press, 2009). See Alien Act, S.L.C. 1794, ch. 5, s. 31; Seditious Meetings Act, S.U.C. 1818, ch. 11, repealed by S.U.C. 1820, ch. 4; see also Greenwood's discussion in F. Murray Greenwood, "The Drafting and Passage of the War Measures Act in 1914 and 1927: Object Lessons in the Need for Vigilance," in *Law & Society: Issues in Legal History*, ed. W. Wesley Pue and Barry Wright (Ottawa: Carleton University Press, 1988), 296–7.

9. The use of the criminal law to regulate political ideology is in keeping with the actions of law enforcement that engaged in "political policing" for much of Canada's history. See Reg Whitaker, Gregory Kealey, and Andrew Parnaby, *Secret Service: Political Policing in Canada from the Fenians to Fortress America* (Toronto: University of Toronto Press, 2010); for more on state power and the shaping of citizens see Mariana Valverde, *The Age of Light, Soap and Water: 19th Century Moral Reform in English Canada* (Toronto: University of Toronto Press, 1991); Enakshi Dua, "The Passage from Subjects to Aliens: Indian Migrants and the Racialization of Canadian Citizenship," *Sociologie et Sociétés* 31, no. 2 (Autumn 1999): 145–62; Franca Iacovetta, *Gatekeepers: Reshaping Immigrant Lives in Cold War Canada* (Toronto: Between the Lines, 2006).

10. *Homo sacer*, or the sacred man, was a classification in Roman law, a person who could be killed but not sacrificed because they were unholy or unclean. Anyone who killed such a figure would not be guilty of a homicide. This classification is similar to the status of an outlaw in early English law. Agamben discusses how only the sovereign is able to construct such beings. Other examples would be Jewish prisoners in

Auschwitz or prisoners accused of terrorism in Guantanamo Bay, Cuba. Both existed "outside the law" in that they received no legal protections other than what their captors allowed them. See Giorgio Agamben, *Homo Sacer: Sovereign Power and Bare Life*, trans. Daniel Heller-Roazen (Stanford: Stanford University Press, 1995), part 2.

11. My comparison of communists, and more specifically immigrant Communists, with Agamben's figure of *homo sacer* is meant to illustrate how the state can exclude individuals from legal protections and the significance of their isolation from society. It is *not* meant to suggest that the Canadian state in the interwar period could dispose of communists at will and by whatever means. The point is that it is the state that ultimately determines the degree of exclusion and not that the killability of communists ever became the defining trait of the Canadian state.

12. Craig Heron, ed., *The Workers' Revolt in Canada, 1917–1925* (Toronto: University of Toronto Press), 35; Ross Lambertson, *Repression and Resistance: Canadian Human Rights Activists, 1930–1960* (Toronto: University of Toronto Press, 2005), 22; Desmond Brown, *The Genesis of the Canadian Criminal Code of 1892* (Toronto: University of Toronto Press, 1989), 152; J.B. Mackenzie, "Section 98 Criminal Code and Freedom of Expression in Canada," *Queen's Law Journal* 4 (1972): 469–83; D.C. Masters, *The Winnipeg General Strike* (Toronto: University of Toronto Press, 1950), 138; Robert Craig Brown and Ramsay Cook, *Canada: A Nation Transformed 1896–1921* (Toronto: McClelland & Stewart, 1976), 314; Greenwood, "The Drafting and Passage of the War Measures Act," 305; Douglas A. Schmeiser, *Civil Liberties in Canada* (Oxford: Oxford University Press, 1964), 217; Thomas R. Berger, *Fragile Freedoms: Human Rights and Dissent in Canada* (Toronto: Clarke, Irwin, 1982), 132–8.

13. Carolyn Strange and Tina Loo, *Making Good: Law and Moral Regulation in Canada, 1867–1939* (Toronto: University of Toronto Press, 1997), 134.

14. Ken Adachi, *The Enemy That Never Was: A History of the Japanese Canadians* (Toronto: McClelland & Stewart, 1991), 355–70; Peter Ward, *White Canada Forever: Popular Attitudes and Public Policy toward Orientals in British Columbia* (Montreal: McGill-Queen's University Press, 1978), 61.

15. Donald Avery, *"Dangerous Foreigners": European Immigrant Workers and Labour Radicalism in Canada, 1896–1932* (Toronto: McClelland & Stewart, 1979), 47, 83–4, 135.

16. Russ McCormack, *Reformers, Rebels and Revolutionaries: The Western Canadian Radical Movement 1899–1919* (Toronto: University of Toronto Press, 1978); Betcherman, *The Little Band*; Gregory S. Kealey, "1919: The Canadian Labour Revolt," *Labour/Le Travail* 13 (Spring 1984): 11–44; Frances Swyripa and John Herd Thompson, eds., *Loyalties in Conflict:*

Ukrainians in Canada during the Great War (Edmonton: Canadian Institute of Ukrainian Study Press, 1983). For more on internment, see Norman Hillmer, Bohdan Kordan, and Lubomyr Luciuk, *On Guard for Thee: War, Ethnicity, and the Canadian State, 1939–1945* (Ottawa: Canadian Government Publishing Centre, 1988); Lubomyr Luciuk, *A Time for Atonement: Canada's First National Internment Operations and the Ukrainian Canadians, 1914–1920* (Kingston: Lime Stone Press, 1988); Franca Iacovetta, Roberto Perin, Angelo Principe, eds., *Enemies Within: Italian and Other Internees in Canada and Abroad* (Toronto: University of Toronto Press, 2000); Linda Kealey, *Enlisting Women for the Cause: Women, Labour and the Left in Canada, 1890–1920* (Toronto: University of Toronto Press, 1998); Andrée Lévesque, *Red Travellers: Jeanne Corbin and Her Comrades* (Montreal: McGill-Queen's University Press, 2006); Joan Sangster, *Dreams of Equality: Women on the Canadian Left, 1920–1950* (Toronto: McClelland & Stewart, 1989); *Regulating Girls and Women: Sexuality, Family and the Law in Ontario, 1920–1960*, 2nd ed. (Toronto: University of Toronto Press, 2001).

17. See, for instance, Reg Whitaker, *Double Standard: The Secret History of Canadian Immigration* (Toronto: Lester & Orpen Dennys, 1987); Roberts, *Whence They Came*.

18. Steve Hewitt, *Spying 101: The RCMP's Secret Activities at Canadian Universities, 1917–1997* (Toronto: University of Toronto Press, 2002); Larry Hannant, *The Infernal Machine: Investigating the Loyalty of Canada's Citizens* (Toronto: University of Toronto Press, 1995).

19. Wesley K. Wark, "Security Intelligence in Canada, 1864–1945: The History of a 'National Insecurity State,'" in *Go Spy the Land: Military Intelligence in History*, ed. Keith Neilson and B.J.C. McKercher (Westport, CT: Greenwood, 1992), 172; Reg Whitaker and Gary Marcuse, *Cold War Canada: The Making of a National Insecurity State, 1945–1957* (Toronto: University of Toronto Press, 1994); Gary Kinsman, Dieter K. Buse, and Mercedes Steedman, eds., *Whose National Security? Canadian State Surveillance and the Creation of Enemies* (Toronto: Between the Lines, 2000).

20. Gary Kinsman, "The Canadian Cold War on Queers: Sexual Regulation and Resistance," in *Love, Hate, and Fear in Canada's Cold War*, ed. Richard Cavell (Toronto: University of Toronto Press, 2004), 109; Mark Kristmanson, *Plateaus of Freedom: Nationality, Culture and State Security in Canada1940–1960* (Toronto: University of Toronto Press, 2002); Strange and Loo, *Making Good*.

21. Iacovetta, *Gatekeepers*.

22. Lambertson, *Repression and Resistance*; Dominique Clement, *Canada's Rights Revolution: Social Movements and Social Change, 1937–82* (Vancouver: University of British Columbia Press, 2008).

23. Whitaker, Kealey, and Parnaby, *Secret Service.*

24. Leland de la Durantaye, *Giorgio Agamben* (Stanford: Stanford University Press, 2009), 345–59.

25. See Agamben, *Homo Sacer* and *State of Exception*, trans. Kevin Attell (Chicago: University of Chicago Press, 2005); *Remnants of Auschwitz: The Witness and the Archive*, trans. Daniel Heller-Roazen (Cambridge, MA: Zone Books, 2002), 18–20.

26. Agamben, *Homo Sacer*, 27, 83.

27. Kevin Bruyneel advances a similar argument in his revised look at Louis Riel; see "Exiled, Executed, Exalted: Louis Riel, *Homo Sacer* and the Production of Canadian Sovereignty," *Canadian Journal of Political Science* 43, no. 3 (2010): 711–32.

28. See Joanna Bourke, *Fear: A Cultural History* (Berkeley: Counterpoint, 2007); Jessica Gienow-Hecht, *Emotions in American History: An International Assessment* (New York: Berghahn Books, 2010); Peter N. Stearns and Carol Z. Stearns, "Emotionology: Clarifying the History of Emotions and Emotional Standards," *American Historical Review* 90, no. 4 (1985): 813–30; William M. Reddy, *The Navigation of Feeling: A Framework for the History of Emotions* (Cambridge: Cambridge University Press, 2001).

29. Phillip Abrams, "Notes on the Difficulty of Studying the State," *Journal of Historical Sociology* 1, no. 1 (March 1988): 58–89. For a similar argument involving the law as ideology, see Douglas Hay, "Property, Authority and the Criminal Law," in A*lbion's Fatal Tree: Crime and Society in Eighteenth Century England*, ed. Douglas Hay et al., 1st ed. (London: Allen Lane / Penguin, 1975).

30. Ian McKay, "Canada as a Long Liberal Revolution," in *Liberalism and Hegemony: Debating the Canadian Liberal Revolution*, ed. Jean-François Constant and Michel Ducharme (Toronto: University of Toronto Press, 2009), 400–1.

31. For more on the contradictions of emergency law in liberal democracy and emergency law's relationship to politics and government policy, see Rande W. Kostal, *A Jurisprudence of Power* (Oxford: Oxford University Press, 2008); Kent Roach, *The 9/11 Effect: Comparative Counter Terrorism* (Cambridge: Cambridge University Press, 2011); Roach, *September 11: Consequences for Canada* (Durham: Acumen, 2003). For more on Canada and liberal order, see Ian McKay, "The Liberal Order Framework: A Prospectus for a Reconnaissance of Canadian History," *Canadian Historical Review* 81, no. 4 (December 2000): 617–45.

32. Agamben, *Homo Sacer*, 115.

33. Jessica Whyte, *Catastrophe and Redemption: The Political Thought of Giorgio Agamben* (Albany: State University of New York Press, 2013), 49.

34. Alan Greer and Ian Radforth, eds., *Colonial Leviathan: State Forma-tion in Mid-Nineteenth-Century Canada* (Toronto: University of Toronto Press, 1992), 10.

35. The term was first used by Mathews and Albino in an article in which they detail their challenge to a law that was used to detain opponents of apartheid in South Africa if an officer suspected an individual of acting on behalf of an unlawful organization, particularly in the case of Nelson Mandela's African National Congress. When that case came to the appel-late division, the court refused to place any restrictions on the "legality of the detentions," and the authors claim that by doing so, the court accepted the "permanence of the temporary," placing South Africa in a permanent state of emergency in which common laws could be passed that allowed the government to operate outside the rule of law. See A.S. Mathews and R.C. Albino, "The Permanence of the Temporary: An Examination of the 90 and 18 Day Detention Laws," *South African Law Journal* 83 (1966): 16–43; David Dyzenhaus, "The Permanence of the Temporary: Can Emergency Powers be Normalized?" in *The Security of Freedom: Essays on Canada's Anti-Terrorism Bill*, ed. Ronald J. Daniels, Patrick Macklem, and Kent Roach (Toronto: University of Toronto Press, 2001). Bill C-36 (the "anti-terrorism bill") in 2001 amended the Criminal Code, the Official Secrets Act, the Canada Evidence Act, and the Proceeds of Crime Act, among others, to "combat terrorism." See Canada, First Session Thirty-Seventh Parliament, Elizabeth II, 2001, 49–50. For more on the legal questions and debates surrounding the bill, see Ronald J. Daniels, Pat-rick Macklem, and Kent Roach, eds., *The Security of Freedom: Essays on Canada's Anti-Terrorism Bill* (Toronto: University of Toronto Press, 2001).

Chapter 1

1. See, for instance, R.C. Brown, *Robert Laird Borden: A Biography*, 2nd ed. (Toronto: Macmillan of Canada, 1980); C.P. Stacey, *Canada in the Age of Conflict*, vol. 1, *1867–1921* (Toronto: University of Toronto Press, 1981); J.L. Granatstein et al., *Nation: Canada since Confederation*, 3rd ed. (Toronto: McGraw-Hill Ryerson, 1990).

2. For more on the First World War and Canada, see Robert Craig Brown and Ramsay Cook, *Canada: A Nation Transformed 1896–1921* (Toronto: McClelland & Stewart, 1976); Daphne Read, ed., *The Great War and Canadian Society: An Oral History* (Toronto: New Hogtown Press, 1978); Robert Bothwell, Ian Drummond, and John English, *Canada 1900–1945* (Toronto: University of Toronto Press, 1987); R.T. Naylor, "The Canadian State, the Accumulation of Capital, and the Great War," *Journal of Canadian Studies* 16 (Fall/Winter 1981): 26–55.

3. Lambertson, *Repression and Resistance: Canadian Human Rights Activists, 1930–1960* (Toronto: University of Toronto Press, 2005), 22; Desmond Brown, *The Genesis of the Canadian Criminal Code of 1892* (Toronto: University of Toronto Press, 1989; J.B. Mackenzie, "Section 98 Criminal Code and Freedom of Expression in Canada," *Queen's Law Journal* 4 (1972); D.C. Masters, *The Winnipeg General Strike* (Toronto: University of Toronto Press, 1950), 138; Brown and Cook, *Canada: A Nation Transformed*, 314.

4. Donald Avery, *"Dangerous Foreigners": European Immigrant Workers and Labour Radicalism in Canada, 1896–1932* (Toronto: McClelland & Stewart, 1979); Gregory S. Kealey, "State Repression of Labour and the Left in Canada, 1914–1920: The Impact of the First World War," *Canadian Historical Review* 73, no. 3 (September 1993): 281–314.

5. Section 98 was originally known as Section 97(a) and (b) in 1919. After a Code restructuring that took place in 1927, Section 97 was renamed Section 98. I will refer to the section as Section 98 throughout the text for consistency and clarity.

6. O'Connor to Borden, 16 October 1911, Robert Borden Papers (hereafter Borden Papers), Library and Archives Canada (hereafter LAC), MG26-H, vol. 154, 82435.

7. W.F. O'Connor, 1914 General Notes, Borden Papers, LAC, MG26-H, vol. 336, 892; see Murray Greenwood's discussion of the creation of the act in "The Drafting and Passage of the War Measures Act in 1914 and 1927: Object Lessons in the Need for Vigilance," in *Law & Society: Issues in Legal History*, ed. W. Wesley Pue and Barry Wright (Ottawa: Carleton University Press, 1988).

8. War Measures Act, S.C. 1914, ch. 2, s. 4.

9. Greenwood, "War Measures Act," 298–303; See M.L. Friedland, *National Security: The Legal Dimensions: A Study Prepared for the Commission of Inquiry Concerning Certain Activities of the Royal Canadian Mounted Police* (Hull: Minister of Supply and Services Canada, 1980), 110; Patricia Peppin, "Emergency Legislation and Rights in Canada: The War Measures Act and Civil Liberties," *Queen's Law Journal* 18, 130 (1993): 133–4.

10. O'Connor, 1914 General Notes.

11. Giorgio Agamben, *Homo Sacer: Sovereign Power and Bare Life*, trans. Daniel Heller-Roazen (Stanford: Stanford University Press, 1995), part 1.

12. Craig Heron and Myer Siemiatycki, "The Great War, the State, and Working-Class Canada," in *The Workers' Revolt in Canada, 1917–1925*, ed. Craig Heron (Toronto: University of Toronto Press, 1998). For more on the war and the home front, see Arthur Marwick, *War and Social Change in the Twentieth Century: A Comparative Study of Britain,*

France, Germany, Russia, and the United States (London: Macmillan, 1974); Modris Eksteins, *Rites of Spring: The Great War and the Birth of the Modern Age* (Toronto: Lester & Orpen Dennys, 1989).

13. Heron and Siemiatycki, "The Great War"; Frances Swyripa and John Herd Thompson, eds., *Loyalties in Conflict: Ukrainians in Canada during the Great War* (Edmonton: Canadian Institute of Ukrainian Study Press, 1983); Lubomyr Luciuk, *A Time for Atonement: Canada's First National Internment Operations and the Ukrainian Canadians, 1914–1920* (Kingston: Lime Stone Press, 1988); Paul Craven, *"An Impartial Umpire:" Industrial Relations and the Canadian State 1900–1911* (Toronto: University of Toronto Press, 1980); Brown and Cook, *Canada 1896–1921.*

14. Previous to the creation of PC 834, the Militia Act required civil authorities who required military assistance to provide a written request to the federal government signed by a local magistrate and two justices of the peace. The government's PC 834 negated these requirements and allowed for direct intervention. See F.M. Auger, "On the Brink of Civil War: The Canadian Government and the Suppression of the 1918 Quebec Easter Riots," *Canadian Historical Review* 89, no. 4 (December 2008): 508–11.

15. Ibid., 525–6.

16. Gregory S. Kealey, "The Parameters of Class Conflict: Strikes in Canada, 1891–1930," in *Class, Community and the Labour Movement: Wales and Canada, 1850–1930,* ed. Deian R. Hopkin and Gregory S. Kealey (Aberystwyth, Wales: Llafur and Canadian Committee on Labour History, 1989), 213–48.

17. Avery, *Dangerous Foreigners*; Reg Whitaker, Gregory S. Kealey, and Andrew Parnaby, *Secret Service: Political Policing in Canada from the Fenians to Fortress America* (Toronto: University of Toronto Press, 2010); Ian Angus, *Canadian Bolsheviks: The Early Years of the Communist Party of Canada,* 2nd ed. (Victoria: Trafford, 2004).

18. Imperial Munitions Board to Borden, 22 February 1918, Borden Papers, LAC, MG26-H, vol. 104, 56597.

19. Geoffrey R. Stone, *Perilous Times: Free Speech in Wartime: From the Sedition Act of 1798 to the War on Terrorism* (New York: W.W. Norton, 2004), 146–7.

20. Temiskaming Mine Managers' Association to Frank Cochrane, 22 March 1918, LAC, MG26-H, vol. 104, 56620.

21. Cawdron to Doherty, 5 March 1918, Borden Papers, LAC, MG26-H, vol. 104, 56612.

22. Avery, *Dangerous Foreigners*; Michiel Horn, "Keeping Canada 'Canadian': Anti-Communism and Canadianism in Toronto, 1928–29," *Canada: A Historical Magazine* 3, no. 3 (September 1975): 34–47; Dennis

G. Molinaro, "'A Species of Treason?' Deportation and Nation-Building in the Case of Tomo Čačić 1931–1934," *Canadian Historical Review* 91, no.1 (March 2010): 61–85; Whitaker, Kealey, and Parnaby, *Secret Service*, 142–4; Lorna McLean, "To Become Part of Us: Ethnicity, Race, Literacy and the Canadian Immigration Act of 1919," *Canadian Ethnic Studies* 36, no. 2 (2004): 1–28.

23. Sherwood to F.A. Acland, Minister of Labour, 9 May 1818, Borden Papers, LAC, MG26-H, vol. 104, 56639.

24. Avery, *Dangerous Foreigners*, 73.

25. Ibid., 74.

26. Cahan to Doherty, 9 February 1912, Borden Papers, LAC, MG26-H, vol. 152, 81830.

27. Borden to Cahan, 19 May 1918, Borden Papers, LAC, MG26-H, vol. 104, 56642.

28. Stone, *Perilous Times*, 157; William H. Thomas Jr, *Unsafe for Democracy: World War I and the U.S. Justice Department's Covert Campaign to Suppress Dissent* (Madison: University of Wisconsin Press, 2008), 89–109.

29. Cahan to Doherty, 20 July 1918, Borden Papers, LAC, MG26-H, vol. 104, 56656.

30. Sherwood to Doherty, 16 June 1918, Borden Papers, LAC, MG26, H, vol. 104, 56651–3.

31. Cahan to Doherty, 14 September 1918, Borden Papers, LAC, MG26-H, vol. 104, 56665–81; Cahan to Doherty, 26 September 1918, Borden Papers, LAC, MG26-H, vol. 104, 56692–6.

32. Cahan to Borden, 20 September 1918, Borden Papers, LAC, MG26-H, vol. 104, 56685–9; see also Gordon Brook-Shepard, *The Ironmaze: Western Intelligence and the Bolsheviks* (London: Macmillan, 1998).

33. Canada, *Proclamations and Orders in Council of the Imperial Government* (Ottawa: J. de Labroquerie Tache, Printer to the King, 1919), lxxvii–lxxx.

34. Ibid.

35. Kealey, "State Repression."

36. William Preston Jr, *Aliens and Dissenters: Federal Suppression of Radicals 1903–1933* (New York: Harper and Row Publishers, 1963), 32.

37. A Canadian citizen was defined in the 1910 Immigration Act as "1) a person born in Canada who had not become an alien" by marrying an alien or acquiring a different citizenship; "2) a British subject who had acquired Canadian domicile," which was three years of residence in Canada in 1910 and later changed to five years of residence in Canada in 1919; "3) a person naturalized as a citizen under Canadian law. Anyone who was not a British subject was an alien." See Barbara Roberts,

Whence They Came: Deportation from Canada 1900–1935 (Ottawa: University of Ottawa Press, 1988), 25.

38. See Ian McKay and Jamie Swift, *Warrior Nation: Rebranding Canada in an Age of Anxiety* (Toronto: Between the Lines, 2012).

39. Ian Milligan, "Sedition in Wartime Ontario: The Trials and Imprisonment of Isaac Bainbridge, 1917–1918," *Ontario History* 100, no. 2 (Autumn 2008): 150–77.

40. Rowell to Borden, 29 October 1918, Borden Papers, LAC, MG26-H, vol. 104, 56708.

41. Whitaker, Kealey, and Parnaby, *Secret Service*, 78.

42. C.H. Cahan to the Honourable Arthur Meighen, Acting Minister of Justice, letter, 28 November 1918, LAC, RG13, vol. 938, file 2715 1918, 1.

43. Whitaker, Kealey and Parnaby, *Secret Service*, 77–8.

44. See Reinhold Kramer and Tom Mitchell, *When the State Trembled: How A.J. Andrews and the Citizens' Committee Broke the Winnipeg General Strike* (Toronto: University of Toronto Press, 2010).

45. Fear also gripped Americans in this period. See Jörg Nagler, "The Mobilization of Emotions: Propaganda and Social Violence on the American Home Front during World War I," in *Emotions in American History: An International Assessment*, ed. Jessica Gienow-Hecht (New York: Berghahn Books, 2010), 66–91.

46. Catherine Mills, "Politics: Biopolitics, Sovereignty and Nihilism," in *The Philosophy of Agamben* (Montreal: McGill-Queen's University Press, 2008), 75.

47. Swyripa and Thompson, eds., *Loyalties in Conflict*.

48. Angus, *Canadian Bolsheviks*, 29.

49. Norman Penner, *Winnipeg 1919: The Strikers' Own History of the Winnipeg General Strike* (Toronto: J. Lewis & Samuel, 1973).

50. Whitaker, Kealey and Parnaby, *Secret Service*, 67. For more on the labour revolt, see, for example, Heron, ed., *The Workers' Revolt*; Kealey, "1919: The Canadian Labour Revolt," *Labour/Le Travail* 13 (Spring 1984): 11–44; Glen Makahonuk, "Class Conflict in a Prairie City: The Saskatoon Working-Class Response to Prairie Capitalism 1906–19," *Labour/Le Travail* 19 (Spring 1987): 89–124; James Naylor, *The New Democracy: Challenging the Industrial Order in Industrial Ontario* (Toronto: University of Toronto Press, 1991); Suzanne Morton, "Labourism and Economic Action: The Halifax Shipyards Strike of 1920," *Labour/Le Travail* 22 (Fall 1988): 67–98. For more on interpreting the strike as a revolt, see Ian McKay, *Reasoning Otherwise: Leftists and the People's Enlightenment in Canada, 1890–1920* (Toronto: Between the Lines, 2008), chapter 7.

51. Kramer and Mitchell, *When the State Trembled*, 142–46. For more on the strike, see Masters, *The Winnipeg General Strike*; J.E. Rea, "The Politics of Class: Winnipeg City Council 1919–45," in *The West and The Nation: Essays in Honour of W.L. Morton*, ed. Carl Berger and Ramsay Cook (Toronto: McClelland & Stewart, 1976), 232–49; David Bercuson, *Confrontation at Winnipeg: Labour, Industrial Relations, and the General Strike*, 2nd ed. (Montreal: McGill-Queen's University Press, 1990); Kenneth McNaught and David Bercuson, *The Winnipeg General Strike* (Don Mills: Longman, 1974); Penner, *Winnipeg 1919*.

52. Canada, *Debates of the House of Commons Second Session Sixteenth Parliament*, vol. 2 (Ottawa: F.A. Acland, Printer to the King, 1928), 2473.

53. Ann Hagedorn, *Savage Peace: Hope and Fear in America, 1919* (New York: Simon & Schuster, 2007), 27–31,184–5, 226–230.

54. Roy L. Garis, *Immigration Restriction: A Study of the Opposition to and Regulation of Immigration into the United States* (New York: Macmillan, 1927), 138–140. See also Paul Avrich, *Sacco and Vanzetti: The Anarchist Background* (Princeton: Princeton University Press, 1991), 130–6.

55. Laura Tabili, *"We Ask for British Justice": Workers and Racial Difference in Late Imperial Britain* (Ithaca, NY: Cornell University Press, 1994).

56. Canada, *Debates of the House of Commons Second Session Thirteenth Parliament*, vol. 4 (Ottawa: J. de Labroquerie Tache, 1919), 3212.

57. Kramer and Mitchell, *When the State Trembled*, 146.

58. Ibid., 182–3.

59. Robertson to Borden, 18 June 1919, Borden Papers, LAC, MG26-H, vol. 104, 62013.

60. Canada, *House of Commons Debates*, 1919, 3285–90.

61. Ibid.

62. Ibid., 3288.

63. Ibid., 3290.

64. Arthur Meighen, Canada, *Debates of the Senate First Session Eighteenth Parliament* (Ottawa: J.O. Patenaude, Printer to the King, 1936), 619–21.

65. Barry Wright and Susan Binnie, eds., *Canadian State Trials*, vol. 3 (Toronto: University of Toronto Press, 2009),15–16.

66. Brown, *Genesis of the Canadian Criminal Code*, 140. See also Brown and Wright, "Codificaton, Public Order and the Security Provisions of the Canadian Criminal Code," in *Canadian State Trials*, vol. 3, ed. Wright and Binnie, 540–6.

67. Brown, *Genesis of the Canadian Criminal Code*, 140.

68. Ibid., 140, 153.

69. Palmer also makes a similar point in noting how state repression during this period was a means of managing the unemployed and containing the "threat" they posed. Bryan D. Palmer, *Working-Class Experience:*

Rethinking the History of Canadian Labour 1800–1991, 2nd ed. (Toronto: McClelland & Stewart, 1992), 262.

70. Agamben, "For a Theory of Destituent Power," *Chronos* 10, 16 November 2013.
71. Canada, *House of Commons Debates*, 1919, 3292.
72. Ibid., 4357.
73. Ibid., 4358.
74. Canada, *Senate Debates*, 1936, 913.
75. Ibid.
76. Ibid., 916.
77. Ibid., 917.
78. R.S.C. 1927, ch. 36.
79. For a discussion on his statements, see Canada, *Debates of the House of Commons First Session Fifteenth Parliament* (Ottawa: F.A. Acland, 1926), 4073.
80. See s. 98(3) in Appendix 2; R.S.C. 1927, ch. 36.
81. See s. 98(8) in Appendix 2; R.S.C. 1927, ch. 36.
82. Ibid.
83. Ibid.
84. Papers examined included the *Vancouver Sun*, the *Toronto Star*, the *Globe*, the *Halifax Chronicle*, the *Montreal Gazette*, the *Calgary Herald*, and the *Winnipeg Free Press*, as well as the *Trades and Labour Congress Journal*.
85. "Free Discussion and Violence," *Toronto Star*, 18 June 1919.
86. "Freedom Not License," *Halifax Chronicle*, 10 June 1919.
87. "House Gets New Light on Labour Conditions," *Toronto Star*, 3 June 1919, , 8.
88. "Premier Borden Appeals to Canadian Labour, Strikes a Danger in After-War Time," *Ottawa Citizen*, 14 January 1919, found in Borden Papers, LAC, MG26-H, vol. 111, 60757.
89. Canada, *Debates of the Senate Second Session Thirteenth Parliament* (Ottawa: J. de Labroquerie Tache, 1919), 673.
90. "Deport Them All Is Power's Plan," *Toronto Daily Star*, 3 June 1919, 8.
91. "Russell Verdict Robs of the Right to Strike," *Toronto Star*, 27 December 1919, 2.
92. See Barry Ferguson, "Before the Citizenship Act: Confronting Canadian Citizenship in the House of Commons, 1900–1947," in *Thinkers and Dreamers: Historical Essays in Honour of Carl Berger*, ed. Gerald Friesen and Doug Owram (Toronto: University of Toronto Press, 2010).
93. Jérôme Ouellet and Frédéric Roussel-Beaulieu, "Les débats parlementaires au service de l'historie politique," *Bulletin d'Historie Politique* 11, no. 3 (2003): 23–40. See also Ferguson, "Before the Citizenship Act."

94. Canada, *Debates of the Senate Fourth Session Thirteenth Parliament* (Ottawa: Thomas Mulvey, Printer to the King, 1920), 462.

95. Ibid.

96. Ibid., 465.

97. Ibid., 468.

98. Ibid., 499.

99. Ibid., 508.

100. Kenneth McNaught, *A Prophet in Politics: A Biography of J.S. Woodsworth* (Toronto: University of Toronto Press, 2001; first published 1959), 165–71. See also Allen Mills, *Fool for Christ: The Political Thought of J.S. Woodsworth* (Toronto: University of Toronto Press, 1991).

101. Canada, *Debates of the House of Commons First Session Fourteenth Parliament* (Ottawa: F.A. Acland, 1922), 865, 3281–3.

102. Canada, *Debates of the House of Commons First Session Fifteenth Parliament* (Ottawa: F.A. Acland, 1926), 4073.

103. Ibid.

104. *House of Commons Debates*, 1922, 3285.

105. Supra note 37.

106. Canada, *Debates of the House of Commons Second Session Fourteenth Parliament* (Ottawa: F.A. Acland, 1923), 2430.

107. Ibid., 2432.

108. "Bulletin No. 39," 2 September 1920, in Gregory S. Kealey and Reg Whitaker, eds., *R.C.M.P. Security Bulletins: The Early Years 1919–1929* (St John's: Canadian Committee on Labour History, 1994), 81.

109. Thomas Geggie, "Britain Takes Steps to Stamp Out Sedition," *Toronto Daily Star*, 27 April 1921.

110. Associated Press, "Seize Activists Deport Aliens London Project," *Toronto Daily Star*, 23 September 1925.

111. Hal O'Flaherty, "Leading Reds Arrested in London Police Swoop," *Toronto Daily Star*, 15 October 1925.

112. David Frank, *J.B. McLachlan: A Biography* (Toronto: James Lorimer, 1999), 231–317.

113. Canada, *Debates of the House of Commons First Session Fifteenth Parliament* (Ottawa: F.A. Acland, 1926), 643.

114. *House of Commons Debates*, 1926, 4071–3.

115. Ibid., 3995.

116. Ibid., 3997.

117. Ibid., 4076.

118. Ibid., 4077.

119. Ibid.

120. Ibid., 4114.

121. Ibid., 4116.

122. Ibid., 2134.
123. Ibid., 4119.
124. Ibid., 245.
125. Ibid., 273.
126. Ibid., 274.
127. Ibid., 271.
128. Ibid., 274.
129. Ibid., 283.
130. Ibid., 3998.
131. T.H. Marshall, *Citizenship and Social Class* (Cambridge: Cambridge University Press, 1950). See also Ferguson, "Before the Citizenship Act," 164; Kenneth Carty and Peter Ward, "The Making of a Canadian Political Citizenship," in *National Politics and Community in Canada*, ed. Carty and Ward (Vancouver: University of British Columbia Press, 1986), 65–79; Robert Bothwell, "Something of Value? Subjects and Citizens in Canadian History," in *Belonging: The Meaning and Future of Canadian Citizenship*, ed. William Kaplan (Montreal: McGill-Queen's University Press, 1993), 25–35.
132. Scholars of the Cold War have put forth similar arguments in regards to political beliefs and citizenship. See, for instance, Franca Iacovetta, *Gatekeepers: Reshaping Immigrant Lives in Cold War Canada* (Toronto: Between the Lines, 2006),19; Reg Whitaker, *Double Standard: The Secret History of Canadian Immigration* (Toronto: Lester & Orpen Dennys, 1987), 188. Kramer and Mitchell also discuss how citizenship was tied to bourgeois and British values in their study on the Citizens' Committee of 1000 during the Winnipeg General Strike in *When the State Trembled*, 70–96.
133. Ferguson, "Before the Citizenship Act," 164.

Chapter 2

1. H. Blair Neatby, *The Politics of Chaos: Canada in the Thirties* (Toronto: Macmillan of Canada, 1972). For more on the Great Depression, see John Kenneth Galbraith, *The Great Crash 1929*, 2nd ed. (Boston: Houghton Mifflin, 1955); John Herd Thompson with Allen Seager, *Canada 1922–1939: Decades of Discord* (Toronto: McClelland & Stewart, 1985); Michiel Horn, *The Dirty Thirties: Canadians in the Great Depression* (Toronto: Copp Clark, 1971); James Struthers, *No Fault of Their Own: Unemployment and the Canadian Welfare State 1914–1941* (Toronto: University of Toronto Press, 1983); J.L. Granatstein et al., eds., *Twentieth Century Canada: A Reader* (Toronto: McGraw-Hill Ryerson, 1986); Laurel Sefton MacDowell

and Ian Radforth, eds., *Canadian Working Class History: Selected Readings* (Toronto: Canadian Scholars' Press, 1992), section 4; Bryan D. Palmer, *Working-Class Experience: Rethinking the History of Canadian Labour 1800–1991*, 2nd ed. (Toronto: McClelland & Stewart, 1992); Katrina Srigley, *Breadwinning Daughters: Young Working Women in a Depression-Era City 1929–1939* (Toronto: University of Toronto Press, 2009); Lara Campbell, *Respectable Citizens: Gender, Family and Unemployment in Ontario's Great Depression* (Toronto: University of Toronto Press, 2009).

2. Ian Angus, *Canadian Bolsheviks: The Early Years of the Communist Party of Canada*, 2nd ed. (Victoria: Trafford, 2004); Ivan Avakumovic, *The Communist Party in Canada: A History* (Toronto: McClelland & Stewart, 1975); William Rodney, *Soldiers of the International: A History of the Communist Party in Canada, 1919–1929* (Toronto: University of Toronto Press, 1968); Joan Sangster, "Robitnytsia, Ukrainian Communists, and the 'Porcupinism' Debate: Reassessing Ethnicity, Gender, and Class in Early Canadian Communism, 1922–1930," *Labour/Le Travail* 56 (Fall 2005): 51–89.

3. Reg Whitaker, Gregory S. Kealey, and Andrew Parnaby demonstrate how authorities were able to successfully strike the CPC, arguing that the "intelligence cycle worked": see *Secret Service: Political Policing in Canada from the Fenians to Fortress America* (Toronto: University of Toronto Press, 2010). For more on the intelligence cycle (the process of planning, collecting, processing, analysing, and disseminating intelligence), see Michael A. Turner, *Why Secret Intelligence Fails* (Dulles, VA: Potomac Books, 2005); Peter Gill and Mark Phythian, *Intelligence in an Insecure World* (Cambridge, UK: Polity Press, 2006); Michael Herman, *Intelligence Power in Peace and War* (Cambridge: Cambridge University Press, 1996).

4. Priya Satia argues that British cultural perceptions shaped the British understanding of "Arabia" during the First World War as the British attempted to pacify the region. Britain was a "state that could not see" and used violence to control a region it did not understand, including through the use of aerial bombardment during peacetime. The British perceived their enemies as intractable. This perception, coupled with the creation of a culture of violence due to the First World War, led to cultural biases against the region. Thus culture shaped how the British imperial state "saw" their targets. See Satia, *Spies in Arabia: The Great War and the Cultural Foundations of Britain's Covert Empire in the Middle East* (New York: Oxford University Press, 2008).

5. Angus, *Canadian Bolsheviks*, 41–6, 64–70.

6. Angus, *Canadian Bolsheviks*, 70. For more on the history of the CPC, see also Norman Penner, *Canadian Communism: The Stalin Years and Beyond* (Toronto: Methuen, 1988); Rodney, *Soldiers of the International*; Avakumovic, *The Communist Party in Canada*; John Manley, "'Starve, Be Damned!' Communists and Canada's Urban Unemployed, 1929–39," *Canadian Historical Review* 79, no. 3 (September 1998): 466–91; Manley, "'Audacity, Audacity, Still More Audacity': Tim Buck, the Party, and the People, 1932–1939," *Labour/Le Travail* 49 (Spring: 2002), 9–41; Andrée Lévesque, "The Canadian Left in Quebec during the Great Depression: The Communist Party of Canada and the CCF in Quebec, 1929–1939" (PhD diss., Duke University, 1972).

7. Avakumovic, *The Communist Party*, 35–8.

8. It is worth noting that Stalin and Bukharin never foresaw the coming Depression. See Kevin McDermott and Jeremy Agnew, *The Comintern: A History of International Communism from Lenin to Stalin* (Basingstoke: Macmillan, 1996), 69; Stewart Smith, *Comrades and Komsomolkas* (Toronto: Lugus Publications, 1993), 120. For more elaboration on the term "social fascists" in reference to social democrats, see G. Pierce, *Socialism and the CCF* (Montreal: Contemporary Publishing Association, 1934), 153–160. See also Angus, *Canadian Bolsheviks*, chapters 14–16.

9. For more perspectives on these debates, see John McIlroy and Alan Campbell, "'Nina Ponomareva's Hats': The New Revisionism, the Communist International, and the Communist Party of Great Britain, 1920–30," *Labour/Le Travail* 49 (Spring 2002):147–87; Bryan D. Palmer, "Rethinking the Historiography of United States Communism," *American Communist History* 2, no. 2 (2003): 139–73; Andrew Thorpe, "Comintern 'Control' of the Communist Party of Great Britain, 1920–43," *English Historical Review* 113 (June 1998): 637–62; James R. Barrett, "The History of American Communism and Our Understanding of Stalinism," *American Communist History* 2, no. 2 (2003): 175–82. The attempts to categorize some works as revisionist and others as traditionalist have also been contested; see, for instance, Ian McKay, "Joe Salsberg, Depression-Era Communism, and the Limits of Moscow's Rule," *Canadian Jewish Studies* 21 (2013 [2014]):130–142 [also in *Oyfn Veg*, a festschrift in honour of Gerald Tulchinsky]; Bryan D. Palmer, "Reading Otherwise: Ian McKay's 'Fairly Straightforward' Misrepresentation of Communist Party Historiography," *Canadian Jewish Studies* 23 (2015).

10. More on the Stalinization of the CPC can be found in a number of histories on the CPC, such as Rodney's *Soldiers of the International*. One of the more detailed treatments of this topic can be found in Angus's *Canadian Bolsheviks*, specifically chapters 11 and 12.

11. Tim Buck, 1926, Organizational Report, Library and Archives Canada (hereafter LAC), Communist International Fonds (hereafter CI Fonds), fond 495, file 33, reel K-273.

12. Avakumovic, *The Communist Party*, 36.

13. Letter from Charlie to Sam (Carr), 22 October 1931, LAC, CI Fonds, fond 495, file 121, reel K-281.

14. Resolution on the Situation and Tasks of District 7, 4 May 1934, LAC, CI Fonds, fond 495, file 63, reel K-287.

15. Ibid.

16. Avakumovic, *The Communist Party*, 94.

17. Executive Committee of the Communist International to the Sixth Congress of the Communist Party of Canada, 22 February 1929, LAC, CI Fonds, fond 495, file 66, reel K-276.

18. Letter of P.B. to District No. 7, 1 October 1932, LAC, CI Fonds, fond 495, file 140, reel K-284.

19. Jim Mochoruk, "'Pop & Co' versus Buck and the 'Lenin School Boys': Ukrainian Canadians and the Communist Party of Canada 1921–1931," in *Re-Imagining Ukrainian Canadians: History, Politics, and Identity*, ed. Rhonda L. Hinther and Jim Mochoruk (Toronto: University of Toronto Press, 2011), 331–75; Ian Radforth, *Bushworkers and Bosses* (Toronto: University of Toronto Press, 1987); Ruth A. Frager, "Sewing Solidarity: The Eaton's Strike of 1912," and Carmela Patrias, "Relief Strike: Immigrant Workers and the Great Depression in Crowland, Ontario," in *A Nation of Immigrants: Women, Workers, and Communities in Canadian History, 1840s–1960s*, ed. Franca Iacovetta, Daula Draper, and Robert Ventresca (Toronto: University of Toronto Press, 1998); Dennis G. Molinaro, "'A Species of Treason?' Deportation and Nation-Building in the Case of Tomo Čačić 1931–1934," *Canadian Historical Review* 91, no. 1 (March 2010): 61–85.

20. Minutes of the Political Bureau, 30 September 1926, LAC, CI Fonds, fond 495, file 40, reel K-274.

21. Minutes of Central Executive Committee Meeting, 7 February 1926, LAC, CI Fonds, fond 495, file 40, reel K-274.

22. Minutes of the Political Bureau, 30 September 1926, LAC, CI Fonds, fond 495, file 40, reel K-274.

23. Minutes of the Political Bureau, 14 March 1926, LAC, CI Fonds, fond 495, file 40, reel K-274.

24. Angus, *Canadian Bolsheviks*, 272–81.

25. Executive Committee of the Communist International to the Canadian Party, 1927, LAC, CI Fonds, fond 495, file 46, reel K-274.

26. Radforth, *Bushworkers*, 109, 111, 123, 132. See also Ruth A. Frager, *Sweatshop Strife: Class, Ethnicity, and Gender in the Jewish Labour*

Movement of Toronto, 1900–1939 (Toronto: University of Toronto Press, 1992); Carmela Patrias, *Patriots and Proletarians: Politicizing Hungarian Immigrants in Interwar Canada* (Montreal: McGill-Queen's University Press, 1994).

27. Manley, "Starve, Be Damned!" 480.
28. Joseph Stalin, *Interviews with Foreign Workers' Delegations* (New York: International Publishers, 1927) 9, 27–9; see also Stalin, "Marxism and the National Question," in *Works* (Moscow: Foreign Languages Publishing House, 1954).
29. Jeremy Smith, *The Bolsheviks and the National Question, 1917–23* (New York: St Martin's Press, 1999), 22–8.
30. Canada, *Supreme Court of Ontario – Rex vs. Tim Buck et al.*, LAC, vol. 738, RG76-B-1-a 71–5, file 513173, 290.
31. Stalin, *Interviews with Foreign Workers' Delegations*, 9; Stalin, "Marxism and the National Question," 378–80.
32. Stalin, "Marxism and the National Question," 323.
33. Ibid., 332–44.
34. In the Jewish case, the Soviet Union had promised an autonomous Jewish republic in eastern Russia called Birobidzhan. It would be a homeland for Jews that would be autonomous, allowing for Jewish emancipation. Though the promise turned out to be a fraud, Jewish Communists in North America supported the idea from the 1920s to the 1950s. See Henry Felix Srebrnik, *Jerusalem on the Amur: Birobidzhan and the Canadian Jewish Communist Movement, 1924–1951* (Montreal: McGill-Queen's University Press, 2008.) For more on the National Question in Canada, see William Burgess, "Canada's Location in the World System: Reworking the Debate in Canadian Political Economy" (PhD diss., University of British Columbia, 2002).
35. Minutes of the Political Bureau, 22 January 1931, LAC, CI Fonds, fond 495, file 117 reel K-281 [capitalization in original].
36. Stalin, "Marxism and the National Question," 323.
37. Ibid.
38. Lévesque, *Red Travellers*, 128–30; "International Women's Day: Draw the Working-Class Women into the Struggle," *Worker*, 28 February 1931.
39. Joan Sangster, *Dreams of Equality: Women on the Canadian Left, 1920–1950* (Toronto: McClelland & Stewart, 1989), 31–2, 45–52. See also Margaret Helen Hobbs and Joan Sangster, *The Woman Worker, 1926–1929* (Toronto: Canadian Committee on Labour History, 1999). For more on women's leagues and leftist activism, see Joan Sangster, "The Communist Party and the Women Question, 1922–1929," *Labour/Le Travail* 15 (Spring: 1985), 25–56; Linda Kealey, *Enlisting Women for the Cause: Women, Labour and the Left in Canada, 1890–1920* (Toronto:

University of Toronto Press, 1998); Frances Swyripa, *Wedded to the Cause: Ukrainian-Canadian Women and Ethnic Identity, 1891–1991* (Toronto: University of Toronto Press, 1993); Frager, *Sweatshop Strife.* For more on women and gender in the CPC, see Nancy Butler, "Mother Russia and the Socialist Fatherland: Women and the Communist Party of Canada, 1932–1941, with Specific Reference to the Activism of Dorothy Livesay and Jim Watts" (PhD diss., Queen's University, 2010). In contrast, Janice Newton argues that the Canadian Left failed to sustain the socialist feminist cause in *The Feminist Challenge to the Canadian Left, 1900–1918* (Montreal: McGill-Queen's University Press, 1995).

40. Lévesque, *Red Travellers*, 134–7.
41. Ibid., 154–5.
42. "Toronto Communists Admit Work against British Empire," *Toronto Daily Star*, 26 May 1927.
43. Stephen L. Endicott, *Raising the Workers' Flag: The Workers' Unity League of Canada, 1930–1936* (Toronto: University of Toronto Press, 2012), 25–6.
44. See, for example, "War in Manchuria Threat against Soviet Union" and "Terror Reign in Ireland Effort to Crush Revolt," *Worker*, 14 November 1931; "Conquest of Yemen Is British Attempt to Strengthen Yoke," *Worker*, 12 May 1934; "Revolt in Philippines," *Worker*, 6 July 1935.
45. "Bulletin No. 48" and "Bulletin No. 332," in Gregory S. Kealey and Reg Whitaker, eds., *R.C.M.P. Security Bulletins: The Early Years 1919–1929* (St John's: Canadian Committee on Labour History, 1994), 266, 338–9.
46. See Gregory S. Kealey, "1919: The Canadian Labour Revolt," *Labour/Le Travail* 13 (Spring 1984): 11–44; Kealey, "The Early Years of State Surveillance of Labour and the Left in Canada: The Institutional Framework of the Royal Canadian Mounted Police Security and Intelligence Apparatus, 1918–26," in *Espionage, Past, Present and Future?* ed. Wesley Wark (New York: Frank Cass, 1994); Steve Hewitt, *Spying 101: The RCMP's Secret Activities at Canadian Universities, 1917–1997* (Toronto: University of Toronto Press, 2002).
47. Lita-Rose Betcherman, *The Little Band: The Clashes between the Communists and the Political and Legal Establishment in Canada, 1928–1932* (Ottawa: Deneau Publishers, 1982).
48. Michiel Horn, "'Free Speech within the Law': The Letter of the Sixty-Eight Toronto Professors, 1931," *Ontario History* 72, no. 1 (March 1980): 27–48.
49. D. Draper, "Good Citizenship," *Empire Club of Canada Addresses Delivered to the Members during the Year 1928* (Toronto: Hunter-Rose, 1929), 174.
50. The Liberals did achieve some success. On 30 April, Bill 187 removed the government's ability to deport British subjects who had acquired

naturalization. Other immigrant activists were a more pressing concern. See Canada, *Debates of the House of Commons Fourth Session Sixteenth Parliament* (Ottawa: F.C. Acland, 1930), 2741.

51. Smith to Bennett, 8 June 1932, R.B. Bennett Papers (hereafter Bennett Papers), LAC, 93151.

52. Strong to Bennett, 27 August 1930, LAC, Bennett Papers, 94419–20.

53. Employers Association of Manitoba to Bennett, 14 April 1931, Bennett Papers, LAC, 94525 [underline in original].

54. Calls for the deportation of undesirables and Communists came from over forty cities across all provinces in the country, such as Orillia, Niagara Falls, Kingston, Port Perry, and Sherbrooke, Quebec, among others. See Carrie M. Johnson to Bennett, 5 May 1931, Bennett Papers, LAC, 94579.

55. "Is Most British City in All This Country Toronto or Kingston?" *Globe*, 13 June 1929. For more on the CPC public speeches and the perceptions of communism as "foreign," see Michiel Horn, "Keeping Canada 'Canadian': Anti-Communism and Canadianism in Toronto, 1928–29," *Canada: A Historical Magazine* 3, no. 3 (September 1975): 34–47.

56. Bennett to MacBrian, 15 December 1931, Bennett Papers, LAC, 94971–4.

57. Neatby also documents a common joke among Canadians in the 1930s in which an angry Bennett was seen talking to himself while onlookers quipped that he must have been having a "cabinet meeting." Neatby, *The Politics of Chaos*, 50–2.

58. Bennett to Ferland, 20 November 1933, Bennett Papers, LAC, 96553; Bennett to Miller, 23 November 1933, Bennett Papers, LAC, 96557.

59. "Me Swear, Me Drink, Me a Canadian, Declares Newcomer," *Globe*, 9 May 1929.

60. Paula Maurutto, "Private Policing and Surveillance of Catholics: Anti-Communism in the Roman Catholic Archdiocese of Toronto, 1920–60," in *Whose National Security? Canadian State Surveillance and the Creation of Enemies*, ed. Gary Kinsman, Dieter K. Buse, and Mercedes Steedman (Toronto: Between the Lines, 2000), 40.

61. J.R. MacNicol, Canada, *Debates of the House of Commons Second Session Seventeenth Parliament*, vol. 4 (Ottawa: F.A. Acland, Printer to the King, 1931), 3477.

62. Gerald B. Winrod, *3 Modern Evils: Modernism, Atheism, Bolshevism* (Wichita, Kansas: Defender Publishers, 1932); found in LAC, Bennett Papers, 93623.

63. W.H. Price as quoted in Canada, *The King vs. Buck and Others: The Judgment of the Court of Appeal of Ontario Concerning the Communist Party in Canada*, ed. W.H. Price, LAC, RG13, vol. 2014, file 1484 1932, 2, 16.

64. W.H. Price, "On Atheism," 12 July 1933, Annual Orange Order Celebration, Kingston, ON, Archives of Ontario (hereafter AO), RG4–2, file 4.26.
65. Betcherman, *The Little Band*, 44.
66. Betcherman, *The Little Band*, 22.
67. "Poisoning the Wells," *Globe*, 7 December 1928.
68. Horn, "Keeping Canada 'Canadian,'" 41.
69. "Only Two Sides to It," *Globe*, 23 January 1931.
70. "Fewer Foreigners and More British," *Mail and Empire*, 10 January 1929.
71. "Keep Canada Canadian," *Toronto Evening Telegram*, 8 June 1928.
72. "What Has Christianity to Do with It?" *Toronto Daily Star*, 31 January 1929.
73. Committee Representing American Federation of Labor to Tim Buck, 27 August 1928, AO, RG4–32, file 3188/31, 290631.
74. Horn, "Keeping Canada 'Canadian,'"45.
75. "Action against Communism Urged," *Hamilton Spectator*, 16 June 1931; found in Bennett Papers, LAC, 94771.
76. Association Representing Ukrainians of Alberta to Bennett, 15 July 1933, Bennett Papers, LAC, 93449.
77. Borbowski to Bennett, 28 March 1931, Bennett Papers, LAC, 94508.
78. G.B. Nicholson, 7 July1931, *House of Commons Debates*, vol. 4, 3482.
79. Brownlee to Bennett, 14 January 1931, Bennett Papers, LAC, 94455.
80. Tolmie to Bennett, 13 June 1931, Bennett Papers, LAC, 94763.
81. Bennett to Tolmie, 13 June 1931, Bennett Papers, LAC, 94765.
82. For more on Taschereau's political career, see Bernard Vigod, *Quebec before Duplessis: The Political Career of Louis-Alexandre Taschereau* (Montreal: McGill-Queen's University Press, 1986).
83. Andrée Lévesque, *Virage à gauche interdit: Les communistes, les socialistes et leurs ennemis au Québec 1929–1939* (Montreal: Boréal, 1984), 122–3.
84. For more on these arrests, see Marcel Fournier, *Communisme et anticommunisme au Québec, 1920–1950* (Montreal: Éditions coopératives Albert Saint-Martin, 1979) and Andrée Lévesque, "Le Québec et le monde communiste: Cowansville 1931," in *Le droit de se taire: Histoire des communistes au Québec, de la Première Guerre mondiale à la Révolution tranquille*, ed. Robert Comeau and Bernard Dionne (Montreal: VLB Éditeur, 1989).
85. Andrée Lévesque, "Red Scares and Repression in Québec 1919–1939," in *Canadian State Trials*, vol. 4, ed. Barry Wright, Susan Binnie, and Eric Tucker (Toronto: University of Toronto Press, 2015). For more on the left in Quebec, see also Lévesque, "The Canadian Left in Quebec."

86. Manley, "Starve, Be Damned!" 466–9.
87. Both the National Employment Commission in 1936 and the Rowell–Sirois Commission in 1937 reported that unemployment was a national problem that the federal government needed the power to deal with under an amended constitution. It was a finding that was initially met with hostility by Prime Minister Mackenzie King. See Neatby, *The Politics of Chaos*, 83–4. For more on the creation of unemployment insurance and the CPC agitation for it, see Struthers, *No Fault of Their Own*; Manley, "Starve, Be Damned!"
88. W.F. Langworthy to E. Bayley, 1 November 1930, AO, RG4 1930, file 3178.
89. The bulk of letter writers from the hardest hit in Canadian society during the Depression (farmers, the unemployed, the elderly, sick, or disabled) to R.B. Bennett reveal that many people sought relief and work during the Depression and not radical social change. Although, as Neatby has argued, many new political parties emerged in the period as Canadians looked for alternatives and reform, but overall there was little appetite for the drastic political changes sought by the CPC. See, for instance, Michael Bliss, ed., *The Wretched of Canada: Letters to R.B. Bennett 1930–35* (Toronto: University of Toronto Press, 1971); Neatby, *The Politics of Chaos*. See also Horn, *The Dirty Thirties*, part 7.
90. See Lara Campbell's discussion of how gender helped shaped expressions of dissent in *Respectable Citizens*, chapter 5.
91. "Reds Rounded Up," *Globe*, 12 August 1931. For more on the context surrounding these clashes, see Michel Beaulieu, *Labour at the Lakehead: Ethnicity, Socialism and Politics, 1900–35* (Vancouver: University of British Columbia Press, 2011).
92. RCMP General Report of the Communist Party of Canada, part 1, AO, RG4, series D-1–1, reel 36, 2–7.
93. *Rex v. Weir*, LAC, Jacob Lawrence Cohen Fonds, MG30-A94, vol. 1, file 6; see also Laurel Sefton MacDowell, *Renegade Lawyer: The Life of J.L. Cohen* (Toronto: University of Toronto Press, 2001), 35–8; Betcherman, *The Little Band*, 76–8.
94. Bayley to Golding, 4 May 1931, AO, RG4–32, file 3188/31, 30L0643–8.
95. Marshall to Draper, 8 June 1931, AO, RG4–32, file 3188/31, 30L0670.
96. Guthrie to Price,18 March 1931, AO, RG4–32, file 3188/31, 30L0637–8.
97. Ibid. For more on the RCMP's obsession with communism, see Hewitt, *Spying 101*; Whitaker, Kealey, and Parnaby, *Secret Service*; Larry Hannant, *The Infernal Machine: Investigating the Loyalty of Canada's Citizens* (Toronto: University of Toronto Press, 1995).

98. The statements were made by Sedgwick in an interview with Betcherman for her book *The Little Band*. See page 162.
99. Starnes to Sedgwick, 1 May 1931, AO, RG4–32, file 3188/31, 30L0641.
100. Betcherman, *The Little Band*, 168–70.
101. Giorgio Agamben, *Remnants of Auschwitz: The Witness and the Archive*, trans. Daniel Heller-Roazen (Cambridge, MA: Zone Books, 2002), 18–20.
102. Price to Sedgwick, 15 August 1931, AO, RG4–32, file 3188/31, 30L0789.
103. See, for instance, Wilkins to Price, 19 August 1931, AO, RG4–32, file 3188/31, 30L0833.
104. Price to Sedgwick, 25 August 1931, AO, RG4–32, file 3188/31, 30L 0875.
105. Supra note 3.
106. "Province Swoops to Oust All Reds," *Toronto Daily Star*, 12 August 1931.
107. Warrant to Arrest, AO, RG4–32, file 3188/31, 28L0026.
108. "Province Swoops to Oust All Reds."
109. Ibid.
110. William Simpson, in Canada, *Rex vs. Tim Buck et al.*, LAC, vol. 738, RG76-B-1-a 71–5, file 513173, 53.
111. John Nimmo, in Canada, *Rex vs. Tim Buck et al.*, 71–5; V.J. LaChance to the Commissioner, 20 August 1931, LAC, Record of Canadian Security Intelligence Service, file 96-A-00149.
112. "Province Swoops to Oust All Reds"; George Fish, in Canada, *Rex vs. Tim Buck et al.*, 85–7.
113. "Ewen Gives Up to Face Charge of Communism," *Toronto Daily Star*, 17 August 1931; Betcherman, *The Little Band*, 178.
114. "Remand Three Red Leaders. Refuse Bail: Police Raid and Arrest in Sudden, Secret Move against Reds in Canada," *Toronto Evening Telegram*, 12 August 1931.
115. See, for instance, George Fish's testimony in *Rex vs. Tim Buck et al.*, 87.
116. Oscar Ryan, *Tim Buck – A Conscience for Canada* (Toronto: Progress Books, 1975), 147–8.
117. See, for instance, Agamben, *Remnants of Auschwitz*, 18–20.

Chapter 3

1. The Crown dropped its case against Golinsky at the conclusion of the trial, claiming it lacked evidence of his involvement in the CPC.

2. The trial has largely received only passing mention in a number of studies that briefly discuss Section 98, most often in the context of human rights and labour history in Canada. See, for instance, Dominique Clement, *Canada's Rights Revolution: Social Movements and Social Change, 1937–82* (Vancouver: University of British Columbia Press, 2008); Eric M. Adams, "Canada's 'Newer Constitutional Law' and the Idea of Constitutional Rights," *McGill Law Journal* 51, no. 435 (2006): 435–74; Richard Fidler, "Proscribing Unlawful Associations: The Swift Rise and Agonizing Demise of Section 98" (unpublished, Osgoode Law School, May 1984); J.B. Mackenzie, "Section 98 Criminal Code and Freedom of Expression in Canada," *Queen's Law Journal* 4 (1972). Desmond Brown mentions the trial in a brief discussion of Section 98; see Brown's *The Genesis of the Canadian Criminal Code of 1892* (Toronto: University of Toronto Press, 1989). One of the most popular discussions of the trial within the context of human rights and labour history occurs in Lita-Rose Betcherman, *The Little Band: The Clashes between the Communists and the Political and Legal Establishment in Canada, 1928–1932* (Ottawa: Deneau Publishers, 1982).

3. Betcherman, *The Little Band*, 179.

4. Laurel Sefton MacDowell, *Renegade Lawyer: The Life of J.L. Cohen* (Toronto: University of Toronto Press, 2001), 44.

5. J.S. Woodsworth protested against Wright's instructions to the jury during a session of Parliament in 1929 in a more general discussion about police repression of activists and free speech. See Woodsworth's comments in Canada, *Debates of the House of Commons Third Session Sixteenth Parliament* (Ottawa: F.C. Acland, Printer to the King, 1929), 2354–5.

6. "Eyes of Masses on Trial of Nine," *Worker*, 7 November 1931, 1.

7. Criminal Code of Canada, R.S.C. 1927, s. 98(3), 30.

8. Joseph Sedgwick to Col. Price, Attorney General of Ontario, Re: *Rex vs. Buck et al.*, 17 October 1931, Archives of Ontario (hereafter AO), RG4–32, file 3188/31, 30L0923–7.

9. No document within the records of the trial is signed as being the brief Edwards produced to the grand jury. However, in the trial records there is a letter from Sommerville to Sedgwick that includes a summary of the Court of Appeal arguments regarding Buck et al.'s appeal. Within that summary is a document that seems very likely to be the brief Edwards prepared, on the basis of the content and description of the brief provided by Sedgwick in his letter to Price. See "Rex vs. Tim Buck et al." in "In the Court of Appeal of Ontario," 19 February 1932, AO, RG4–32, file 3188/31.

10. Ibid.

11. Ibid.
12. Sedgwick's letter that details the meeting and events does not explicitly state what type of meeting this was or whether defence lawyers were present. See Sedgwick to Price, 17 October 1931.
13. Sedgwick to Price, 17 October 1931. Parliament never revised Section 98 in the next session following the trial, likely because they did not need to once Buck et al. were convicted and the party became unlawful. The "and/or" issue was never revisited until the Liberals repealed Section 98 in 1936. See chapter 6.
14. Rowell to Borden, 29 October 1918, Borden Papers, LAC, MG26-H, vol. 104, 56708.
15. Hugh Macdonald in *Supreme Court of Ontario – Rex vs. Tim Buck et al.*, Library and Archives Canada (hereafter LAC), vol. 738, RG76-B-1-a 71–5, file 513173, 3.
16. Ibid.
17. Ibid., 7.
18. Ibid., 8.
19. Ibid., 10.
20. Ibid.
21. Norman Sommerville, *Rex vs. Tim Buck et al.*, 16.
22. Bill of Particulars, AO, RG4–32, file 3188/31.
23. *Rex vs. Tim Buck et al.*, 22.
24. Henry Wright, *Rex vs. Tim Buck et al.*, 27.
25. "Judge Scores Conduct of Two Defers Sentence," *Toronto Daily Star*, 3 November 1931.
26. "Seven Reds Get Five Year Terms, One Two," *Toronto Evening Telegram*, 13 November 1931.
27. "Nearly 100 Rejected at Communist Trial," *Toronto Daily Star*, 3 November 1931.
28. Sommerville Re: Buck et al., Opening to the Jury, RG 4–32, file 3188/31, 28L 0137.
29. Ibid.
30. Ibid., 28L 0138.
31. See John Nimmo's testimony in *Rex vs. Tim Buck et al.*, 71–5, and George Fish, 85–7.
32. George Fish, *Rex vs. Tim Buck et al.*, 87.
33. Andrew Parnaby and Gregory S. Kealey, "How the 'Reds' Got Their Man: The Communist Party Unmasks an RCMP Spy," *Labour/Le Travail*, 40 (Fall 1997), 253–67; Steve Hewitt, "Royal Canadian Mounted Spy: The Secret Life of John Leopold/Jack Esselwein," *Intelligence and National Security* 15, no. 1 (2000): 144–68.
34. Sommerville, *Rex vs. Tim Buck et al.*, 98.

35. A.E. Smith, *Rex vs. Tim Buck et al.*, 109.
36. Anthony Rasporich, "Tomo Čačić: Rebel without a Country," *Canadian Ethnic Studies* 10, no. 2 (1978): 86–93.
37. Macdonald, *Rex vs. Tim Buck et al.*, 116.
38. Ibid., 120.
39. Ibid.
40. John Leopold, *Rex vs. Tim Buck et al.*, 125.
41. Ibid., 130–1.
42. Wright, *Rex vs. Tim Buck et al.*, 161.
43. Sommerville, *Rex vs. Tim Buck et al.*, 168 [underline in original].
44. Leopold, *Rex vs. Tim Buck et al.*, 170.
45. Sommerville, *Rex vs. Tim Buck et al.*, 173.
46. *Rex vs. Tim Buck et al.*, 176.
47. *Rex vs. Tim Buck et al.*, 199D–199E.
48. Leopold, *Rex vs. Tim Buck et al.*, 242.
49. *Rex vs. Tim Buck et al.*, 246–8.
50. Paul Avrich, *Sacco and Vanzetti: The Anarchist Background* (Princeton: Princeton University Press, 1991).
51. Macdonald, *Rex vs. Tim Buck et al.*, 251.
52. Leopold, *Rex vs. Tim Buck et al.*, 251.
53. *Rex vs. Tim Buck et al.*, 253.
54. Wright, *Rex vs. Tim Buck et al.*, 257.
55. These were organizations that represented the different ethnic groups within the party.
56. The Communist International (CI) had its suspicions that the Canadians were modelling their case on the UK prosecution, although in the UK case, the CPGB leaders were charged as individuals; the party itself was not outlawed as a result of the convictions of the leaders, unlike in the Canadian trial. See "The Imprisonment of the Leaders of the CP of C and the Declaration of the Illegality of the Party," LAC, Communist International Fonds, fond 495, file 126. For more on the Zinoviev letter, see Gill Bennett, *Churchill's Man of Mystery* (New York: Routledge, 2007); Nigel West, *At Her Majesty's Secret Service: The Chiefs of Britain's Intelligence Agency, MI6* (London: Greenhill Books, 2006).
57. *Rex vs. Tim Buck et al.*, 356–61.
58. Ibid.
59. Ibid., 365–7.
60. The sale of Communist material could warrant a Section 98 charge after the Buck trial. See Saul Feigelman, "Jailed for Selling La Vie Ouvriere," *Worker*, 1 December 1934. The RCMP kept a close watch on the case; see "No. 711 Weekly Summary Report on Revolutionary Organizations and Agitators in Canada," in Gregory S. Kealey and Reg Whitaker, eds.,

R.C.M.P. Security Bulletins: The Depression Years Part 1, 1933–1934 (St John's: Canadian Committee on Labour History, 1993), 89; "Police Grab Whole French Paper Issue," *Worker*, 12 May 1934; "La Vie Ouvriere Starts Campaign," *Worker*, 30 June 1934; Canada, *Debates of the House of Commons First Session Eighteenth Parliament* (Ottawa: J.G. Patenaude, Printer to the King, 1936), 4231–3.

61. Papers examined include the *Toronto Daily Star*, the *Globe*, the *Ottawa Citizen*, the *Winnipeg Free Press*, the *Calgary Herald*, the *Vancouver Sun*, the *Montreal Gazette*, the *Worker*, and the *Halifax Chronicle*.

62. "Canadian Secession Alleged Studied by Moscow," *Globe*, 5 November 1931; "Reds Planned Armed Revolt," *Montreal Gazette*, 5 November 1931; "Mountie 9 Years as Red," *Vancouver Sun*, 4 November 1931; "'R.C.M.P. Detective Who Operated as Communist Seemed Reddest of Reds," 5 November 1931, *Winnipeg Free Press*; "Communists Planned Revolt Says Counsel," *Winnipeg Free Press*, 4 November 1931; "Militant Communist Group Organized Here, R.C.M.P. Officer Says," *Toronto Daily Star*, 5 November 1931; "Policeman Acted as Red Leader," *Calgary Daily Herald*, 4 November 1931.

63. "Foster Race Hostility Among Quebec Workers Moscow's Alleged 'Line,'" *Globe*, 6 November 1931; "Canadian Reds Look to Russia as Fatherland," *Montreal Gazette*, 10 November 1931; "Communism in Quebec," *Gazette*, 9 November 1931; "Red Activities Stand Exposed," *Calgary Daily Herald*, 9 November 1931.

64. "Communist Leaders Are Found Guilty," *Winnipeg Free Press*, 13 November 1931; "Russia Before Canada," *Vancouver Sun*, 11 November 1931.

65. Frederick Griffin, "Sgt. Leopold Real Mountie Served in Sub-Arctic Post," *Toronto Daily Star*, 6 November 1931.

66. Ibid.

67. Frederick Griffin, "Mountie Was Afraid He'd Talk in His Sleep to Agent of Soviet," *Toronto Daily Star*, 7 November 1931.

68. See "Declaration of the Worker Jury Regarding the Trial, the Conviction and Sentence of Eight Leaders of Working Class," *Worker*, 21 November 1931; towards the end of the article, the "workers' jury" calls for Section 98's repeal.

69. Macdonald, *Rex vs. Tim Buck et al.*, 377.

70. Wright, *Rex vs. Tim Buck et al.*, 377.

71. Ibid., 378.

72. Tim Buck, *Rex vs. Tim Buck et al.*, 402.

73. Macdonald, *Rex vs. Tim Buck et al.*, 425.

74. Wright, *Rex vs. Tim Buck et al.*, 426.

75. Buck, *Rex vs. Tim Buck et al.*, 427.

76. Ibid., 429.

77. Ibid., 440.
78. Ibid., 441.
79. *Rex vs. Tim Buck et al.*, 448–50.
80. Ibid.
81. Ibid., 452–3.
82. Ibid.
83. Macdonald, *Rex vs. Tim Buck et al.*, 453.
84. *Rex vs. Tim Buck et al.*, 472–3.
85. Ibid., 522.
86. Tom Ewen, *Rex vs. Tim Buck et al.*, 591.
87. Ibid., 598.
88. Ibid., 607.
89. *Rex vs. Tim Buck et al.*, 612.
90. Ibid., 735.
91. Ibid., 767.
92. Tim Buck, *An Indictment of Capitalism* (Toronto: Canadian Labor Defense League, 1932). Norman Penner notes how the prosecution and imprisonment of the accused led to Buck receiving far more attention and praise; see Penner, *Canadian Communism: The Stalin Years and Beyond* (Toronto: Methuen, 1988), 110, and "Canada May Set Precedent in Communism, Buck Says," *Toronto Daily Star*, 11 November 1931.There was truth in Buck's statement. For instance, although the leaders of the Communist Party of Great Britain were charged with seditious conspiracy in 1925 and later convicted, the charges were against the individuals, and the party itself was never classified as unlawful. According to F.R. Scott, after the Buck et al. trial and convictions, Canada joined Japan, Italy, Poland, and the more "reactionary Balkan states" in outlawing the Communist party. See F.R. Scott, "The Trial of the Toronto Communists," *Queen's Quarterly* 39 (1932): 512–27.
93. "Violence Said Alien to Eight Accused," *Toronto Daily Star*, 12 November 1931.
94. Sommerville, "Trial Importance of Trial Position of Jury," AO, RG4–32, file 3188/31, 28 L 0145.
95. Sommerville, Closing Address to the Jury, AO, RG4–32, file 3188/31, 28 L0147.
96. Ibid., 28 L 0158.
97. Ibid., 28 L 0174.
98. Ibid., 28 L 0175 [capitalization in original].
99. For more on gender and the state, see Yasmeen Abu-Laban, *Gendering the Nation-State: Canadian and Comparative Perspectives* (Vancouver: University of British Columbia, 2009).

100. Wright, *Rex vs. Tim Buck et al.*, 783–4.
101. Macdonald, *Rex vs. Tim Buck et al.*, 798.
102. Wright, *Rex vs. Tim Buck et al.*, 800–02.
103. For more on hegemony and the state in the Canadian context, see Ian McKay, "The Liberal Order Framework: A Prospectus for a Reconnaissance of Canadian History," *Canadian Historical Review* 81, no. 4 (December 2000): 617–45.
104. "Canada Sentences 8 Reds for Sedition; Prison Terms and Deportation Are Decreed – All Communist Property Will Be Seized. 4000 More Face Arrest Ontario Attorney General Sends Party Rolls to All the Other Provinces," *New York Times*, 13 November 1931.
105. "Seven Communists Get Five Year Terms: Communism Is Dealt Death-Blow by Sentences To-Day," *Toronto Daily Star*, 13 November 1931.
106. "In the Court of Appeal for Ontario," found in Sommerville to Sedgwick, 19 February 1932, AO, RG4–32, file 3188/31; "Appeal Court Hears Case of Workers' Leaders – Judgment Reserved," *Worker*, 16 January 1932.
107. *The King vs. Buck and Others: The Judgment of the Court of Appeal of Ontario Concerning the Communist Party in Canada*, ed. W.H. Price, LAC, RG13, vol. 2014, file 1484 1932, 2, 16; "'Communists' Fail in Their Appeal against Sentences," *Globe*, 20 February 1932.
108. Giorgio Agamben, *Remnants of Auschwitz: The Witness and the Archive*, trans. Daniel Heller-Roazen (Cambridge, MA: Zone Books, 2002), 18–20.

Chapter 4

1. See Barbara Roberts, *Whence They Came: Deportation from Canada 1900–1935* (Ottawa: University of Ottawa Press, 1988). Much of the historical literature on political deportation has focused on particular historical events and has dealt with government policy. See, for instance, Anthony Rasporich, "Tomo Čačić: Rebel without a Country," *Canadian Ethnic Studies* 10, no. 2 (1978): 86–93; Ann Pratt, *Securing Borders: Detention and Deportation in Canada* (Vancouver: University of British Columbia Press, 2005). New approaches to studying deportation have emerged from a number of different disciplines and have influenced historical studies. See Giorgio Agamben, *Homo Sacer: Sovereign Power and Bare Life*, trans. Daniel Heller-Roazen (Stanford: Stanford University Press, 1995) and *State of Exception*, trans. Kevin Attell (Chicago: University of Chicago Press, 2005); Nicholas De Genova, "The Deportation Regime: Sovereignty, Space and the Freedom of Movement," in *The Deportation Regime: Sovereignty, Space*

and the Freedom of Movement, ed. Nicholas De Genova and Nathalie Peutz (Durham: Duke University Press, 2010); Linda Bosniak, *The Citizen and the Alien: Dilemmas of Contemporary Membership* (Princeton, NJ: Princeton University Press, 2006); Sean Mills, "Quebec, Haiti, and the Deportation Crisis of 1974," *Canadian Historical Review* 94, no. 3 (September 2013): 405–35; Cynthia Wright, "The Museum of Illegal Immigration: Historical Perspectives on the Production of Non-Citizens and Challenges to Immigration Controls," in *Producing and Negotiating Non-Citizenship: Precarious Legal Status in Canada*, ed. Luin Goldring and Patricia Landolt (Toronto: University of Toronto Press, 2013); Dennis G. Molinaro, "'A Species of Treason?' Deportation and Nation-Building in the Case of Tomo Čačić 1931–1934," *Canadian Historical Review* 91, no. 1 (March 2010): 61–85; Yasmeen Abu-Laban and Nisha Nath, "From Deportation to Apology: The Case of Maher Arar and the Canadian State," *Canadian Ethnic Studies* 39, no. 3 (2007): 71–98. For more on *homo sacer* in a Canadian context, see Kevin Bruyneel, "Exiled, Executed, Exalted: Louis Riel, *Homo Sacer* and the Production of Canadian Sovereignty," *Canadian Journal of Political Science* 43, no. 3 (2010): 711–32; Christine Elie, "The City and the Reds: Leftism, the Civic Politics of Order, and a Contested Modernity in Montreal, 1929–1947" (PhD diss., Queen's University, 2015).

2. See Agamben, *Homo Sacer*. For more on transnational activists, see Donna R. Gabaccia and Franca Iacovetta, eds., *Women, Gender, and Transnational Lives: Italian Workers of the World* (Toronto: University of Toronto Press, 2002); Donna R. Gabaccia and Fraser M. Ottanelli, *Italian Workers of the World: Labor Migration and the Formation of Multiethnic States* (Champaign, IL: University of Illinois Press, 2001); Travis Tomchuk, *Transnational Activists: Italian Anarchist Networks in Southern Ontario and the Northeastern United States, 1915–1940* (PhD diss., Queen's University, 2010). The state's power to shape citizens has been discussed in a number of contexts. See Iacovetta, *Gatekeepers: Reshaping Immigrant Lives in Cold War Canada* (Toronto: Between the Lines, 2006); Mariana Valverde, *The Age of Light, Soap and Water: 19th Century Moral Reform in English Canada* (Toronto: University of Toronto Press, 1991); Enakshi Dua, "The Passage from Subjects to Aliens: Indian Migrants and the Racialization of Canadian Citizenship," *Sociologie et Sociétés* 31, no. 2 (Autumn 1999): 145–62; Himani Bannerji, *The Dark Side of the Nation: Essays on Multiculturalism, Nationalism and Gender* (Toronto: Canadian Scholars' Press, 2000).

3. See chapter 1, note 11.

4. Joseph Sedgwick to Col. Price Re: *Rex vs. Buck et al.*, 17 October 1931, Archives of Ontario (hereafter AO), RG4–32, file 3188/31, 30L0923–27.

For more on the trial of Buck et al., see Molinaro, "'A Species of Treason?'"; Lita-Rose Betcherman, *The Little Band: The Clashes between the Communists and the Political and Legal Establishment in Canada, 1928–1932* (Ottawa: Deneau Publishers, 1982); Reg Whitaker, Gregory S. Kealey, and Andrew Parnaby, *Secret Service: Political Policing in Canada from the Fenians to Fortress America* (Toronto: University of Toronto Press, 2010). On "dangerous foreigners," see Donald Avery, *"Dangerous Foreigners": European Immigrant Workers and Labour Radicalism in Canada, 1896–1932* (Toronto: McClelland & Stewart, 1979).

5.   "Kommunistijahtien laajentamiseen valmistaudutaan," *Vapaus*, 16 November 1931; "Komuniści Skazani Na Więzienie i Deportację," *Gazeta Katolicka w Kanadzie*, 18 November 1931.

6.   J.H. MacBrien to the Officer Commanding D Division, Winnipeg, 11 December 1931, Library and Archives Canada (hereafter LAC), Record of Canadian Security Intelligence Service (hereafter CSIS), RG146, vol. 3470, file 175/P3470.

7.   Roberts, *Whence They Came*, 134–8.

8.   "Sudbury Men's Arrest Part of Wide Round-Up Rumored at Ottawa," *Toronto Star*, 5 May 1932. See also Roberts's discussion of the Halifax Ten in *Whence They Came*, 140–8.

9.   "Secret Deportation Plan Crowds Halifax," *Toronto Star*, 7 May 1932.

10.   See J.H. MacBrien to the Officer Commanding D Division, Winnipeg, and Roberts, *Whence They Came*, 141–2.

11.   On 6 June 1919, Section 41 was amended during the Winnipeg General Strike to enable the deportation of British-born immigrants, a response to the labour revolt. The amendments were heavily influenced by American legislation but were later removed in 1928. Roberts, *Whence They Came*, 18–19; Reinhold Kramer and Tom Mitchell, *When the State Trembled: How A.J. Andrews and the Citizens' Committee Broke the Winnipeg General Strike* (Toronto: University of Toronto Press, 2010).

12.   Dennis G. Molinaro, "Section 98: The Trial of Rex v. Buck et al. and the 'State of Exception' in Canada, 1919–1936," in *Canadian State Trials*, vol. 4, ed. Barry Wright, Susan Binnie, and Eric Tucker; Kramer and Mitchell, *When the State Trembled*; Roberts, *Whence They Came*, 18–19, 29–36.

13.   Roberts, *Whence They Came*, 29–36.

14.   For instance, in the case of Tomo Čačić, a memorandum to the minister of justice outlines how his deportation could be challenged; see Frederick P. Varco, Memorandum for the Minister of Justice, 1 December 1933, LAC, RG13, vol. 2014, file 1484 1932. For more on Čačić's deportation, see Molinaro, "'A Species of Treason?'"; Rasporich, "Rebel without a Country."

15. "Local Lawyer Retained for Man Held Here," *Halifax Chronicle*, 29 December 1933, found in LAC, Record of CSIS, RG146, vol. 4670, file 96-A-00149.

16. Arvo Vaara, Board of Inquiry, 7 May 1932, LAC, RG76-I-A-1, vol. 376, file 513116, and Dan Chomicki, Board of Inquiry, 6 May 1932, LAC, RG76-I-A-1, vol. 376, file 513111. See also LAC, RG76-B-1-a, vol. 738, file 513057.

17. The challenge represented all but Stahlberg and Zurcher. It is unclear if the CLDL represented them in a separate challenge or was hoping to set a precedent by securing the release of the others. See "In the Supreme Court of Nova Scotia in Banco Re: Steven Worozcyt and Seven Others,"1932, LAC, RG76-B-1-a, vol. 738, file 513057.

18. *Supreme Court of Canada – A.Vaara et al. v. the King*, 4 August 1932, LAC, RG13, vol. 2465, 9-A-3008.

19. Ibid.

20. De Genova, "The Deportation Regime," 35.

21. Catherine Mills, "Politics: Biopolitics, Sovereignty and Nihilism," in *The Philosophy of Agamben* (Montreal: McGill-Queen's University Press, 2008), 75.

22. Agamben, *Homo Sacer*, 128.

23. For more on Finnish workers and sojourning, see Ian Radforth, *Bushworkers and Bosses* (Toronto: University of Toronto Press, 1987).

24. Vaara, Board of Inquiry, 7 May 1932.

25. Ivan Avakumovic, *The Communist Party in Canada: A History* (Toronto: McClelland & Stewart, 1975); Norman Penner, *Canadian Communism: The Stalin Years and Beyond* (Toronto: Methuen, 1988); Angus, *Canadian Bolsheviks: The Early Years of the Communist Party of Canada*, 2nd ed. (Victoria: Trafford, 2004), 272–3; Vaara, Board of Inquiry, 7 May 1932.

26. Betcherman, *The Little Band*, chapter 3.

27. Varpu Lindström, "The Finnish Canadian Communities during the Decade of the Depression," in *Karelian Exodus: Finnish Communities in North America and Soviet Karelia during the Depression Era*, ed. Ronald Harpelle, Varpu Lindström, and Alexis Pogorelskin (Toronto: Aspasia Books, 2004); Evgeny Efremkin, "'Karelian Project' or 'Karelian Fever'? Orders from Above, Reaction from Below: Conflicting Interests in Kremlin, Karelia and Canada," in *North American Finns in Soviet Karelia in the 1930s*, ed. Irina Takala and Ilya Solomeshch (Petrozavodsk: Petrozavodsk State University Press, 2008), 55–82.

28. Lindström, "The Finnish Canadian Communities."

29. Conrad Cesinger, Board of Inquiry, 6 May 1932, LAC, Record of CSIS, RG146, vol. 3470, file 175/P3470.

30. A. Grenke, "From Dreams of the Worker State to Fighting Hitler: The German Canadian Left from the Depression to the End of World War II," *Labour/Le Travail* 25 (Spring 1995), 65–105. For other examples of immigrant communities combining culture and politics, see Radforth, *Bushworkers and Bosses*; Ruth A. Frager, "Sewing Solidarity: The Eaton's Strike of 1912," and Carmela Patrias, "Relief Strike: Immigrant Workers and the Great Depression in Crowland, Ontario," in *A Nation of Immigrants: Women, Workers, and Communities in Canadian History, 1840s–1960s*, ed. Franca Iacovetta, Daula Draper, and Robert Ventresca (Toronto: University of Toronto Press, 1998); Jim Mochoruk, "'Pop & Co' versus Buck and the 'Lenin School Boys': Ukrainian Canadians and the Communist Party of Canada 1921–1931," in *Re-Imagining Ukrainian Canadians: History, Politics, and Identity*, ed. Rhonda L. Hinther and Jim Mochoruk (Toronto: University of Toronto Press, 2011), 331–75.

31. Cesinger, Board of Inquiry.

32. T. Dann, Inspector Manitoba District, Personal History File, 8 April 1927, Record of CSIS, RG146 vol. 4283, file 175/P 2783; Dan Chomicki, Board of Inquiry, 6 May 1932.

33. Holmes to Carr, 23 March 1931, LAC, RG76-I-A-1, vol. 376, file 513111 [underline in original].

34. For more on Polish immigrants and the CPC, see Patryk Polec, "From Hurrah Revolutionaries to Polish Patriots: The Rise of Polish Canadian Radicalism," *Polish American Studies* 68, no. 2 (Autumn 2011): 43–66.

35. R.H. Munroe to Joliffe Re: Ivan Sembaj, 14 May 1932, LAC, RG 76-B-1-a, vol. 738, file 513057.

36. See Justice Wright's closing remarks in *Supreme Court of Ontario – Rex vs. Tim Buck et al.*, LAC, vol. 738, RG76-B-1-a 71–5, file 513173, 800–02.

37. R.H. Munroe to Joliffe Re: Gottfried Zurcher, 14 May 1932, LAC, RG76-B-1-a, volume 738, file 513057; "Mrs. Zurcher to Be Deported," *Worker*, 21 May 1932.

38. Roberts, *Whence They Came*, 114–17. Similar deportations occurred in the United States, which Canada modelled. See Deirdre M. Moloney, "Women, Sexual Morality, and Economic Dependency in Early U.S. Deportation Policy," *Journal of Women's History* 18, no. 2 (Summer 2006): 95–122.

39. R.H. Munroe to Joliffe Re: Stefan Worozcyt, 14 May 1932, LAC, RG76-B-1-a, vol. 738, file 513057.

40. R.H. Munroe to Joliffe Re: Hans Kist, 14 May 1932, LAC, RG76-B-1-a, vol. 738, file 513057.

41. E.D. Wilkins to Col. Price, 19 August 1931, AO, RG4–32, file 3188/31, 30L0923–7.

42. R.H. Munroe to Joliffe Re: Martin Parker, 14 May 1932, LAC, RG76-B-1-a, vol. 738, file 513057.

43. "Secret Deportation Plan Crowds Halifax," *Toronto Star*, 7 May 1932.

44. J.A. McGibbon to Col. Price, 17 August 1931, AO, RG4–32, file 3188/31, 30L0923–7.

45. R.H. Munroe to Joliffe Re: John Farkas, 14 May 1932, LAC, RG76-B-1-a, vol. 738, file 513057.

46. R.H. Munroe to Joliffe Re: Toivo Stahlberg, 14 May 1932, LAC, RG76-B-1-a, vol. 738, file 513057.

47. Ibid.

48. Tomo Čačić quoted in S. Balen, "Razgovor sa Tomom Čačićem," *Jedinstvo*, 8 January 1957.

49. Ibid.

50. Franjo Ugrin, "Moja sjećanja," *Jedinstvo*, 18 November 1966, 2.

51. Tomo Čačić, "Pismo Tome Čačića," *Jedinstvo*, 13 January 1967.

52. Tomo Čačić quoted in S. Balen, "Razgovor sa Tomom Čačićem."

53. See, for instance, Robert Ventresca and Franca Iacovetta, "Virgilia D'Andrea: The Politics of Protest and the Poetry of Exile," in *Women, Gender, and Transnational Lives: Italian Workers of the World*, ed. Donna R. Gabaccia and Franca Iacovetta (Toronto: University of Toronto Press, 2002).

54. Ian Radforth argues that while a number of "Red Finns" immigrated to Canada and were active in the socialist movement, "a significant proportion" of "apolitical" immigrants became radicalized after their arrival in Canada. See Radforth, "Finnish Radicalism and Labour Activism in the Northern Ontario Woods," in *A Nation of Immigrants: Women, Workers, and Communities in Canadian History, 1840s–1960s*, ed. Franca Iacovetta, Daula Draper, and Robert Ventresca (Toronto: University of Toronto Press, 1998).

55. Rasporich, "Rebel without a Country."

56. Karl Marx, *Capital: A Critique of Political Economy*, vol. 1, 1867, trans. Ben Fowkes (New York: Penguin Books, 1976). See also De Genova, "The Deportation Regime," 56.

57. "Conrad Cesinger verhaftet," *Deutsche Arbeiterzeitung* (hereafter *DAZ*), 16 May 1932.

58. "Żądają Zwolnienia Więźniów W Halifax," *Glos Pracy*, 15 June 1932.

59. "Manifest," *Glos Pracy*, 1 June 1932.

60. "Nowa Fala Teroru W Polscl," *Budzik*, 2 December 1931; "Što Će Se Desiti Tomi Čačiću Ako Dozvolimo Da Ga Deportiraju," *Borba*, 13 December 1933 1.

61. "Workers' Leaders Spirited Away, Being Held for Immediate Deportation by Ottawa," *Worker*, 7 May 1932.

62. "Only Mass Protest Can Save Workers Held in Halifax from Deportations!" *Worker*, 21 May 1932.

63. "Eight Communist Leaders Have Spent Two Years in Kingston Hell Hole," *Worker*, 4 November 1933.

64. The *Worker* and the CLDL claimed that an inmate in Collins Bay who had alleged that Čačić was attempting to organize inmates to overthrow the prison (which resulted in him being sent to the hole and later his early probation being denied) was a former stockbroker who received early parole. See "No Hole in Kingston Says Bennett in Letter," *Worker*, 9 December 1933, 2; Richard Wright and Robin Endres, eds., *Eight Men Speak, and Other Plays from the Canadian Workers' Theatre* (Toronto: New Hogtown Press, 1976), 64.

65. "'Czarlike': Declare Liberals, Slam Deportation Method," *Toronto Star*, 7 May 1932.

66. Roberts, *Whence They Came*, 148–9.

67. "Held over Year for Deportation," *Toronto* Star, 12 July 1933.

68. "Report Deportee Beaten to Death," *Toronto Star*, 9 April 1936.

69. "Hans Kist von Nazis ermordet," *DAZ*, 1 December 1933.

70. Andrij Makuch, "Fighting for the Soul of the Ukrainian Progressive Movement in Canada: The Lobayites and the Ukrainian Labour-Farmer Temple Association," in *History, Politics, and Identity*, ed. Rhonda L. Hinther and Jim Mochoruk (Toronto: University of Toronto Press, 2011), 377–9.

71. Toivo J. Stahlberg, "Ainoastaan Työläisten Joukkotoiminta Voi Lopettaa Terrorion," *Vapaus*, 3 January 1933.

72. "Vaara ja Parker lähettäneet tervehdyksen työläisille," *Vapaus*, 5 January 1933.

73. "Päivän Pakina: Hieman asiallisuutta, olkaa hyvä," *Vapaus*, 10 May 1958.

74. Ibid.

75. "Conrad Cesinger in Deutschland," *Volksstimme*, August 1947.

76. Conrad Cesinger, "Das Leben im heutigen Deutschland," *Volksstimme*, December 1947.

77. Ibid.

78. "Dan Chomicky Receives Red Army Award," *Ukrainske Slovo*, 17 October 1945.

79. "Лист Від Дена Хоміцького," *Ukrainske Slovo*, 13 March 1946.

80. Marie Chomicki to Prime Minister Mackenzie King, 21 July 1947, LAC, RG76-I-A-1, vol. 376, file 513111.

81. L.H. Nicholson to C.E.S. Smith, LAC, Record of CSIS, RG146, vol. 4283 file, 175/P 2783.

82. "Return to Canada of Mary Ann Chomicki and Her Daughter Marie Antoinette," 15 January 1958, LAC, RG76-I-A-1, vol. 376, file 513111.

83. Leslie Morris, "Dan Holmes," *Canadian Tribune*, 19 August 1957.

84. Tomo Čačić, "Drug Tomo Čačić opisuje [illegible] veličanstvenog 'Metro' u Moskvi," *Borba*, 11 June 1935, 1; see also Rasporich, "Rebel without a Country," 91.

85. "'O' Division Translator's Report," 10 March 1942, LAC, Record of CSIS, RG146, vol. 4670, file 96-A-00149.

86. Michael Petrou, *Renegades: Canadians in the Spanish Civil War* (Vancouver: University of British Columbia Press, 2008), 35.

87. Tomo Čačić, "Moji Doživljaji Od Kako Sam Se Rastao S Drugovima U Kanadi," *Jedinstvo*, 22 October 1956, 1.

88. Ibid. Čačić would support decolonization movements eloquently in his later years.

89. Ibid.

90. Ibid.

91. Ibid.

92. Ibid.; Rasporich, "Rebel without a Country," 92.

93. *Jedinstvo* Report, 30 May 1961, LAC, Record of CSIS, RG146, vol. 4670, file 96-A-00149; *Slobodna Misao* Report, 28 March 1940, LAC, Record of CSIS, RG146, vol. 4670, file 96-A-00149.

94. "Tomo Čačić," *Jedinstvo*, 19 September 1969, 1.

95. Vaara, Board of Inquiry, 7 May 1932.

Chapter 5

1. Stephen L. Endicott, *Bienfait: The Saskatchewan Miners' Struggle of 1931* (Toronto: University of Toronto Press, reprinted 2002); Paul Axelrod, "Spying on the Young in the Depression and War: Students, Youth Groups and the RCMP, 1935–1942," *Labour/Le Travail* 35 (Spring 1995), 43–63; Gordon Hak, "Red Wages: Communists and the 1934 Vancouver Island Loggers Strike," *Pacific Northwest Quarterly* 80, no. 3 (July 1989): 82–90; Michael Lonardo, "Under a Watchful Eye: A Case Study of Police Surveillance during the 1930s," *Labour/Le Travail* 35 (Spring 1995): no. 11–41; Andrew Parnaby, *On the Hook: Welfare Capitalism on the Vancouver Waterfront, 1919–1939* (PhD diss., Memorial University, 2001); Bill Waiser, *All Hell Can't Stop Us: The On-to-Ottawa Trek and Regina Riot* (Calgary: Fifth House, 2003); Reg Whitaker, Gregory S. Kealey, and Andrew Parnaby, *Secret Service: Political Policing in Canada from the Fenians to Fortress America* (Toronto: University of Toronto Press, 2010), chapter 5; Andrée Lévesque, "Red Scares and Repression in Québec 1919–1939," in *Canadian State Trials*, vol. 4, ed. Barry Wright, Susan Binnie, and Eric Tucker (Toronto: University of Toronto Press, 2015).

2. City of Prince Albert Police Committee to Bennett, 4 March 1933, LAC, R.B. Bennett Papers (hereafter Bennett Papers), 93336.

3. Ukrainian Sporting Association to Bennett, 18 June 1933, LAC, Bennett Papers, 93430.
4. Ralph Webb to W.L. Gordon, 21 March 1934, LAC, Bennett Papers, 93792.
5. J.C. MacCorkindale to Wesley Gordon, 18 April 1932, LAC, Bennett Papers, 92972.
6. J.R. Smith to Bennett, 19 December 1932, LAC, Bennett Papers, 94850.
7. Bennett to Jean, 6 June 1935, LAC, Bennett Papers, 93967.
8. Bennett to Lockwood, 8 July 1935, LAC, Bennett Papers, 93972.
9. W.H. Price, "The Possibility of Peaceful Economic and Political Development with a Consideration in That Regard of Section 98 of the Criminal Code," 1933, Archives of Ontario (hereafter AO), RG4–2, file 4.27.
10. For more on relief and gender during the Depression, see Lara Campbell, *Respectable Citizens: Gender, Family and Unemployment in Ontario's Great Depression* (Toronto: University of Toronto Press, 2009); Nancy Christie, *Engendering the State: Family, Work and Welfare in Canada* (Toronto: University of Toronto Press, 2000).
11. W.H. Price, "Address by the Honourable Col. W.H. Price Attorney General of Ontario at the Annual Meeting of the Liberal-Conservative Association of Toronto," 9 November 1932, AO, RG4–2, file 4.6.
12. F. Murray Greenwood, "The Drafting and Passage of the War Measures Act in 1914 and 1927: Object Lessons in the Need for Vigilance," in *Law & Society: Issues in Legal History*, ed. W. Wesley Pue and Barry Wright (Ottawa: Carleton University Press, 1988), 305–6.
13. Unemployment and Farm Relief Act, S.C. 1931, ch. 58, 21–2.
14. Canada, *Debates of the House of Commons Fourth Session Seventeenth Parliament* (Ottawa: F.C. Acland, Printer to the King,1931), 4278, 4286.
15. For more on the Unemployment and Farm Relief Act of 1931 and its connection to fighting left-wing activism, see Waiser's discussion in *All Hell Can't Stop Us*, 16–17; Larry A. Glassford, *Reaction & Reform: The Politics of the Conservative Party under R.B. Bennett 192–1938* (Toronto: University of Toronto Press, 1992), 122; John Herd Thompson with Allen Seager, *Canada 1922–1939: Decades of Discord* (Toronto: McClelland & Stewart, 1985), 213–215.
16. Canada, *Debates of the House of Commons Fourth Session Seventeenth Parliament* (Ottawa: F.C. Acland, 1933), 256.
17. Ibid., 2188.
18. Ibid., 2102.
19. "Conviction of the Communists," *Canadian Bar Review* 9 (1931), 655–6.
20. Minutes of the Political Bureau, 24 October 1931, LAC, Communist International Fonds (hereafter CI Fonds), fond 495, file 126, reel K-281.
21. "Resolutions on the Tasks of the CP of C," 22 October 1932, LAC, CI Fonds, Fond 495 File 131 Reel K-283.

22. CP of Canada Reports, 16 July 1932, LAC, CI Fonds, fond 495, file 136, reel K-283.
23. Ibid.
24. "Methods of Illegal Work in the CP of C," 8 August 1932, LAC, CI Fonds, fond 495 file 136, reel K-283.
25. Sedgwick to Price, 28 February 1933, AO, RG4–32, file 4.13.
26. Ibid.
27. Ibid.
28. Bennett to H. Ferland, 22 November 1933, LAC, Bennett Papers, 96553.
29. Bennett to J.A. Miller, 23 November 1933, LAC, Bennett Papers, 96557.
30. N.E. Macfarlane, Extract from, or Precis of, Communication Dated 31 May 1932, LAC, Record of Canadian Security Intelligence Service (hereafter CSIS), RG146, vol. 4670, file 94-A-00006. Inspector Mead of the RCMP regarded Evans as an "extreme radical." See S.T. Wood to the Commissioner, 11 April 1932, LAC, Record of CSIS, RG146, vol. 4670, file 94-A-00006.
31. For more on the WUL organizing during this period, see Stephen L. Endicott, *Raising the Workers' Flag: The Workers' Unity League of Canada, 1930–1936* (Toronto: University of Toronto Press, 2012); Manley, "Starve, Be Damned!"; Manley, "Communism and the Canadian Working Class in the Great Depression: The Workers' Unity League, 1930–1936" (PhD diss., Dalhousie University, 1984).
32. "Workers' Unity League Meeting," 23 September 1932, LAC, Record of CSIS, RG146, vol. 4670, file 94-A-00006.
33. Campaign Bulletin, University Archives of University of British Columbia (hereafter UA of UBC), Arthur Evans Fonds, RBC-ARC-1181, series B, file 2–6; Ben Swankey and Jean Evans Sheils, *"Work and Wages!" A Semi-Documentary Account of the Life and Times of Arthur H. (Slim) Evans 1890–1944* (Vancouver: Granville Press, 1977), 39.
34. William John Thomson, *Rex v. Evans*, UA of UBC, Arthur Evans Fonds, RBC-ARC-1181, series B, file 2–7, 7–14.
35. Witness Statement of Mary Dorothy Hewitt, 20 December 1933, UA of UBC, Arthur Evans Fonds, RBC-ARC-1181, series B, file 2–6.
36. S.T. Wood to Inspector Cruickshank, 8 December 1932, and J.H. McMullin to S.T. Wood, 9 December 1932 in LAC, Record of CSIS, RG146, vol. 4670, file 94-A-00006. See also S.T. Wood to the Commissioner of the RCMP, 20 December 1932, LAC, Record of CSIS, RG146, vol. 4670, file 94-A-00006.
37. W.A. Macdonald, Charge to the Jury, 12 September 1933, UA of UBC, Arthur Evans Fonds, RBC-ARC-1181, series B, file 2–8, 8.
38. Swankey and Evans Sheils, *"Work and Wages!"* 48–57.
39. *Rex v. Evans*, 1–5.

40. Ibid., 7–14; supra note 35.
41. Ibid., 47.
42. Ibid., 18–19, 24.
43. Ibid., 68–70.
44. See, for instance, W.A. Macdonald's comments, *Rex v. Evans*, 166–7.
45. Gordon Grant, *Rex v. Evans*, 120.
46. See, for instance, *Rex v. Evans*, 134–41.
47. W.A. Macdonald, Charge to the Jury, 4–5.
48. Swankey and Evans Sheils, *"Work and Wages!"* 68–9.
49. Kyle Franz points out that Blairmore, Alberta, had elected in 1933 a Communist town council. How such a council could exist following the CPC trial was largely due to the efforts of individuals to deny their linkages to the formal CPC, which had been outlawed, and to avoid language that could bring them within reach of Section 98. See Franz, "Alberta's Red Democrats: The Challenge and Legacy of Blairmore Communism, 1921–1936 (PhD diss., Queen's University, 2013).
50. See, for instance, the arrest of twenty-nine marchers in a hunger march in Edmonton in 1933, the arrest of over eighty strikers in a lumber strike in Rouyn, Quebec, in 1933, or the fifty-one arrested in Port Arthur because of a lumber worker strike, also in 1933. See *Rex v. John Gager et al.*, 16 January 1933, Provincial Archives of Alberta, GR1983.0001, file 8645; CLDL Hunger March Defense Committee, "The Alberta Hunger-March and the Trial of the Victims of Brownlee's Police Terror," Provincial Archives of Alberta, PR1999.0626; "Socialists and Labor Party Continue Attack on Workers Section 98 May Be Charged," *Worker*, 14 January 1933; "Bail Increased to Keep CLDL Organizer in Jail," *Worker*, 23 December 1933; "Fifty-One in Port Arthur Jail," *Worker*, 23 December 1933.
51. The incident is described by H. Blair Neatby in *The Politics of Chaos: Canada in the Thirties* (Toronto: Macmillan of Canada, 1972), 64.
52. "Section 98 Invoked for Carrying a Button," *Worker*, 25 June 1932; "Escapes Section 98 Conviction," *Worker*, 2 July 1932.
53. "Section 98 Charge Collapses in Alta," *Worker*, 26 November 1932.
54. "Section 98 Appears in Port Arthur; All Property Seized Is Forfeited," *Worker*, 17 December 1932.
55. "Socialists and Labor Party Continue Attack on Workers."
56. Sedgwick to Bayly,13 June 1932, AO, RG4–32, file 1552.
57. "Arrest of Joe Derry Is Threat against Young Communist League," *Worker*, 29 April 1933; "Sec. 98 Attack on YCL Is an Attack on Working Class," *Worker*, 27 May 1933; "Section 98 Used in Attack on Young Communist League," *Worker*, 2 May 1933.

58. "Derry Audiences Show Hatred of Section 98," *Worker*, 2 September 1933.

59. "Section 98 Charge against Joe Derry Fails in Toronto," *Worker*, 19 December 1934.

60. Lévesque, "Red Scares and Repression in Québec, 1919–1939."

61. "Emergency Committee for the Protection of Civil Liberties," 12 February 1934, LAC, Francis Reginald Scott Fonds (hereafter F.R. Scott Fonds), vol. 9, file 8.

62. See Béatrice Richard, "Peril communiste au Temiscamingue: 1933–1934," in *Le droit de se taire: Histoire des communistes au Québec, de la Première Guerre mondiale à la Révolution tranquille*, ed. Robert Comeau and Bernard Dionne (Montreal: VLB Éditeur, 1989); Andrée Lévesque, *Red Travellers: Jeanne Corbin and Her Comrades* (Montreal: McGill-Queen's University Press, 2006).

63. J.E. Keith, "The Fascist Province," *Canadian Forum*, April 1934; Keith, "Quebec's Iron Heel," *Canadian Forum*, November 1936.

64. Supra note 60.

65. Canada, *Debates of the House of Commons First Session Eighteenth Parliament* (Ottawa: J.G. Patenaude, Printer to the King, 1936), 4231–33; "Le Roi vs. Saul Feigelman – Ann Feigelman, Cour du Banc Du Roi – Montreal," Bibliothèque et Archives nationals du Québec.

66. Canada, *House of Commons Debates*, 1936, 4232.

67. Saul Feigelman, "Jailed for Selling La Vie Ouvrière," *Worker*, 1 December 1934.

68. "No. 711 Weekly Summary Report on Revolutionary Organizations and Agitators in Canada," in Gregory S. Kealey and Reg Whitaker, eds., *R.C.M.P. Security Bulletins: The Depression Years Part 1, 1933–1934* (St John's: Canadian Committee on Labour History, 1993), 89.

69. "Police Grab Whole French Paper Issue," *Worker*, 12 May 1934; "La Vie Ouvriere Starts Campaign," *Worker*, 30 June 1934.

70. Lévesque, *Red Travellers*, 148.

71. Endicott, *Bienfait: The Saskatchewan Miners' Struggle of 1931*, 118–123.

72. Michiel Horn, *The Dirty Thirties: Canadians in the Great Depression* (Toronto: Copp Clark, 1971), 10.

73. See "The Iron Heel in Canada First Quarter 1934," *Canadian Labor Defender*, June 1934, 10; "The Iron Heel in Canada 1933," *Canadian Labor Defender*, May 1934, 10; "1931 - A Year of Sharpest Terror against Struggling Canadian Masses," *Canadian Labor Defender*, January 1932, 4; "Notes: 1932 and Now," *Canadian Labor Defender*, January/February 1933, 2.

74. Dominion Bureau of Statistics to F.R. Scott, 22 May 1933, LAC, F.R. Scott Fonds, vol. 10.

75. Judy Fudge and Eric Tucker, *Labour Before the Law: The Regulation of Workers' Collective Action in Canada, 1900–1948* (Toronto: Oxford University Press, 2001), 157.
76. "The Uses of Section 98," *Worker*, 29 July 1933.
77. Norman Keys, "Section 98 of the Criminal Code," *Fortnightly Law Journal* 3 (June 1933).
78. "Police Claim Officer Justified in Shooting," *Toronto Star*, 7 March 1933.
79. Ibid.
80. "Constable Exonerated in Fatal Shooting," *Toronto Star*, 8 March 1933.
81. "Zynchuck Case," notes found in LAC, F.R. Scott Fonds, vol. 30.
82. Supra note 77.
83. "Zynchuck Case."
84. "Police Armed with Tear Gas Guns at Zynchuck Inquest," *Montreal Gazette*, 9 March 1933.
85. Ibid.
86. Ibid.
87. Ibid.
88. Ibid.
89. "Investigation Is Sought in the Zynchuck Case," *Toronto Star*, 13 March 1933.
90. Ibid.; "Police Over-Awe Crowd at Funeral," *Toronto Star*, 13 March 1933; "As Verdun Jobless Marched to Funeral," *Montreal Daily Herald*, 11 March 1933; "Women Kicked by Policemen as 20,000 Dispersed," *Montreal Daily Herald*, 11 March 1933; "Communism Denied by Verdun Workers," *Montreal Daily Herald*, 13 March 1933; "Police Fists and Feet Kept Busy at Zynchuck Funeral," *Montreal Gazette*, 13 March 1933.
91. "A Blot on the Police Escutcheon," *Montreal Daily Herald*, 13 March 1933.
92. "Hot News, Officer Assaults Another," *Montreal Gazette*, 14 March 1933; "A Word for the Police," *Montreal Gazette*, 18 March 1933.
93. "Pastor Makes Protest," *Montreal Gazette*, 13 March 1933; "Citizens Discuss Recent Disorders," *Toronto Star*, 16 March 1933; "Cossack Conduct Blamed on Police," *Montreal Gazette*, 18 March 1933; "Minister Protests Police Brutality," *Montreal Daily Herald*, 13 March 1933.
94. "Pastor Makes Protest," "Citizens Discuss Recent Disorders," "Cossack Conduct Blamed on Police, "Minister Protests Police Brutality."
95. "No Trouble Anywhere, Declares Inspector in Charge of Police," *Toronto Star*, 13 March 1933.

96. "Preliminary Step in Zynchuck Probe," *Montreal Gazette*, 13 March 1933.

97. David Arnason, introduction to *Right Hand Left Hand: A True Life of the Thirties: Paris, Toronto, Montreal, the West and Vancouver. Love, Politics, the Depression and Feminism*, by Dorothy Livesay, ed. Arnason and Kim Todd (Erin, ON: Press Porcepic), 16; Ross Lambertson, *Repression and Resistance: Canadian Human Rights Activists, 1930–1960* (Toronto: University of Toronto Press, 2005), 33.

98. "Call Defense Witnesses in Zynchuck Inquiry," *Toronto Star*, 21 March 1933.

99. Ibid.; "Witnesses Claim Zappa Menaced," *Toronto Star*, 23 March 1933.

100. "Court Refuses to Issue Warrant for Officer's Arrest," *Montreal Gazette*, 24 March 1933; "Premier Refuses Zappa Case Probe," *Toronto Star*, 23 March 1933. For more on the incident, see Christine Elie, "The City and the Reds: Leftism, the Civic Politics of Order, and a Contested Modernity in Montreal, 1929–1947" (PhD diss., Queen's University, 2015).

101. Michel Foucault, *Discipline and Punish: The Birth of the Prison*, trans. Alan Sheridan (New York: Vintage Books, 1995), 304. See also Foucault, "About the Concept of the 'Dangerous Individual' in Nineteenth Century Legal Psychiatry," in *Power: Essential Works of Foucault 1954-1984*, vol. 3, ed. James Faubion (New York: New Press/Penguin, 2000).

102. Walter Benjamin, "Critique of Violence," in *Reflections* (New York: Shocken Books, 1978), 277–300.

103. Giorgio Agamben, "Sovereign Police," in *Means without End* (Minneapolis: Minnesota University Press, 2000), 103–4.

104. Arendt argues that violence is "instrumental" and that while violence can "destroy power," power can never "grow out of it." See Hannah Arendt, *On Violence* (New York: Harcourt Brace and World Publishers, 1970), 52–3.

105. For instance, Agamben posits that the basis for the state of exception is the Latin phrase *Necessitas legem non habet* or "Necessity has no law." See Agamben, "Sovereign Police," 103–4.

106. In a similar argument, Arendt argues that state violence occurs when a loss of power is perceived by authorities. See *On Violence*.

107. Agamben argues that only sovereign power has the ability to kill or sanction killing and not be guilty of homicide. See *Homo Sacer: Sovereign Power and Bare Life*, trans. Daniel Heller-Roazen (Stanford: Stanford University Press, 1995), part 2.

Chapter 6

1. See Dominique Clement, *Canada's Rights Revolution: Social Movements and Social Change, 1937–82* (Vancouver: University of British Columbia Press, 2008), 38. Ross Lambertson regards the CLDL as "at best" a "proto-civil liberties organization" because it sought the protection of only workers' rights when the state was repressing them and was usually "narrowly focused" on "defending the rights of 'foreigners.'" See Lambertson, *Repression and Resistance: Canadian Human Rights Activists, 1930–1960* (Toronto: University of Toronto Press, 2005), 24–5.

2. For examples of this type of literature, see Andrew Thorpe, "Comintern 'Control' of the Communist Party of Great Britain, 1920–43," *English Historical Review* 113 (June 1998): 637–62; James R. Barrett, "The History of American Communism and Our Understanding of Stalinism," *American Communist History* 2, no. 2 (2003): 175–82. In the Canadian context, see Ian McKay, "Joe Salsberg, Depression-Era Communism, and the Limits of Moscow's Rule," *Canadian Jewish Studies* 21 (2013 [2014]):130–142,

3. J. Petryshyn, "Class Conflict and Civil Liberties: The Origins and Activities of the Canadian Labour Defence League, 1925–1940," *Labour/Le Travail* 10 (Autumn 1982): 40–2.

4. Ibid.

5. Ibid.; Canadian Labor Defense League (hereafter CLDL), *Constitution* (Toronto: CLDL, 1927).

6. Petryshyn, "Class Conflict and Civil Liberties"; CLDL, *Constitution*.

7. Central Organization Department Report, 30 June 1931, Library and Archives Canada (hereafter LAC), Communist International Fonds (hereafter CI Fonds), fond 495, file 122, reel K-281.

8. Andrée Lévesque, *Red Travellers: Jeanne Corbin and Her Comrades* (Montreal: McGill-Queen's University Press, 2006), 146.

9. Central Organization Department Report, 14 July 1931, LAC, CI Fonds, fond 495, file 122, reel K-281.

10. "Mobilize for the Repeal of Section 98," *Worker*, 21 November 1931 [capitalization in original].

11. CLDL, "Report: First National Convention," 17 July 1933, Thomas Fisher Rare Book Library (hereafter TFL), Robert S. Kenny Collection, MS179 (hereafter Kenny MS179), box 39, file 11.

12. A.E. Smith to R.B. Bennett, 21 February 1933, LAC, CI Fonds, fond 495, file 154, reel K-286.

13. Hugh Guthrie, 14 February 1933, Canada, *Debates of the House of Commons Fourth Session Seventeenth Parliament* (Ottawa: F.C. Acland, Printer to the King, 1933), 2100–2.

14. Report on the CLDL, 1932 October, LAC, CI Fonds, fond 495, file 146, reel K-285.
15. CLDL, "Report: First National Convention," 17 July 1933.
16. "Workers of the Border Cities!" October 1933, TFL, Kenny MS179, box 39, file 18.
17. Ibid.
18. A.E. Smith to All Workers and Farmers Organizations and All Trade Unions, 29 September 1933, TFL, Kenny MS179, box 39, file 18.
19. CLDL, "Joe Derry Committed for Trial," 2 May 1933, TFL, Kenny MS179, box 39, file 18.
20. CLDL, "Repeal Conference Call," December 1932, TFL, Kenny MS179, box 39, file 18.
21. CLDL, Resolution Re: Section 98 of the Criminal Code of Canada, n.d., Kenny MS179, box 39, file 18.
22. Smith to Woodsworth, 22 April 1931, James Shaver Woodsworth Papers (hereafter Woodsworth Papers), LAC, MG27 III C7, vol. 5, file 9.
23. Woodsworth to Smith, 23 April 1931, Woodsworth Papers, LAC, MG27 III C7, vol. 5, file 9.
24. See the Research Committee of the League for Social Reconstruction, *Social Planning for Canada* (Toronto: Thomas Nelson & Sons, 1935); Michiel Horn, "Frank Underhill's Early Drafts of the Regina Manifesto 1933," *Canadian Historical Review* 54, no. 4 (December: 1973): 393–418; Horn, *The League for Social Reconstruction: Intellectual Origins of the Democratic Left in Canada 1930–1942* (Toronto: University of Toronto Press, 1980); S.M. Lipset, *Agrarian Socialism: The Cooperative Commonwealth Federation in Saskatchewan* (Berkeley: University of California Press, 1959); Walter Young, *The Anatomy of a Party* (Toronto: University of Toronto Press, 1969); Alan Whitehorn, *Canadian Socialism: Essays on the CCF-NDP* (Toronto: Oxford University Press, 1992); J. William Brennan, ed., *Building the Co-operative Commonwealth: Essays on the Democratic Socialist Tradition in Canada* (Regina: University of Regina Press, 1985); Sean Mills, "When Democratic Socialists Discovered Democracy: The League for Social Reconstruction Confronts the 'Quebec Problem,'" *Canadian Historical Review* 86, no. 1 (March 2005): 53–81.
25. Buhay to Woodsworth, 19 May 1933, LAC, Woodsworth Papers MG27 III C7, vol. 5, file 9.
26. Smith makes this claim in his autobiography. See A.E. Smith, *All My Life: An Autobiography* (Toronto: Progress Books, 1977), 145.
27. Ibid., 165.
28. Ibid., 168.
29. Young, *Anatomy of a Party*, chapter 9. Whitehorn argues that Woodsworth's disciplining of CCF members for cooperating with Communists

reveals how the CCF was always structured as a party and not as a "protest movement becalmed," as Young argues. See Whitehorn, *Canadian Socialism*. Other examples of cooperation between the CCF and Communists occurred in the Canadian Youth Congress (CYC) initiative led by the CPC. As James Naylor observes, the CYC was more effective than the former CPC group, the League against War and Fascism, in attracting CCF youth in the Co-operative Commonwealth Youth Movement. See Naylor, "Socialism for a New Generation: CCF Youth in the Popular Front Era," *Canadian Historical Review* 94, no. 1 (March 2013): 69–70.

30. For more on the popular front in Canada, see John Manley, "Communists Love Canada! The Communist Party of Canada, the People and the Popular Front, 1933–1939," *Journal of Canadian Studies* 36, no. 4 (Winter 2002): 59–86; Manley, "Red or Yellow? Canadian Communists and the 'Long' Third Period, 1927–36," in *In Search of Revolution: International Communist Parties in the Third Period*, ed. Matthew Worley (London: I.B. Tauris, 2004), 220–46.

31. Resolution on the Tasks of the CP of C, 22 October 1932, LAC, CI Fonds, fond 495, file 131, reel K-283.

32. Norman to S, 7 April 1934, LAC, CI Fonds, fond 495, file 162, reel K-287.

33. CP of Canada Reports, 16 July 1932, LAC, CI Fonds, fond 495, file 136, reel K-283.

34. Resolution on Present Situation and CLDL Tasks, 16 November 1934, LAC, CI Fonds, fond 495, file 166, reel K-288.

35. CLDL, Constitution of the CLDL, 1932, found in LAC, Francis Reginald Scott Fonds (hereafter F.R. Scott Fonds), MG30 211, vol. 9, file 8.

36. See, for instance, Mark Leier, *Where the Fraser River Flows: The Industrial Workers of the World in British Columbia* (Vancouver: New Star Books, 1990); Ruth A. Frager and Carmela Patrias, "Human Rights Activists and the Question of Sex Discrimination in Postwar Ontario," *Canadian Historical Review* 93, no. 4 (2012): 583–610; Patrias, *Jobs and Justice: Fighting Discrimination in Wartime Canada, 1939–1945* (Toronto: University of Toronto Press, 2012).

37. CP of Canada Reports, 16 July 1932, LAC, CI Fonds, fond 495, file 136, reel K-283.

38. Sandra Djwa, *The Politics of the Imagination: A Life of F.R. Scott*, (Toronto: McClelland & Stewart, 1987), chapters 1 and 17.

39. Andrée Lévesque, "Red Scares and Repression in Québec 1919–1939," in *Canadian State Trials*, vol. 4, ed. Barry Wright, Susan Binnie, and Eric Tucker (Toronto: University of Toronto Press, 2015).

40. See, for instance, Horn, "Frank Underhill's Early Drafts of the Regina Manifesto."

41. Eric M. Adams, "Canada's 'Newer Constitutional Law' and the Idea of Constitutional Rights," *McGill Law Journal* 51, no. 435 (2006): 439.

42. J.S. Woodsworth, 19 June 1936, Canada, *Debates of the House of Commons First Session Eighteenth Parliament* (Ottawa: J. O. Patenaude, Printer to the King, 1936), 4233.

43. F.R. Scott, "The Trial of the Toronto Communists," *Queen's Quarterly* 39 (1932): 512.

44. Ibid., 514.

45. Ibid., 520, 524–5.

46. F.R. Scott, *Essays on the Constitution: Aspects of Canadian Law and Politics* (Toronto: University of Toronto Press, 1977), 69.

47. Young, *Anatomy of a Party*, 137.

48. F.R. Scott, "Communists, Senators, and All That," *Worker*, 10 August 1935.

49. Scott to King, 8 March 1936, LAC, F.R. Scott Fonds, MG30 211, vol. 9, file 9. For more on the conflicts and cooperation between Communists and more moderate progressives, see Lambertson, *Repression and Resistance*, chapter 1.

50. Lambertson, *Repression and Resistance*, 24–35.

51. Ibid., 31; see also Scott to Timbres, 29 May 1933, LAC, F.R. Scott Fonds, MG30 211, vol. 9, file 8.

52. Lambertson, *Repression and Resistance*, 34–5.

53. Frank Underhill, *Regina Manifesto*, found in LAC, F.R. Scott Fonds, MG30 211, vol. 12, file 8.

54. Larry A. Glassford, "Retrenchment – R.B. Bennett Style: The Conservative Record before the New Deal, 1930–34," *American Review of Canadian Studies* 19, no. 2 (1989): 141–57.

55. In correspondence with like-minded citizens, Bennett reassured them that unemployed trekkers would not get more relief, just an opportunity "to do some work if they really wanted." He believed "communists" were at the root of troubles in the relief camps and that they had "excellent shelter" and "better food than families in Canada." See Bennett to Webber, 4 June 1935, and Bennett to J.T. Simpson, 16 July 1935, in R.B. Bennett Papers (hereafter Bennett Papers), LAC, MG26-K, 496515 and 496984. See also H. Blair Neatby, *The Politics of Chaos: Canada in the Thirties* (Toronto: Macmillan of Canada, 1972); Bill Waiser, *All Hell Can't Stop Us: The On-to-Ottawa Trek and Regina Riot* (Calgary: Fifth House, 2003), chapter 1; James Struthers, *No Fault of Their Own: Unemployment and the Canadian Welfare State 1914–1941* (Toronto: University of Toronto Press, 1983), chapter 2. For more on the RCMP perspective of Communists and the unemployed, see Reg Whitaker, Gregory S. Kealey, and Andrew Parnaby, *Secret Service: Political Policing in Canada from*

the Fenians to Fortress America (Toronto: University of Toronto Press, 2010), 131–6.

56. For more on the creation of the camps, see Waiser, *All Hell Can't Stop Us*, 24; Struthers, *No Fault of Their Own*, 75–81.

57. Waiser, *All Hell Can't Stop Us*, 35–7.

58. Ibid.

59. Ibid.

60. Ibid., chapter 4. See also Ronald Liversedge, *Recollections of the On-to Ottawa Trek* (Montreal: McGill-Queen's University Press, 1973); Michiel Horn, *The Dirty Thirties: Canadians in the Great Depression* (Toronto: Copp Clark, 1971); Victor Howard, *We Were the Salt of the Earth: The On-to-Ottawa Trek and Regina Riot* (Regina: Canadian Plains Research Center, 1985), 88, 96.

61. McGeer to Bennett, 21 May 1935, Bennett Papers, LAC, MG26-K, 496509–11.

62. Waiser, *All Hell Can't Stop Us*, 69.

63. Ibid., 75, 95, 134–5. See also Whitaker, Kealey, and Parnaby, *Secret Service*, 131–8. For Arthur Evans's account of the meeting, see Swankey and Evans Sheils, *"Work and Wages!"* 144–6.

64. Waiser, *All Hell Can't Stop Us*, 142.

65. Ibid., 154.

66. Ibid., 171–84, 200, 203, 212.

67. Ibid., 59.

68. See, for instance, "8th Enlarged Plenum of CCCP," June 1935, LAC, CI Fonds, fond 495, file 177.

69. *The King vs. A. Evans, G. Black, et al.*, 1935, Saskatchewan Archives, R-304.1, file 15b.

70. See, for instance, testimony from Ibid., 147–50.

71. Ibid., 209–12.

72. Ibid., 356–7.

73. Ibid., 387–90.

74. Ibid., 657.

75. Ibid., 658.

76. Ibid., 658–60.

77. Ibid., 66.

78. Steve Hewitt, "Royal Canadian Mounted Spy: The Secret Life of John Leopold/Jack Esselwein," *Intelligence and National Security* 15, no. 1 (2000), 154–5.

79. *The King v. A. Evans, G. Black, et al.*, 690–2.

80. Ibid., 710–11, 719.

81. Ibid., 711–26.

82. Waiser, *All Hell Can't Stop Us*, 232.

83. Ibid., 245–6.
84. Ibid., 253–5.
85. Neatby, *The Politics of Chaos*, 75–83.
86. "Excerpt from Mr. King's Second Radio Broadcast," 2 August 1935, William Lyon Mackenzie King Papers (hereafter King Papers), LAC, MG26-J4, vol. 156, C112114 [capitalization in original].
87. Edwards to Lapointe, 17 January 1936, and Edwards to Lapointe, 16 March 1936, in LAC, RG13, vol. 2809, file 136061.
88. Subsection 8 stipulated that anyone who ". . . prints, publishes, edits, issues, circulates, sells, or offers for sale or distribution any book, newspaper, periodical, pamphlet, picture, paper, circular, card, letter, writing, print, publication or document of any kind, in which is taught, advocated, advised or defended, or who shall in any manner teach, advocate or advise or defend the use, without authority of law, force, violence, terrorism, or physical injury to person or property, or threats of such injury, as a means of accomplishing any governmental, industrial or economic change . . . shall be guilty of an offense . . ." See Criminal Code of Canada, R.S.C. 1927, s. 98(8).
89. Edwards to King, 11 June 1936, King Papers, LAC, MG26-J4, vol. 156, C112108; Edwards to Lapointe, 16 March 1936, LAC, RG13, vol. 2809, file 136061.
90. Edwards to King, 11 June 1936; Memorandum Re: Repeal of Section 98 and Amendment of Section 133 of the Criminal Code, LAC, RG13, vol. 2809, file 136061; Edwards to King, 12 June 1936, King Papers, LAC, MG26-J4, vol. 156, C112119–21.
91. Memorandum Re: Repeal of Section 98.
92. Ernest Lapointe, *House of Commons Debates*, 1936, 4225–7.
93. Ibid., 4228.
94. Ibid., 4230.
95. J.S. Woodsworth, *House of Commons Debates*, 1936, 4230, 4232–5.
96. C.H. Cahan, *House of Commons Debates*, 1936, 4237.
97. Herbert Wilton, *House of Commons Debates*, 1936, 4243–4.
98. R.B. Bennett, *House of Commons Debates*, 1936, 4245–51.
99. Arthur Meighen, Canada, *Debates of the Senate* (Ottawa: J.O. Patenaude, 1936), 619–21.
100. John Haig, *Senate Debates*, 1936, 621–2.
101. George Gordon, *Senate Debates*, 1936, 622.
102. "Section 98 Is Gone," *Toronto Saturday Night*, 27 June 1936.
103. Meighen, *Senate Debates*, 1936, 622.
104. Grant Dexter, "Liquidation of Winnipeg Strike," *Winnipeg Free Press*, 7 July 1936.
105. "Section 98 and After," *Montreal Gazette*, 14 July 1936; "Croll, Roebuck, Section 98 and Communists," *Mail and Empire*, 9 July 1936.

106. "Reds to Celebrate Section 98 Repeal," *Montreal Gazette*, 3 July 1936; "Buck Asks Erasure of Conviction," *Globe*, 3 July 1936.
107. "The Late Section 98," *Toronto Star*, 14 July 1936.
108. "Section 98 Done at Last," 25 June 1936, *Toronto Evening Telegram*.
109. "Rikoslain 98 pykälän peruuttaminen voitettiin joukkotoiminnan kautta," *Vapaus*, 24 June 1936; "Drakońska Sekcja 98 Ma Być Skreślona," *Glos Pracy*, 13 June 1936; "Das Parlament verhandelt ueber die Abschaffung Sektion 98," 17 June 1936, *Deutsche Arbeiterzeitung*.
110. A.E. Smith, "Notes on Civil Liberties," TFL, Kenny MS179, box 38, file 12, 17 [capitalization in original].
111. See Criminal Code of Canada, R.S.C. 1985, ch. C-46, s. 59(4a), 59(4b).

Conclusion

1. Hugh Guthrie to Bennett, 17 May 1935, R.B. Bennett Papers, LAC, reel M-989, 94340.
2. See F.R. Scott, "The Padlock Act and the Criminal Code" and "Canadian Civil Liberties Union to Governor-General," 27 January 1938, found in LAC, Francis Reginald Scott Fonds, vol. 10, file 10.
3. G.A. Coughlin, "The Quebec 'Padlock Law,'" *L'Oeuvre des tracts* 234 (December 1938): 1–10.
4. An officer who did not commit the act of disaffection would have to prove they had no knowledge of the actions of the guilty member. Regulation 62's amendment also gave the government the power to consider an organization unlawful if an officer was found guilty of disaffection. All of the members would then be considered guilty of an offence. See R.S. Lambert, *This Freedom: A Guide to Good Citizenship in a Time of War* (Toronto: Canadian Association for Adult Education, 1940), addendum to page 9.
5. See Canada, Public Order Regulations 1970, SOR/70-444, s. 3, 4.
6. See Criminal Code of Canada, R.S.C. 1985, ch. C-46, s. 59(4a), 59(4b). For the Anti-Terrorism Act, 2015, see Anti-Terrorism Act, R.S.C. 2015.
7. For instance, Justice Minister Anne McLellan, in arguing against a "sunset clause" in Bill C-36, the "anti-terrorism bill," stated that "we cannot expect terrorism to disappear in a few years" and that legislation should be in place for an "extended" period. See Anne McLellan, "Letters to the Editor: Anti-Terrorism Act," *Globe and Mail*, 25 October 2001.
8. Jesse McLean, Robert Benzie, and Tanya Talaga, "'No Extra Powers' Granted to Police during G20 Summit: Liberals," *Toronto Star*, 30 June 2010; Jill Mahoney and Ann Hui, "G20-Related Mass Arrests Unique in Canadian History," 28 June 2010, *Globe and Mail*; Sidhartha Banerjee,

"Mass Quebec Protest Arrests Set to Overwhelm Province's Justice System," *National Post*, 25 May 2012.

9. See, for instance, Greg Weston, Glenn Greenwald, and Ryan Gallagher, "CSEC Used Airport Wi-Fi to Track Canadian Travellers: Edward Snowden Documents," *CBC News*, 30 January 2014.

10. Mark Mazzetti, "Panel Faults C.I.A. over Brutality and Deceit in Terrorism Interrogations," *New York Times*, 9 December 2014; Nazim Baksh and Terrance McKenna, "Documents Show CSIS and RCMP's Role in Post-9/11Torture of Three Canadians in Syria," *CBC News*, 19 September 2016, http://www.cbc.ca/news/canada/terrorism-torture-syria-canadians-1.3669425.

11. For instance, Agamben argues that "the state or the sovereign retains this potential to suspend the rule of law even when not doing so, just as we might say that in the stabilized form of constituted power the state retains the potentiality for exercising its full power to suspend the rule of law." See Leland de la Durantaye, *Giorgio Agamben* (Stanford: Stanford University Press, 2009), 232.

12. See, for instance, Robert Wright's analysis of Canadian media following the attacks in which he argues that the inability of individuals to analyse the event without being portrayed as anti-American reinforced the "view that September 11th existed outside of history." It is a view that has achieved "hegemonic" status. See Wright, *Virtual Sovereignty: Nationalism, Culture and the Canadian Question* (Toronto: Canadian Scholars' Press, 2004), 253. Such views were also often expressed by American policy-makers responsible for the creation of new security measures and laws, such as former secretary of state Condoleezza Rice, who in 2009 defended George W. Bush's government's support for exceptional security measures and interrogations, stating, "Anything that was legal and was going to make this country safe the president wanted to do . . . unless you were there, in a position of responsibility after September 11th, you cannot possibly imagine the dilemmas that you faced in trying to protect Americans." See Glen Kessler, "Rice Defends Enhanced Interrogations," *Washington Post*, 30 April 2009.

13. The law provides for the deportation of undocumented residents of Haitian descent regardless of whether they were born in the Dominican Republic. It is also retroactive to 1929. See Lorgia García-Peña, "Suddenly, Illegal at Home," *New York Times*, 12 December 2013. Bill C-43 makes it easier for the Canadian government to deport permanent residents if convicted of a criminal offence, including minor offences. Any permanent resident, no matter the length of time spent in Canada, with a past criminal conviction can be eligible for deportation. The Canadian Bar Association has urged the government to abandon the bill or significantly revise it. See

Nicholas Keung, "Thousands Could Face Deportation for Minor Crimes under Tory Bill: Permanent Residents Could Lose Status, Immigration Lawyers Say," *Toronto Star*, 4 October 2012; "CBA Says Most Changes to Bill C-43 Are 'Unjustified,'" *Targeted News Service* (Washington, DC), 8 November 2012. On 19 June 2014, Bill C-24, or the Strengthening Canadian Citizenship Act, achieved royal assent. The new law gives the government the power to strip citizenship from dual nationals or people born in Canada but eligible to acquire dual citizenship. For commentary on the law, see "Bill C-24 Is Wrong: There Is Only One Kind of Canadian Citizen," *Globe and Mail*, 30 June 2014. The Trudeau government has retained a number of the Conservative changes to the Citizenship Act, such as having government bureaucrats rather than judges decide citizenship applications. See Evan Dyer, "Trudeau Government Revoking Citizenship at Much Higher Rate than Conservatives," 9 October 2016, *CBC News*, http://www.cbc.ca/news/politics/citizenship-revocation -trudeau-harper-1.3795733. Countries such as France and Britain have also increased their ability to revoke citizenship. See Steven Meurrens, "Analyzing the Liberal Changes to Canada's Citizenship Act," *Policy Options*, 29 February 2016, http://policyoptions.irpp.org/2016/02/29/ analyzing-the-liberal-changes-to-canadas-citizenship-act/.

14. Angelique Chrisafis, "France Seeks to Extend State of Emergency Until End of July," *Guardian*, 20 April 2016, https://www.theguardian.com/ world/2016/apr/20/france-seeks-to-extend-state-of-emergency-until-end-of-july; Massimo Calabresi, "The War on Terror Is Over – Long Live the War on Terror," *Time*, 16 June 2014, http://time.com/2873297/ boko-haram-iraq-bergdahl-war-terror/; Ross Douthat, "Thoughts on the Boston Lockdown," *New York Times*, 22 April 2013, http://douthat.blogs .nytimes.com/2013/04/22/thoughts-on-the-boston-lockdown/; Glenn Greenwald, "Chilling Legal Memo from Obama DOJ Justifies Assassination of U.S. Citizens," *Guardian*, 5 February 2013, https://www.theguardian. com/commentisfree/2013/feb/05/obama-kill-list-doj-memo.

15. See Agamben, *State of Exception*, trans. Kevin Attell (Chicago: University of Chicago Press, 2005) and *Homo Sacer: Sovereign Power and Bare Life*, trans. Daniel Heller-Roazen (Stanford: Stanford University Press, 1995).

16. Walter Benjamin, "Theses on the Philosophy of History," in *Walter Benjamin: Illuminations*, 2nd ed., ed. Hannah Arendt (London: Fontana Press, 1992), 248–9.

17. de la Durantaye, *Giorgio Agamben*, 341–5, 359, 387–9.

Bibliography

Archival and Manuscript Collections

Archives of Ontario

RG 4–2: Office of the Attorney General Correspondence and Subject Files
RG 4–32: Attorney General Central Registry Criminal and Civil Files

Bibliothèque et Archives nationals du Québec

TP9: Archives judiciaries, Fonds Cour du banc du roi/de la reine

Library and Archives Canada

Government Archives Division
RG6: Department of the Secretary of State of Canada
RG13: Department of Justice
RG26: Department of Citizenship and Immigration
RG27: Department of Labour
RG73: Department of the Solicitor General
RG76: Department of Immigration
RG85: Northern Affairs Program
RG146: Canadian Security Intelligence Service
Manuscript Division
MG10-K3: Communist International Fonds
MG26-H: Robert Borden Papers
MG26-K: Richard Bedford Bennett Papers
MG28-IV4: Communist Party of Canada Fonds
MG30-D211: Francis Reginald Scott Fonds
MG32-G3: Tim Buck Collection
MG30-A94: Jacob Lawrence Cohen Fonds

MG27 III C7: James Shaver Woodsworth Papers
MG26-J4: William Lyon Mackenzie King Papers

Provincial Archives of Alberta

GR1983.0001: Edmonton Judicial District, Supreme Court Criminal Case Files
PR1999.0626: Canadian Labour Defence League Fonds

Saskatchewan Archives

GR11-Collection R-304.1: Department of the Attorney General, Regina
Judicial Centre Court Records

Thomas Fisher Rare Book Library

MS179: Robert S. Kenny Collection

University Archives of the University of British Columbia

RBC-ARC-1181: Arthur H. Evans Fonds

Newspapers

Borba (Croatian; Toronto, 12 Oct. 1932–19 Sept. 1936)
Jedinstvo (Croatian; Toronto, 1955–1969)
Slobodna Misao (Croatian; Toronto, 1936–1940)
Vapaus (Finnish; Sudbury, 1931–1958)
Deutsche Arbeiterzeitung (German; Winnipeg, 1931–6)
Volksstimme (German; Toronto, 1946–7)
Budzik (Polish; Toronto, 1931–2)
Gazeta Katolicka w Kanadzie (Polish; Winnipeg, 1931–6)
Glos Pracy (Polish; Toronto, 1932–6)
Ukrainske Slovo (Ukrainian; 1945–6)
Calgary Herald (Calgary, 1919–1936)
Halifax Chronicle (Halifax, 1919–1936)
Montreal Gazette (Montreal, 1919–1936)
New York Times (New York, 1931; 2010–2016)
Ottawa Citizen (Ottawa, 1919–1936)
Canadian Forum (Toronto, 1933–4)
Canadian Labor Defender (Toronto, 1931–4)
Globe (Toronto, 1919–1936, 2010–2014)
Mail and Empire (Toronto, 1931–6)
National Post (Toronto, 2010–2014)
Toronto Evening Telegram (Toronto, 1931–6)
Toronto Saturday Night (Toronto, 1936)
Toronto Star (Toronto, 1919–1936, 2010–2014)
Worker (Toronto, 1926–1936)
Vancouver Sun (Vancouver, 1919–1936)
Washington Post (Washington, DC, 2009)

Winnipeg Free Press (Winnipeg, 1919–1936)
CBC News (www.cbc.ca/news, 2010–2014)
Guardian (www.theguardian.com, 2012–2016)
Time (www.time.com, 2014)

Other Primary Sources

Canada. *Debates of the House of Commons*, 1919–36.
Canada. *Debates of the Senate*, 1919–36.
Canada. *Proclamations and Orders in Council of the Imperial Government*, 1919.
Canada. *Provincial Statutes of Canada*, 1848.
Canada. *Statutes of Canada*, 1919, 1927, 1936, 1985, 2001, 2015.
Canada. *Public Order Regulations*, 1970.

Secondary Materials

Books and Book Chapters

Abu-Laban, Yasmeen. *Gendering the Nation-State: Canadian and Comparative Perspectives*. Vancouver: University of British Columbia Press, 2009.
Adachi, Ken. *The Enemy That Never Was: A History of the Japanese Canadians*. Toronto: McClelland & Stewart, 1991.
Agamben, Giorgio. *Homo Sacer: Sovereign Power and Bare Life*. Translated by Daniel Heller-Roazen. Stanford: Stanford University Press, 1995.
– *Means without End*. Translated by Cesare Casarino. Minneapolis: Minnesota University Press, 2000.
– *Remnants of Auschwitz: The Witness and the Archive*. Translated by Daniel Heller-Roazen. Cambridge, MA: Zone Books, 2002.
– *State of Exception*. Translated by Kevin Attell. Chicago: University of Chicago Press, 2005.
Angus, Ian. *Canadian Bolsheviks: The Early Years of the Communist Party of Canada*. 2nd ed. Vancouver: Trafford Publishing, 2004.
Arendt, Hannah. *On Violence*. New York: Harcourt Brace and World Publishers, 1970.
Arnason, David. Introduction to *Right Hand Left Hand: A True Life of the Thirties: Paris, Toronto, Montreal, the West and Vancouver. Love, Politics, the Depression and Feminism*, by Dorothy Livesay. Edited by David Arnason and Kim Todd. Erin, ON: Press Porcepic, 1977.
Avakumovic, Ivan. *The Communist Party in Canada: A History*. Toronto: McClelland and Stewart, 1975.
Avery, Donald. *"Dangerous Foreigners": European Immigrant Workers and Labour Radicalism in Canada, 1896–1932*. Toronto: McClelland & Stewart, 1979.
Bauman, Zygmunt. *Socialism the Active Utopia*. London: George Allen & Unwin, 1976.

Benjamin, Walter. "A Critique of Violence." In *Reflections: Essays, Aphorisms, Autobiographical Writings*, translated By Edmond Jephcott, edited by Peter Demetz, 277–300. New York: Shocken Books, 1986.

– "Theses on the Philosophy of History." In *Iluminations*, 2nd ed., translated by Harry Zohn, edited by Hannah Arendt, 245–55. London: Fontana Press, 1992.

Bannerji, Himani. *The Dark Side of the Nation: Essays on Multiculturalism, Nationalism and Gender.* Toronto: Canadian Scholars' Press, 2000.

Beaulieu, Michel. *Labour at the Lakehead: Ethnicity, Socialism and Politics, 1900–35.* Vancouver: University of British Columbia Press, 2011.

Bennett, Gill. *Churchill's Man of Mystery.* New York: Routledge, 2007.

Bercuson, David. *Confrontation at Winnipeg: Labour, Industrial Relations, and the General Strike.* 2nd ed. Montreal: McGill-Queen's University Press, 1990.

Berger, Thomas R. *Fragile Freedoms: Human Rights and Dissent in Canada.* Toronto: Clarke, Irwin, 1982.

Betcherman, Lita-Rose. *The Little Band: The Clashes between Communists and the Political and Legal Establishment in Canada, 1928–1932.* Ottawa: Deneau Publishers, 1982.

Bliss, Michael, ed. *The Wretched of Canada: Letters to R.B. Bennett 1930–35.* Toronto: University of Toronto Press, 1971.

Bosniak, Linda. *The Citizen and the Alien: Dilemmas of Contemporary Membership.* Princeton, NJ: Princeton University Press, 2006.

Bothwell, Robert. "Something of Value? Subjects and Citizens in Canadian History." In *Belonging: The Meaning and Future of Canadian Citizenship*, edited by William Kaplan. Montreal: McGill-Queen's University Press, 1993.

Bothwell, Robert, Ian Drummond, and John English. *Canada 1900–1945.* Toronto: University of Toronto Press, 1987.

Bourke, Joanna, *Fear: A Cultural History*. Berkeley: Counterpoint, 2007.

Brennan, J. William, ed. *Building the Co-operative Commonwealth: Essays on the Democratic Socialist Tradition in Canada.* Regina: University of Regina Press, 1985.

Brook-Shepard, Gordon. *The Ironmaze: Western Intelligence and the Bolsheviks.* London: Macmillan, 1998.

Brown, Lorne A., and Caroline Brown. *An Unauthorized History of the RCMP.* Toronto: James Lorimer, 1973.

Brown, Robert Craig, and Ramsay Cook. *Canada: A Nation Transformed.* Toronto: McClelland & Stewart, 1974.

Brown, Robert Craig. *Robert Laird Borden: A Biography.* 2nd ed. Toronto: Macmillan of Canada, 1980.

Brown, Desmond. *The Genesis of the Canadian Criminal Code of 1892.* Toronto: University of Toronto Press, 1989.

Brown, Desmond, and Barry Wright. "Codification, Public Order and the Security Provisions of the Canadian Criminal Code." *Political Trials and Security Measures, 1840–1914.* Vol. 3 of *Canadian State Trials*, edited by Barry Wright and Susan Binnie. Toronto: University of Toronto Press, 2009.

Buck, Tim. *An Indictment of Capitalism.* Toronto: Canadian Labor Defense League, 1932.

– *Yours in the Struggle: Reminiscences of Tim Buck.* Toronto: NC Press, 1977.

Campbell, Lara. *Respectable Citizens: Gender, Family and Unemployment in Ontario's Great Depression.* Toronto: University of Toronto Press, 2009.

Canadian Labor Defense League. *Constitution.* Toronto: Canadian Labor Defense League, 1927.

Careless, J.M.S. *Union of the Canadas: The Growth of Canadian Institutions, 1841–1857.* Toronto: McClelland & Stewart, 1967.

Carr, E.H. *The Russian Revolution from Lenin to Stalin, 1917–1929.* New York: Palgrave Macmillan, 2004.

Carty, Kenneth, and Peter Ward. "The Making of a Canadian Political Citizenship." In *National Politics and Community in Canada*, edited by Kenneth Carty and Peter Ward. Vancouver: University of British Columbia Press, 1986.

Chan, Anthony B. *Gold Mountain: The Chinese in the New World.* Charlottesville: University of Virginia Press, 1983.

Clark, Katrina. *The Soviet Novel: History as Ritual.* Chicago: University of Chicago Press, 1981.

Clement, Dominique. *Canada's Rights Revolution: Social Movements and Social Change, 1937–82.* Vancouver: University of British Columbia Press, 2008.

Craven, Paul. *"An Impartial Umpire": Industrial Relations and the Canadian State, 1900–1911.* Toronto: University of Toronto Press, 1980.

De Genova, Nicholas. "The Deportation Regime: Sovereignty, Space and the Freedom of Movement." In *The Deportation Regime: Sovereignty, Space and the Freedom of Movement*, edited by Nicholas De Genova and Nathalie Peutz. Durham: Duke University Press, 2010.

de la Durantaye, Leland. *Giorgio Agamben.* Stanford: Stanford University Press, 2009.

Daniels, Ronald J., Patrick Macklem, and Kent Roach, eds. *The Security of Freedom: Essays on Canada's Anti-Terrorism Bill.* Toronto: University of Toronto Press, 2001.

Djwa, Sandra. *The Politics of the Imagination: A Life of F.R. Scott.* Toronto: McClelland & Stewart, 1987.

Draper, Denis C. "Good Citizenship." In *Empire Club of Canada Addresses Delivered to the Members during the Year 1928*, 173–8. Toronto: Hunter-Rose, 1929.

Dyzenhaus, David. "The Permanence of the Temporary: Can Emergency Powers Be Normalized?" In *The Security of Freedom: Essays on Canada's Anti-Terrorism Bill*, edited by Ronald J. Daniels, Patrick Macklem, and Kent Roach. Toronto: University of Toronto Press, 2001.

Eaden, James, and David Renton. *The Communist Party of Great Britain since 1920*. New York: Palgrave, 2002.

Efremkin, Evgeny. "'Karelian Project' or 'Karelian Fever'? Orders from Above, Reaction from Below: Conflicting Interests in Kremlin, Karelia and Canada." In *North American Finns in Soviet Karelia in the 1930s*, edited by Irina Takala and Ilya Solomeshch. Petrozavodsk: Petrozavodsk State University Press, 2008.

Eksteins, Modris. *Rites of Spring: The Great War and the Birth of the Modern Age*. Toronto: Lester & Orpen Dennys, 1989.

Endicott, Stephen L. *Bienfait: The Saskatchewan Miners' Struggle of 1931*. Toronto: University of Toronto Press, reprinted 2002.

– *Raising the Workers' Flag: The Workers' Unity League of Canada, 1930–1936*. Toronto: University of Toronto Press, 2012.

Ewen, Tom. *The Forge Glows Red: From Blacksmith to Revolutionary*. Toronto: Progress Books, 1974.

Fecteau, Jean-Marie, and Douglas Hay. "'Government by Will and Pleasure Instead of Law': Military Justice and the Legal System in Quebec, 1775–83." *Law, Politics, and Security Measures, 1608–1837*. Vol. 1 of *Canadian State Trials*, edited by F. Murray Greenwood and Barry Wright. Toronto: University of Toronto Press, 1996.

Ferguson, Barry. "Before the Citizenship Act: Confronting Canadian Citizenship in the House of Commons, 1900–1947." In *Thinkers and Dreamers: Historical Essays in Honour of Carl Berger*, edited by Gerald Friesen and Doug Owram. Toronto: University of Toronto Press, 2010.

Fitzpatrick, Sheila. *The Cultural Front: Power and Culture in Revolutionary Russia*. Ithaca, NY: Cornell University Press, 1992.

Forgacs, David, ed. *The Antonio Gramsci Reader: Selected Writings 1916–1935*. New York: New York University Press, 2000.

Foucault, Michel. "About the Concept of the 'Dangerous Individual' in Nineteenth Century Legal Psychiatry." *Power*. Vol. 3 of *Essential Works of Foucault, 1954–1984*, edited by James Faubion. New York: New Press/ Penguin, 2000.

– *Discipline and Punish: The Birth of the Prison*, translated by Alan Sheridan. New York: Vintage Books, 1995.

– "Governmentality." In *The Foucault Effect: Studies in Governmentality*, edited by Graham Burchell, Colin Cordon, and Peter Miller. Chicago: University of Chicago Press, 1991.

– *Madness and Civilization: A History of Insanity in the Age of Reason.* New York: Vintage, 1988.

Fournier, Marcel. *Communisme et anticommunisme au Québec, 1920–1950.* Montreal: Éditions coopératives Albert Saint-Martin, 1979.

Frager, Ruth A. "Sewing Solidarity: The Eaton's Strike of 1912." In *A Nation of Immigrants: Women, Workers, and Communities in Canadian History, 1840s –1960s,* edited by Franca Iacovetta, Daula Draper, and Robert Ventresca. Toronto: University of Toronto Press, 1998.

– *Sweatshop Strife: Class, Ethnicity, and Gender in the Jewish Labour Movement of Toronto, 1900–1939.* Toronto: University of Toronto Press, 1992.

Frank, David. *J.B. McLachlan: A Biography.* Toronto: James Lorimer, 1999.

Friedland, M.L. *National Security: The Legal Dimensions: A Study Prepared for the Commission of Inquiry Concerning Certain Activities of the Royal Canadian Mounted Police.* Hull: Minister of Supply and Services Canada, 1980.

Fudge, Judy, and Eric Tucker. *Labour Before the Law: The Regulation of Workers' Collective Action in Canada, 1900–1948.*Toronto: Oxford University Press, 2001.

Gabaccia, Donna R., and Fraser M. Ottanelli. *Italian Workers of the World: Labor Migration and the Formation of Multiethnic States.* Champaign, IL: University of Illinois Press, 2001.

Galbraith, John Kenneth. *The Great Crash, 1929.* 2nd ed. Boston: Houghton Mifflin, 1955.

Ghetti, Pablo S. "World and Waste, or the Law of Liquidity." In *Liquid Society and Its Law,* edited by Jiří Přibáň. Burlington, VT: Ashgate Publishing, 2007.

Gill, Peter, and Mark Phythian. *Intelligence in an Insecure World.* Cambridge, UK: Polity Press, 2006.

Glassford, Larry A. *Reaction & Reform: The Politics of the Conservative Party under R.B. Bennett 1927–1938.* Toronto: University of Toronto Press, 1992.

Goldman, Wendy Z. *Women at the Gates: Gender and Industry in Stalin's Russia.* Cambridge: Cambridge University Press, 2002.

Granatstein, J.L., ed. *Nation: Canada since Confederation.* 3rd ed. Toronto: McGraw-Hill Ryerson, 1990.

– *Twentieth Century Canada: A Reader.* Toronto: McGraw-Hill Ryerson, 1986.

Greenwood, F. Murray, and Barry Wright, eds. *Law, Politics, and Security Measures, 1608–1837.* Vol. 1 of *Canadian State Trials.* Toronto: University of Toronto Press, 1996.

– *Rebellion and Invasion in the Canadas, 1837–1839.* Vol. 2 of *Canadian State Trials.* Toronto: University of Toronto Press, 2002.

Greenwood, F. Murray. "The Drafting and Passage of the War Measures Act in 1914 and 1927: Object Lessons in the Need for Vigilance." In *Canadian Perspectives on Law & Society: Issues in Legal History,* edited by

W. Wesley Pue and Barry Wright, 291–327. Ottawa: Carleton University Press, 1988.

Greer, Alan, and Ian Radforth, eds. *Colonial Leviathan: State Formation in Mid-Nineteenth-Century Canada*. Toronto: University of Toronto Press, 1992.

Guglielmo, Jennifer. *Living the Revolution: Italian Women's Resistance and Radicalism in New York City, 1880–1945*. Chapel Hill: University of North Carolina Press, 2010.

Hannant, Larry. *The Infernal Machine: Investigating the Loyalty of Canada's Citizens*. Toronto: University of Toronto Press, 1995.

Hay, Douglas. "Civilians Tried in Military Courts: Quebec, 1759–64." *Law, Politics, and Security Measures, 1608–1837*. Vol. 1 of *Canadian State Trials*, edited by F. Murray Greenwood and Barry Wright . Toronto: University of Toronto Press, 1996.

– "Property, Authority and the Criminal Law." In *Albion's Fatal Tree: Crime and Society in Eighteenth Century England*, edited by Douglas Hay, Peter Linebaugh, John G. Rule, E.P. Thompson, and Cal Winslow. 1st ed. London: Allen Lane/Penguin, 1975.

Herman, Michael. *Intelligence Power in Peace and War*. Cambridge: Cambridge University Press, 1996.

Heron, Craig, ed. *The Workers' Revolt in Canada, 1917–1925*. Toronto: University of Toronto Press, 1998.

Heron, Craig, and Myer Siemiatycki. "The Great War, the State, and Working-Class Canada." In *The Workers' Revolt in Canada 1917–1925*, edited by Craig Heron. Toronto: University of Toronto Press, 1998.

Hewitt, Steve. *Spying 101: The RCMP's Secret Activities at Canadian Universities 1917 –1997*. Toronto: University of Toronto Press, 2002.

Hillmer, Norman, Bohdan Kordan, and Lubomyr Luciuk. *On Guard for Thee: War, Ethnicity, and the Canadian State, 1939–1945*. Ottawa: Canadian Government Publishing Centre, 1988.

Hobbs, Margaret Helen, and Joan Sangster. *The Woman Worker, 1926–1929*. Toronto: Canadian Committee on Labour History, 1999.

Horn, Michiel, ed. *The Dirty Thirties: Canadians in the Great Depression*. Toronto: Copp Clark, 1972.

– *The League for Social Reconstruction: Intellectual Origins of the Democratic Left in Canada 1930–1942*.Toronto: University of Toronto Press, 1980.

Howard, Victor. *We Were the Salt of the Earth: The On-to-Ottawa Trek and Regina Riot*. Regina: Canadian Plains Research Center, 1985.

Iacovetta, Franca. *Gatekeepers: Reshaping Immigrant Lives in Cold War Canada*. Toronto: Between the Lines, 2006.

– "Recipes for Democracy? Gender, Family and Making Female Citizens in Cold War Canada." In *Moral Regulation and Governance in Canada:*

History, Context and Critical Issues, edited by Amanda Glasbeek. Canadian Scholars' Press, 2006.

Kanstroom, Daniel. *Deportation Nation: Outsiders in American History.* Cambridge: Harvard University Press, 2007.

Kealey, Gregory S. "The Parameters of Class Conflict: Strikes in Canada, 1891–1930." In *Class, Community and the Labour Movement: Wales and Canada, 1850–1930*, edited by Deian R. Hopkin and Gregory S. Kealey. Aberystwyth, Wales: Llafur and Canadian Committee on Labour History, 1989.

– "The Early Years of State Surveillance of Labour and the Left in Canada: The Institutional Framework of the Royal Canadian Mounted Police Security and Intelligence Apparatus, 1918–26." In *Espionage, Past, Present and Future?* edited by Wesley Wark. New York: Frank Cass, 1994.

Kealey, Gregory S., and Reg Whitaker, eds. *R.C.M.P. Security Bulletins: The Early Years, 1919–29*. Canadian Committee on Labour History: St John's, 1994.

– *R.C.M.P. Security Bulletins: The Depression Years, Part 1, 1933–34*. Canadian Committee on Labour History: St John's, 1993.

– *R.C.M.P. Security Bulletins: The Depression Years, Part 2, 1935*. Canadian Committee on Labour History: St John's, 1995.

Kelley, Ninette, and Michael Trebilcock. *The Making of the Mosaic: A History of Canadian Immigration Policy.* Toronto: University of Toronto Press, 1998.

Kinsman, Gary, Dieter K. Buse, and Mercedes Steedman, eds. *Whose National Security? Canadian State Surveillance and the Creation of Enemies.* Toronto: Between the Lines, 2000.

Kolasky, John. *The Shattered Illusion: The History of Ukrainian Pro-Communist Organizations in Canada.* Toronto: Peter Martin Associates, 1979.

Kostal, Rande W. *A Jurisprudence of Power.* Oxford: Oxford University Press, 2008.

Kramer, Reinhold, and Tom Mitchell. *When the State Trembled: How A.J. Andrews and the Citizens' Committee Broke the Winnipeg General Strike.* Toronto: University of Toronto Press, 2010.

Kristmanson, Mark. *Plateaus of Freedom: Nationality, Culture and State Security in Canada 1940–1960.* Toronto: Oxford University Press, 2003.

Lambert, R.S. *This Freedom: A Guide to Good Citizenship in a Time of War.* Toronto: Canadian Association for Adult Education, 1940.

Lambertson, Ross. *Repression and Resistance: Canadian Human Rights Activists 1930–1960.* Toronto: University of Toronto Press, 2005.

Lampe, John. *Yugoslavia as History: Twice There Was a Country.* Cambridge: . Cambridge University Press, 2000.

Leier, Mark. *Where the Fraser River Flows: The Industrial Workers of the World in British Columbia.* Vancouver: New Star Books, 1990.

Leslie, R.F., ed. *The History of Poland since 1863*. London: Cambridge University Press, 1980.

Lévesque, Andrée. "Le Québec et le monde communiste: Cowansville 1931." In *Le droit de se taire: Histoire des communistes au Québec, de la Première Guerre mondiale à la Révolution tranquille*, edited by Robert Comeau and Bernard Dionne. Montreal: VLB Éditeur, 1989.

– "Red Scares and Repression in Québec, 1919–1939." *Security, Dissent, and the Limits of Toleration in War and Peace, 1914–1939*. Vol. 4 of *Canadian State Trials*, edited by Barry Wright, Susan Binnie, and Eric Tucker. Toronto: University of Toronto Press, 2015.

– *Red Travellers: Jean Corbin and Her Comrades*, translated by Yvonne Klein. Montreal: McGill-Queen's University Press, 2006.

– *Virage à gauche interdit: Les communistes, les socialistes et leurs ennemis au Québec 1929–1939*. Montreal: Boréal, 1984.

Lindström, Varpu. "The Finnish Canadian Communities during the Decade of the Depression." In *Karelian Exodus: Finnish Communities in North America and Soviet Karelia during the Depression Era*, edited by Ronald Harpelle, Varpu Lindström, and Alexis Pogorelskin. Toronto: Aspasia Books, 2004.

– "'Heaven or Hell on Earth?' Soviet Karelia's Propaganda War of 1934–1935 in the Finnish Canadian Press." In *North American Finns in Soviet Karelia in the 1930s*, edited by Irina Takala and Ilya Solomeshch. Petrozavodsk: Petrozavodsk State University Press, 2008.

Lipset, S.M. *Agrarian Socialism: The Cooperative Commonwealth Federation in Saskatchewan*. Berkeley: University of California Press, 1959.

Liversedge, Ronald. *Recollections of the On-to-Ottawa Trek*. Montreal: McGill-Queen's University Press, 1973.

Lower, Arthur. *History of Canada*. 5th ed. Toronto: McClelland & Stewart, 1977.

Luciuk, Lubomyr. *A Time for Atonement: Canada's First National Internment Operations and the Ukrainian Canadians, 1914–1920*. Kingston: Lime Stone Press, 1988.

MacDowell, Laurel Sefton. *Renegade Lawyer: The Life of J.L. Cohen*. Toronto: Osgood Society for Canadian Legal History, 2001.

MacDowell, Laurel Sefton, and Ian Radforth, eds. *Canadian Working Class History: Selected Readings*. Toronto: Canadian Scholars' Press, 1992.

Makuch, Andrij. "Fighting for the Soul of the Ukrainian Progressive Movement in Canada: The Lobayites and the Ukrainian Labour-Farmer Temple Association." In *Re-Imagining Ukrainian Canadians: History, Politics, and Identity*, edited by Rhonda L. Hinther and Jim Mochoruk .Toronto: University of Toronto Press, 2011.

Manley, John. "Red or Yellow? Canadian Communists and the 'Long' Third Period, 1927–36." In *In Search of Revolution: International Communist*

Parties in the Third Period, edited by Matthew Worley. London: I.B. Tauris, 2004.

Marshall, T.H. *Citizenship and Social Class*. Cambridge: Cambridge University Press, 1950.

Martynowych, Orest T. *Ukrainians in Canada: The Formative Period, 1891–1924*. Edmonton: Canadian Institute of Ukrainian Studies Press, 1991.

Marwick, Arthur. *War and Social Change in the Twentieth Century: A Comparative Study of Britain, France, Germany, Russia, and the United States*. London: Macmillan, 1974.

Marx, Karl. Vol. 1 of *Capital: A Critique of Political Economy*. 1867. Translated by Ben Fowkes. New York: Penguin, 1990.

– "Towards a Critique of Hegel's Philosophy of Right: Introduction." In *Karl Marx: Selected Writings*, edited by David McLellan. 2nd ed. Oxford: Oxford University Press, 2000.

Masters, D.C. *The Winnipeg General Strike*. Toronto: University of Toronto Press, 1950.

Maurutto, Paula. "Private Policing and Surveillance of Catholics: Anti-Communism in the Roman Catholic Archdiocese of Toronto, 1920–60." In *Whose National Security? Canadian State Surveillance and the Creation of Enemies*, edited by Gary Kinsman, Dieter K. Buse, and Mercedes Steedman. Toronto: Between the Lines, 2000.

McDermott, Kevin, and Jeremy Agnew. *The Comintern: A History of International Communism from Lenin to Stalin*. Basingstoke: Macmillan, 1996.

McKay, Ian. "Canada as a Long Liberal Revolution." In *Liberalism and Hegemony: Debating the Canadian Liberal Revolution*, edited by Jean François Constant and Michel Ducharme. Toronto: University of Toronto Press, 2009.

– *Reasoning Otherwise: Leftists and the People's Enlightenment in Canada, 1890–1920*. Toronto: Between the Lines, 2008.

– *Rebels, Reds, Radicals: Rethinking Canada's Left History*. Toronto: Between the Lines, 2005.

McNaught, Kenneth. *A Prophet in Politics: A Biography of J.S. Woodsworth*. Toronto: University of Toronto Press, 2001. First published 1959.

McNaught, Kenneth, and David Bercuson. *The Winnipeg General Strike*. Don Mills: Longman, 1974.

Mills, Allen. *Fool for Christ: The Political Thought of J.S. Woodsworth*. Toronto: University of Toronto Press, 1991.

Mills, Catherine. *The Philosophy of Agamben*. Montreal: McGill-Queen's University Press, 2008.

Mochoruk, Jim. "'Pop & Co' versus Buck and the 'Lenin School Boys': Ukrainian Canadians and the Communist Party of Canada 1921–1931." In *Re-Imagining Ukrainian Canadians: History, Politics, and Identity*, edited by Rhonda L. Hinther and Jim Mochoruk. Toronto: University of Toronto Press, 2011.

Molinaro, Dennis G. "Section 98: The Trial of Rex v. Buck et al. and the 'State of Exception' in Canada, 1919–1936." *Security, Dissent, and the Limits of Toleration in War and Peace, 1914–1939*. Vol. 4 of *Canadian State Trials*, edited by Barry Wright, Susan Binnie, and Eric Tucker. Toronto: University of Toronto Press, 2015.

Nagler, Jörg. "The Mobilization of Emotions: Propaganda and Social Violence on the Home Front during World War I." In *Emotions in American History: An International Assessment*, edited by Jessica Gienow-Hecht. New York: Berghahn Books, 2010.

Naylor, James. *The New Democracy: Challenging the Industrial Order in Industrial Ontario*. Toronto: University of Toronto Press, 1991.

Neatby, H. Blair. *The Politics of Chaos: Canada in the Thirties*. Toronto: Macmillan, 1972.

Newton, Janice. *The Feminist Challenge to the Canadian Left, 1900–1918*. Montreal: McGill-Queen's University Press, 1995.

Ngai, Mae N. *Impossible Subjects: Illegal Aliens and the Making of Modern America*. Princeton: Princeton University Press, 2004.

Palmer, Bryan D. *Working-Class Experience: Rethinking the History of Canadian Labour 1800–1991*. 2nd ed. Toronto: McClelland & Stewart, 1992.

Patrias, Carmela. *Jobs and Justice: Fighting Discrimination in Wartime Canada, 1939–1945*. Toronto: University of Toronto Press, 2012.

– "Relief Strike: Immigrant Workers and the Great Depression in Crowland, Ontario." In *A Nation of Immigrants: Women, Workers, and Communities in Canadian History, 1840s–1960s*, edited by Franca Iacovetta, Daula Draper, and Robert Ventresca. Toronto: University of Toronto Press, 1998.

– *Patriots and Proletarians: Politicizing Hungarian Immigrants in Interwar Canada*. Montreal: McGill-Queen's University Press, 1994.

Penner, Norman. *Canadian Communism: The Stalin Years and Beyond*. Toronto: Methuen, 1988.

– *Winnipeg 1919: The Strikers' Own History of the Winnipeg General Strike*. Toronto: J. Lewis & Samuel, 1973.

Perry, Adele. "Whose Sisters and What Eyes? White Women, Race, and Immigration to British Columbia, 1849–1871." In *Sisters or Strangers? Immigrant, Ethnic, and Racialized Women in Canadian History*, edited by Franca Iacovetta, Frances Swyripa, and Marlene Epp. Toronto: University of Toronto Press, 2004.

Petrou, Michael. *Renegades: Canadians in the Spanish Civil War*. Vancouver: University of British Columbia Press, 2008.

Pierce, G. *Socialism and the CCF*. Montreal: Contemporary Publishing Association, 1934.

Pratt, Ann. *Securing Borders: Detention and Deportation in Canada*. Vancouver: University of British Columbia Press, 2005.

Preston, William. *Aliens and Dissenters: Federal Suppression of Radicals, 1903–1933*. New York: Harper Torchbooks, 1963.

Radforth, Ian. *Bushworkers and Bosses*. Toronto: University of Toronto Press, 1987.

– "Finnish Radicalism and Labour Activism in the Northern Ontario Woods." In *A Nation of Immigrants: Women, Workers, and Communities in Canadian History, 1840s–1960s*, edited by Franca Iacovetta, Daula Draper, and Robert Ventresca. Toronto: University of Toronto Press, 1998.

Ramet, Sabrina P. *The Three Yugoslavias: State-Building and Legitimation, 1918–2005*. Bloomington: Indiana University Press, 2006.

Rasporich, Anthony W. *For a Better Life: A History of the Croatians in Canada*. Toronto: McClelland & Stewart, 1982.

Razack, Sherene. "Abandonment and the Dance of Race and Bureaucracy in Spaces of Exception." In *States of Race: Critical Race Feminism for the 21st Century*, edited by Sherene Razack, Malinda Smith, and Sunera Thobani. Toronto: Between the Lines, 2010.

Rea, J.E. "The Politics of Class: Winnipeg City Council 1919–45." In *The West and the Nation: Essays in Honour of W.L. Morton*, edited by Carl Berger and Ramsay Cook. Toronto: McClelland & Stewart, 1976.

Read, Daphne, ed. *The Great War and Canadian Society: An Oral History*. Toronto: New Hogtown Press, 1978.

Reddy, William M. *The Navigation of Feeling: A Framework for the History of Emotions*. Cambridge: Cambridge University Press, 2001.

Research Committee of the League for Social Reconstruction. *Social Planning for Canada*. Toronto: Thomas Nelson & Sons, 1935.

Richard, Béatrice. "Peril communiste au Temiscamingue: 1933–1934." In *Le droit de se taire: Histoire des communistes au Québec, de la Première Guerre mondiale à la Révolution tranquille*, edited by Robert Comeau and Bernard Dionne. Montreal: VLB Éditeur, 1989.

Roach, Kent. *September 11: Consequences for Canada*. Durham: Acumen, 2003.

– *The 9/11 Effect: Comparative Counter Terrorism*. Cambridge: Cambridge University Press, 2011.

Roberts, Barbara. *Whence They Came: Deportation from Canada, 1900–1935*. Ottawa: University of Ottawa Press, 1988.

Rodney, William. *Soldiers of the International: A History of the Communist Party of Canada, 1919–1929*. Toronto: University of Toronto Press, 1968.

Ryan, Oscar. *Deported! The Struggle against Deportations and for the Defense of the Foreign-Born Workers: The Case of the Ten Prisoners in Halifax, of the Thousands Who Face Deportation*. Toronto: Canadian Labor Defense League, 1932.

– *The Sedition of A.E. Smith*. Toronto: Canadian Labor Defense League, 1934.

– *Tim Buck: A Conscience for Canada*. Toronto: Progress Books, 1975.

Sangster, Joan. *Dreams of Equality: Women on the Canadian Left, 1920–1950.* Toronto: McClelland & Stewart, 1989.

– *Regulating Girls and Women: Sexuality, Family and the Law in Ontario, 1920–1960.* 2nd ed. Toronto: University of Toronto Press, 2001.

Satia, Priya. *Spies in Arabia: The Great War and the Cultural Foundations of Britain's Covert Empire in the Middle East.* New York: Oxford University Press, 2008.

Schmeiser, Douglas A. *Civil Liberties in Canada.* Oxford: Oxford University Press, 1964.

Scott, F.R. *Essays on the Constitution: Aspects of Canadian Law and Politics.* Toronto: University of Toronto Press, 1977.

Singleton, Fred. *A Short History of the Yugoslav Peoples.* London: Cambridge University Press, 1985.

Smith, A.E. *All My Life: An Autobiography.* Toronto: Progress Books, 1977.

Smith, Jeremy. *The Bolsheviks and the National Question, 1917–23.* New York: St Martin's Press, 1999.

Smith, Stewart. *Comrades and Komsomolkas.* Toronto: Lugus Publications, 1993.

Srebrnik, Henry Felix. *Jerusalem on the Amur: Birobidzhan and the Canadian Jewish Communist Movement, 1924–1951.* Montreal: McGill-Queen's University Press, 2008.

Srigley, Katrina. *Breadwinning Daughters: Young Working Women in a Depression-Era City 1929–1939.* Toronto: University of Toronto Press, 2009.

Stacey, C.P. *Canada in the Age of Conflict.* Vol. 1, *1867–1921.* Toronto: University of Toronto Press, 1981.

Stachura, Peter D. *Poland in the Twentieth Century.* Basingstoke: Macmillan, 1999.

Stalin, Joseph. *Interviews with Foreign Workers' Delegations.* New York: International Publishers, 1927.

– "Marxism and the National Question." In *Works.* Moscow: Foreign Languages Publishing House, 1954.

Stalin, Joseph. *Our Foreign Policy: Stalin, Molotov, Litvinov.* Moscow: Co-operative Publishing Society of Foreign Workers in the USSR, 1934.

Stone, Geoffrey R. *Perilous Times: Free Speech in Wartime: From the Sedition Act of 1798 to the War on Terrorism.* New York: W.W. Norton, 2004.

Strange, Carolyn, and Tina Loo. *Making Good: Law and Moral Regulation in Canada, 1867–1939.* Toronto: University of Toronto Press, 1997.

Struthers, James. *No Fault of Their Own: Unemployment and the Canadian Welfare State, 1914–1941.*Toronto: University of Toronto Press, 1983.

Swankey, Ben, and Jean Evans Sheils. *"Work and Wages!" A Semi-Documentary Account of the Life and Times of Arthur H. (Slim) Evans 1890–1944*. Vancouver: Granville Press, 1977.

Swyripa, Frances, and John Herd Thompson, eds. *Loyalties in Conflict: Ukrainians in Canada during the Great War*. Edmonton: Canadian Institute of Ukrainian Studies Press, 1983.

Thobani, Sunera. *Exalted Subjects: Studies in the Making of Race and Nation in Canada*. Toronto: University of Toronto Press, 2012.

Thomas, William H., Jr. *Unsafe for Democracy: World War I and the U.S. Justice Department's Covert Campaign to Suppress Dissent*. Madison: University of Wisconsin Press, 2008.

Thompson, John Herd, with Allen Seager. *Canada 1922–1939: Decades of Discord*. Toronto: McClelland & Stewart, 1985.

Thorpe, Andrew. *The British Communist Party and Moscow, 1920–43*. Manchester: Manchester University Press, 2000.

Tucker, Robert C. *Stalin in Power: The Revolution from Above, 1928–1941*. New York: W.W. Norton, 1990.

Turner, Michael A. *Why Secret Intelligence Fails*. Dulles, VA: Potomac Books, 2005.

Valverde, Mariana. *The Age of Light, Soap and Water: 19th Century Moral Reform in English Canada*. Toronto: University of Toronto Press, 1991.

Vasiliadis, Peter. *Dangerous Truth: Immigrant Communities and Ethnic Minorities in the United States and Canada*. New York: AMS Press, 1989.

Ventresca, Robert, and Franca Iacovetta. "Virgilia D'Andrea: The Politics of Protest and the Poetry of Exile." In *Women, Gender, and Transnational Lives: Italian Workers of the World*, edited by Donna R. Gabaccia and Franca Iacovetta. Toronto: University of Toronto Press, 2002.

Vigod, Bernard. *Quebec before Duplessis: The Political Career of Louis-Alexandre Taschereau*. Montreal: McGill-Queen's University Press, 1986.

Waiser, Bill. *All Hell Can't Stop Us: The On-to-Ottawa Trek and Regina Riot*. Calgary: Fifth House, 2003.

Ward, Peter. *White Canada Forever: Popular Attitudes and Public Policy toward Orientals in British Columbia*. 3rd ed. Montreal: McGill-Queen's University Press, 2002.

Wark, Wesley. "Security Intelligence in Canada, 1864–1945: The History of a 'National Insecurity State.'" In *Go Spy the Land: Military Intelligence in History*, edited by Keith Neilson and B.J.C. McKercher. Westport, CT: Praeger, 1992.

West, Nigel. *At Her Majesty's Secret Service: The Chiefs of Britain's Intelligence Agency, MI6*. London: Greenhill Books, 2006.

Whitaker, Reg. *Double Standard: The Secret History of Canadian Immigration*. Toronto: Lester & Orpen Dennys, 1987.

Whitaker, Reg, Gregory S. Kealey, and Andrew Parnaby. *Secret Service: Political Policing in Canada from the Fenians to Fortress America*. Toronto: University of Toronto Press, 2012.

Whitaker, Reg, and Gary Marcuse. *Cold War Canada: The Making of a National Insecurity State, 1945–1957*. Toronto: University of Toronto Press, 1994.

Whitehorn, Alan. *Canadian Socialism: Essays on the CCF-NDP*. Toronto: Oxford University Press, 1992.

Whyte, Jessica. *Catastrophe and Redemption: The Political Thought of Giorgio Agamben*. Albany: State University of New York Press, 2013.

Worley, Matthew. *Class against Class: The Communist Party in Britain between the Wars*. London: I.B. Tauris, 2002.

Wright, Barry, and Susan Binnie, eds. *Political Trials and Security Measures, 1840–1914*. Vol. 3 of *Canadian State Trials*. University of Toronto Press, 2009.

Wright, Cynthia. "The Museum of Illegal Immigration: Historical Perspectives on the Production of Non-Citizens and Challenges to Immigration Controls." In *Producing and Negotiating Non-Citizenship: Precarious Legal Status in Canada*, edited by Luin Goldring and Patricia Landolt. Toronto: University of Toronto Press, 2013.

Wright, Richard, and Robin Endres, eds. *Eight Men Speak, and Other Plays from the Canadian Workers' Theatre*. Toronto: New Hogtown Press, 1976.

Young, Walter. *The Anatomy of a Party*. Toronto: University of Toronto Press, 1969.

Articles

Abrams, Phillip. "Notes on the Difficulty of Studying the State." *Journal of Historical Sociology* 1, no. 1 (March 1988): 58–89.

Abu-Laban, Yasmeen, and Nisha Nath. "From Deportation to Apology: The Case of Maher Arar and the Canadian State." *Canadian Ethnic Studies* 39, no. 3 (2007): 71–98.

Adams, Eric M. "Canada's 'Newer Constitutional Law' and the Idea of Constitutional Rights." *McGill Law Journal* 51, no. 435 (2006): 435–74.

Agamben, Giorgio. "For a Theory of Destituent Power." *Chronos* 10, 16 November 2013.

Auger, F.M. "On the Brink of Civil War: The Canadian Government and the Suppression of the 1918 Quebec Easter Riots." *Canadian Historical Review* 89, no. 4 (December 2008): 503–40.

Avery, Donald. "Continental European Immigrant Workers in Canada 1896–1919: From 'Stalwart Peasants' to Radical Proletariat." *Canadian Review of Sociology and Anthropology* 12, no. 1 (1975): 53–64.

Axelrod, Paul. "Spying on the Young in the Depression and War: Students, Youth Groups and the RCMP, 1935–1942." *Labour/Le Travail* 35 (Spring 1995): 43–63.

Barrett, James R. "The History of American Communism and our Understanding of Stalinism." *American Communist History* 2 (December 2003): 175–82.

Bruyneel, Kevin. "Exiled, Executed, Exalted: Louis Riel, *Homo Sacer* and the Production of Canadian Sovereignty." *Canadian Journal of Political Science* 43, no. 3 (2010): 711–32.

Coughlin, G.A. "The Quebec 'Padlock Law.'" *L'Oeuvre des tracts* 234 (December 1938): 1–10.

Dua, Enakshi. "The Passage from Subjects to Aliens: Indian Migrants and the Racialization of Canadian Citizenship." *Sociologie et Sociétés* 31, no. 2 (Autumn 1999):145–62.

Frager, Ruth A., and Carmela Patrias. "Human Rights Activists and the Question of Sex Discrimination in Postwar Ontario." *Canadian Historical Review* 93, no. 4 (2012): 583–610.

Glassford, Larry A. "Retrenchment – R.B. Bennett Style: The Conservative Record before the New Deal, 1930–34." *American Review of Canadian Studies* 19, no. 2 (1989): 141–57.

Gordon, Todd. "Towards an Anti-Racist Marxist State Theory: A Canadian Case Study." *Capital & Class* 91 (2007): 1–29.

Grenke, Art. "From Dreams of the Worker State to Fighting Hitler: The German Canadian Left from the Depression to the end of World War II." *Labour/Le Travail* 25 (Spring 1995): 65–105.

Hak, Gordon. "Red Wages: Communists and the 1934 Vancouver Island Loggers Strike." *Pacific Northwest Quarterly* 80, no. 3 (July 1989): 82–90.

Harney, Robert. "Montreal's King of Italian Labour: A Case Study of Padronism." *Labour/Le Travail* 4 (1979): 57–84.

Hay, Douglas. "Tradition, Judges and Civil Liberties in Canada." *Osgoode Hall Law Journal* 41, no. 2/3 (Summer/Fall 2003): 319–22.

Hewitt, Steve. "Royal Canadian Mounted Spy: The Secret Life of John Leopold/ Jack Esselwein." *Intelligence and National Security* 15, no. 1 (Spring 2000): 154–5.

Horn, Michiel. "Frank Underhill's Early Drafts of the Regina Manifesto 1933." *Canadian Historical Review* 54, no. 4 (December 1973): 393–418.

– "'Free Speech within the Law': The Letter of the Sixty-Eight Toronto Professors, 1931." *Ontario History* 72, no. 1 (March 1980): 27–48.

– "Keeping Canada 'Canadian': Anti-Communism and Canadianism in Toronto, 1928–29." *Canada: A Historical Magazine* 3, no. 3 (September 1975): 34–47.

Kealey, Gregory S. "919: The Canadian Labour Revolt." *Labour/Le Travail* 13 (1984): 11–44.

- "State Repression of Labour and the Left in Canada, 1914–20: The Impact of the First World War." *Canadian Historical Review* 7, no. 3 (September 1993): 281–314.

Kealey, Gregory S., and Andrew Parnaby. "The Origins of Political Policing in Canada: Class, Law, and the Burden of Empire." *Osgoode Hall Law Journal* 41, no. 2/3 (Summer/Fall 2003): 211–40.

Keshen, Jeffrey. "All the News That Was Fit to Print: Ernest J. Chambers and Information Control in Canada, 1914–1919." *Canadian Historical Review* 73, no. 3 (September 1992): 315–43.

Keys, Norman. "Section 98 of the Criminal Code." *Fortnightly Law Journal* 3 (June 1933).

Lonardo, Michael. "Under a Watchful Eye: A Case Study of Police Surveillance during the 1930s." *Labour/Le Travail* 35 (Spring 1995):11–41.

Mackenzie, J.B. "Section 98 Criminal Code and Freedom of Expression in Canada." *Queen's Law Journal* 4 (1972): 469–83.

Makahonuk, Glen. "Class Conflict in a Prairie City: The Saskatoon Working-Class Response to Prairie Capitalism 1906–19." *Labour/Le Travail* 19 (Spring 1987): 89–124.

Manley, John. "'Audacity, Audacity, Still More Audacity': Tim Buck, the Party, and the People, 1932–1939."*Labour/Le Travail* 49 (Spring 2002): 9–42.

- "Moscow Rules? 'Red' Unionism and 'Class against Class' in Britain, Canada, and the United States, 1928–1935." *Labour/Le Travail* 56 (Fall 2005): 9–50.

- "'Starve, Be Damned!' Communists and Canada's Urban Unemployed, 1929–1939." *Canadian Historical Review* 79, no. 3 (September 1998): 466–91.

- "Communists Love Canada! The Communist Party of Canada, the People and the Popular Front, 1933–1939." *Journal of Canadian Studies* 36, no. 4 (Winter 2002): 59–86.

Mathews, A.S., and R.C. Albino. "The Permanence of the Temporary: An Examination of the 90 and 18 Day Detention Laws." *South African Law Journal* 83 (1966): 16–43.

McKay, Ian. "For a New Kind of History: A Reconnaissance of 100 Years of Canadian Socialism." *Labour/Le Travail* 46 (Fall 2000): 69–125.

- "Joe Salsberg, Depression-Era Communism, and the Limits of Moscow's Rule." *Canadian Jewish Studies* 21 (2013 [2014]): 130–42.

- "The Liberal Order Framework: A Prospectus for a Reconnaissance of Canadian History." *Canadian Historical Review* 81, no. 3 (September 2000): 617–45.

McLean, Lorna. "To Become Part of Us: Ethnicity, Race, Literacy and the Canadian Immigration Act of 1919." *Canadian Ethnic Studies* 36, no. 2 (2004): 1–28.

McIlroy, John, and Alan Campbell. "'Nina Ponomareva's Hats': The New Revisionism, the Communist International, and the Communist Party of Great Britain, 1920–30." *Labour/Le Travail* 49 (Spring 2002): 147–87.

Milligan, Ian. "Sedition in Wartime Ontario: The Trials and Imprisonment of Isaac Bainbridge, 1917–1918." *Ontario History* 100, no. 2 (Autumn 2008): 150–77.

Mills, Sean. "Quebec, Haiti, and the Deportation Crisis of 1974." *Canadian Historical Review* 94, no. 3 (September 2013): 405–35.

– "When Democratic Socialists Discovered Democracy: The League for Social Reconstruction Confronts the 'Quebec Problem.'" *Canadian Historical Review* 86, no. 1 (March 2005): 53–81.

Molinaro, Dennis G. "'A Species of Treason?' Deportation and Nation-Building in the Case of Tomo Čačić." *Canadian Historical Review* 91, no. 1 (March 2010): 61–85.

Moloney, Deirdre M. "Women, Sexual Morality, and Economic Dependency in Early U.S. Deportation Policy." *Journal of Women's History* 18, no. 2 (Summer 2006): 95–122.

Morton, Suzanne. "Labourism and Economic Action: The Halifax Shipyards Strike of 1920." *Labour/Le Travail* 22 (Fall 1988): 67–98.

Naylor, James. "Socialism for a New Generation: CCF Youth in the Popular Front Era." *Canadian Historical Review* 94, no. 1 (March 2013): 69–70.

Naylor, R.T. "The Canadian State, the Accumulation of Capital, and the Great War." *Journal of Canadian Studies* 16 (Fall/Winter 1981): 26–55.

Ouellet, Jérôme, and Frédéric Roussel-Beaulieu. "Les débats parlementaires au service de l'histoire politique." *Bulletin d'Histoire Politique* 11, no. 3 (2003): 23–40.

Palmer, Bryan D. "Reading Otherwise: Ian McKay's 'Fairly Straightforward' Misrepresentation of Communist Party Historiography." *Canadian Jewish Studies* 23 (2015).

– "Rethinking the Historiography of United States Communism." *American Communist History* 2 (December 2003): 139–73.

Parnaby, Andrew, and Gregory S. Kealey. "How the 'Reds' Got Their Man: The Communist Party Unmasks an RCMP Spy." *Labour/Le Travail* 40 (Fall 1997): 253–67.

Peppin, Patricia. "Emergency Legislation and Rights in Canada: The War Measures Act and Civil Liberties." *Queen's Law Journal* 18, no. 130 (1993): 129–90.

Petryshyn, J. "Class Conflict and Civil Liberties: The Origins and Activities of the Canadian Labour Defence League, 1925–1940." *Labour/Le Travail* 10 (Autumn 1982): 39–64.

– "R.B. Bennett and the Communists, 1930–1935." *Journal of Canadian Studies* 9, no. 4 (1974): 43–55.

Polec, Patryk. "From Hurrah Revolutionaries to Polish Patriots: The Rise of Polish Canadian Radicalism." *Polish American Studies* 68, no. 2 (Autumn 2011): 43–66.

Pue, W. Wesley. "The War on Terror: Constitutional Governance in a Permanent State of Warfare?" *Osgoode Hall Law Journal* 41 (2003): 267–92.

Rasporich, Anthony W. "Tomo Čačić: Rebel without a Country." *Canadian Ethnic Studies* 10, no. 2 (1978): 86–93.

Reid, Susan E. "All Stalin's Women: Gender and Power in Soviet Art of the 1930s." *Slavic Review* 57, no. 1 (1998): 133–73.

Roberts, Barbara. "Shovelling Out the 'Mutinous': Political Deportation from Canada before 1936." *Labour/Le Travail* 18 (Fall 1986): 77–110.

Sangster, Joan. "Robitnytsia, Ukrainian Communists, and the 'Porcupinism' Debate: Reassessing Ethnicity, Gender, and Class in Early Canadian Communism, 1922–1930." *Labour/Le Travail* 56 (Fall 2005): 51–89.

– "The Communist Party and the Women Question, 1922–1929." *Labour/Le Travail* 15 (Spring 1985) 25–56.

Scott, F.R. "The Trial of the Toronto Communists." *Queen's Quarterly* 39 (August 1932): 512–27.

Stearns, Peter N., and Carol Z. Stearns. "Emotionology: Clarifying the History of Emotions and Emotional Standards." *American Historical Review* 90, no. 4 (1985): 813–30.

Switzer, Jack. "The Ordeal of Sophie Sheinin." *Alberta History* (January 2008): 19–21.

Thorpe, Andrew. "Comintern 'Control' of the Communist Party of Great Britain, 1920–43." *English Historical Review* 113 (June 1998): 637–62.

Unpublished and Theses

Burgess, William. "Canada's Location in the World System: Reworking the Debate in Canadian Political Economy." PhD diss., University of British Columbia, 2002.

Butler, Nancy. "Mother Russia and the Socialist Fatherland: Women and the Communist Party of Canada, 1932–1941, with Specific Reference to the Activism of Dorothy Livesay and Jim Watts." PhD diss., Queen's University, 2010.

Elie, Christine. "The City and the Reds: Leftism, the Civic Politics of Order, and a Contested Modernity in Montreal, 1929–1947." PhD diss., Queen's University, 2015.

Fidler, Richard. "Proscribing Unlawful Associations: The Swift Rise and Agonizing Demise of Section 98." Unpublished, Osgoode Law School, May 1984.

Franz, Kyle. "Alberta's Red Democrats: The Challenge and Legacy of Blairmore Communism, 1921–1936." PhD diss., Queen's University, 2013.

Lévesque, Andrée. "The Canadian Left in Quebec during the Great Depression: The Communist Party of Canada and the CCF in Quebec, 1929–1939." PhD diss., Duke University, 1972.

Manley, John. "Communism and the Canadian Working Class in the Great Depression: The Workers' Unity League, 1930–1936." PhD diss., Dalhousie University, 1984.

Parnaby, Andrew. "On the Hook: Welfare Capitalism on the Vancouver Waterfront, 1919–1939." PhD diss., Memorial University, 2001.

Tomchuk, Travis. "Transnational Radicals: Italian Anarchist Networks in Southern Ontario and the Northeastern United States, 1915–1940." PhD diss., Queen's University, 2010.

Index

Agamben, Giorgio, 8, 12–13, 15–16,
  39, 118, 218, 233; *homo sacer*, 8–9,
  12–13, 15–16, 120–1, 125, 145, 222,
  224, 230; protection of law, 12, 56
alien(s), 24, 26, 28, 34, 40, 50, 57, 60,
  77, 84, 103, 125, 223
Aliens Restriction Act (1919), 34
American Protective League (APL),
  26–7
Andrews, A.J., 34, 35
anti-terrorism: 2001 Act (Canada), 18;
  2015 Act, 4, 227, 229; Amendments,
  228; Bill C-51, 227; laws, 3, 226
Anti-terrorism Act, 2015. *See* anti-
  terrorism
Arendt, Hannah, 183; violence, 183;
  power, 183

Benjamin, Walter, v, 12, 182, 229, 233
Bennett, R.B., 5, 15, 21, 51, 53, 57, 69,
  70–2, 74–7, 147–8, 150–1, 153–4,
  161–2, 169, 170, 176, 186, 189,
  191–2, 198, 200–3, 205–6, 210,
  215–16, 223, 225–6
Bill C-51. *See* anti-terrorism
Bill 153, 51–3
Blair, Chief Bill, 229
Borba, 131–3, 143
Borden, Robert, 19, 20–2, 24, 26–7,
  29–31

Boychuk, John, 81, 86, 88, 95, 97, 98
Bruce, Malcolm, 81, 86, 88, 97, 102, 113
Buck, Tim, 59, 60, 68, 71–2, 78, 81,
  86–9, 91, 94, 97, 110–12, 114–15,
  119, 120–4, 130–1, 135, 138, 147,
  151–2, 156, 158–61, 163–4, 167,
  169–72, 184–5, 187–94, 197–8,
  206–9, 218–19, 224–5
Buhay, Becky, 66, 168, 188, 192
Buller, Annie, 66, 168, 169
Bureau of Investigation, 29

Čačić, Tomo, 81–2, 86, 88, 95–7, 114,
  116, 121, 125, 131–5, 138, 142–4, 224
Cahan, C.H., 26–32, 34, 214–15
Canadian Labor Defense League
  (CLDL), 97, 114, 124, 128–9, 130,
  134–5, 137, 140, 142, 151, 153–4,
  162, 164–6, 168–70, 174, 176–7,
  179–81, 185–95, 198–201, 216, 219,
  220, 225
Canadian Security Intelligence Service
  (CSIS), 10
Carr, Sam, 67, 81, 86, 88, 97
CCF (Co-operative Commonwealth
  Federation), 191–6, 198–200, 205,
  211, 216, 220
Cesinger, Conrad, 122, 127, 134, 140,
  141, 143
Charlie Hebdo attacks, 232

Charter challenge, 221, 229
Chomicki, Dmytro, 122, 127–8, 132,
    134, 138, 141–3; Holmes, Dan (also
    known as), 122, 127
CIA (Central Intelligence Agency), 230
citizenship, 6, 8, 46, 49, 54, 74–5, 121,
    125, 126, 145, 150, 174, 231
Citizenship Act, 231
civilian communications, 229
civil liberty, 10, 48, 96, 119, 165–6,
    185–6, 199, 200, 216, 219, 225–6,
    228, 232–3
Cohen, J.L., 77, 88, 89, 188
Cold War, 10, 15, 140, 226, 228
Communications Security Establishment
    (CSE), 229
communism, 6–7, 9, 10, 13–14, 28, 43,
    52, 55, 58–9, 65–6, 68, 70–8, 80, 84,
    86–7, 91, 101, 104, 106, 113–15, 117,
    119–21, 126–7, 130, 139, 140, 142,
    145–9, 151, 153, 155, 159–60, 164,
    167, 172–3, 182–4, 194, 201, 205,
    209–15, 217, 220, 223, 225–7
Communist International (CI), 58–60,
    62–3, 65–7, 70, 81, 93–4, 97, 99–101,
    103, 105, 111–16, 118, 151–2, 160,
    186–7, 188–9, 191, 193–5, 205, 220
Communist Party of Canada (CPC),
    5–6, 14, 17, 42, 51, 56–69, 71,
    74–81, 83–9, 91–124, 126–35,
    139, 142, 145–7, 151–8, 160–1,
    163–4, 168, 171, 181, 184, 186–8,
    190–1, 193–5, 201–2, 205–9, 219–20,
    223–4; ethnicity in CPC, 61–5; tied to
    Communist International (CI), 59–61;
    women in CPC, 65–6
conscription, 21, 24
Conservative Party, 21, 24, 26, 34, 40,
    49, 50, 51, 52, 53, 54, 57, 69, 72, 78,
    84, 105, 147–9, 151, 161, 186, 191,
    199, 201, 214, 215–17, 219, 231
Corbin, Jeanne, 66, 165, 168, 188
corn law riots, 197
Criminal Code of Canada: Section
    83.28, 4; Section 97, 41; Section 98,
    6–9, 11–20, 22, 33, 36, 41–9, 51–3,
    55–6, 68–71, 78, 80, 82–95, 98–9,
    101, 104, 108, 109, 111–12, 114–20,
    123–4, 145–9, 151–4, 156–72, 181,

183–201, 203, 205–7, 210–20, 222–8,
    231–2; Section 133, 37–8, 41, 49, 54,
    90, 94, 211–21, 226; Section 134, 37,
    211, 212
CSIS (Canadian Security Intelligence
    Service), 10

David Bill, 168, 171, 200
Deutsche Arbeiterzeitung (DAZ), 134,
    138–9
deportation, 5, 8, 14, 29–30, 34–6, 40,
    44, 46–7, 49, 50, 52, 54, 70, 74–5,
    79, 116, 119–25, 127–32, 134–6,
    138–40, 142, 145–7, 148, 151, 153–4,
    162, 170, 187–9, 191–2, 194–5,
    197–8, 208, 211, 223–4, 228, 231;
    antideporation, 162, 188
Defense of the Realm Act (DORA). See
    under United Kingdom
Donahue, Jerry, 165

Easter Riots, 24
Edwards, W. Stewart, 90, 211–13
Eight Men Speak (play), 135
emergency measures, 6–9, 14–17, 37,
    44, 45, 50, 55–6, 75, 84, 135, 145–6,
    150, 184, 214, 217, 218, 225, 228–9,
    231
emergency powers, 8, 16, 54, 55, 57,
    119, 149, 204, 223, 226, 229, 231
Emergency Powers Act (1920). See
    United Kingdom
emergency state, 9, 15, 123, 228, 232,
    233; non-emergency state, 9, 229
Espionage Act, 25, 30–1, 34, 223
Evanik, Annie, 165
Evans, Arthur "Slim", 147, 154–61,
    163–4, 184, 190, 201–2, 204–6,
    209–10, 224
Ewen, Tom, 82, 86, 88–9, 95, 97,
    112–13, 207
exclusion, 12–13, 15, 18, 186, 218,
    222–5, 230; and inclusion, 12, 230
Executive Council of Ontario, 229

Farkas, John, 122, 130–1
FBI. See Bureau of Investigation
Finnish Organization of Canada (FOC),
    64, 122, 126–7, 131

First World War. *See* World War I
Foucault, Michel, 10, 12, 182; dangerous
    individual, 182–3

G20 (summit, and riots, Toronto), 229
Gastown Riot, 10
Geneva Conventions, 230
Glos Pracy, 128, 134, 219
Golinsky, Mike, 82, 86, 88, 95–7, 114,
    164
Gouzenko affair, 228
Guantanamo Bay. *See under* torture
Guthrie, Hugh, 34–40, 70, 78, 148, 171,
    189, 192, 203, 226

Halifax Ten, the, 121, 123
Harper, Stephen, 231
heightened security, 8, 17, 227–8
Hill, Amos T., 81–2, 86, 88, 97, 113
Hobbes, Thomas, 47
homo sacer. *See* Agamben, Giorgio

Immigration Act (1903) US: Section
    2, 29
Immigration Act (1910) Canada, 6, 20,
    29, 31, 34–6, 43–4, 46–9, 51, 53, 121,
    123–5, 147, 223–4; Section 15 1919
    amendments, 35; Section 41, 6, 20,
    29, 30–1, 35, 40, 43–51, 53, 56, 68,
    121–5, 145, 197, 213, 224
Indigenous peoples, 194, 230
Industrial Workers of the World (IWW),
    24–8
insecurity state, 10, 228
internment, 23, 28, 79, 226
interwar period, 5, 7–9, 15–17, 41, 68,
    133, 230, 232

Ķarelia, 126, 140
Kellock-Taschereau Commission, 226, 228
King, William Lyon Mackenzie, 48, 51,
    69, 142, 149–50, 186, 189, 201, 210,
    220
Kingston Penitentiary riot (1932), 192
Kist, Hans, 122, 128–30, 138–9

Lapointe, Ernest, 48, 51–2, 69, 211,
    213–15, 219
lapsed powers, 229

League for Social Reconstruction, 180,
    185, 192, 196, 225
Leopold, John, 68, 79, 96–7, 99,
    100, 102–8, 110, 118, 123–4, 145,
    164, 205, 207–9; undercover, Jack
    Esselwein, 68, 96, 107
liberal democracy, 11, 13, 196, 230;
    Canada, 186; society, 4; state, 12, 18,
    218, 223, 230; theory, 12
Liberal Party, 21–2, 24, 39, 41, 48, 51,
    69, 142, 186, 199–200, 210–17, 225
liberal society, 11, 13, 17, 117, 186, 218,
    221, 228, 232
liberalism, 11–12, 17, 198–9, 211, 230
Locke, John, 11, 47; criticism of
    authority, 38; inalienable rights, 11

MacBrien, James, 202
Macdonald, Hugh, 88, 89, 92–102, 104,
    109–14, 116–17
Magna Carta, 47
marginalized, 60, 65, 84
Meighen, Arthur, 31, 34–5, 38–40, 43,
    49, 52, 216–18
Military Services Act, 24, 27
minorities (racial, ethnic, and/or
    linguistic), 11, 55, 61–4, 194–5, 230

nation building, 6–9, 15, 19, 30, 45, 55,
    118–20, 145, 171, 183–4, 205, 214,
    217–18, 220, 222, 224, 228, 230, 232;
    through repression, 6, 55, 184, 217,
    228. *See also* state formation
Newlove, Tom H., 205–10
normalizing emergency measures,
    6, 14, 44, 55, 145, 146, 184, 214,
    228; emergency laws, 39, 104, 222;
    exceptional powers, 80; repression,
    222; the emergency, 171

Obama, Barack, 232
O'Connor, William Francis, 21–2, 31
October Crisis, 10, 227–8
On-to-Ottawa Trek, 5, 186, 201–6,
    209–10, 220, 225

Padlock Act, 10, 226, 228
Patriot Act, 17
PC 834, 24

PC 2384, 6, 9, 29, 30–2, 35, 37, 41,
44–5, 55–6, 86, 90–1, 116, 118–19,
213–14, 223
peacetime, 6, 14, 16, 22, 28, 34, 35, 45,
56, 75, 80, 86, 118–19, 146, 150, 171,
214, 218, 226, 229–31
Perry, A.B., 28, 35, 36
Pohjansalo, Martin, 122, 130, 139, 140,
145
police, 3–5, 10, 15–17, 28, 30, 51, 58, 60,
68–70, 72–3, 75–6, 78, 80–2, 84, 88,
94–6, 102–5, 108, 113, 130–1, 142,
146–7, 152, 155–66, 168, 171–4, 176–
84, 198, 200–6, 209, 223, 225, 229,
232; Dominion Police, 25–7; Royal
Canadian Mounted Police (RCMP),
5, 10, 15, 28, 42, 50, 58, 68, 71–2,
75–82, 96, 103–5, 108, 122–4, 127–8,
132–4, 142–6, 153–7, 161, 164,
168–9, 169, 202–4, 206–10, 214–15,
225; Royal Northwest Mounted Police
(RNWMP), 25, 28, 30, 35, 103
policing, 10, 39, 105–6; political
policing, 10, 29
Popovich, Matthew, 81, 86, 88, 95, 97,
99, 115
preventative arrests, 3–4, 8, 82–3, 231
preventative security measures, 10
Price, William (H.), 72–3, 77–9, 83, 87,
130, 131, 148–9, 153, 189
protection of law. See Agamben, Giorgio

Quebec student protests (2012), 229

Raketti, Harry, 165
reds, 46, 50, 69, 71–2, 74, 77, 79, 82,
105, 148, 160
Regina Manifesto, 192, 196, 200
Regina Riot, 5, 201, 209, 210
Relief Camp Worker's Union (RCWU),
201–2, 206–9
Renan, Ernest, v, 233
rendition, 230
RCMP. See under police
Riot Act, 181

Schmitt, Carl, v, 12, 233
Scott, F.R., 75, 165, 170, 178, 180,
185–6, 192, 196–200, 226
Second World War. See World War II

Special Committee Report on Sedition
1919: Section 2, 37
secret hearings, 229
security crisis(es), 55, 228
Sedgwick, Joseph, 79, 87–8, 91, 97, 100,
117, 153, 154, 163
Sembaj, Ivan, 122, 128, 133, 138–9, 145
September 11th, 2001, 3, 17, 229–30,
231, 232
Sherwood, Percy, 26–8
Smith, Adam, 47
Smith, A.E., 81, 97, 154, 189–93,
219–20, 233; freedom of the mind,
220, 233
Snowden, Edward, 229
Social Credit Party, 57, 211
Social Democratic Party (SDP), 25,
27–8, 30, 91
Sommerville, Norman, 87–8, 90–5,
97–100, 102–4, 111–17
Stahlberg, Toivo "John", 122, 130–1, 139
Starnes, Cortlandt, 78, 79
state formation, 11, 228, 230. See also
nation building
state of emergency, 12, 16–17, 19–20,
56, 204, 223, 232–3
state of exception, 12–13, 15–17, 56,
182, 222–3, 225, 228, 230, 232–3

Taschereau, Louis-Alexandre, 75, 106,
164–5, 167, 172, 181, 226, 228
terror, 41, 48, 55, 139, 147, 160, 177,
183–5, 190–1, 194, 200, 217, 224, 230;
Nazi terror, 233; war on terror, 232
terrorism, 4, 7, 17, 48, 55, 227, 230, 231;
attacks, 3; threats, 232
The Eight, 86, 116–18, 154, 188, 192,
224; Eight Men Speak (play), 135
The Ten, 121, 123
Third Period (of communism), 14, 58–60,
62, 64, 66, 83, 126, 131, 192, 193
torture, 134–5, 139, 230; Guantanamo
Bay, 230; waterboarding, 230
Trudeau, Justin, 231
Trudeau, Pierre Elliott, 227

Ukrainian Labour-Farmer Temple
Association (ULFTA), 61, 64, 122, 127–9
United Kingdom (UK), 34–5, 50, 54,
66–9, 79, 84, 103, 142; Defence of the

Realm Act (DORA), 21–2, 31, 148, 223;
   Emergency Powers Act (1920), 149
United States of America, 8, 17, 25–6,
   28–9, 31, 36, 38, 44–5, 46, 52, 70, 74,
   79, 102, 108, 111, 123, 129, 131, 139,
   143, 144, 154, 187, 198, 208, 214,
   223, 228, 230–2

Vaara, Arvo, 89, 122, 126–8, 130, 132,
   134, 139–40, 145
Vapaus, 62, 89, 113, 122, 126–7, 130–1,
   134, 139, 140, 219

War Measures Act (WMA), 6, 16, 19,
   21, 28, 56, 149, 150, 213, 220, 223;
   Section 2, 149; Section 4, 22
war on terror. *See* terror
waterboarding. *See* torture
Winnipeg General Strike, 5, 20, 31, 33,
   35–6, 41, 43, 44, 46, 48–9, 70, 148, 218

Wood, S.T., 156, 203–4, 209
Woodsworth, J.S., 48–9, 51–2, 151,
   167, 186, 189, 191–3, 196–7, 199,
   214, 220
Worker's Unity League (WUL), 59,
   81, 95, 97, 112, 154–7, 161, 163,
   165, 168, 176, 193, 194, 201–2, 205,
   207–9
World War I, 10, 13, 16, 19–20, 23, 32,
   57, 96, 127, 134, 200, 230
World War II, 9–10, 143, 219, 226–7,
   229–30
Worozcyt (Worebek), Steve, 122, 128–9,
   138

Zappa, Joseph, 172–6, 179–83
Zurcher, Gottfried, 122, 128–9, 138
Zynchuck, Nicholas, 147, 172–84,
   193, 200, 225, 229; funeral, 176–80,
   182–4, 225

PUBLICATIONS OF THE OSGOODE SOCIETY FOR CANADIAN LEGAL HISTORY

2017   Constance Backhouse, *Claire L'Heureux-Dubé: A Life*
       Dennis G. Molinaro, *An Exceptional Law: Section 98 and the Emergency State, 1919–1936*
2016   Lori Chambers, *A Legal History of Adoption in Ontario, 1921–2015*
       Bradley Miller, *Borderline Crime: Fugitive Criminals and the Challenge of the Border, 1819–1914*
       James Muir, *Law, Debt, and Merchant Power: The Civil Courts of Eighteenth-Century Halifax*
2015   Barry Wright, Eric Tucker, and Susan Binnie, eds., *Canadian State Trials, Volume IV: Security, Dissent, and the Limits of Toleration in War and Peace, 1914–1939*
       David Fraser, *"Honorary Protestants": The Jewish School Question in Montreal, 1867–1997*
       C. Ian Kyer, *A Thirty Years' War: The Failed Public/Private Partnership that Spurred the Creation of the Toronto Transit Commission, 1891–1921*
       Dale Gibson, *Law, Life, and Government at Red River: Settlement and Governance, 1812–1872*
2014   Christopher Moore, *The Court of Appeal for Ontario: Defining the Right of Appeal, 1792–2013*
       Paul Craven, *Petty Justice: Low Law and the Sessions System in Charlotte County, New Brunswick, 1785–1867*
       Thomas G.W. Telfer, *Ruin and Redemption: The Struggle for a Canadian Bankruptcy Law, 1867–1919*
       Dominique Clément, *Equality Deferred: Sex Discrimination and British Columbia's Human Rights State, 1953–1984*
2013   Roy McMurtry, *Memoirs and Reflections*
       Charlotte Gray, *The Massey Murder: A Maid, Her Master, and the Trial That Shocked a Nation*
       C. Ian Kyer, *Lawyers, Families, and Businesses: The Shaping of a Bay Street Law Firm, Faskens 1863–1963*
       G. Blaine Baker and Donald Fyson, eds., *Essays in the History of Canadian Law, Volume XI: Quebec and the Canadas*

2012   R. Blake Brown, *Arming and Disarming: A History of Gun Control in Canada*

Eric Tucker, James Muir, and Bruce Ziff, eds., *Property on Trial: Canadian Cases in Context*

Shelley Gavigan, *Hunger, Horses, and Government Men: Criminal Law on the Aboriginal Plains, 1870–1905*

Barrington Walker, ed., *The African Canadian Legal Odyssey: Historical Essays*

2011   Robert J. Sharpe, *The Lazier Murder: Prince Edward County, 1884*

Philip Girard, *Lawyers and Legal Culture in British North America: Beamish Murdoch of Halifax*

John McLaren, *Dewigged, Bothered, and Bewildered: British Colonial Judges on Trial, 1800–1900*

Lesley Erickson, *Westward Bound: Sex, Violence, the Law, and the Making of a Settler Society*

2010   Judy Fudge and Eric Tucker, eds., *Work on Trial: Canadian Labour Law Struggles*

Christopher Moore, *The British Columbia Court of Appeal: The First Hundred Years*

Frederick Vaughan, *Viscount Haldane: 'The Wicked Step-father of the Canadian Constitution'*

Barrington Walker, *Race on Trial: Black Defendants in Ontario's Criminal Courts, 1858–1958*

2009   William Kaplan, *Canadian Maverick: The Life and Times of Ivan C. Rand*

R. Blake Brown, *A Trying Question: The Jury in Nineteenth-Century Canada*

Barry Wright and Susan Binnie, eds., *Canadian State Trials, Volume III: Political Trials and Security Measures, 1840–1914*

Robert J. Sharpe, *The Last Day, the Last Hour: The Currie Libel Trial* (paperback edition with a new preface)

2008   Constance Backhouse, *Carnal Crimes: Sexual Assault Law in Canada, 1900–1975*

Jim Phillips, R. Roy McMurtry, and John T. Saywell, eds., *Essays in the History of Canadian Law, Volume X: A Tribute to Peter N. Oliver*

Greg Taylor, *The Law of the Land: The Advent of the Torrens System in Canada*

Hamar Foster, Benjamin Berger, and A.R. Buck, eds., *The Grand Experiment: Law and Legal Culture in British Settler Societies*

2007 Robert Sharpe and Patricia McMahon, *The Persons Case: The Origins and Legacy of the Fight for Legal Personhood*

Lori Chambers, *Misconceptions: Unmarried Motherhood and the Ontario Children of Unmarried Parents Act, 1921–1969*

Jonathan Swainger, ed., *A History of the Supreme Court of Alberta*

Martin Friedland, *My Life in Crime and Other Academic Adventures*

2006 Donald Fyson, *Magistrates, Police, and People: Everyday Criminal Justice in Quebec and Lower Canada, 1764–1837*

Dale Brawn, *The Court of Queen's Bench of Manitoba, 1870–1950: A Biographical History*

R.C.B. Risk, *A History of Canadian Legal Thought: Collected Essays*, edited and introduced by G. Blaine Baker and Jim Phillips

2005 Philip Girard, *Bora Laskin: Bringing Law to Life*

Christopher English, ed., *Essays in the History of Canadian Law: Volume IX – Two Islands: Newfoundland and Prince Edward Island*

Fred Kaufman, *Searching for Justice: An Autobiography*

2004 Philip Girard, Jim Phillips, and Barry Cahill, eds., *The Supreme Court of Nova Scotia, 1754–2004: From Imperial Bastion to Provincial Oracle*

Frederick Vaughan, *Aggressive in Pursuit: The Life of Justice Emmett Hall*

John D. Honsberger, *Osgoode Hall: An Illustrated History*

Constance Backhouse and Nancy Backhouse, *The Heiress versus the Establishment: Mrs Campbell's Campaign for Legal Justice*

2003 Robert Sharpe and Kent Roach, *Brian Dickson: A Judge's Journey*

Jerry Bannister, *The Rule of the Admirals: Law, Custom, and Naval Government in Newfoundland, 1699–1832*

George Finlayson, *John J. Robinette, Peerless Mentor: An Appreciation*

Peter Oliver, *The Conventional Man: The Diaries of Ontario Chief Justice Robert A. Harrison, 1856–1878*

2002 John T. Saywell, *The Lawmakers: Judicial Power and the Shaping of Canadian Federalism*

Patrick Brode, *Courted and Abandoned: Seduction in Canadian Law*

David Murray, *Colonial Justice: Justice, Morality, and Crime in the Niagara District, 1791–1849*

F. Murray Greenwood and Barry Wright, eds., *Canadian State Trials, Volume II: Rebellion and Invasion in the Canadas, 1837–1839*

2001 Ellen Anderson, *Judging Bertha Wilson: Law as Large as Life*

Judy Fudge and Eric Tucker, *Labour before the Law: The Regulation of Workers' Collective Action in Canada, 1900–1948*

Laurel Sefton MacDowell, *Renegade Lawyer: The Life of J.L. Cohen*

2000 Barry Cahill, *'The Thousandth Man': A Biography of James McGregor Stewart*

A.B. McKillop, *The Spinster and the Prophet: Florence Deeks, H.G. Wells, and the Mystery of the Purloined Past*

Beverley Boissery and F. Murray Greenwood, *Uncertain Justice: Canadian Women and Capital Punishment*

Bruce Ziff, *Unforeseen Legacies: Reuben Wells Leonard and the Leonard Foundation Trust*

1999 Constance Backhouse, *Colour-Coded: A Legal History of Racism in Canada, 1900–1950*

G. Blaine Baker and Jim Phillips, eds., *Essays in the History of Canadian Law: Volume VIII – In Honour of R.C.B. Risk*

Richard W. Pound, *Chief Justice W.R. Jackett: By the Law of the Land*

David Vanek, *Fulfilment: Memoirs of a Criminal Court Judge*

1998 Sidney Harring, *White Man's Law: Native People in Nineteenth-Century Canadian Jurisprudence*

Peter Oliver, *'Terror to Evil-Doers': Prisons and Punishments in Nineteenth-Century Ontario*

1997 James W. St.G. Walker, *'Race,' Rights and the Law in the Supreme Court of Canada: Historical Case Studies*

Lori Chambers, *Married Women and Property Law in Victorian Ontario*

Patrick Brode, *Casual Slaughters and Accidental Judgments: Canadian War Crimes and Prosecutions, 1944–1948*

Ian Bushnell, *The Federal Court of Canada: A History, 1875–1992*

1996 Carol Wilton, ed., *Essays in the History of Canadian Law: Volume VII – Inside the Law: Canadian Law Firms in Historical Perspective*

William Kaplan, *Bad Judgment: The Case of Mr Justice Leo A. Landreville*

Murray Greenwood and Barry Wright, eds., *Canadian State Trials: Volume I – Law, Politics, and Security Measures, 1608–1837*

1995   David Williams, *Just Lawyers: Seven Portraits*

Hamar Foster and John McLaren, eds., *Essays in the History of Canadian Law: Volume VI – British Columbia and the Yukon*

W.H. Morrow, ed., *Northern Justice: The Memoirs of Mr Justice William G. Morrow*

Beverley Boissery, *A Deep Sense of Wrong: The Treason, Trials, and Transportation to New South Wales of Lower Canadian Rebels after the 1838 Rebellion*

1994   Patrick Boyer, *A Passion for Justice: The Legacy of James Chalmers McRuer*

Charles Pullen, *The Life and Times of Arthur Maloney: The Last of the Tribunes*

Jim Phillips, Tina Loo, and Susan Lewthwaite, eds., *Essays in the History of Canadian Law: Volume V – Crime and Criminal Justice*

Brian Young, *The Politics of Codification: The Lower Canadian Civil Code of 1866*

1993   Greg Marquis, *Policing Canada's Century: A History of the Canadian Association of Chiefs of Police*

Murray Greenwood, *Legacies of Fear: Law and Politics in Quebec in the Era of the French Revolution*

1992   Brendan O'Brien, *Speedy Justice: The Tragic Last Voyage of His Majesty's Vessel Speedy*

Robert Fraser, ed., *Provincial Justice: Upper Canadian Legal Portraits from the Dictionary of Canadian Biography*

1991   Constance Backhouse, *Petticoats and Prejudice: Women and Law in Nineteenth-Century Canada*

1990   Philip Girard and Jim Phillips, eds., *Essays in the History of Canadian Law: Volume III – Nova Scotia*

Carol Wilton, ed., *Essays in the History of Canadian Law: Volume IV – Beyond the Law: Lawyers and Business in Canada, 1830–1930*

1989   Desmond Brown, *The Genesis of the Canadian Criminal Code of 1892*

Patrick Brode, *The Odyssey of John Anderson*

1988   Robert Sharpe, *The Last Day, the Last Hour: The Currie Libel Trial*

John D. Arnup, *Middleton: The Beloved Judge*

1987   C. Ian Kyer and Jerome Bickenbach, *The Fiercest Debate: Cecil A. Wright, the Benchers, and Legal Education in Ontario, 1923–1957*

1986 Paul Romney, *Mr Attorney: The Attorney General for Ontario in Court, Cabinet, and Legislature, 1791–1899*

Martin Friedland, *The Case of Valentine Shortis: A True Story of Crime and Politics in Canada*

1985 James Snell and Frederick Vaughan, *The Supreme Court of Canada: History of the Institution*

1984 Patrick Brode, *Sir John Beverley Robinson: Bone and Sinew of the Compact*

David Williams, *Duff: A Life in the Law*

1983 David H. Flaherty, ed., *Essays in the History of Canadian Law: Volume II*

1982 Marion MacRae and Anthony Adamson, *Cornerstones of Order: Courthouses and Town Halls of Ontario, 1784–1914*

1981 David H. Flaherty, ed., *Essays in the History of Canadian Law: Volume I*

THE CANADIAN SOCIAL HISTORY SERIES

Terry Copp,
*The Anatomy of Poverty: The Condition of
the Working Class in Montreal, 1897–1929,*
1974.
ISBN 0-7710-2252-2

Alison Prentice,
*The School Promoters: Education and
Social Class in Mid-Nineteenth Century
Upper Canada,* 1977.
ISBN 0-8020-8692-6

John Herd Thompson,
*The Harvests of War: The Prairie West,
1914–1918,* 1978.
ISBN 0-7710-8560-5

Joy Parr, Editor,
*Childhood and Family in Canadian
History,* 1982.
ISBN 0-7710-6938-3

**Alison Prentice and Susan Mann
Trofimenkoff, Editors,**
*The Neglected Majority: Essays in Cana-
dian Women's History,* Volume 2, 1985.
ISBN 0-7710-8583-4

Ruth Roach Pierson,
*"They're Still Women After All": The
Second World War and Canadian Wom-
anhood,* 1986.
ISBN 0-7710-6958-8

Bryan D. Palmer,
*The Character of Class Struggle: Essays
in Canadian Working Class History,
1850–1985,* 1986.
ISBN 0-7710-6946-4

Alan Metcalfe,
*Canada Learns to Play: The Emergence
of Organized Sport, 1807–1914,* 1987.
ISBN 0-7710-5870-5

Marta Danylewycz,
*Taking the Veil: An Alternative to Mar-
riage, Motherhood, and Spinsterhood in
Quebec, 1840–1920,* 1987.
ISBN 0-7710-2550-5

Craig Heron,
*Working in Steel: The Early Years in
Canada, 1883–1935,* 1988.
ISBN 978-1-4426-0984-6

**Wendy Mitchinson and Janice Dickin
McGinnis, Editors,**
*Essays in the History of Canadian Med-
icine,* 1988.
ISBN 0-7710-6063-7

Joan Sangster,
*Dreams of Equality: Women on the Canadian
Left, 1920–1950,* 1989.
ISBN 0-7710-7946-X

Angus McLaren,
*Our Own Master Race: Eugenics in
Canada, 1885–1945,* 1990.
ISBN 0-7710-5544-7

Bruno Ramirez,
*On the Move: French-Canadian and
Italian Migrants in the North Atlantic
Economy, 1860–1914,* 1991.
ISBN 0-7710-7283-X

Mariana Valverde,
*'The Age of Light, Soap and Water':
Moral Reform in English Canada,
1885–1925,* 1991.
ISBN 978-0-8020-9595-4

Bettina Bradbury,
*Working Families: Age, Gender, and
Daily Survival in Industrializing
Montreal,* 1993.
ISBN 978-0-8020-8689-1

Andrée Lévesque,
*Making and Breaking the Rules: Women
in Quebec, 1919–1939,* 1994.
ISBN 978-1-4426-1138-2

Cecilia Danysk,
*Hired Hands: Labour and the Develop-
ment of Prairie Agriculture, 1880–1930,*
1995.
ISBN 0-7710-2552-1

Kathryn McPherson,
Bedside Matters: The Transformation of Canadian Nursing, 1900–1990, 1996.
ISBN 978-0-8020-8679-2

Edith Burley,
Servants of the Honourable Company: Work, Discipline, and Conflict in the Hudson's Bay Company, 1770–1870, 1997.
ISBN 0-19-541296-6

Mercedes Steedman,
Angels of the Workplace: Women and the Construction of Gender Relations in the Canadian Clothing Industry, 1890–1940, 1997.
ISBN 978-1-4426-0982-2

Angus McLaren and Arlene Tigar McLaren,
The Bedroom and the State: The Changing Practices and Politics of Contraception and Abortion in Canada, 1880–1997, 1997.
isbn 0-19-541318-0

Kathryn McPherson, Cecilia Morgan, and Nancy M. Forestell, Editors,
Gendered Pasts: Historical Essays in Femininity and Masculinity in Canada, 1999.
ISBN 0-978-0-8020-8690-7

Gillian Creese,
Contracting Masculinity: Gender, Class, and Race in a White-Collar Union, 1944–1994, 1999.
ISBN 0-19-541454-3

Geoffrey Reaume,
Remembrance of Patients Past: Patient Life at the Toronto Hospital for the Insane, 1870–1940, 2000.
isbn 978-1-4426-1075-0

Miriam Wright,
A Fishery for Modern Times: The State and the Industrialization of the Newfoundland Fishery, 1934–1968, 2001.
ISBN 0-19-541620-1

Judy Fudge and Eric Tucker,
Labour Before the Law: The Regulation of Workers' Collective Action in Canada, 1900–1948, 2001.
ISBN 978-0-8020-3793-0

Mark Moss,
Manliness and Militarism: Educating Young Boys in Ontario for War, 2001.
ISBN 0-19-541594-9

Joan Sangster,
Regulating Girls and Women: Sexuality, Family, and the Law in Ontario 1920–1960, 2001.
ISBN 0-19-541663-5

Reinhold Kramer and Tom Mitchell,
Walk Towards the Gallows: The Tragedy of Hilda Blake, Hanged 1899, 2002.
ISBN 978-0-8020-9542-8

Mark Kristmanson,
Plateaus of Freedom: Nationality, Culture, and State Security in Canada, 1940–1960, 2002.
isbn 0-19-541866-2 (cloth)
ISBN 0-19-541803-4 (paper)

Robin Jarvis Brownlie,
A Fatherly Eye: Indian Agents, Government Power, and Aboriginal Resistance in Ontario, 1918–1939, 2003.
ISBN 0-19-541891-3 (cloth)
ISBN 0-19-541784-4 (paper)

Steve Hewitt,
Riding to the Rescue: The Transformation of the RCMP in Alberta and Saskatchewan, 1914–1939, 2006.
ISBN 978-0-8020-9021-8 (cloth)
ISBN 978-0-8020-4895-0 (paper)

Robert K. Kristofferson,
Craft Capitalism: Craftworkers and Early Industrialization in Hamilton, Ontario, 1840–1871, 2007.
ISBN 978-0-8020-9127-7 (.cloth)
ISBN 978-0-8020-9408-7 (paper)

Andrew Parnaby,
*Citizen Docker: Making a New Deal on
the Vancouver Waterfront, 1919–1939,*
2008.
ISBN 978-0-8020-9056-0 (cloth)
ISBN 978-0-8020-9384-4 (paper)

J.I. Little,
*Loyalties in Conflict: A Canadian
Borderland in War and Rebellion,
1812–1840,* 2008.
ISBN 978-0-8020-9773-6 (cloth)
ISBN 978-0-8020-9525-1 (paper)

Pauline Greenhill,
*Make the Night Hideous: Four English
Canadian Charivaris, 1881–1940,*
2010.
ISBN 978-1-4426-4077-1 (cloth)
ISBN 978-1-4426-1015-6 (paper)

Rhonda L. Hinther and Jim Mochoruk,
*Re-imagining Ukrainian-Canadians:
History, Politics, and Identity,*
2010.
ISBN 978-1-4426-4134-1 (cloth)
ISBN 978-1-4426-1062-0 (paper)

Reinhold Kramer and Tom Mitchell,
*When the State Trembled: How A.J.
Andrews and the Citizens' Committee
Broke the Winnipeg General Strike,*
2010.
ISBN 978-1-4426-4219-5 (cloth)
ISBN 978-1-4426-1116-0 (paper)

Barrington Walker,
*Race on Trial: Black Defendants in Ontario's
Criminal Courts, 1858–1958,* 2010.
ISBN 978-0-8020-9909-9 (cloth)

**Lara Campbell, Dominique Clément,
and Greg Kealey,**
Debating Dissent: Canada and the 1960s
ISBN 978-1-4426-4164-8 (cloth)
ISBN 978-1-4426-1078-1 (paper)

Janis Thiessen,
*Manufacturing Mennonites: Work and
Religion in Post-War Manitoba*
ISBN 978-1-4426-4213-3 (cloth)
ISBN 978-1-4426-1113-9 (paper)

Don Nerbas,
*Dominion of Capital: The Politics of Big
Business and the Crisis of the Canadian
Bourgeoisie, 1914–1947*
ISBN 978-1-4426-4545-5 (cloth)
ISBN 978-1-4426-1352-2 (paper)

Kirk Niergarth,
*"The Dignity of Every Human Being": New
Brunswick Artists and Canadian Culture be-
tween the Great Depression and the Cold War*
ISBN 978-1-4426-4560-8 (cloth)
ISBN 978-1-4426-1389-8 (paper)

Dennis G. Molinaro,
*An Exceptional Law: Section 98 and the
Emergency State, 1919–1936*
ISBN 978-1-4426-2957-8 (cloth)
ISBN 978-1-4426-2958-5 (paper)